PLAYING THE GAME

THE BRITISH JUNIOR INFANTRY OFFICER ON THE WESTERN FRONT 1914-18

Christopher Moore-Bick

Helion Studies in Military History Number 4

Helion & Company Ltd

Dedication: For Kathryn, with love.

Helion Studies in Military History
No 1 *Learning from Foreign Wars. Russian Military Thinking 1859-73*
      Gudrun Persson (ISBN 978-1-906033-61-3)
No 2 *A Military Government in Exile. The Polish Government-in-Exile 1939-45, a Study of Discontent* Evan McGilvray (ISBN 978-1-906033-58-3)
No 3 *From Landrecies to Cambrai. Case Studies of German Offensive and Defensive Operations on the Western Front 1914-17* Capt G.C. Wynne (ISBN 978-1-906033-76-7)
No 4 *Playing the Game. The British Junior Infantry Officer on the Western Front 1914-18* Christopher Moore-Bick (ISBN 978-1-906033-84-2)
No 5 *The History of the British Army Film & Photographic Unit in the Second World War* Dr Fred McGlade (ISBN 978-1-906033-94-1)

Helion & Company Limited
26 Willow Road
Solihull
West Midlands B91 1UE
England
Tel. 0121 705 3393
Fax 0121 711 4075
Email: info@helion.co.uk
Website: www.helion.co.uk

Published by Helion & Company 2011

Designed and typeset by Farr out Publications, Wokingham, Berkshire
Cover designed by Farr out Publications, Wokingham, Berkshire
Printed by Gutenberg Press Limited, Tarxien, Malta

Text © Christopher Moore-Bick.
Photographs as individually credited.

ISBN 978 1 906033 84 2

British Library Cataloguing-in-Publication Data.
A catalogue record for this book is available from the British Library.

Front cover: 'The Dispatch (The Captain's Dugout)', painting by Marjorie Violet Watherston, oil on canvas, dated 1917. (Imperial War Museum ART 5199)
Rear cover: Photographs of Captain Samuel James Paget, 1895-1918, and sport at Winchester College. (Private archive)

For details of other military history titles published by Helion & Company Limited contact the above address, or visit our website: http://www.helion.co.uk.

We always welcome receiving book proposals from prospective authors.

Contents

List of Illustrations

Acknowledgements

I would like to take this opportunity to express my most sincere thanks to the many people and organisations who have made this book possible. As it is scarcely possible to name everybody who has in some way influenced this work, I would like to begin by offering thanks – and apologies – to anybody whom I have failed to name. I am none the less grateful.

Duncan Rogers at Helion & Co. Ltd. deserves special mention for inviting me to write this book in the first place, and for assisting and guiding me through the process. I had not appreciated how much I would enjoy the task, and without Duncan's intervention I might never have found out. My thanks also to Ann Farr at Farr out Publications for her work on the design and typesetting. Dr Peter Martland, my postgraduate supervisor, has continued to provide unfailing support and advice, for which I am very grateful. My thanks also to Professor David Reynolds and Dr Stephen Badsey, who both provided extremely helpful comments on draft text, and to Dr Patrick Zutshi and Dr Daniel Todman, who provided assistance and advice. My managers and colleagues at the Ministry of Defence have been unfailingly supportive. In particular, my military colleagues have patiently tolerated and assisted with my many questions about specific aspects of Army life. All errors are, of course, my own but I apologise particularly to them for any factual mistakes concerning all things military. I fear they will think their kind efforts have been in vain, although I know I have profited greatly by their instruction. I must further offer them my apologies for reproducing passages of original text which are critical or disparaging of certain regiments or corps. Needless to say, they should not be taken as expressing my own views!

My father- and mother-in-law, Brian and Linda, have been immensely kind and supportive, assisting particularly with their comments on early drafts and, in Linda's case, inspiring the title of this book. Last, but by no means least, I would like to thank my parents, for their unfailing support and encouragement, and my wife, Kathryn. I don't think either of us appreciated what a big commitment this project would be, but she has cheerfully tolerated all of the disruptions and difficulties and provided invaluable assistance in the production of the finished manuscript. As with many things, I could not have done it without her.

The writings of young British officers are at the very heart of this project, and its success very much depended on my ability to locate and access high-quality material. I am therefore very grateful to all those who have enabled me to read and reproduce the necessary material. I owe very special thanks to the late Mrs Verily Paget Anderson, who kindly gave me full access to the collected letters and war scrapbook of her late brother-in-law, Captain Samuel Paget, and to Eddie Anderson for his permission to use extracts from this collection in this book. This previously unstudied resource provided an exciting starting point for my research and yielded some extremely valuable material, so I am indebted to Mrs Paget Anderson for her generosity, hospitality and encouragement, and very sad about her recent passing, not least because it has deprived me of the pleasure of knowing what she thinks of the end result.

The documents held in the Imperial War Museum collection were a vital resource. I am grateful to the Trustees of the Imperial War Museum for granting access to this fantastic archive, and to Tony Richards and the other staff at the museum for their assistance. I am similarly grateful to the staff at the National Archives, the Churchill Archive Centre, Cambridge, and the Syndics of the Cambridge University Library for allowing me to use their collections.

I would like to express my thanks to the Warden and Scholars of Winchester College for granting me access to the Winchester College Archives, and to Dr James Webster, Dr Roger Custance, Suzanne Foster and Jenni Sundheim, who all assisted with the search for material and the hunt for permissions. My thanks also to James Sabben-Clare, for permission to quote from his book *Winchester College: After 600 Years, 1382-1982*, to the Headman, Ralph Townsend, for permission to use extracts from *The Wykehamist*, and to P&G Wells for likewise giving their consent. Patrick Maclure and the Winchester College Development Office deserve special thanks for allowing me to place a short article in the alumni publication *The Trusty Servant* appealing for primary sources still in private hands. I am grateful to all those who answered the call expressing an interest in my work, many of whom made suggestions and kindly offered useful material which I sadly did not find time to investigate fully.

For access to or permission to use material to which they hold the rights I would like to thank the following: Lyn Albrighton, for the papers of Lt. D Neilson-Terry; Rodney Allan, for the papers of Major Rayner Stowell; Andrew Baines, for the papers of Captain John Stanhope Baines; Victoria Baker, for the papers of William Baker; Mike Bickersteth, for the papers of the Bickersteth family; Charles Brims, for the diaries of Captain R.C. Smith; the Viscount Chandos, for the papers of Oliver Lyttelton (1st Viscount Chandos); John D'Arcy, for the papers of James Edmund H. Neville; Alex de Jonge, for interesting information relating to his father and his permission to reprint it; Professor Freeman Dyson, for a letter from Sir George Dyson; Owen Evans, for the papers of Major H.K.D. Evans; Graham Ferguson, for the papers of Alan Ferguson; Sir Edward Ford, for the memoir of 2nd Lieutenant Gilbert Talbot; General Sir David Fraser, for the letters and diaries of the Hon. William Fraser; Janet Grimes, for the papers of Captain A.B. Pick; Gerry Harrison, for the papers of Captain Charles May; Valerie Hawgood, for the papers of 2nd Lt. Bernard Long; F. Nigel Hepper, for the papers of Captain E.R. Hepper; Adrian House, Simon House and Julia Chappell, for the papers of Major H.W. House; Christopher Jerram, for the diaries of Brigadier-General G.N.B. Forster; Jennifer Keeling, for the papers of Captain Arthur Gibbs; Mrs Nicola Kent, for the papers of Lt. Wilbert Spencer; Mrs Rosemary Lenanton, for the papers of Sir Gerald Lenanton; Peter Luttman-Johnson, for the papers of Frederic Luttman-Johnson; George Medley, for the papers of Bertram Medley; Ian Miller, for the papers of Lt. Roderick Swayne; Michael Milligan, for the papers of 2nd Lt. A. Milligan; Yarnton Mills, for the poems and letters of 2nd Lt. W.R.G. Mills, and Oliver Mills for permission to reproduce extracts from this collection; David and William Paton, for the writings of Captain John Eugene Crombie; Mrs Rosemary Pearson, for the papers of Major R.S. Cockburn; Hugh Peppiatt, for the war diary of Major Leslie Peppiatt; Mrs Peggy Pike, for the papers of J.R. Monsell; P.C.B.

Pockney, for notes relating to his father; Andy Pratt, for the papers of Major T.D. Pratt; Max Rendall, for permission to include letters written by the Winchester headmaster Monty Rendall; Julia Rhys, for the papers of Cosmo Clark published as *The Tin Trunk: Letters and Drawings 1914-1918*; Karen Sellick and Barbara Gatehouse, for the papers of Kennard Bliss; Jean Shaw, for the papers of Geoffrey and Lesley Holt; John Scott, for the Worthington family archive; Peter Stormonth Darling, for the memoir of Lt.-Col. John Collier Stormonth Darling; Gerald Towell, for his assistance with the papers of Kennard Bliss; David Vellacott, for the papers of Captain John Loudon Strain; Peter Waugh, for the papers of Alec Waugh; F.E.B. Witts, for the papers of Major-General F.V.B. Witts; and Peter Yarrow, for the papers of Captain L.D. Spicer.

I include the following copyright notices in grateful acknowledgement of the permissions I have been granted to include copyrighted material: B. Bairnsfather, *"The Bystander's" Fragments from France*, © 2011 Barbara Bruce Littlejohn, all rights reserved, reproduced with permission from Barbara Bruce Littlejohn; I.R. Bet-El, *Conscripts – Lost Legions of the Great War*, first published by Sutton Publishing, 1999, reproduced with permission of The History Press; extract from the papers of X. Marcel Boulestin © X. Marcel Boulestin, reproduced by permission of PFD (www.pfd.co.uk) on behalf of the Estate of X. Marcel Boulestin; *Dismembering the Male: Men's Bodies, Britain and the Great War* by Joanna Bourke (Reaktion Books, London, 1996) © Joanna Bourke, 1996; M. Browne, *A Dream Of Youth – An Etonian's Reply to "The Loom of Youth"*, London, Longmans, 1918, reproduced with permission of Pearson Education Ltd.; O.S. Buckmaster, *Roundabout – The Autobiography of Viscount Buckmaster*, Witherby, 1969, reproduced with permission of Witherby Publishing Group Ltd.; G.A. Burgoyne, *The Burgoyne Diaries*, reproduced with permission of Thomas Harmsworth Publishing; H. Cecil & P.H. Liddle (eds.), *Facing Armageddon – The First World War Experienced*, Leo Cooper, 1996, reproduced with permission of Pen & Sword Books Ltd.; extracts from *A Passionate Prodigality – Fragments of Autobiography* by Guy Chapman © Guy Chapman, reproduced by permission of PFD (www.pfd.co.uk) on behalf of the Estate of Guy Chapman; R. Chickering & S. Förster (eds.), *Great War, Total War – Combat and Mobilization on the Western Front, 1914-1918*, Cambridge University Press, 2000, reproduced with permission of Cambridge University Press; Crown copyright material appears with permission of the National Archives; R. Devonald-Lewis (ed.), *From the Somme To The Armistice – The Memoirs of Captain Stormont Gibbs, MC*, Kimber, 1986, reproduced with permission of Gliddon Books; J.C. Dunn, *The War the Infantry Knew, 1914-1918*, Jane's, 1987, reproduced with permission of The Royal Welch Fusiliers Association, Wrexham; R. Feilding, *War Letters to a Wife, France and Flanders, 1915-1919* reproduced with permission of Spellmount Publishers Limited; J. Golder Burns, *Through A Padre's Spectacles*, London, J. Clarke & Co., 1917, reproduced with permission of J. Clarke & Co.; G.H. Greenwell, *An Infant In Arms*, Dickson & Thompson, 1935, reproduced with permission of Penguin Books Ltd.; A. Gregory, *The Last Great War – British Society and the First World War*, Cambridge University Press, 2008, reproduced with permission of Cambridge University Press; extracts from *The Harrovian* reproduced by permission of the Harrow School Archive; F.C. Hitchcock, *"Stand To" – A Diary of the Trenches 1915-1918*, Hurst & Blackett, 1937, reproduced with permission of Gliddon Books; extracts from *A War Imagined – The First World War and English Culture* by Samuel Hynes, published by Bodley Head, reprinted by permission of The Random House Group Ltd.; L.E. Jones, *An Edwardian Youth*, Macmillan & Co., 1956, reproduced with permission of Palgrave Macmillan; extract from the *Journal of Modern History* reproduced with permission of the University of Chicago Press; E. Leed, *No Man's Land – Combat & Identity in World War I*, Cambridge University Press, 1979, reproduced with permission of Cambridge University Press; H.N. McCartney, *Citizen Soldiers – The Liverpool Territorials in the First World War*, Cambridge University Press, 2005; reproduced with permission of Cambridge University Press; J. Mangan, *Athleticism in the Victorian and Edwardian public school*, Cambridge University Press, 1981, reproduced with permission of Cambridge University Press; *Warrior Nation: Images of War in British Popular Culture, 1850-2000* by Michael Paris (Reaktion Books, London, 2000) © Michael Paris, 2000; P. Parker, *The Old Lie – The Great War and the Public School Ethos*, Constable, 1987, reproduced by kind permission of Continuum International Publishing Group; M. Ponsonby, *Visions and Vignettes of War*, London, Longmans & Co., 1917, reproduced with permission of Pearson Education Ltd; T. W. Pym and G. Gordon, Papers from Picardy, Constable, 1917, reproduced with permission of Constable & Robinson Ltd.; T. Quinn, *Tales of the Old Soldiers. Ten Veterans of the First World War Remember Life and Death in the Trenches*, first published by Sutton Publishing, 1993, reproduced with permission of The History Press; M. Roper, *The Secret Battle – Emotional Survival in the Great War*, Manchester University Press, 2009, reproduced with permission of Manchester University Press; G.D. Sheffield, *Officer-Man Relations, Morale and Discipline in the British Army in the Era of the First World War*, 2000, Palgrave Macmillan, reproduced with permission of Palgrave Macmillan; G.D. Sheffield & G.I.S. Inglis (eds.), *From Vimy Ridge to the Rhine – The Great War Letters of Christopher Stone DSO MC*, Crowood, 1989, reproduced with permission of The Crowood Press; C.R. Stone, 'A Decca Romance', taken from the August 1923 issue of *Gramophone Magazine* which continues to be published monthly. For more information visit www.Gramophone.co.uk; E. Talbot, "War and Conscience", *The Contemporary Review*, 1914 reproduced with permission of The Contemporary Review Co. Ltd.; E.C. Vaughan, *Some Desperate Glory – The diary of a young officer, 1917*, London, Warne, 1981, reproduced with permission of Pen & Sword Books Ltd.; J.S.K. Watson, *Fighting Different Wars – Experience, Memory, and the First World War in Britain*, Cambridge University Press, 2004, reproduced with permission of Cambridge University Press; H. Williamson, *A Fox Under My Cloak*, reproduced with permission of the Henry Williamson Literary Estate; J.M. Winter, *The Great War and the British People*, 1986, Palgrave Macmillan, reproduced with permission of Palgrave Macmillan; J.M. Winter & E. Sivan (eds.), *War and Remembrance in the Twentieth Century*, Cambridge University Press, 1999, reproduced with permission of Cambridge University Press; A. Wolff (ed.), *Subalterns of the Foot – Three World War I Diaries of Officers of the Cheshire Regiment*, reproduced with permission of Square One Publications.

Despite my best efforts I have been unable to contact all copyright holders. I offer my apologies to anybody whose permission has not been obtained and encourage them to contact me, care of Helion & Co. Ltd, so that I can address any issues and correct any omissions. Likewise, if I have inadvertently infringed anybody's copyrights I offer my sincere apologies and invite those concerned to get in touch.

Introduction

If you ask somebody a question about the First World War you are likely to be told about the misery and suffering of men herded to their deaths in appalling conditions, or about the callous incompetence of the senior commanders and politicians who allowed it to happen. The experience of the Western Front is consequently defined predominantly as a conflict between the interests or fortunes of those at the top and those at the bottom of the hierarchy. This understanding has very profoundly influenced much of the history of the war. Writers have concentrated on questions of military competence and strategy (and the associated praise or condemnation) or on the experience of the ordinary Tommy. This book is not about either. It is the story of the men who occupied a position in between, the infantry subalterns and captains who had to translate the orders of the higher command into operational detail. Thousands of them were drawn from the middle and upper classes of Edwardian society. Brought up according to an ethos which was substantially unchanged since its creation in the Victorian public schools, they had to make the difficult transition from civilians to responsible commanders. Their ability to do this was a critical element of the story of the Western Front. Without them, the army could not possibly have held together and enjoyed eventual success. To understand their role, it is necessary to understand their experience of the war, an experience which was in its own way as distinct from that of the ordinary Tommy with whom they shared a trench, as it was from the châteaux generals of legend.

Gaining a clear understanding of that experience has been made more difficult by the passage of time. Reactions to the death in July 2009 of Harry Patch, the last man in Britain to have experienced the trenches of the Western Front, highlighted the nature of the challenge. His celebrity reflected the continuing public fascination with the war, but also the sense of incongruity which fuels that interest. The First World War has long seemed a uniquely unfathomable event, not in the sense that we cannot explain what happened, but because we cannot somehow believe that it did. How could men have endured the conditions and the horror? How could generals and politicians have allowed it to continue in such a way for so long? How could the war be seen as anything other than a defeat, a black mark and a scar on the history of British arms? The arrival of new generations who have not, thankfully, had to experience war directly in the way their ancestors did, has surely heightened this sense of unreality.

A prevailing popular narrative of the war which emphasises mud, futility and appalling bloodshed is apparently both clear and well understood and it is our difficulty in coming to terms with it which sustains public fascination. Amidst all this public incredulity Harry Patch was that tremendous anomaly, a voice in the 21st century for whom these events were not a mystery, but a sadly-remembered reality. When he went through those trenches and battles he would have been conscious of a similar process of separation from those servicemen and civilians who did not share his experience. This sense of otherness, what the Germans knew as *fronterlebnis*, was potent then.[1] Time has amplified that status.

It is hardly surprising, then, that even after writing this book I still feel that there is something different about the Western Front, something that will forever place it at least some way beyond our understanding as historical observers. While this makes the First World War particularly intriguing, it is obviously far from its sole appeal. It had a profound impact on the 20th Century and the modern world and continues to fascinate because its legacy and ramifications are as present in everyday life as the thousands of war memorials which continue to define our public spaces. The particular characteristics which contributed to this effect – such as mass mobilisation, technological conflict, trench deadlock and the ensuing high casualty rates – have provided generations of historians with fertile ground for investigation and debate. It is also a ripe source of controversy, the inevitable consequence of a potent mix of death and destruction, class considerations, politics and family ties. People continue to care about the war because their relatives who fought and died, though long gone, are still present in their thoughts. This was powerfully demonstrated recently in July 2010 on the occasion of the dedication of a new war cemetery at Fromelles. Ninety-four years after they died, troops buried in a mass grave were reinterred with full military honours. A Channel 4 documentary, *WW1: Finding the Lost Battalions*, followed the work of recovering and identifying the bodies. Relatives of men lost at Fromelles participated in the programme, movingly describing their emotions when considering the fate of these soldiers.

Programmes like this one tend to adhere faithfully to the prevailing popular narrative – war as painful quasi-defeat, loss that cannot be justified. In this case the sombre tone was undoubtedly apt, given the solemnity of the occasion, but it made the now-traditional emphasis on the idea of combatants as helpless victims even more apparent. Admittedly the casualty lists at a place like Fromelles speak for themselves, but there is something peculiar in depicting armed assault troops in this way. This, of course, reflects those other great conventions of First World War description – futility, bungling, the betrayal of youth – which were firmly locked into the public mind in the 1960s. The military history of the war became dominated by interpretations which castigated and condemned generals; the British Army was a blunt and intransigent beast, chewing up its human resources rather than learning lessons and adapting.

A number of historians have successfully challenged this unsophisticated interpretation over the course of the last two decades, although their efforts show little sign of achieving a genuine strategic breakthrough (outside historical circles, at least). Indeed, so tenacious is the popular perception built on *Oh! What a Lovely War* and *Blackadder Goes Forth* that it has proved effective for revisionist writers like Gary Sheffield and Gordon Corrigan to present their work as a frontal assault on what they perceive to be the most egregious myths.[2] Nevertheless, in the field of military history there is now a much better understanding of the context in which strategic and tactical decisions were taken and a far greater appreciation of the extent to which the army overcame problems and evolved, developing advanced capabilities which would enable it to win a series of crucial engagements in 1918.

There have also been big advances in the field of social and cultural history. Dedicated exploration of the everyday experiences of First World War servicemen began in the 1970s when writers began examining the wealth of primary sources available in the form of letters, diaries, personal accounts and the testimony of surviving veterans.[3] These works have been partly superseded by more recent publications such as Richard

Holmes' *Tommy – The British Soldier on the Western Front 1914-1918* (2004), which have been able to acknowledge and reflect the developments in military historiography. It is, of course, essential that they should do so. The business of cultural historians is the exploration of the complexity and detail of soldiers' everyday experiences. Context is therefore extremely important. A vast array of factors, ranging from the changing character of military campaigns to variations in the nature of enemy weapons and tactics can all have a dramatic effect on the lives of individual soldiers. An infantryman in the trenches in 1915 had a very different experience to a later soldier taking part in the more open warfare of 1918. Even wider questions concerning the competence of strategists and tacticians are significant since soldiers' attitudes towards their work are likely to be affected by their perception of their own and their commanders' abilities.

These newer histories of the experience of war typically cover a lot of ground, illuminating many different facets of the lives of the men who fought. Others across the disciplines of both military and cultural history have taken a different tack, focusing on narrower subject areas. Joanna Bourke, through her unflinching examinations of both the psychology of killing and bodily issues, has demonstrated the importance of seeing the subjects of cultural histories as real people, with all the implied idiosyncrasies and imperfections, rather than the plaster saints they have sometimes become through repeated memorialisation.[4] John Fuller has looked in detail at the importance of working-class culture in the war-zone, providing a new cross-disciplinary perspective on questions of morale and combat motivation.[5] More recently, Michael Roper has explored the challenges of emotional survival while, on the military side of the equation, studies of issues like logistics and the practicalities of command at different levels have further demonstrated the value of using smaller building blocks to add to the big picture.[6]

Despite all these impressive contributions, however, junior British officers, the lieutenants and captains who led the army in the field, have typically been peripheral figures in the history of the First World War. They often receive detailed attention only when historians consider three subjects: controversy surrounding the efficacy of their public-school backgrounds and ideals; the concept (or myth) of the 'Lost Generation'; and the maintenance of discipline and morale – the question of the relationships between leader and led. Moreover, these debates, especially the latter, often only consider officers as a factor affecting overall unit performance rather than as individuals worthy of study in their own right. John Lewis-Stempel's recent *Six Weeks – The Short and Gallant Life of the British Officer in the First World War* (2010) is a welcome addition to the historiography, tackling this marginalisation head on.[7]

The tendency to sideline the junior officers may have several explanations. First, subsequent national experiences established different narratives of conflict, especially the concept of the 'people's war'. The Second World War was as much the story of the evacuated child or the blitzed family as of the front-line soldier. There may consequently have been a tendency amongst historians to see the experience of the man in the ranks as the 'true' experience of the First World War. The pyramidal structure of the military hierarchy, then as now, certainly meant that it was the more common. Secondly, the historians of the 1970s did excellent work in contrasting the lifestyles of junior officers and their men, highlighting particular privileges afforded the former.[8] This may have created an impression that the officers' experiences had already been adequately explored, although it is often the case that we only know in quite general terms about such subjects as their social habits. Thirdly, researchers may have been influenced by the domination of modern interpretations of the First World War by a select group of war poets and writers – most of whom served as officers. The provision of such a powerful intellectual framework may have encouraged historians to look elsewhere, imagining that junior officers had already written their own histories.

Men like Siegfried Sassoon and Wilfred Owen, however, were arguably unusual by the standards of the day.[9] If they are at (or near) one end of the spectrum – the voices of bitterness and disillusionment – it should be remembered that there was another extremity inhabited by those who actually enjoyed the war (or at least professed to have enjoyed it). In between there were, of course, thousands of disparate individuals with varying perspectives. Their different attitudes and experiences are available to researchers in sometimes startling clarity, thanks to the volume and quality of surviving primary sources. Junior officers were typically well educated. Many were diligent correspondents or diarists. They were less subject to official censorship than their men and often wrote with great candour.

Like their men, they were part of a remarkable citizen army. Britain's achievement in developing a force eventually capable of prevailing on the Western Front (not to mention successes in other theatres) was extraordinary, as many histories have made clear. Building on only a small pre-war professional force (which was, in any case, largely smashed in the opening months of the conflict), the military had to take civilians – initially volunteers, later conscripts – and turn them into soldiers in less time and under less favourable circumstances than would previously have been required. Those who became junior officers were, of course, an important part of that process of force generation; their performance in inspiring and leading men was a major determinant of success. If this set them apart from the men who fought in the ranks, they were still 'civilians in uniform' like them, different in some important respects from pre-war Regulars. Many had no notion of a military career and were only committed to the war effort and the military for as long as it took to defeat Germany. Yet while they could not be entirely like the Regulars they still had to become soldierly and build new identities, both in order to do their jobs properly and to enable them to understand and interpret their circumstances.

This book seeks to analyse the wartime lives and experiences of First World War junior officers in detail, paying particular attention to this transition from civilian to soldier. It does not, however, attempt to tackle this vast subject in its entirety. Instead, I have chosen to focus on the Western Front because of the way in which it has always dominated British perceptions and interpretations of the war. I have also restricted myself to the infantry because they were the principal trench combatants, making their experiences arguably *the* seminal form of war service. In making these choices I certainly do not mean to disparage other forms of service and combat. I do not doubt that the contributions of other junior officers on the Western Front in the artillery, the Royal Flying Corps or many other occupations were hugely important; likewise the service of all types of officers in other theatres of war. I feel sure that they would make for fascinating study, but it seemed appropriate to exclude certain types of service because they could be expected to have their own distinct characteristics. Artillery officers, for example, typically had very different routines and responsibilities to their infantry counterparts. Hopefully these other forms of service will receive appropriate attention in due course.

Despite this comparatively narrow focus, some of the topics addressed clearly have wider relevance. Certain aspects of the transition, particularly its early stages, will have been similarly experienced by men bound for other destinations and other types of service. The social activities and networks described in Chapter 8 seem likewise to reflect class and generational characteristics as well as some infantry particularities. There are equally instances where I have used material written by non-infantry officers. Such cases are justified on the grounds that they illuminate situations and truths which applied to many different types of soldier equally or because the circumstances described were also relevant to the infantry. Different branches of the army overlapped at various points both in terms of their duties and their experiences. Engineers working in forward trenches or gunners serving as observers may, on occasion, be considered to have provided insights which help historians to understand their infantry colleagues. This is even more the case when considering more personal aspects of the lives and experiences of junior officers which are not inherently anything to do with the nature of their military service.

This claim to wider applicability – of both the analysis of infantry officers and certain sources that fall (strictly speaking) outside this remit – makes it all the more necessary, however, to note that none of the experiences described in this book were universal. Its conclusions are inevitably almost entirely generalizations, as they must be when talking about the lives and fates of many thousands of individuals all of whom were plucked from different personal circumstances and served at different times, in different sectors of the line, following different career arcs.

Diversity of experience creates its own challenges, to which must be added the difficulties of interpreting the primary sources on which this book is based. The letters and diaries written contemporaneously have certain advantages over memoirs or accounts written long after the event since they tend to focus more on daily happenings and sensations rather than well-remembered incidents. Over a period of time they can reflect changing moods and attitudes and can shed valuable light on the minutiae of life on the Western Front. They may also be a more accurate reflection of personal circumstances, since their creators have (usually) not had the opportunity to mull over their experiences or historicise their experiences – but they are not unproblematic. In the first place, the value of sources is highly variable. A correspondent may write interestingly and discriminatingly about weighty personal or military issues or he may confine himself to platitudes, pleasantries and requests for clean socks. Naturally, historians will gravitate towards those individuals who have something to say. Can any understanding gained from these sources be complete if it is disproportionately based on the testimony of these more thoughtful and revealing characters?

Then there is the problem of editorial intrusion. Letters and diaries are invariably edited in some way or other before publication. Historians and editors nowadays tend to focus on providing context and are likely to be aware of the potential issues that their interventions may cause. More problematic by far are the numerous collections published by families in the aftermath of a death. The explicitly commemorative function of these books raises questions about their contents. Even collections deposited in public archives are not immune, as there is no knowing what may have been removed before they were handed over. There is, for that matter, no way of knowing what may have been lost or destroyed by accident, whether during the war or subsequently.

Another problem particularly associated with Western Front sources concerns the use of language and the ways in which messages were conveyed to certain audiences. Essentially, there is frequently a significant representational gulf between the way in which correspondents write in letters about active service and the notorious images of mud and slaughter. The same is true of many diaries of the period, since many sources using that format or title were, in fact, rather more like regular despatches to the family or home than a truly private journal. The war is often described as 'topping fun', or a 'marvellous experience', and so forth. Soldiers claim that they have never felt so fit, or that they would not want to be anywhere else. Can any of these more positive statements be taken at face value, or are writers shielding their audience from the truth? Are they using this elevating vocabulary because they think social conventions demand it, or do they sincerely think in these ways? The answer may be different for every individual. Some historians have argued that there was a general tendency for soldiers to represent their experiences as positive and to shield their families from the true horrors. No doubt this was sometimes the case, but far from universal, judging by the large numbers of correspondents prepared to include graphic details. What is the greater distorting factor: their use of language or our verdict on what they *should* have written? How can we recreate the true opinions of those who experienced the war and avoid the pitfall identified by Peter Simkins – that the cultural weight accorded to the bitter writings of the war poets and our own squeamishness persuade us to translate our view of how it *should* have been into our understanding of how it was?[10] The answer is that there can be no strict rules determining the interpretation of these sources. Janet Watson, in an extensive discussion of the problem, rightly notes that 'letters should not be treated as transparent windows into their authors' minds' but also that surprising statements should not be dismissed out of hand.[11] The historian must therefore exercise care and judgement while recognising that conclusions remain subjective.

Later accounts and memoirs have also been used because they frequently provide excellent descriptions of events which might not feature in letters to family or a diary. Their use in gaining an insight into the contemporary or changing attitudes of soldiers, however, is much more problematic. Oral history provided by veterans can be affected by subsequent events, attitudes and narratives – occasionally even to the extent of fabricating memories.[12] The writers of memoirs are vulnerable to the influence of post-war developments in personal, social or historical perspectives on the war. While this does not render them useless as historical sources it is important to use them carefully.

In addition to those primary sources which have been cited and listed in the bibliography, there were many others which were read but not used because they did not provide any additional insights. In combination, however, with the secondary literature – itself rich in extracts from primary sources – this material contributed to an overall process of familiarisation with the period and the sources. I have relied on this familiarisation to draw certain conclusions which, although not supported by any preponderant weight of evidence, appear to be in accordance with my overall experience of the sources.

In order to explore the different experiences and attitudes of junior officers, this book focuses on the process of transition from civilian to soldier and the construction of a soldierly identity. This process was the essence of Britain's force generation during the war, as the authorities had to build an army, not simply a crowd of civilians wearing uniform. A focus on personal chronologies of wartime service and the ensuing development of a soldier character has had some influence on the selection of sources. In the first few years of the war the army predominantly commissioned men from a public-school background. Of those, it might be expected that the growth of a new military persona would be most evident in those who went straight from school or university into the army. These men from the upper- and middle-classes could generally be expected to have had less experience of the realities of adult life than those who were older or who, because of their different circumstances, might have had to accept working and family responsibilities by the same age. As Harold Mellersh of Berkhamstead School observed, 'being a schoolboy when it started, I entered the Army with my mind very much the equivalent of a blank sheet.' He took a temporary commission in the 3rd Battalion of the East Lancashire Regiment in June 1915, shortly after his 18th birthday.[13] The letters and diaries of his contemporaries form the backbone of this analysis. This has several further advantages for a study of transition. This cohort of young men came from relatively homogenous backgrounds. When examining any journey, in this case the journey from civilian to officer, it is important to know as much as possible about the point of departure. A common public-school background supplies a basis for what follows.

Moreover, while not all First World War infantry officers went to public school by any means, the values of such institutions and the Edwardian society they reflected were deemed to be ideal for military leaders. While the exclusivity of this mindset has rightly failed to stand the test of time, the army took it seriously. Once the social base of the officer corps began to get broader, it did everything possible to ensure that the officer corps retained this particular cultural and ideological standard, even to the extent of training officers from other backgrounds how to behave.[14] As Gary Sheffield has argued, these new officers 'soaked up public-school values through education, training and socialisation. As a result, the lower-middle-class and working-class officers of the latter part of the war were imbued with much the same values as their public-school-educated predecessors.'[15] While this forced homogeneity is useful when attempting to draw some broad conclusions about officers on the Western Front, these social and cultural changes did have a big impact, as did structural changes like the introduction of conscription. I have tried to remain mindful of the distinctions and the important changes in the composition of the officer corps and have attempted to address them as thoroughly as possible throughout.

The process of transition is defined by its temporal nature and consequently the first three chapters follow what might be called the usual stages of the junior officer's career in a roughly chronological fashion. Chapter 1 examines the social, cultural and educational backgrounds which nurtured the traditional officer class: the children of the upper- and middle-classes. It is primarily concerned with the pre-war world, the factors which contributed to the decision of thousands of young men fresh from public school and university to volunteer in those early months of the war and the nature of the military system which accepted them into its officer hierarchy. Since many future officers remained at school beyond the outbreak of war, Chapter 1 also examines the effect which the conflict had on educational institutions and their pupils.

Chapter 2 is concerned with the process of getting a commission and the earliest stages of the transition from civilian to soldier. The decision to participate in the war may be seen as an important initial step and moment of self-definition, the prospective officer thinking (perhaps for the first time) of himself as a potential soldier rather than just a civilian. Questions of perception and self-validation, introduced in this context, are consistently important throughout a young officer's military career. The process of developing a soldierly character begins in earnest, however, with the assumption of military duties and the receipt of military training.

With the transition underway and having received some training, Chapter 3 describes the young officer's introduction to the Western Front and the stages of initiation into the role of front-line combatant. Whatever their subsequent thoughts about trench warfare, it is striking that young officers were strongly influenced by a perception that only in the trenches could a man fully satisfy certain expectations of what it meant to be a fighter. Their desire to achieve that initiation made them keen to experience the line and certain key activities, such as experiencing some kind of threat. This was, however, essentially a relatively brief phase, after which new officers had to learn their craft. This period of the transition was increasingly characterised by the discarding of initial assumptions and expectations in favour of attitudes based more on experience. It is also at this point that growing professionalism emerges as one of the defining features of junior officers' development, transforming their attitudes towards the military and the roles they should perform as part of the broader war effort.

Subsequent chapters move away from a chronological approach to the transition in order to deal with issues which might be encountered by an officer at any point in his career. There is, however, an assumption of a degree of experience of military life since most of the topics covered suppose that the newly-initiated warrior has progressed from his initially rather volatile reactions to novel events, sights and eventualities – in other words that he has settled down into his new life. Chapters 4 and 5 are concerned with professional and personal challenges which officers encountered. They had to navigate rites of passage involving violent activity, learning to kill and wound and living with all the repercussions of battle while shouldering the burden of responsibility. Complicating their transformation into fully practised soldiers were the personal problems which beset all young adults, including the temptations of alcohol and sex.

Chapters 6 and 7 consider the officer's relationships with his numerous colleagues, initially within companies and battalions. Young officers needed to learn about the group dynamics of infantry work and establish good working relationships not only with their fellow subalterns and captains but also with those characters within any given unit who wielded real power over them; these people were not always those with the highest rank. Questions of seniority and promotion quickly became important, since these official gradations mediated all military interactions. They could, however, provide a source of friction within a unit, potentially affecting the ability of officers to work together efficiently. As the focus moves beyond the officer's immediate world, it considers his attitude towards and relationships with the other units, formations and types of officer which populated the Western Front. The infantry was divided into regular, Territorial and New Army battalions, all with distinctive characteristics. Subalterns also had to establish working relationships with auxiliaries such as Royal Engineers and with senior officers operating on the staffs of higher formations. A final important element is the officer's relationship with his charges in the ranks. The rapid expansion of the army, initially through a process of popular volunteering and subsequently through conscription, had overturned the traditional social structure of the infantry. There could be no guarantee that a platoon contained men who came from lower social classes or possessed a lower standard of education. A private might be equal or even superior to his officer in these respects, complicating their relationship and potentially rendering the inexperienced officer's task of leadership much more difficult.

Whether dealing with the challenges of providing leadership or simply finding ways of coping with the pressures of life on active service, it is apparent that many officers relied on a strong element of continuity with their previous civilian lives. Their backgrounds and, in many cases, experiences of public schools or Edwardian society more generally provided them with useful transposable skills or conceptual frameworks which could be used to make life more supportable. The extent to which they relied on elements of the familiar is nowhere more apparent than in their social activities, discussed in Chapter 8. Sociability was an important glue binding the officer corps together and giving its members emotional support, thanks in large measure to the importation of pre-existing social networks and sociable practices. These activities were facilitated by distinctive patterns of consumption, which are discussed in Chapter 9. Although valuable as a means of augmenting the benefits of communal activities, they were also important for an individual officer and his ability to make himself comfortable on active service, further buttressing himself against the privations of life on the Western Front.

The question of personal endurance is much more complicated than just access to comforts and luxuries, as is evident by the numerous different theories and contributions which have been advanced to explain the fact that the British army did not experience any large-scale problems with discipline. A key problem was the retention of a positive soldierly attitude within a theatre of war which was characterised by impersonal forces and has frequently been assessed to have been uniquely psychologically challenging for the combatants. The central argument in Chapter 10 is that junior officers were fortunate in possessing a greater ability, compared to other front-line soldiers, to create and maintain positive conceptions of their work and their status as soldiers by adapting familiar practices and ideas. This was due partly to their elevated status as officers and partly to their backgrounds and educations, despite claims that the public-school ethos was decidedly unsuited to conditions on the Western Front and actually represented more of a hazard than a help.

Chapter 11 finds junior officers at the end of their transition from civilians to soldiers, contemplating the war's meaning and implications. Attitudes are expressed by veterans with experience of the totality of life on the Western Front rather than by the callow young men they had formerly been. Traditional understandings of this class of officer have stressed the emergence of disillusionment, expressed so eloquently by the likes of Sassoon and Owen. This chapter acknowledges and examines that possibility. It also recognises, however, the degree to which faith in the justice of their cause and a traditional belief in honour, glory and the virtues of self-sacrifice sustained officers throughout years of war.[16] The retention of these values can be attributed partly to the destructive nature of the Western Front and the toll it took on a relatively well-defined group within British society and partly to the professionalism which many junior officers developed over the course of the service. They did not cling blindly to traditional but outmoded values, but adapted the ethos on which they had been raised. This enabled it to maintain its relevance, and consequently its ability to inspire and support, despite the awful suffering of the Western Front.

The idea that high concepts of glory and honour could be anything other than deceitful in such a context is seldom heard nowadays, while Wilfred Owen's scathing *Dulce et Decorum Est* is a staple part of many an education (my own included). This book certainly does not advance an argument that war *should* be regarded in these Victorian terms. Rather, it suggests that such debates need not obscure the men who might have subscribed to these values or imply that they could not have been sincere in their views. They were not the inbred, ineffectual fops of some popular mythology, neither were they the undifferentiated plaster saints created by some commemorative practices. They were simply individuals who were asked, in the words of Henry Newbolt's *Vitaï Lampada*, to 'Play up! play up! and play the game!' If we want to understand the generation who answered that call we need to look behind the stereotype and consider afresh how they did in fact set about 'playing the game'.

1

Education and Upbringing

Samuel Paget seemed destined to enjoy a comfortable and, quite possibly, a prestigious life. Born in 1895, he was undoubtedly well connected – the son of Henry Luke Paget, later Bishop of Stepney and Chester, and nephew of Samuel Hoare, the prominent Conservative politician who held offices including Home and Foreign Secretary and was ennobled in 1944 as Viscount Templewood. He was also talented, winning a scholarship to Winchester College, placed 6th on the roll of those taking the school's 'election' exams. During his final year at the school young Sam was a member of the 1st XI cricket team (known as Lords) and Prefect of Hall, the scholars' equivalent of head boy. He was also awarded the King's Gold Medal for Latin Verse. In December, 1913, he was elected a scholar of New College, Oxford.

His younger brother Paul found success and fame as an architect, but life was to take Sam down a very different path. The Great War intervened before he could take up his Oxford scholarship and, like many thousands of others, he joined the Army, taking a commission in the Norfolk Regiment. Even then, he seemed destined to rise. His obituary in school magazine *The Wykehamist* noted 'the extreme promise of his military career'. Mentioned in despatches in April 1916, he became first an instructor in the Fourth Army School and then a staff officer with the same formation. Appointed Brigade Major 149 Infantry Brigade in March 1918, he was reported 'missing, believed killed' shortly afterwards.[1]

Paget's fate was a common one, both in the sense that he was only one of hundreds of thousands of British soldiers who died and because, like many from his class and educational background, he had entered the military by taking a commission. The mass army created to fight a major continental land war had to be led, and the officer corps swelled dramatically from 28,060 at the declaration of hostilities to a final strength of 164,255 when the Armistice was signed.[2] Tens of thousands more were killed or invalided out. The demand for officers, which became acute almost immediately despite the Army's best efforts to comb out men from training or administrative posts or retirement, made the commissioning of large numbers of new leaders essential. Cadets from Sandhurst and Woolwich were hurried into their first professional postings, but this was never going to be enough to satisfy demand.[3] Fortunately, thousands of young men were coming forward to volunteer, and many of them seemed like promising officer material.

From the outset, the War Office had a clear policy for the selection of new officers which was to have a profound impact on the wartime experiences of men like Paget. The authorities had a long-standing belief in the importance of placing troops under the command of 'gentlemen', a term which would have needed very little explanation in Victorian and Edwardian Britain. Gentlemen were a social elite, identified by precise codes of deportment and conduct. The deferential way in which they were typically treated was balanced by the expectation that they would conform to these standards.

Captain Samuel James Paget, 1895-1918. (Private archive)

Their supposed moral standing and innate authority meant that gentleman were seen as naturally suited to leadership roles.[4] A recruitment drive that began on 10 September 1914 sought to attract men with these qualities and prior military experience in an Officer Training Corps. The call also went out for 'other young men of good general education', in other words, those who were already thought to possess the right non-military attributes. A good general education, in this context, did not exclusively mean attendance at a public school, but these institutions were particularly identified with the creation of gentlemen. When more detailed instructions were issued in April 1915 they specified 'a public school education or its equivalent'.[5]

Although attendance at a public school was highly correlated with social class, this never meant that the officer corps was itself defined by class. Official guidelines were always fairly elastic and pragmatic considerations remained important. As Gary Sheffield has argued, it would also be entirely wrong to imagine that there was no social broadening of the officer corps from the outset. In his haste to supply his New Army with leaders, the Secretary of State for War, Lord Kitchener, almost immediately reached beyond the usual social elites.[6] This willingness to look beyond traditional cohorts became more important as the war progressed and the demand for new officers outstripped the supply of candidates from traditional sources. Views about the importance of character traits inculcated by a public-school style education persisted but the army did not respond to the shortage by seeking in some way to make class itself a criterion for leadership. Instead it chose to become a provider of those traits to men who were suitable in other regards, usually those who had already demonstrated military skills and an aptitude for leadership in the field.

The decision in 1914 and 1915 to commission on a basis which was almost intrinsically biased towards the upper classes was, however, entirely in keeping with practical considerations, established practices, prevailing class attitudes and military beliefs about the qualities which an officer required. These policies resulted in the commissioning of thousands of young men with public-school and university backgrounds. This chapter examines the factors underpinning this official choice. This is an essential starting point for a study of the junior leaders of the First World War because of the degree of cultural homogeneity which persisted within the officer class throughout the conflict. The public-schoolboys who came of age before or shortly after the start of the war had absorbed ideas through their lessons, sports, extra-curricular activities and entertainments. This conditioning created the starting point for a process of transition which took them from the civilian world to a new military life. Those from a similar background who came of age after the start of the war were usually subjected to a heightened process of militarization as the public schools threw themselves enthusiastically behind the war effort, encouraging the creation of a communal identity which would ultimately play a significant role amid the trials of the Western Front, but the doctrine was largely unchanged. It was the same creed which the army endeavoured to teach to a new generation of officers, although this is a subject for Chapter 7.

᠉

Throughout the 19th Century the British army was subject to the professionalizing forces at work in other areas of national life.[7] These significantly altered its social composition, professional abilities and attitudes. Its officer corps was not exempt. Close connections between the Regular Army and social elites, in particular the landed aristocracy, had historically been ensured by the system of purchase of commissions and promotions. Once this system had been abolished by the Cardwell reforms of 1871, the officer corps became altogether more professional and officers' backgrounds became more socially varied.[8] By 1899, whilst significant numbers were still drawn from the aristocracy and the landed gentry, approximately half of all military officers came from the middle-classes, many from professional, clerical or military families.[9]

Under the new system, the public schools became an increasingly important source of officers. The army that fought in the Boer War was largely commanded by public-school-educated officers who comprised a calculated 62 per cent of the total. Eleven per cent came from Eton alone.[10] The percentage of Sandhurst entrants with public-school backgrounds increased from 12 per cent in 1883 to 55.4 per cent between 1896 and 1900.[11] By the Edwardian era, Gary Sheffield notes, this type of education had almost become a prerequisite.[12] Given the increasing domination of the officer corps by the middle and professional classes, this was due in large measure to the schools' successes in promoting themselves as the preferred educators of these demographics.

Although the schools and the officer corps were much less socially exclusive by the end of the Victorian era they were still dominated by an ethos derived from the landed classes and the aristocracy, reflecting the highly conformist nature of Victorian and Edwardian society in which traditional elites largely remained the arbiters of taste and social mores. The persistence of notably elite enclaves in both systems was probably influential as well. Within the public-school system, Eton and Harrow were clearly at the top of the pile, attracting the upper and wealthier middle classes.[13] Other public schools naturally attempted to emulate the more esteemed institutions. An ensuing educational homogeneity was carried over into the officer corps, where the dominance of upper-class values and ideals was further promoted by the character of the most prestigious units. The percentage of aristocratic officers in the Household Cavalry and the Brigade of Guards was actually higher in 1912 than it had been in either 1830 or 1852.[14]

The public schools' success was also due to the high correlation between the attitudes and ideas prized by the military and the public schools.[15] The military establishment, adhering adamantly to a heroic, chivalric and classical conception of warfare throughout much of the 19th Century, had laid great weight on the value of character and morale rather than on intellect and application.[16] The public schools did likewise. Their influence was highly acceptable to the army since the emphasis they placed on 'character', inspired by Thomas Arnold and muscular Christianity, was considered to impart all that prospective officers required short of actual military knowledge, and that learning to be a gentleman was all the training in leadership that was necessary.[17] The public schools also taught their pupils to accept that status carried with it some social obligations. A sense of responsibility offset the privilege of landed society in the 19th Century and was considered important in maintaining the social order. The officer corps had internalised this lesson by Edwardian times, institutionalising the paternalistic attitude towards their men which was to be such an asset during the war.[18]

Given the close relationship that already existed between the public schools and the officer corps, it is perhaps unsurprising that the War Office should have turned to the products of the public schools at the outbreak of war. An alternative source of officers might have been non-commissioned officers of the Regular Army, many of whom were fulfilling important leadership roles and were highly proficient soldiers. NCOs were given commissions in the Victorian and Edwardian army, although not in particularly large numbers unless a major conflict was taking place. During the Crimean War, for example, 252 NCOs were commissioned.[19] A few famous figures such as Sir William Robertson – who enlisted in 1877, was commissioned nine years later and served as Chief of the Imperial General Staff from 1915 to 1918 – enjoyed illustrious careers which began in the ranks.[20] More commonly, however, senior NCOs who joined the officer corps rose no further than the rank of captain, and frequently accepted posts with no prospect of promotion, such as those of quartermaster or riding master.[21]

This was not, in any case, the War Office's preferred method of providing leaders. Nevertheless, despite persistent beliefs about the importance of social considerations, recruitment policies were undergoing a process of reassessment prior to the start of the First World War. In 1913 the Army Council was contemplating a substantial increase in the number of commissions given to NCOs and hoped to benefit from the experience of the French Army. As early as the 1870s, one third or more of France's entire establishment of officers was being sourced from the ranks of its *sous officiers,* whereas the British never obtained more than five per cent.[22] Major M. Earle was tasked with investigating the French system of educating NCOs selected for commissions and visited their training establishments at Saumur (Cavalry), St Maixent (Infantry), Versailles (Engineers) and Fontainebleau (Artillery). His report was forwarded to the Chief of the Imperial General Staff, Sir John French, in February 1914 and to J.E.B. Seely, Secretary of State for War, the following month.

Earle had been instructed to look at ways of overcoming educational and social deficiencies in exceptional men considered appropriate for commissions, rather than to look at training in specifically military skills. His report illuminated the shared French and British belief that NCOs required training in officer-like behaviour in addition to knowledge of an officer's duties if they were to inspire confidence in their men. One part of this instruction involved inculcating appropriate moral virtues:

> The French also make a great point of instructing their NCOs in what they call 'Morale'. It is not easy to define shortly what is meant by the word, unless it is 'how one should behave in peace and war'. The lecture I heard on 'Morale' at St Maixent dealt with the arguments of the anti-militarists and pacifists, classes of persons sometimes to be met with in the ranks of a national army. In every army, however, the officers should be acquainted with the history and policy of their fellow citizens who are opposed to the profession of arms. The subject of 'Morale' deals with questions of behaviour towards seniors, juniors and civilians, honour, truthfulness, uprightness, sobriety, health, the attitude of crowds, courage, fear, panics, grumbling, ambition, etc., etc. It struck me as an important subject for all young officers, and although it is one we entirely omit from the curriculum at our cadet colleges, we should do well to introduce it at a school for NCOs.[23]

The use by a French lecturer of the story of Captain Scott's ill-fated polar expedition as an example of manly virtues similarly demonstrates the amount of common cultural ground.[24] The emphasis on behaviour towards the members of society's different strata is also significant; the hallmark of the idealised Edwardian social system was deference and the appropriate treatment of the lower classes by their superiors. It is quite possible that Earle stopped short of recommending its inclusion on the usual officers' curriculum because he assumed that so many of the 'lessons' would (or should) already have been mastered by those seeking commissions. He also noted with approval the methods adopted by the French to diminish or remove social stigmas:

> A great point is made in all schools for Non-Commissioned Officers in France, save perhaps in that of the cavalry at Saumur where the students are of a higher standard socially and educationally, of teaching the mother tongue. Every effort is made at all times to correct vulgarity or commonness of speech, but in addition distinct lessons in French are given to assist candidates to speak and write properly. It is possible that impurities in the language and provincialisms in France are more common than in England, and they are certainly more tolerated in that country than with us, but in spite of this the French General Staff devote time to correcting them.[25]

This point is given added emphasis by Earle's analysis of the essential differences between the British and French systems of messing:

> **In France** the officers' mess is a very simple affair. A regiment is permanently quartered in the same town. Officers of different classes, tastes or means may take root in different parts of the town, and perhaps do not associate off duty …

In England the mess stands for much. King's Regulations lay down that all single members shall be dining members. In fact the members of a mess must be one family, especially is this the case when the unit goes abroad.[26]

By ensuring that its officers would socialise closely as a matter of course, the British army placed a premium on social homogeneity or, at least, the ability of its officers to maintain effective and harmonious relations. This, Earle clearly believed, would be challenged by introducing untutored members of the lower classes into the mix. Extolling the virtues of the French system, he warned that 'A cockney NCO coming to join the officers' mess of one of our regiments would be somewhat handicapped.' The contemporary truth of this caution is borne out by the following comment from an Old Etonian, surveying his Edwardian youth from the 1950s: 'If birds of a feather flock together, with young Englishmen it is largely a question of pronunciation. We could respect any one of our fellow-undergraduates; but a man going up to Oxford does not want respect, he wants social equality, and for that – I tell of the past – must speak the Queen's English with a specific accent and intonation. Or rather, he must *not* speak it in certain ways; for while a Scottish accent can be so easy upon the ear that the speaker actually endears himself for that alone, and Yorkshire vowels can charm, a Cockney voice, in any of its variations, is a sad bar to social acceptance.'[27]

Potential problems of this sort seem to have been uppermost in Earle's mind when he offered a judgement on one potential solution to the practical problem of how best to educate candidates: setting aside part of the facility at Sandhurst.

In this case we should have great difficulty in dealing with 2 classes of students requiring different systems of instruction; we should have the inconvenience of cadets paying fees up to £150 p.a. and the NCOs being, I presume, educated *gratis*. But most serious of all to my mind might be the social question. The public-school boy is very intolerant, and it is possible that the 600 cadets might not behave sympathetically to the NCOs. I do not recommend this course.[28]

The Chief of the Imperial General Staff clearly had similar concerns about social mixing. Sir John French's practical opposition to the creation of a system for large-scale promotion from the ranks on the French model was partly influenced by considerations of affordability – the necessity of 'Cutting our coat according to our cloth' – and utility. Since NCOs were required to possess a First Class Certificate of Education before they could be considered for a commission, they already possessed much of the education which the French NCO only received as part of his officer training. He was also, however, opposed to the scheme on social grounds, arguing that it was inadvisable to alter the class dynamic which supported officer-man relations: 'Having regard to the methods by which we recruit our army, our great military traditions, and the incalculable value of preserving the exceptionally happy relations which exist between commissioned and non-commissioned ranks, founded on the experience and work almost of centuries, I am very strongly of opinion that it would be unwise and unsuitable under existing conditions to increase the proportion of officers promoted from the ranks to anything like that which obtains in France.'[29] He did not completely agree with Earle's judgement on the Sandhurst option and the need to segregate NCOs and other students, arguing that the

Major's objections were perhaps overstated and might very possibly be overcome, but he was concerned that 'to act upon the suggestion at once would mean giving up all hope of the required number of cadets being forthcoming, which we certainly should not do just yet.'[30]

Since such senior figures in the army were not convinced that it was necessary to take a step that some clearly regarded as drastic, it is not surprising that no such idea came to the fore in the early months of the war. The NCO scheme had only been considered as a way of overcoming a shortfall in applications for commissions from precisely the public-school men who volunteered in their thousands after August 1914. There were also practical considerations. It would have been extremely difficult to have retrieved NCOs from the front during the first few chaotic months of fighting, where they were urgently needed. Although many NCOs and privates were being commissioned within a few months, this was not in itself indicative of a social revolution within the officer corps since the ranks of the New Armies contained thousands of public-school-educated men who had opted to enlist. It was not until this reserve began to grow scarce in 1916 that more radical steps had to be taken.[31]

The junior officers of the First World War grew up in a society in which the aristocracy and wealthy landed interests, having weathered the processes of industrialisation and urbanisation without any serious popular unrest, still held influential positions in the establishment, the Church, Parliament and the Army. The composition of that elite, however, was changing. By the end of the 19th Century, as Oscar Wilde's Lady Bracknell observed in 1895, land had 'ceased to be either a profit or a pleasure. It gives one position, and prevents one from keeping it up.'[32] An international collapse in agricultural prices caused estate rentals to fall dramatically and land values to plummet correspondingly whilst output declined. Average incomes from land fell by approximately 30 per cent in the last two decades of the 19th Century.[33] Wheat production contracted severely under the pressure of North American and Russian competition.[34] Despite a steadying of the agricultural sector in the Edwardian period, the combination of this downturn and increased taxation, especially death duties, threatened to destroy the position and influence of the landed elite – a feat which the Great War subsequently largely achieved – whilst increased democratic participation, brought about by the Reform Acts of 1867 and 1884 and the Parliament Act of 1911, challenged its grip on power.[35]

Simultaneously, the population was becoming increasingly urban. By 1911, 78 per cent of the approximately 36 million Britons lived in towns or cities, compared with 44.6 per cent in 1861.[36] Industry and new service sectors created fortunes for families which did not belong to the ranks of the landed elite.[37] Their arrival might have been a serious challenge to the dominance of these traditional leaders of society, even threatening to supplant them altogether at the top of the social order. Unlike Germany, however, where a later and more sudden industrial revolution hampered the attempts of the new industrial bourgeoisie to enter into and be absorbed by the old system, the early and gradual process of modernisation in Britain afforded ample opportunities for the incorporation of new elites into the old order rather than the replacement of the latter by the former.[38] There were no rigid boundaries between the two groups. During the Edwardian era the new plutocrats virtually completed their fusion with a traditional governing class which increasingly resembled them.[39] Richer landowners were diversifying and survived the fall in agricultural incomes by spreading their assets through investments, typically overseas.[40] Moreover, industrialisation had brought great wealth not only to entrepreneurs and members of the middle- and business-classes but also to the aristocracy, many of whose members owned valuable real estate or lands containing raw materials. By 1914, for example, the Duke of Northumberland was earning nearly 60 per cent of his net income from mineral deposits whilst the Duke of Westminster, then as now, received a large income from his urban estate.[41] Thanks to this flexibility within the upper echelons of British society, the established order remained outwardly stable despite numerous sources of trouble and turmoil, ranging from industrial unrest to suffragette agitation.

Perhaps because of this fusion, the weight of cultural and social influence largely remained with the ranks of the aristocracy. Reacting to a prevalent anti-industrialist prejudice, the *nouveau riche* and middle-classes aspired to become like the traditional arbiters of social mores rather than establishing an alternative.[42] The fervent ambition of many aspirant businessmen and professionals was that they and their families be absorbed into the best established social circles, a quest for gentility that was satirised in George and Weedon Grossmith's *The Diary of a Nobody* in 1892. Although the process of absorption accelerated in the second half of the 19th Century, the path to genuine acceptance was, nevertheless, fraught with difficulties.[43] The upper echelons of Edwardian society could be extremely regimented and unbending. Knowledge of the correct protocol was vital. Wilfrid Ewart's novel *Way of Revelation*, published in 1921, looked back at this restrictive pre-war environment, where the threat of 'excommunication' hung over those who transgressed against a narrow sartorial or social code. Those seeking to gain acceptance had to avoid numerous hidden pitfalls:

> One night a provincial lady with more ambition than knowledge of the world she aspired to enter, gave an extremely expensive party and invited a large number of people (very few of whom she knew by sight). Thoughtfully but still provincially she introduced programmes for the convenience of the guests. What is more, they were convenient. However, the thing was a perfect scandal and the ball a failure from start to finish. Everybody said "Programmes! How perfectly awful! Who are these people? Did you ever see such a show? Let's flee!" And they did.

Such sensitivities created an environment in which, Ewart writes, an Englishman was terrified of 'differing from his neighbour', creating an 'unvarying similarity in outlook and appearance'.[44] No doubt there were hide-bound Edwardians for whom the minutest detail of sartorial and social etiquette was sacrosanct, and Ewart's use of melodramatic religious vocabulary highlights the absurdity of the system when taken to extremes. Emphasis on these arbitrary strictures should not, however, obscure the fact that these club rules served a purpose. All social groupings establish these gradations to greater or lesser extents and use them to identify people with common values and ideas. What mattered to the middle and upper classes of Victorian and Edwardian Britain was the existence of a mechanism for the transmission and preservation of their standards and the accompanying value system. Public schools undoubtedly provided a highly efficient system for inculcating this homogeneity of form and outlook.

The many educational establishments which might be deemed 'public schools' were not themselves homogenous, despite their effectiveness in satisfying the exacting requirements of their patrons. Private education had developed and flourished in Victorian Britain, creating a wide range of schools which defies rigid classification. J.A. Mangan, writing in 1981, found that he could not improve on the analysis done by Vivian Ogilvie in 1957:

> Ogilvie assures us that the principal characteristics of a public school are: it is for the well-to-do, expensive, predominantly boarding, independent of the state, but neither privately owned nor profit making. He points out, however, that there are illustrious public schools which fall out of line in one or other particular: these constitute exceptions within the general rule.[45]

A variety of different types of school could therefore be considered to fit the mould. Undoubtedly the most prestigious were the so-called 'Great Public Schools' which were investigated by the Clarendon Commission, set up in 1861. These schools – Eton, Harrow, Rugby, Winchester, Shrewsbury, Charterhouse, Westminster, St Paul's and Merchant Taylors' – all had their particular character and idiosyncrasies, as did the large numbers of denomination schools, such as Leys, Ampleforth and Bishop's Stortford, and proprietary schools initially financed by shareholders, such as Cheltenham, Marlborough and Malvern.[46] Another factor which might define the public school could be membership of the Headmaster's Conference, founded in 1869. Perhaps the most important feature that most (if not all) of these establishments had in common, however, was a relatively consistent brand identity. They deliberately courted the custom of the upper classes, tailoring their product to satisfy contemporary expectations and social distinctions.[47] At the same time, the continuing influence of the great school reformers such as Thomas Arnold ensured that public-school practices and idiosyncrasies were widely emulated by many different types of school.[48] Consequently, public-school status was either a matter of self-definition or successful self-promotion.

The same was true, to some extent, of public-school men. Although the concept of 'gentleman' was widely understood, it was less clear to whom it actually applied. This uncertainty, Philip Mason has argued, actually underpinned its success, especially since the definition of a gentleman was not predicated on any factor like birth which might prevent others from joining.[49] There existed a broad constituency whose members either felt that they were themselves included within the category or could hope that they or their descendants eventually would do. Members of the middle classes eagerly conformed to and supported upper class values and modes of behaviour in the hope that they too could be numbered among the elite.

This ambiguity encouraged a range of schools to cater for families of different means and social gradations, creating cohorts of 'Old public-schoolboys' who did not belong to a definite social class but nevertheless constituted a distinctive grouping whose members shared similar attitudes and comported themselves in a common fashion.[50] A public-school background consequently acted as a social passport, providing new acquaintances with immediate reassurance that they were likely to be socially and ideologically compatible.[51]

Sam Paget (back row, 3rd from left) with fellow sportsmen
at Winchester College. (Private archive)

The techniques employed by the public schools to create this uniformity have been much criticised.[52] The centrality of Classics within the academic syllabus has been particularly controversial. In the mid-19th Century boys might spend over three times as long studying classics as they did mathematics, modern languages and science combined.[53] This dominance did not go unremarked in the latter half of the 19th Century. The Clarendon Commission Report of 1864, although commenting on their 'intrinsic excellence as an instrument of education', stated that the teaching of arithmetic and mathematics was deficient and that the virtual exclusion of science was 'a plain defect and a great practical evil'.[54] By the Edwardian era the public schools had recognised the importance of a more varied curriculum, and were beginning to modernise. Criticisms of traditional methods, combined with pressures from an expanding state sector and middle-class parents anxious to get their money's worth, stimulated the development of a broader curriculum within the public-school sector.[55] They did not, by any means, correct all of the faults associated with the old classical regime. On the eve of the First World War it was still possible for a schoolboy like Paul Jones to lament the prestige still given to Latin and Greek, but improvements were made.[56] Schools were typically divided into a 'Classical' and a 'Modern' side, which gave more attention to languages, sciences and mathematics. An institutional bias was still usually all too obvious; Paul Jones, though head of the 'Modern' side, was not eligible for the captaincy of the school, as that office was rigidly reserved for a Classicist.

Equally controversial, both contemporaneously and subsequently, was the emphasis placed by the public schools on sport. Originally introduced in the early 19th Century as a mechanism, in combination with the prefect system, for controlling frequently unruly pupils and providing them with some positive recreation, athleticism took on a life of its own.[57] By the Edwardian era, it had taken over the schools' energies and essence to an extent that many critics considered absolutely unjustifiable.[58] While its predominance may have been completely out of proportion to its educational value, it was not, however, entirely illogical for sport to occupy an important place in the timetable. The upper classes had evolved a value system in which sporting and gentlemanly values were closely entwined. The schools existed, at least in part, to further the social aims of the middle-classes.[59] Since skill in games secured entry to and even a leading position in the privileged circle, it was rational for parents to recognise the benefits that might accrue from extensive physical education.[60] The school that did not emulate the great public schools in their devotion to sport would be handicapped in the educational marketplace.

Despite such social dividends, there can be little doubt that the public schools could have provided better intellectual training for their pupils by concentrating less on sport and more on modern subjects. The military was especially poorly served. The system's particular deficiencies in preparing young men for commissions in the late 19th Century were reflected in the number of boys sent to special 'crammers' to get ready for the Sandhurst and Woolwich entrance exams.[61] In 1902 a committee on army education found that few public-schoolboys could enter these colleges without them.[62] A contemporary military commentator, William Cairnes, saw the associated expense as a further obstacle to broadening the social base of the officer corps. He also argued that the cramming mentality was perpetuated by the army's own systems for examination, with the result that the whole system of military education was becoming 'daily less and less practical. The examinations which were instituted in order to periodically test the fitness of officers for the rank which they held and for promotion to a higher grade have gradually become more and more farcical, till at the present day, instead of being a test of the real knowledge of an officer, they merely test his capacity for rapidly accumulating a mass of undigested information, available only for a short period, by the aid of one of those military crammers'.[63] Any improvements in the public-school system which may have been made during the Edwardian period did not knock the crammer from its important step on the educational ladder. Billy Congreve, who took a commission in the Rifle Brigade in 1911, attended one of these institutions in London before winning his place at Sandhurst, despite being educated previously at Eton.[64]

A public-school education may, it seems, have lacked intellectual rigour and overlooked important modern subjects, but classics and games arguably did compliment each other as tools for the development of particular desired traits.[65] Activities in the classroom and on the playing fields were both intended to provide a moral education. As the Clarendon Commission noted, the classics supplied 'the most graceful and some of the noblest poetry, the finest eloquence, the deepest philosophy, the wisest historical writing'. Though the Commissioners also praised the technical benefits of a classical education, commenting that 'there are few educated men who are not sensible of the advantages they gained as boys from the steady practice of composition and translation, and from their introduction to etymology', it was the virtuous examples propounded in their texts which made them all the more suitable, in the views of schoolmasters, for the purpose of building 'character'. Classical literature was rich in useful imagery and moral content. It supplied Ciceronian notions of civic duty and honour and Homeric values of heroism and sacrifice, and was all the more useful for its descent, as the Clarendon Commissioners noted, 'from the periods of their highest perfection, comparatively untouched by the inevitable process of degeneration and decay', which gave it an added sense of gravity and permanence.[66]

Sport, which could easily be imbued with a similar ethos, was the chosen method for creating a shared outlook and developing 'character'.[67] Manliness was also encouraged by regimes of cold baths, cross-country runs and generally Spartan conditions intended to develop physical hardiness.[68] Other techniques included such simple practices as closeting boys together in boarding houses and establishing self-regulating hierarchies – exemplified by the prefect system of schoolboy governance – which ensured conformity to exacting standards of dress, deportment and behaviour which reflected traditional upper-class values.[69] Additional emphasis on school traditions and the maintenance of an 'old boy' presence within school social life – for example at occasions such as Eton Match day at Winchester College – constantly reminded pupils of their membership of an elite order whose standards they must always strive to maintain. When they went out into the world this *esprit de corps* was maintained by special societies, London clubs and the Old School Tie.[70]

This education also had political and imperial dimensions. It was axiomatic that the public-school class had a responsibility to provide leadership for the country, both at home and in its imperial endeavours. The schools sought to impart the discipline which was considered necessary for men who were to dedicate themselves to the maintenance and increase of the nation's overseas possessions. Sport, argued Bernard Darwin in his 1929 book *The English Public School*, was a useful mechanism for teaching this self-control, routinely subordinating players to the wider interests of their team.[71] Many former pupils did find employment abroad in the years before the First World War.[72] Recruitment was apparently assisted by a Colonial Office tendency to select on the basis of interview and general school record.[73] This imperial ideology complemented the latent anti-individualism of the schools, since it viewed the world in terms of nation states locked together in Darwinian competition, affording little place to the individual who did not believe in doing his duty.[74]

A further conditioning influence was provided by the military component of education, the Officer Training Corps. This organisation, which had its junior divisions in the schools and its senior in the universities, had been formed under the direction of the then Secretary of State for War, Richard Haldane, in 1907 from the old universities' volunteer corps and the public schools' cadet corps.[75] They were widely accepted within public-school life, although it is harder to gauge whether they were actually popular. Peter Parker has argued that they were not:

> Officially there was no compulsion to join the OTC, but quite how voluntary these organisations were in practice is open to doubt. The pressure to conform and evidence of coercion suggests that some of the recruits were less eager than their COs would have us believe. Figures suggest a keenness which is absent from reminiscences.[76]

Be that as it may, there can be no doubt that the OTCs, the reports of whose training days can be found regularly in the pages of school magazines, fitted neatly alongside the other tools used by public-school educators to mould character. They also ensured that military influences were present at an early stage in the lives of unwitting future soldiers. Nearly 10,000 public-schoolboys were in summer camps when the war began.[77]

The public schools also fostered awareness and consideration of public affairs (to which many public-schoolboys will also have been exposed by broader family and social contacts.) Between September 1913 and March 1914, for example, Wykehamists debated subjects as varied as Lloyd George's land scheme, the merits of the Polar expedition, Ulster, vivisection and labour relations.[78] Edmund Blunden recalled learning about the troubles in Ireland in the school dayroom from the papers in which matters of war and foreign policy were vigorously debated.[79] This does not mean public-school men sensed impending disaster. In this, as Samuel Hynes has concluded, they were like the rest of the population.[80] It did, however, mean that they probably had some basis on which to make rational judgements when the crisis came.

The universities were, in many respects, similar to the public schools from which their students were predominantly drawn.[81] In certain cases the connections were explicit; Winchester College and New College, Oxford, share both a founder (the 14th Century bishop William of Wykeham) and strikingly similar architectural features. More important, however, were the shared educational and cultural characteristics. The dominance of the Classics was only just beginning to crumble in the Edwardian period, and most universities placed the same emphasis on duty, manliness and 'character'. The cult of athleticism, with its equally didactic functions, similarly held sway. Universities had come to attach great importance to sporting prowess to the detriment, some felt, of their academic standing.[82] Life, however, was less rigid than it had been at school. The possession of a private room instead of a dormitory, an absence of timetabled lessons, less formal relationships with fellows and tutors than with teachers, and a lack of inhibiting rules governing one's extra-curricular activities created an atmosphere in which the more independently-minded could reject certain aspects of the formula and break away from the traditional school power structures. For some undergraduates, therefore, a university career could provide an important opportunity for character development and a broadening of horizons, although only within the strict boundaries laid down by conventional Edwardian society.

The degree to which universities – like the public schools – encouraged, or perhaps failed to discourage, a spirit of patriotic self-sacrifice can be seen in the numbers of those who volunteered at the start of the war. By Christmas 1914 almost half the students in residence in Christ's College, Cambridge, in 1913-14 had volunteered.[83] Many university men were able to obtain commissions immediately at the start of the war, having served in their university OTCs. These organisations operated on similar lines to their public-school counterparts, although they also regularly prepared candidates for commissions in the regular army.[84] University contingents could include infantry, cavalry, engineer, medical and artillery sections – the latter at Cambridge apparently attracting the most ardent members of the sporting fraternity.[85] Although they did useful practical work in training a military reserve, Alan Haig-Brown, writing during the war, argued that perhaps their greatest contribution was psychological: 'the suggestion in the name of "The Officers Training Corps" that there really was a need for officers, and that every member was to be trained to fit himself as a leader of men and as an important and desired servant of the Empire, was sufficient and more than sufficient to arouse both the undergraduate and the schoolboy mind.'[86]

⁊⹀

At the same time, developments within broader British society and politics were also exerting an influence, both on the schools and universities and on the younger generations. In the years after the Diamond Jubilee of 1897 – arguably the high-point of British confidence and self-assurance – a number of factors contributed to a growing national sense of vulnerability and, with it, concern about impending conflict. The unification of Germany in 1870, accompanied by the military humiliation of France, and its emergence alongside the United States as an economic power had suggested that a new world order was rising in which it could not be taken for granted that Britain was master of her own fate.[87] The Boer War crystallised many of these apprehensions. The British Army, which had, in recent years, only fought minor colonial conflicts, found itself locked in a difficult and humiliating struggle. At its start in October 1899 some thought (as others initially did in August 1914) that it would be over by Christmas. It dragged on, however, for another 29 months at a cost of £201 million and required the services of 256,340 regular soldiers, 109,048 from the Militia, Yeomanry and Volunteers, 30,633 from the colonies and another 50-60,000 raised in South Africa.[88]

When the national inquest began, considerable national anxiety was aroused by assertions that significant elements within the population were physically unfit for military service and that this was the reason for the failures of the military campaign.[89] The glittering statue of Britannia seemed as though she might have crumbling feet of clay, the mood of alarm reinforced, Nicoletta Gullace argues, by that seemingly staple British concern: that modern living, with its luxuries and extravagances was promoting the moral decline of the younger generation.[90] The Inter-Departmental Committee on Physical Deterioration of 1903-4 did not accept the worst of the accusations, but it was readily apparent that there were severe social problems within the cities of Britain. This realisation had a profound effect on the Edwardian psyche, eventually stimulating the programme of Liberal welfare legislation after that party's election victory in 1906. Samuel Hynes has identified a mixed mood in the country at the end of Victoria's reign, a combination of pining for a bygone age and of anxiety.[91] Some of those looking back with the benefit of an increasing understanding of the problems created by urbanisation experienced a longing for what they believed to have been a more traditional rural lifestyle, imagined as part of a wider revolt against modernity.[92] This idyll of a more stable social order in which men could live a more Spartan, healthy lifestyle away from the unnatural urban environment could almost have been a realisation of the public-school ethos.

Many who looked forward feared invasion. War was considered to be a possibility all through the first years of the new century.[93] Germany was cast in the role of potential conqueror. Successive British governments had reached accommodations with France and Russia in order to safeguard imperial possessions. Germany, on the other hand, was newly unified and had a rapidly expanding economy. She was increasingly anxious to obtain overseas possessions and assert herself as a great European power. The Kaiser's

Weltpolitik and Admiral Tirpitz's expansion of the German navy created a potential rival to the Royal Navy's pre-eminence and a threat to Britain's security. Technical advancements and the launching of the first dreadnought in 1906 – an act which rendered all earlier warships obsolete – raised the very real prospect that the *Hochseeflotte* might be able to dominate the North Sea unless Britain exceeded Germany's level of spending.[94] The Edwardian popular perception that Germany was a threat to the United Kingdom was therefore easily understandable, even though Germany had abandoned any tentative invasion plans by 1897.[95]

Public agitation in response to the naval scare reflected the degree to which militaristic thinking and geo-strategic concerns had become important elements within the national psyche. The outcry against the inadequacy of Liberal defence plans was led by organisations such as the Navy League. This group, along with the military National Service League, was attracting an increasingly large membership and made the national state of preparation for war a major political issue, much debated in newspapers, Parliament – and school and university debating societies. The upper classes, because of their long association with British politics, were prominent in these debates, especially in the ranks of the proponents of compulsory national military service, advocated most forcefully by the Boer War hero Lord Roberts. These movements may have talked about preventing or deterring invasion but their discourse, in conjunction with fears about national degeneration, increasingly encouraged an identification of military virtues – closely associated with public-school virtues – as ideal national qualities.[96]

Simultaneously, various intellectual and philosophical movements were beginning to argue that conflict itself should be viewed as decidedly beneficial. At one end of the spectrum were movements such as Vorticism and Futurism which saw violence as creative and hygienic.[97] These did not gain widespread currency, but there was a strong undercurrent of similar ideas across society. Conscriptionists argued that one of the principle benefits, alongside military preparedness, would be a more robust national masculinity.[98] There was an inherent link between the physical and the spiritual, and some elements within organised religion began to espouse similar theories of purification. This became particularly apparent when the war came; there was a widespread view within the Church of England that the conflict presented an outstanding opportunity for national moral development.[99]

A sense of the acceptability and even desirability of warfare was reflected in popular culture, particularly the juvenile literature which was the staple entertainment of generations of schoolboys. The so-called 'penny dreadfuls', which had been particularly popular in the 1840s, were frequently both gothic and gory.[100] What they stimulated, however, was the publication of material intended to be rather more improving and edifying. It was through these texts that some of the strongest Victorian and Edwardian ideals were transmitted. Publications like *The Boy's Own Paper*, which was first published in 1879 by the Religious Tract Society and achieved a circulation of approximately 250,000 within four years, deliberately aimed to be wholesome and improving, patriotically promoting proper Christian values.[101]

By the 1890s, schoolboy literature tended to stress manliness, preparedness and positive ideas about the heroic, purgative and glorious nature of conflict.[102] The heroes of writers like G.A. Henty usually fulfilled their imperial or national duty through violence, displaying their masculine virtues most visibly through their conquest of inferior, usually foreign, opponents.[103] Their personalities and values also increasingly conformed to a certain archetype. Patrick Howarth has coined the expression 'Newbolt Man' to describe this idealised hero who was seen to epitomise the values encapsulated in Sir Henry Newbolt's famous 1897 poem *Vitaï Lampada*. The true Victorian and Edwardian hero was gallant but fundamentally innocent sexually, enjoyed a vigorous and adventurous lifestyle, embodied the classical morals of the era and believed in gentlemanly values rather than the more modern, professional attitude.[104] Since his exploits were read by almost all classes of boys they not only reinforced the homogeneous outlook within the public schools but also spread that same ethos more widely throughout British society.

By the late 19th Century, a large canon of suitably moralistic and improving literature was already available to supplement the character instruction afforded by the Classics.[105] These selections, which included enduringly popular tales such as Sir Walter Scott's *Ivanhoe* (1819), were constantly being extended prior to the outbreak of war by the publication of new works by the likes of Sir Arthur Conan Doyle, Sir Henry Rider Haggard and Baroness Orczy. Whether it was King Richard hacking down the evil knight Sir Reginald Front-de-Boeuf or Alan Quartermain and Sir Henry Curtis fighting to install Umbopa as king of the Kukuanas en route to *King Solomon's Mines* (1885), public-school boys were absorbing a positive conception of violence from an early age. Even Kenneth Graham's *The Wind in the Willows* (1908) can be interpreted, Michael Paris argues, as a parable justifying the use of violence to preserve the established social order: 'Such stories both reflected and reinforced contemporary anxieties over national defence, and helped spread the belief among the nation's youth that the "great war" was imminent and that they would have a major role to play in it.'[106]

Warlike vocabulary and imagery were not confined to stories set in unreal, foreign or historical climes. The heroes of Kipling's *Stalky & Co.* are said to have learned 'the elements of strategy' through 'three years' skirmishing against a hard and unsympathetic peasantry.'[107] In public-school fiction, however, lessons about the utility and morality of violence are typically presented in less dramatic ways. The use of force is governed by ethical codes and power structures. The bullying of small boys is usually presented as immoral.[108] The right of those in authority to dispense merited corporal punishment is absolute. Violence is also presented sometimes as a moral currency used to balance accounts. For example, there is an episode in *Stalky & Co.* in which Mullins, the head of games, is punishing boys for non-attendance. The unfortunate Jevons is found to have been gulled by Babcock tertius into 'shirking his footer': "'I bet Babcock told you that old Pot 'ud let you off because it was the first time." Another nod with a ghost of a smile in it. "All right." Mullins picked Jevons up before he could guess what was coming, laid him on the table with one hand, with the other gave him three emphatic spanks, then held him high in air. "Now you tell Babcock tertius that he's got you a licking from me, and see you jolly well pay it back to him … Cut along."'[109]

More explicitly militaristic messages, such as articles about military music, could be found alongside fiction in the various boys magazines.[110] Militaristic influences were also evident in the development of children's toys. In 1893 mass-produced toy soldiers cast in lead alloy were launched. They were originally modelled on British Army regiments, but the range soon expanded to include heroes of contemporary events such as the Boer War. By 1905 over 100 different figures were available and five million of them were being cast each year. The name of this company, significantly given the jingoistic nature of the national climate, was Britain's Ltd, and their products quickly eclipsed previous favourites like model trains.[111] Additionally, big department stores sold a range of military uniforms for children. Gamages, one of the capital's top toy stockists, included Lancer, Grenadier Guard's and Royal Horse Artillery uniforms in its 1912-13 range.[112] During the war it stocked replica army uniforms for children.[113]

Public-schoolboys were consequently brought up amidst a flurry of social and cultural influences which presented masculinity as inherently vigorous and physical, international relations as a competition to further national interest, and violence (within certain parameters) as noble and moral. As Mark Girouard has noted, the ethos created clear codes of conduct and expectations of courageous, gallant and honourable behaviour.[114] Episodes like the sinking of the *Titanic* or Captain Scott's tragic expedition to the Arctic were fêted because those involved seemed to have demonstrated the required qualities – even if the reality was rather different – and because the narratives fitted the stock language used to describe the behaviour of a gentleman.[115]

The upper classes were also taught that they had an inherent responsibility to provide leadership and to believe in the virtue of sacrificing themselves for the right cause. They belonged to that section of society which had traditionally provided notable support to the volunteer movements and the militia. Following the disbanding of the Volunteer units and the creation of the new Territorial Army by Haldane in 1907, the continued participation of social elites in non-regular military forces was partly assured by both the junior and the senior divisions of the OTCs which were intended to provide large numbers of officers for the Special Reserve and Territorial Force.[116] The public-school classes may also have been influenced by perceived threats to the continuation of the social order such as the People's Budget of 1909, the Parliament Act of 1911, the emergence of a nascent Labour party and unrest in Ireland – where many of the landed elite had holdings. When the war came it provided them with an opportunity to discharge their social obligations and, in so doing, prove the value of the old hierarchy. In this they were supported by popular reactions to the 'rape of Belgium' and propaganda which presented the Germans as barbarous because they threatened traditional and family values.[117]

The public schools continued to play an important role in the development of junior officers even after the start of the war, for the obvious reason that they were constantly producing fresh candidates for commissions. Thanks to the natural rhythms of recruitment and personal impulses, numerous boys who were old enough to serve left school to join up only after several months of warfare had passed. Those who matured in time to take commissions before the end of the war experienced a programme of social conditioning that was an intensified version of that experienced by their predecessors in peacetime. As Adrian Gregory has argued, jingoism and anti-German sentiment did not cause the war, but they were massively increased by it.[118] The public schools were particularly affected because they were naturally predisposed to identify with the conflict and the values which were linked to participation in it.

These institutions effectively became adjuncts to the government recruitment and propaganda drive, reflecting the impetus which the conflict naturally gave to proselytising, the pro-war opinions of powerful sections of the British establishment and the pressures which acted on all members of the public-school and officer classes at this time. The schools were assisted (consciously or otherwise) in this work by former pupils who continued to be an important constituent in an emotionally tight-knit but geographically dispersed community. The pupils were profoundly influenced by this sense of belonging. The sense of obligation to colleagues and predecessors which it created played a crucial role in the development of their attitudes towards the war and their roles within it. The public schools co-opted them into the process of indoctrination, placing particular emphasis on reports of the military careers, triumphs and tragedies of former pupils, some of whom had only recently left. This similarly reinforced a powerful sense of duty in the minds of younger prospective officers.

This work took place against a backdrop of change. The war had a significant and immediate impact on many schools. Familiar faces disappeared as many of the younger schoolmasters volunteered alongside those older pupils who had only a short period of schooling left to them.[119] Some institutions subsequently experienced a significant fall in pupil numbers, a combination of this voluntary impulse and the financial constraints imposed upon increasing numbers of middle-class households as the war progressed. However, some attracted new custom. Cheltenham College, for example, recovered from an early slump in numbers, the increase largely accounted for by entrants to the Military side.[120]

The military dimension of school life was typically greatly encouraged and the operations of the OTCs expanded significantly. Peter McIntosh has suggested that this expansion was essentially at the expense of the athleticism which had traditionally been dominant, although they continued to play their pedagogic moral function.[121] For many schoolmasters, this change in emphasis was not a concession to militarism but a furthering of moral ends.[122] It appears, however, that the OTCs may have been slow to appreciate the changed nature of warfare on the Western Front. A cheerful report of a Harrow field day describes how 'after some miles of fighting in which we crossed hill and dale, wood and moor, we ended on the golf course with a charge, shoulder to shoulder, on an impregnable position, and we were annihilated to the last man.'[123] What might have been understandable in late 1914 is frankly alarming in the context of November 1916. The account suggests that the exercises cannot have provided particularly effective combat training. This did not, however, stop General Sir Henry Horne from acknowledging the contribution made by the OTC when he visited the school in June 1919.[124] His comments were not unreasonable, since any prior education in matters of drill, deportment and duties would certainly have eased an officer's entry into active service.

The issues posed by the war found their way onto some curricula. 'Though it seems rather late now to begin to study the positions of and problems between England and Germany we are constantly being given books to read and tasks to write on the subject,' wrote Gerald Lenanton in October 1914. 'I have read Cramb, Bernhardi, and von Bülow and now I am just going to start *The Anglo-German Problem* by a Belgian named Sarolea.'[125] Schools also routinely welcomed guest speakers. Before the war Field Marshal Lord Roberts had been a frequent visitor at many public schools, emphasising the need to prepare for conflict.[126] Robert Baden-Powell was also active on this lecture circuit, and his opening remarks to an audience of Wykehamists in October 1913 were entirely in keeping with the public-school ethos:

Sir Robert said that he had never been at Winchester before but it had always had a special attraction for him, since there was preserved King Arthur's Round Table. Knights, and the Age of Chivalry, had always been the *beau ideal* of Boy Scouts, for they were the types of gentlemen. He was not there to call upon us to become Scouts ourselves so much as to ask us to give them a helping hand in what ways we could, for by our superior training we could teach them what was good form, and a sense of honour.[127]

In wartime, these lectures tightened their focus. Many were deliberately aimed at encouraging a pro-war attitude and cultivating an appreciation of the nature of the crisis within the schoolboy community. Within months of the start of the war, Harrovians received presentations from Lord Curzon and the writer Hilaire Belloc. Belloc's theme was military strategy and the possible course of the campaign. Various observations, including his comment that his audience should not put much faith in the much-vaunted might of the Russian army, suggest an underlying message about the commitment that would be necessary.[128] Curzon was more direct, stressing the moral imperative for service and the idea that a man who sacrificed himself for his country could live on through the continuing life of the nation.[129] Others concentrated on fostering a favourable impression of the military's work while retaining a pedagogic aspect. This example is from the report in *The Harrovian* of a lecture given in 1916 by General Wilkinson on the Battle of Loos: 'The lecturer told us of the wonderful dash and endurance displayed by each and all of his officers and men, and wound up with some remarks on discipline, which, he said, was not only obedience to orders, but prompt and intelligent obedience to the spirit, and not necessarily the letter, of those orders.'[130]

These formal methods of indoctrination were probably less effective, however, than the examples set by Old Boys. Schools took great pride in their alumni in uniform, tracking them assiduously and ensuring that their service records were widely publicised. Casualty lists of both the dead and the wounded were commonly read out in chapels and published, alongside obituaries, citations for bravery, awards, promotions and other announcements about military careers, in school magazines.[131] Circumstances which rendered a death even more glorious received special prominence. The announcement of the posthumous award of the Victoria Cross to Captain Walter Stone occupied pride of place in *The Harrovian* of 2 March 1918.[132] To some extent schools were appropriating these details to burnish their own credentials. Service demonstrated institutional effectiveness in fostering the required values and the national contribution the schools were making; pupils' willingness (as it was presented) to sacrifice themselves for their country brought glory. Meritorious performances brought credit to the school and were a source of considerable pride. 'It is splendid that Sam should be a Captain before 20,' wrote Winchester College headmaster Monty Rendall to Bishop Paget in March 1915. 'We have one other school-boy Captain (Norton): We shall all be very proud of them. It is splendid that he is converting great powers & energies so wisely & well to such high service – But my heart aches always!'[133] As Rendall's words illustrate, the schools paid a high cost. Alumni were cherished members of a community. The high casualty rates amongst junior officers naturally therefore also brought very deep sorrow to schools throughout the country as well as to families. Acts of celebration and commemoration consequently reflected a need to find ways of coping with bereavement, as well as providing an example to the next generation.

Gallantry untarnished by sacrifice was even more enthusiastically welcomed. Montague Moore was educated at Bedford School and went to Sandhurst in January 1916. In November 1917, while serving as a Second Lieutenant in the Hampshire Regiment, he was awarded the Victoria Cross for taking 28 prisoners, two machine guns and a light field gun and holding the captured position under continual bombardment for 36 hours before retiring wounded.[134] It did not take long for news to reach friends still at his old school. In December he was contacted by schoolboy R.W. Rice: 'Our hearty congratulations to you on your latest performance. We almost feel here as if you learnt how to do it in Cm iii! The Chief gave us a half, which increased your popularity to a vast extent; and my room has been inundated with people demanding to see your photo which appears in the summer of 1912.'[135] It is significant that the whole school should have celebrated this award, the 'chief's' half-holiday institutionalising the collective pride in Moore's achievement and also ensuring that it resonated throughout the school community rather than being limited to Moore's own circle of acquaintances.

As well as being exposed daily to such heroic examples, wartime pupils could also benefit directly from the experiences and opinions of those who had gone before. School publications frequently carried material written by serving officers. Some accounts, like this anonymous tale of the Royal Flying Corps written in April 1916, employed the heroic idiom of traditional war narratives: 'I have had a lot of excitement crowded into this week. To-day I and my observer (Major D. who usually goes with me now), had a fight with a German machine, my fourth in 5 days, and we brought him down. It is a most extraordinary bit of luck having so many fights as we often go for days or weeks without one. ... I think a fight in the air is the most glorious thing in the world, especially when you have the advantage in height and can dive at the other man.'[136] Others provided pupils with more detailed descriptions of service life. 'London Scottish' wrote of sentry duty, rain, digging and the different 'war-sounds'.[137] These narratives are still quite thoroughly sanitised, as one might expect in an official school publication. Whether pupils learned more from direct personal contact with servicemen is unclear, but they certainly did not lack opportunities. Officers on leave in England (either from the front or home duties) frequently included old friends amongst pupils and staff when drawing up a social programme. Sam Paget made a point of travelling to Winchester in May 1915 when he was unexpectedly able to secure some leave from his training in Colchester.[138] Others found themselves with time to spare back in 'Blighty' while recovering from wounds or illness. Gerald Lenanton, another Wykehamist, wrote the following in a letter to his mother in October 1914: 'I wonder if I told you – last Sunday we had in to brew an old member of Kingsgate House who was shot in the shoulder at the Marne at the end of the second day of the allies' advance, was invalided back to England and is now convalescent hoping to return to the front in about a fortnight.'[139] Boys were therefore able to learn the values of duty and heroism at first hand from men who had experienced the fighting. In many cases their mere presence in military regalia must have been enough to impress and achieve propagandist effect.[140]

❧

Naturally, there were conflicting opinions and views about the war within the world of the public schools, especially as the war progressed. Bereavement, although carefully couched in the language of worthy and noble sacrifice by the schools, would still have been difficult to deal with. Not all soldiers training, on leave or convalescing in Britain would have expressed beliefs in accordance with the public-school philosophy. Unsurprisingly, the schoolboys themselves were not always particularly enthusiastic.[141] Alec Waugh, who was educated at Sherborne and gained notoriety for the publication of his account *The Loom of Youth*, wrote in later life that 'The OTC was, with us, practically compulsory; ninety-seven per cent of the school was in it, and that three per cent was garrisoned with doctors' certificates. Like all compulsory things it was extremely unpopular. We used to employ elaborate devices to get leave off.'[142]

On rare occasions some dissenting voices were raised from within the system. In October 1915 *The Harrovian* reported a school debate with the motion 'That international arbitration is not only impossible, but also undesirable'. The votes at the end were tied.[143] Repton schoolmasters Victor Gollancz and David Somervell set out to radicalise their pupils, encouraging them to rebel against the received notions of their education.[144] Their efforts were eventually stifled, however, and the overwhelming impression is of a system resolutely dedicated to the maintenance of its traditional values and to supporting those of its sons who were living up to its ideals. The public schools largely reinforced the government propaganda to which pupils were as susceptible as the rest of the population, and reflected a society and national media which limited the possibilities for open public dissent.[145]

After the introduction of conscription in 1916, it was no longer necessary to convince public-schoolboys to volunteer, but they were still conditioned to support the conflict and accept that they were bound for military service. The war loomed large in their lives. The following anecdote was related, apparently without bitterness, to Alex de Jonge in the 1970s by his father in response to an enquiry about life at Bedford School during the war: 'Future? The future was easy. Every Sunday we'd go to chapel and hear the names of last term's school leavers who'd been killed in France. We all knew our future. We'd leave school, join up, go to France and be killed.'[146] Increasingly, there was no future for young, healthy British males that did not involve fighting. As this admittedly rather pessimistic assessment indicates, for many it was only a matter of time before they had to commit themselves.

2

Commission and Preparation
for a Military Career

The 2010 television series *Downton Abbey* portrayed the First World War literally interrupting an aristocratic Edwardian garden party, a striking visual metaphor for the conflict's intrusion into a settled and ordered world. Popular myth remembers a wave of patriotic fervour in early August 1914 and a rush to join the Colours. In reality, Adrian Gregory argues, the national response was more nuanced, with peak enlistment actually occurring in early September. This reflected the fact that men were impelled by many different factors (or techniques) to enlist.[1] The same was true of those who volunteered to fill the junior ranks of the officer corps. Prospective subalterns did not charge in a body to the nearest recruiting station. They made their way there in their own time and for their own reasons. It is frequently impossible to identify accurately what may have motivated any given individual since letters and diaries so typically start once the new officer is in training or on active service abroad. The beginning of a new military life and period of separation from friends and family so often seems to have provided the inspiration for correspondence, although for many a public-schoolboy or student it was simply a case of returning to the habit of regular letter writing developed at school or university. Despite this gap in many a private record, it is nevertheless likely that personal and family circumstances and political views all played their part together in determining what decision was taken, even though it is apparent from some sources that the imperative was frequently neither understood nor fully analysed. Perhaps, as Samuel Hynes has suggested, the simple fact that there is a war is enough to inspire the younger generation to join in.[2] Certainly a range of explanations can be found in the writings that are available. Thomas Pratt, who was gazetted as Second Lieutenant to the 4th Battalion Duke of Wellington's Regiment in September 1914, thought that 'the whole thing seemed very remote and I thought at the time that this merely meant that our fleet might have work to do. The despatch of an Expeditionary Force to France never entered my head. As I had gained my 'A' certificate in the Officers Training Corps I felt that I had no honourable alternative but to give my name in for a commission.'[3] Alfred Pollard confessed that his life prior to the outbreak of war revolved around 'Rugger in the winter, tennis in the summer, and dancing all year round.' 'Was it Patriotism that stirred me?' he asked rhetorically in his memoir. 'That is the name for it, I suppose, but what did I, a mere boy, know of the danger in which my country stood? Everyone took it as a matter of course that we should be victorious.'[4]

The sense of duty that might be felt by a public-school man was given clearer expression by Donald Hankey, a Rugbeian: 'His whole training, the traditions of his kind, had prepared him for that hour. From his earliest school days he had been taught that it was the mark of a gentleman to welcome danger, and to regard the risk of death as the most piquant sauce to life.'[5] In addition to personal honour codes there were social expectations, which were essentially a wider expression of the same philosophy. Throughout the war, men experienced particular pressures to participate as soldiers, rather than by performing some other necessary but non-military wartime function.[6] The requirement for a response defined in masculine terms of physicality and violence was a product of Victorian and Edwardian ideals. This was reinforced by depictions of the invasion of Belgium and France which appropriated the image of violated femininity.[7] At such a time a man should be in uniform. This was a simple test. In the months before the introduction of conscription certain women manifested this expectation publicly by handing out white feathers to men of fighting age in civilian clothes who could therefore easily be identified as defaulters.

Yet more were attracted by the perceived 'romance' of war. Others found themselves drawn in by acquaintances or old ties. Not for the last time, a public-school background could exert a powerful influence beyond simply marking out suitable officer material. Shortly after the outbreak of war Douglas Wimberley received a letter from the teacher at Wellington College who had commanded the OTC. Another Old Wellingtonian was raising a new battalion of the Devonshire Regiment. 'As I had been an NCO in the Corps, Mr. Bryant, the master concerned, thought I would be among those suitable, and so he enclosed an application form for a commission, with the query "Would I like to be considered". Would I not! I was that month a bare eighteen years old, so could it be wondered at that I was delighted. All boyhood ideas of the Cameron Highlanders, and the fact that I had no connection with Devonshire, were, I fear, hardly considered in the excitement of the moment.'[8] In these many and varied ways several generations of public-school men were drawn into the developing conflict. The emerging evidence of a school or college's response added an extra pressure. The collectivist spirit which they promoted encouraged pupils, staff and alumni alike to think in terms of the *institution's* contribution to the cause as much as the individual's. Sam Paget quickly stepped forward to do his bit, but clearly also took pride in the fact that Winchester's senior cricket team of 1914 had 'done well', all being in uniform apart from those still at the school.[9] A source of pride for Paget, it is easy to see how a sense of obligation could have weighed on those who had not already volunteered.

There was no standard process at the start of the war for gaining entry into the armed forces. This was partly because the usual systems were unable to cope with force generation on the scale that was being attempted. In 1917 a committee on officers' conditions of service, chaired by Winston Churchill, noted the chaotic circumstances:

It was for many months hardly possible for the formations at home to keep pace with the overwhelming influx of recruits. Battalions were in many cases no sooner raised than they had to be subdivided or new sister battalions at once formed. The various ranks, senior and junior alike, had to be filled under emergency conditions from any source available. Men of character and local influence, though without regular military training, rapidly acquired high rank and command; retired officers of all categories and all ages hastened to rejoin, and provided in many cases the sole professional experience of their units; men of all ages and no previous service found themselves almost immediately in command of companies, and thus, in one way or another, the very considerable forces now at the disposal of the Crown were officered, organized and brought into being.[10]

Young men wanting to join up could choose various different routes according to their personal circumstances and preferences.[11] For many, the quickest way into the armed forces was enlisting despite possessing educational qualifications which marked them out in official eyes as potential officers. Hasty moves to join the ranks were often prompted by concern that the conflict might be over before there was any chance to see action.[12] This form of service was also the choice of many who participated in group decisions to join up and wished to fight together. Many regiments established Public Schools Battalions to take advantage of their eagerness.

Some of those who enlisted rather than seek to become officers subsequently declined to apply for commissions because they were comfortable where they were or were apprehensive about taking on additional responsibilities.[13] A few rejected commissions on ideological grounds.[14] Frederick Keeling – although educated at Winchester and Trinity College, Cambridge, and therefore possessing impeccable officer potential by the standards of the day – served in the ranks of the Duke of Cornwall's Light Infantry until his death in August 1916. At school he had 'refused to join the Corps for two terms in which he was the only boy in the House in that position'. His Fabian convictions prompted him to enlist and he consistently refused to contemplate becoming an officer. 'People at home who talk glibly about one's "taking a commission"', he wrote, 'don't seem to realise anything about the hundred ties and associations which bind a man to his unit in any soldiering worthy of the name.'[15]

Many men in a similar position ultimately decided that these ties did not compel them to stay in the ranks. The reality of life in the ranks, even in training, unsurprisingly caused many to reconsider the value of a commission, especially once it had become all too obvious that the war was not going to reach a rapid conclusion. Keeling's friend Rupert Brooke was one of these, a fact Keeling lamented. In a letter dated 24 August 1914 he wrote disconsolately 'Rupert Brooke has dropped out. He wants a commission after all, and thinks he can get one through pushing in various quarters.'[16] Some men were influenced by families or friends appalled at the idea of their men serving in any capacity other than as a commissioned officer. Dennis Wheatley had only got as far as putting his name down for a new second-line regiment which might be formed within the Honourable Artillery Company before his father, himself influenced by an officer friend, intervened.[17] Christopher Stone initially enlisted and only applied for a commission because of pressure from his wife.[18] P.G. Heath was simply told one day that he was now an officer, a relative having applied for a commission on his behalf.[19] Those who had already made it as far as the front line might have particularly strong incentives. John Brown left Oxford in the summer of 1914 with a third class degree in Classical Moderations and Litterae Humaniores and enlisted in the 9th Battalion Royal Scots. At first he seemed to be reasonably satisfied with his new life, calling it 'extraordinarily dull, but healthy' in a letter to his parents in February 1915. Scrubbing floors and pans, route marching, digging trenches – all were cheerfully accepted as part of the 'simple life' he professed to appreciate so much.[20]

His outlook changed relatively quickly, however. On 31 March he wrote to his father asking if there was any chance of getting a commission 'either in a regiment out here or coming out quite soon.' His correspondence contains such a catalogue of justifications that it is clear that the question had become something of an obsession. 'I want to see both sides', he wrote. 'By the time I get it, I would have been out here as a private at least two months and would know my way about. As a private you get so little freedom when not fighting that you can't get any fun. If you are maimed you get no pension, and having a much harder time you are more likely to get ill. As for added danger, there is little in it. The majority of fire is at random, and it is all chance. I don't think it calculable either way. My two friends are going into the Machine-gun section, and there is little of the old section left. One has just got a commission and gone home. If the war were to last in to next winter it would be an awful business sticking it, and when the war is over, before we are disbanded. Besides, at least I have been under fire, and there will be a great want of officers, and I am not at all sure that it is good for oneself to give up one's initiative so completely. With a little luck I would get home for a little. Of course it would be no use taking one in some battalion not coming out for months. That would not be playing the game.'[21] He was, in other words, mindful of the material advantages of being an officer, ignorant of the statistically greater risks, and conscious to a degree of his class-derived duty. At the same time his loyalty to his unit had been weakened by the departure of colleagues. The same themes were apparent in subsequent letters. To his Mother, he wrote in April 1915 that he thought he had 'quite a right' to a commission after 'sticking nearly three months of it' as a private: 'I was too proud to take a commission, and well I am suffering for it now ... I was a fool.'[22] 'You did the right thing in taking a commission', he wrote to a friend in May. 'The constant drudgery, carrying and digging, leaves one always tired and gets on your nerves worse than the firing, when you are used to brain work, and you haven't the relief of being able to write what you think about it ... My joining as a private was like my going in for Mods. – all pride with a combination of diffidence. I think it must be inherited from my religious ancestors, who liked to be hard on themselves.'[23]

An absence of close friends and the sheer physical toll – apparently a major pre-occupation for the Edwardian gentleman – are strong recurring ideas, but Brown's most revealing comment is about the Tommy himself: 'My experience of last week has given me enormous respect for the British Tommy. I have come across a lot of them. They are very generous, giving you bread, etc., if you happen to be short. The poorer a man is the more generous he seems to be.'[24] Although he is himself a private soldier at this time, and would be indistinguishable from the other Tommies to a casual observer, he clearly does not identify with his colleagues in the ranks. In his own mind, he is officer class. Why, then, did he enlist? A former tutor, writing a eulogy in 1920, describes the decision as being 'like him'. The context for this comment suggests a sense of duty, perhaps also a tendency to think little of the consequences for himself. This was a characteristic commonly attributed to the fallen of the war, an elevation of each life through the emphasis of its moral qualities. Anything, however, other than eagerness to make a contribution as quickly as possible (which is somehow not conveyed) raises questions, when juxtaposed with Brown's enduring class consciousness, about the effects of initial war enthusiasm on perceptions of social hierarchy. It is a tribute of sorts to the novelty and perceived romance of the unfolding conflagration and to the success of the public schools in inculcating patriotic notions that they could have overwhelmed such deeply ingrained class prejudices, persuading men of Brown's background to act in this way. Paradoxically, enlistment could be both entirely characteristic (when measured against the precepts of the Edwardian upbringing) and aberrant (considering the elite status for which public-school men were told they were destined). That the submersion of class instinct did not, in many cases, last for a very long time provides some indication as to which was the more enduring.

Many found themselves in the same position as Brown, Stone or Brook, if not always for the same reasons, and numerous applications for commissions were sent to the War Office. It was reportedly common for young men to start training as privates with newly-formed units only to disappear after a short time to become officers: 'Gaps appeared, and the absence of familiar faces began to be noted from day to day,' wrote Geoffrey Fildes during his early weeks in the ranks of the Artists Rifles. 'These indicated the arrival of commissions for the more fortunate of us. One, we would learn, had gone to join a brother in his Regular battalion; another had had access to the colonel of a Territorial unit in process of formation.'[25] Many newly-enlisted men clearly used their own initiative to realise their officer potential, but they were not the only drivers of this process. As the shortage of officers became increasingly acute, the War Office realised that potentially valuable human resources were being wasted within the ranks. Campaigns were instituted to encourage suitable candidates to put their names forward for commissions, whilst battalion or brigade commanders were ordered to identify specified numbers of men whose names could then be submitted. Attention naturally also focused on those units with disproportionately high numbers of eligible men, particularly Public Schools Battalions of the New Army and the more prestigious Territorial Force regiments, or 'class corps', such as the London Scottish, the London Rifle Brigade and the Honourable Artillery Company – where 'every man was a potential officer', according to recruit Alfred Pollard.[26] As Charles Messenger argues, the maintenance of these entities as fighting units undoubtedly hindered attempts to find officers for the rapidly-expanding army.[27] The authorities had an insatiable appetite for potential leaders from within their ranks. By the end of 1914 350 men from the Middlesex Regiment's Public Schools Battalion had taken commissions. The War Office demanded another 150 in January 1915.[28] The process of commissioning was sometimes rather perfunctory. According to Pollard, after Christmas 1914 'the brigade was depleted of officers through casualties and sickness. The Brigadier called on Colonel Treffry. Twenty of our privates were at once selected and given commissions. After three months in France, without any additional training, they took their places at the head of regular platoons. In their privates' uniforms, with only a star on their shoulders to distinguish them from their followers, they went straight into action.'[29]

Tapping into the officer potential within the ranks, however, was not always straightforward. In Pollard's case a call for volunteers had to take the place of the more usual process of identifying suitable candidates from amongst the NCOs since so many of them had recently been commissioned.[30] Others found that getting their applications through the system could be an extremely lengthy process. Arthur Pick enlisted in August 1914. A letter sent to his parents in late January 1915 highlights the number of his contemporaries already leaving to take up commissions, juxtaposed with an account of the lengthy periods the young private had been required to spend on guard. (It is unclear from the context whether this is in any way related to his desire for a commission. Since he wanted his father to petition a Colonel Oliver on his behalf he may have been trying to impress on his parents the unworthy nature of the work to which he had been set and hence the importance of becoming an officer as quickly as possible.) Subsequent letters sent in February instructed his parents in the administrative steps which had to be taken and contained a description of at least one reversal when Pick was told by his Colonel that no more men were being sent to the Reserves. The matter dragged on through June and July, by which time he was on active service. More paperwork had to be completed, more signatures obtained, and by late August he was undergoing officer training in Leeds. Pick's letters do not betray any particular frustration at this chain of events; in fact, he talks in one letter of his belief that things were progressing steadily.[31] The prominence of this process in his correspondence suggests, however, that it was a major pre-occupation and possibly also a source of considerable stress.

Administrative delays and problems could be exacerbated by the active obstruction of some officers. Many commanders were anxious to retain their units' fighting strength and participate in combat. They soon realised that if they acceded to every application and request from the War Office then it might seriously impair the readiness of the unit as a whole.[32] When Colonel Cairns of the London Rifle Brigade was asked in late 1914 if he could recommend any men for a commission he reportedly declined because, as almost all his men were suitable, it would effectively turn his unit into an OTC.[33] COs might even prevent men under their command from going (as Cairns himself appears to have done). In these circumstances it might still be possible to get away, perhaps while recovering from wounds or when back in Britain on leave, but it seems likely that some potential officers were prevented from realising their ambitions because they were already caught up in the system. Many who could have acquired commissions comparatively easily were eventually killed or disabled serving in the ranks.

Those who, like Brown or Pick, did eventually become officers having begun their careers in the ranks at the start of the war usually found the transition relatively easy. They were accustomed to the private soldier's conditions and these are generally considered to have been substantially inferior to the officer's.[34] Brown called life as an officer 'a picnic' compared to his previous experience in the ranks.[35] They were also automatically ready in social terms to enter the officer corps. The biggest change was the assumption of far greater responsibilities, although they were arguably no less well equipped than any of their fellows who had taken commissions straight away. Many, in fact, would have been better prepared, having seen and gained some understanding of active service and the inner workings of the army. Men with public-school backgrounds who received commissions after serving in the ranks also had the advantage of a closer knowledge of ordinary soldiers.[36] They might consequently know the tricks which were employed to hoodwink inexperienced platoon commanders. Douglas Bell was one who was not going to be fooled, having passed from the ranks of the London Rifle Brigade to a commission in the Queen's Own Cameron Highlanders and therefore knowing all of the subterfuges that the men might try to use.[37] Whether he and other officers with similar experiences could genuinely empathise any better with the lot of the ordinary Tommy is a moot point. Bell had admittedly started in a 'class corps', but did spend time in the trenches alongside what he referred to as 'the Regular Tommies'. Like Brown, however, he clearly either saw himself as very much distinct from the rank and file or slipped easily into the officer's mode of thought and discourse once commissioned, judging by the speed with which he began writing about his men in the patronising manner which was entirely typical of public-school men who had never served outside the officer corps.[38]

Although civilians who wanted to become officers theoretically had a choice between regular and permanent commissions, and service in the regular, territorial or New

Armies, these distinctions must, at the time, have been relatively insignificant to most. Getting into the Army was, for a while, simply a matter of finding somebody willing to take them.[39] Other considerations were often secondary. The chaotic circumstances did not, however, necessarily make it easy to get a commission. Securing any given position might be difficult, as competition for available places could be intense. The possession of any military knowledge counted strongly in an applicant's favour, especially since many New Army units lacked any experienced officers or NCOs. Numerous undergraduates possessed sufficient OTC training to be commissioned and set to work almost immediately, receiving further training on the job. Schoolboys with OTC experience were also snapped up. Although not possessing the higher qualifications available to undergraduates, they might still have valuable experience.[40] The process was also complicated by the retention, in many cases, of pre-war recruiting standards. Would-be subalterns had to satisfy certain requirements if they wished to join particular units. Recruits had to satisfy size criteria and be able to ride if they wanted to be accepted by the cavalry. Aspiring artillery officers required appropriate mathematical knowledge. There might also be social considerations. The right connections and family background were probably needed to secure an opening in the elite infantry regiments. Henry Dundas wished to join the Scots Guards and was fortunate. 'None of his nearest relatives were or had ever been in the Army, but for an Eton boy the matter was easy to arrange.'[41] Harold Macmillan's mother was instrumental in securing him a place in the Grenadier Guards.[42]

Those with access to appropriate advice or contacts could sometimes manipulate the already flexible system to their advantage. Dennis Wheatley's efforts to secure a territorial commission, having abandoned attempts to enlist with the Honourable Artillery Company, began to gain some momentum thanks to a chance meeting between his father and his bank manager, recently given an administrative job in the Territorial Army as a full colonel. When the Colonel intimated that he might be in a position to help, Wheatley's father promptly pressed his son's case. Wheatley went for an interview at the War Office, but it did not quite work out the way he might have imagined, thereby also demonstrating the potential importance of contacts in determining the officer's fate. When Colonel Buchan heard that his friend's son wanted to become an infantry officer he immediately did his best to dissuade him, horrified at the prospect of having to operate on foot.[43] Impressed by this argument, Wheatley applied instead for the territorial field artillery, where he was readily accepted thanks, in part, to a chit from Buchan. On the whole, those seeking commissions – both from civilian life and from the ranks – understood the potential importance of connections. Both Arthur Pick and John Brown told their fathers that they might have a significant role to play in helping to secure commissions for their sons through lobbying senior officers on their behalf.

A relatively small number obtained places at Sandhurst prior to receiving permanent commissions in the regular army. Others applied to local recruiting officers and waited until the army found room for them. Many more simply hunted for the easiest and quickest route, exploiting whatever contacts or opportunities came their way. Ignorant of the variations that existed in the diverse world of regiments and corps, they were often unconcerned about their choice of unit. Fresh from school, Wilfred House was sent by Rugby's OTC commander to a camp on Salisbury Plain for prospective officers: 'We were told that if we did not specify a particular regiment, we should get our commission sooner, so most of us simply put in at once for a commission in the infantry or cavalry or whatever branch we preferred; and then we went home.'[44] House ended up in the 7th Battalion East Lancashire Regiment. Others preferred to exercise a preference for a particular unit. When Sam Paget applied for a temporary commission in September 1914 he expressed a preference 'to serve in infantry, specifically the Norfolk Regiment', which is where he ended up. Administrative standards were apparently fairly lax at this time.[45] Paget's suitability was attested to by Lt. Col. Y.N. Buzzard, OTC Camp Tidworth Pennings, who commented that 'this form has not been sent to the parent for signature, as time presses, but I believe the parent consents.'[46]

Once the initial backlog of volunteers had been dealt with, and the War Office and army had adapted to the needs of the new warfare, procedures became smoother and better regulated. Over time, as it became increasingly difficult to maintain the necessary supply of fresh officers, the authorities began to relax the educational (and hence largely social) criteria for officer selection, recruiting more and more from the ranks and lower class backgrounds. The criteria of April 1915 were sufficiently elastic to allow for greater class heterogeneity, while leaving recruiters and the officer corps in general in no doubt as to

Wartime physical training in the tennis courts of Claire and Trinity College, Cambridge. Officer Cadet Battalions were often based in university facilities, reinforcing links between the war effort and the educational institutions of the upper classes. (Imperial War Museum Q 30299)

the persisting desirability of certain traits and behaviours (either inherent or learned) in officers.

Officer Cadet Battalions were created in February 1916 and from that point onwards the majority of temporary officers commissioned served first in the ranks and then completed the four months' OCB course.[47] Even after the introduction of compulsory military service, however, direct application for a commission could still be made to the War Office. The Military Service Acts were, of course, introduced primarily to ensure the participation of men who, despite being of military age and physically fit, had declined to volunteer. Numerous men would still have volunteered in and after 1916 had these acts not been passed, amongst whom would have been large numbers of public-school men who only reached a suitable age for military service after the start of the war. Bearing in mind the continued work of indoctrination carried on by the public schools during the war, compulsion can have made little difference to men like Frank Paish who became officers after the introduction of conscription. He was very clear in his memoirs there was no question for school-leavers of his generation but that they would serve and seek commissions in order to do so.[48]

Not only were their motivations similar, but conscription-era candidates could still apparently hope to obtain their preferred form of military employment. Public-schoolboys continued to exercise a degree of influence through the traditional medium of connections and patronage. When Arthur Gibbs wrote to his father in April 1916 he clearly expected that there was a realistic prospect that his advice could be acted upon:

> Mother said that you had spoken to somebody in the Irish Guards about getting Bryan into that regiment. For goodness sake, don't let him go into the Irish. They are a very bad regiment even in England, and out here are considered rather worse than some of the best line regiments. Far better get him into the Coldstream, which is a fine regiment, or the Life Guards.[49]

Anecdotal evidence suggests, however, that there may have been some broad changes in the units that they tried to join. An unidentified Wykehamist officer in the 6th Battalion King's Royal Rifle Corps, commenting on a perceived shift in recruiting patterns, told a friend: 'The CO is always asking me why so few from Winchester are coming along now. Everyone seems to be going into the Guards or the Flying Corps. I must do some recruiting when I come down.'[50] There is also some evidence of a shift in the types of occupation deemed most desirable. Frank Paish applied for a commission in the field artillery. He may have been genuinely attracted to the work, and there was certainly strong demand for gunners, given the sevenfold increase in the size of the Royal Artillery alone during the war.[51] It is perhaps more likely, judging by the recommendations of others, that public-school men became more circumspect about trench service. There can be no doubt that they were at least partially aware of what trench life entailed. Acquaintances might also advise them against the infantry. Even before the introduction of conscription Robert Hamilton, who served with the London Regiment as both private and officer, had the following suggestion:

> About young Leon, if he can pick and choose any, let him take my advice and try for all he's worth for the artillery. It's slightly better paid, not so much physical

work, and a thousand times safer, and just as important. Honestly I do not advise the infantry – before this war is over 90% of Captains and subalterns of infantry regiments will be washed out, as will 50% of the men.[52]

After conscription was introduced, Arthur Pick of the Leicestershire Regiment twice advised his parents that his elder brother Sydney should 'try for the artillery if he has to go, or something like that.'[53]

Once a young man joined the army he embarked on a process of transition. The soldier is not merely a civilian in uniform; he has been through an extended process of training and habituation which enables him to function in specific roles and perform tasks which 'civilised' man is taught to eschew.[54] The early months of a new officer's career were frequently something of a crash-course within which the gradations of achievement and acceptance into the military world were relatively clearly delineated. These various landmarks are important because they reveal the ways in which participation in the conflict were imagined by individuals and by society more widely, and indicate different stages in the construction of a soldierly identity.

The decision to volunteer was itself a hugely significant act in the construction of a new character, both for the individual and in the eyes of others. Ilana Bet-El has highlighted the importance, later in the war, of the distinction between those who were conscripted and those who volunteered; no single soldierly identity could be truly shared by both groups because the volunteer's self-motivation was so central in defining his status as masculine warrior.[55] While her primary focus is the conscripted private, the same certainly applied to officers. 'Old hands' faced with new arrivals were inclined to wonder why it was that they had not put on khaki sooner.[56] For volunteer officers, so powerfully motivated by concepts of duty and sacrifice, this was particularly important. The man who had apparently shirked his duties would find acceptance much harder, his identity as a soldier compromised. Having made the decision to volunteer, however, determining exactly where and in what capacity one was to serve was both the visible (and publicly notable) starting point for and a key component of the transition. The decisions taken in attempting to gain entry into the armed forces reveal a good deal about the individual's attitude to the war and his initial perceptions of soldierly values. Those like Douglas Wimberley who were drawn in by ties to particular social groups or educational institutions may have placed a greater emphasis from the outset on the importance of peer-group solidarity. Those like Dennis Wheatley who hunted around for an access point with little defined preference perhaps demonstrated less nascent soldierliness than those who had a more fixed idea about what they wanted to do (and hence what sort of soldier they saw themselves becoming). They may also have been disadvantaged by the haphazard processes through which they eventually secured their commissions. Bureaucratic delay or rejections on the grounds of eyesight, physical fitness, or the lack of certain key competences may have frustrated or undermined their attempts to develop soldierly identities. Their actions, choices and random successes also ultimately played a significant role in shaping their new identities, since different regiments and types of commissions with regular, territorial or New Army battalions all produced their own subtle variations of officer. This much is evident throughout the war in the different tribes and cliques created by defined group identities. The young man fortunate enough to obtain a commission in a socially-prestigious or elite regiment would also acquire different standards and expectations.

Selection for a commission was usually accompanied quite quickly by the adoption of the military guise which definitively created the public image of the soldier. Whether serving in the infantry or in some other branch of the armed forces, the act of putting on uniform for the first time was a major landmark in the transition from civilian to soldier, endowed with tremendous symbolic and personal importance.[57] This is demonstrated in part by the way in which men like Gerald Lenanton felt it necessary to comment on the lack of military attire when writing to relatives: 'We of course have not got any of our uniform yet,' he wrote to his mother while undergoing training at the Royal Military Academy, Woolwich, 'but that is expected in the course of the next fortnight'.[58]

Uniform was such a potent symbol that, in the days before proper kit issue, possession of even an old leather belt or a forage cap 'gave an air of conspicuous distinction to its proud wearer', in the view of Geoffrey Fildes.[59] The author Rudyard Kipling may well have been correct in his assessment in 1915 that 'When the New Army gets all its new uniform, it will gaze at itself like a new Narcissus.'[60] Dressing like a soldier was especially significant to men who failed to get into a combat arm because of physical deficiencies. Paul Jones experienced great difficulty in joining the army because of poor eyesight. Having been rejected categorically by the infantry, and undergone the doubtless humiliating experience of admitting that he would be helpless if his spectacles were lost or broken, he finally obtained a commission in the Army Service Corps. Though a non-combatant – a source of much distress and frustration until he eventually succeeded in transferring to the Tank Corps – he was reportedly 'very proud to don the King's uniform.'[61] Uniform demonstrated his acceptance into a fellowship and ensured public recognition of his desire to serve, although this particular uniform – that of the non-combatant ASC – was to define him in ways which eventually became intolerable.

The masculine and heroic status conferred by a uniform – even that of a non-combatant arm – in a country still swept by romantic and chivalric notions of warfare was a valuable social commodity, and newly-commissioned officers delighted in the opportunity to parade themselves publicly in front of (often female) acquaintances.[62] Henry Williamson's novel *A Fox Under My Cloak*, published in the 1950s, was a fictionalised account of war service, but the main preoccupation of his hero Phillip – 'full of visions of himself in officer's uniform' – was presumably shared by many other young men: 'prices were nothing to him; all that mattered was, would the uniform be ready by Saturday, so that on Sunday morning, after church on the Hill, Helena Rolls and her parents could see him in it.'[63] Of course, the officer's uniform was also the visible symbol of the commission, which carried significant responsibilities as well as privileges and status. During the war many young men achieved that rank earlier than they would previously have done. Major-General Thomas Pilcher highlighted the consequences when he published his collection *A General's Letters To His Son On Obtaining His Commission* in May 1917:

'in normal times you also would have been a good deal older before you donned the King's uniform; but whatever you may be in years you must remember that henceforth it is up to you to acquit yourself as a man. You have had the liberty which accompanies man's estate given to you somewhat suddenly, for it is not long since you left school. I know that many temptations will offer themselves to you, for the hundred-and-one things in order to do which you have longed to be a man are now open to you; but you must always bear in mind that your time, your brain, and your life are now no longer your own, but the State's, which is in urgent need of them.[64]

In the early days of commissioned service in the UK this may have had little resonance for the average young officer, but this juxtaposition of new-found liberty with obligation introduces a new theme: the uniform as liability. Although initially the proud token of service, it literally marked the officer out. This proved to be a tactical disadvantage which caused many deaths as German marksmen targeted the distinctive outline. The Army eventually ordered officers to disguise themselves as Tommies when attacking to overcome this problem.[65] Uniform might also quite quickly become a badge of servitude. Since it symbolised separation from the man's peace-time existence and an acceptance of certain corporate values, it could become the embodiment of his negative feelings about the army. An officer in the Welsh Guards who witnessed a particularly drunken and disgraceful mess dinner was provoked into declaring that 'he would welcome the day when he could burn his uniform and become once more a civilised civilian.'[66] Doubtless many others wished to recover their individuality for far more serious reasons once they had endured life on the Western Front. However, this sort of rejection was distant, if indeed it ever came. Uniform in the early months of the war was a mark of distinction and many young officers relished the chance to obtain and then show off their new outfits.

Like all Edwardian gentlemen, they needed a full wardrobe.[67] The appropriate outfits could be obtained from various outlets widely advertised in newspapers and ranging from large economical department stores to exclusive tailoring firms. The choice of outfitter reflected both a civilian and a nascent soldierly identity, being influenced both by past experience and means and by perceptions of military appropriateness and social correctness. Thus it was that Dennis Wheatley went to a tailor recommended by his colonel, a policy of falling in line with regimental norms advocated later in the war by at least one 'bluffers guide', *Customs of the Army – A Guide for Cadets and Young Officers*. His friend Douglas Gregson, the son of a distinguished solicitor who lived in a big house in Kensington, went to his usual tailor in Savile Row. Bertie Davis, a newly-qualified solicitor clearly occupying a lower social stratum, had to take a cheaper option.[68] Familiar outfitters like Burberry and Aquascutum were also on hand to satisfy demand from thousands of new officers and more and more businesses entered the market.[69] By November 1918 an official list of firms authorised to produce and sell officers' clothes contained 105 manufacturers, 184 woollen merchants and approximately 4,000 tailors.[70] A government-operated scheme ensured that inflated prices were in most cases reduced and stabilised, although advertisements offering a choice of twill flannel, taffeta cloth or wool are indicative of the effects of shortages.[71] The dress codes themselves were always exacting. Military regulations may have been straightforward enough, but there was the additional burden of avoiding any social *faux pas*, especially in those years before the upper classes really began to relax their grip on the officer corps. 'Do not buy very cheap things,' warned *Customs of the Army*, 'as such articles as khaki collars will probably become almost white when washed. This is a very common mistake of junior officers of to-day, who think that the lighter a collar is in shade the smarter they look.'[72] Those destined for more exclusive units were advised to take particular care over their purchases, as mistakes were more likely both to be noticed and to do substantial damage to an officer's chances of social acceptance.

Officers were also expected to equip themselves for active service, paying for both kit and uniform with an allowance from the War Office. The authorities provided Harold Mellersh with £50 in an account at Cox's Bank and a schedule of what was required, 'uniform, binoculars, prismatic compass and so forth'.[73] Not everybody received this helpful information and it was, in any case, difficult for inexperienced officers to know what they might actually *need* on active service. Many had to judge for themselves or rely on eager shop-assistants who often worked on commission and to whom the war had come as a god-send.[74] The War Office encouraged the publication of pamphlets like *Customs of the Army* to address concerns about the social behaviour and abilities of temporary officers, but they were also useful in providing some guidance in practical matters like kit procurement, listing items deemed necessary for home and active service.[75] The inclusion of pyjamas and slippers on the active service list, however, suggests that even this inventory was idealised rather than entirely realistic.[76] Catalogues like the Junior Army and Navy Stores' 'Special Equipment Booklet' – available post free – could also be used to conquer ignorance, but the officer might also have to overcome practical difficulties.[77] In particular, those who were commissioned from the ranks, and were therefore often serving in France when appointed, might have substantial problems obtaining their kit. John Nettleton complained that 'people who got commissions at home could get everything in London, even if they couldn't get them in their own towns, but if you got a commission in the field, everyone behaved as though only your immediate presence at the front could save the nation from defeat. We were allowed *one* day at St Omer, where there was an officers' shop, to fit ourselves out.'[78]

On reporting for duty (with or without uniform) officers had to acquire some infantry training and acclimatise to army life. Those with experience of an OTC summer camp may have found the process more familiar, and young officers straight from school probably had an advantage over their older colleagues in adapting to military routine. John Nettleton, who volunteered for the Army shortly after turning 18, reflected that 'to me, joining the army was something like going to a new school. One had to learn a new set of rules and, ridiculous though they might be, they were really no more ridiculous than the rules one had learned to live with at one's last school. To a man who had been out in the world on his own for some time since leaving school, this was not so. The absurd side of army regulations struck him forcible as being just plain absurd and he was naturally inclined to kick against them. That made it just that much more difficult for him to settle down and accept things as they were than for us younger men.'[79]

The provision of training varied widely depending on timing and circumstances. In the early months, the chaos already witnessed in the matter of commissioning similarly affected the provision of basic training.[80] New subalterns often had to learn the rudiments of drill alongside their men.[81] Many also found themselves thrust somewhat prematurely into the role of teacher. 'These last few days we have done little but lecture as the men are on "light duty" after vaccination,' wrote Sam Paget to his mother in

Born 1897, Wilbert Spencer was educated at Glasgow High School and Dulwich College. He was killed at Neuve Chapelle in March 1915. (Imperial War Museum)

December 1914. 'It is a strain on one's scanty store of military knowledge, but it is good practice & teaches the lecturer as much as the audience!'[82] In contrast Wilbert Spencer, having been gazetted to the Special Reserve of the Wiltshire Regiment in November 1914, was fortunate enough to benefit from a training course at the Royal Military College, Sandhurst, where his extensive curriculum included Military Account Keeping for Law and Administration.[83] Both seemed to be enjoying the life. Paget described one particular week as 'strenuous and pleasant' while Spencer called his education 'very healthy and extraordinarily interesting'. Clearly there was a good deal of physical exertion most of the time; practising digging trenches soon became a staple part of any training regime alongside more traditional physical training.

From January 1915 candidates initially went on four-week courses organised by OTCs and units such as the Artists Rifles. If successful, they moved on to a Young Officers' Company attached to a reserve brigade, and subsequently to their own units.[84] This was succeeded from 1916 by the system of Officer Cadet Battalions – credited by Robert Graves with preserving the cohesion of the army in France.[85] The content of the various courses remained, Gary Sheffield argues, fairly constant throughout the war. By this time most of the cadets had started their military careers in the ranks. Central to the process therefore was socialising students into the officer's role, ensuring that they possessed the characteristics deemed necessary by the War Office, and ensuring they could think like officers, issuing orders rather than simply obeying them.[86] The programme for a four-month course in 1916 included training in anti-gas measures, open warfare, field engineering (including the siting and laying out of trenches and the construction of tunnels and dug-outs), interior economy (covering a wide range of administrative and logistical matters), military law, reconnaissance, musketry, map-reading and bombing.[87]

❧

Once posted to his unit, the new officer then had to wait for the next stage of the transition from civilian to soldier – crossing the Channel. For many this was a defining event, imbued with immense significance because it literally set clear water between him and the uninitiated. Having passed the most immediate public test and demonstrated his masculinity by joining up, a new soldier was faced with another watershed. Physical separation from the theatre of operations with its perceived hardships and dangers was an obvious barrier to the true fulfilment of the soldierly role as popularly conceived. Men who had been to the continent were clearly distinguished in terms of their achievements and experiences from those who had not. Going overseas was consequently especially highly valued by those like Paul Jones who, to their mortification, were judged unfit for combat duties and feared spending the whole war in ignominy back in Britain: 'I can't stand receiving the salutes of men who have fought or are going out to fight while I spend my time about wharves and warehouses,' he told his father Harry Jones shortly after obtaining his ASC commission. Harry noted that 'To his intense delight he received orders to go abroad a couple of months later.'[88] Sadly for Jones, and as he became all too well aware, the transition from civilian to soldier was a series of such moments. Crossing the Channel was an interim step, not the culmination of the process. As Chapter 3 will note, soldiers on active service were promptly re-categorised in the public mind according to whether or not they had been in the firing line.

In the latter stages of the war many officers did not have to wait long before departing to join a unit on the continent – manpower shortages and requirements saw to that. In the early phases, however, officers sometimes waited for months before being dispatched. Some could not be spared from their units or found there were no vacancies abroad. Others belonged to units which seemed destined not to depart for some time, perhaps because they were still forming and preparing. There were ways in which sufficiently bold and motivated officers could manipulate the system to satisfy their impatience. Geoffrey Fildes, who obtained a territorial commission in a battalion of the London Regiment, was able to transfer to the Special Reserve of the Coldstream Guards in order to proceed overseas more quickly.[89] A small number, trapped in red tape, were kept back until they were deemed old enough. Charles Douie clearly resented this terribly:

> I experienced a great disappointment early in 1915, when it was discovered that I had attained the mature age of eighteen only in the late autumn of the year before. My name had been high in the list of subalterns ready for service at the front, and I had just missed a draft for Cape Helles. The inexorable decree of the War Office in regard to my age was brought to my notice and my name was removed. For months I haunted the orderly room and, in my bitter disappointment and my sure expectation of the early termination of the war, contemplated the resignation of my commission and enlistment as a private soldier. I had observed that the affairs of the private soldier and more especially his age were not subjected to the same scrutiny as the affairs of the young officer.[90]

Kipling's son John felt similarly humiliated at being left behind, despite only having to wait until his 18th birthday.[91]

Whether held back by bureaucracy or some other chance, this waiting was deeply frustrating for men who were anxious to use their training, perform the task they had joined up for and emulate friends and colleagues who were already serving abroad. On 14 March 1915 2nd Lt. Robert Hamilton expressed his dissatisfaction in a letter to his cousin Peyton: 'I have been very unsettled since I nearly got away. I wish to goodness I could get out. It seems footling to mess about a house here when there's such crowds going over.'[92] In the earliest months of the war this anxiety was bound up with the fear that the war might end before it was possible to see action.[93] Dennis Neilson-Terry wrote that 'We hope to get out, I doubt it, it needs must depend on the length of the War & perhaps if officers are killed we shall have to be hurried up, I hope so.'[94]

Once fighting had settled into the trench stalemate, officers were reassured that they were unlikely to miss out and no longer expressed fears of this sort. They were, however, no less impatient. Many officers felt excited about the prospect of entering into the next stage of their adventures even when they did not have to cope with the frustrations of being held back. Edwin Campion Vaughan was surprised to realise that he was affected in this way when he came to leave Britain. He had supposed that the chief sentiment would be sadness at leaving his accustomed world and home life behind, but found that 'the excitement of the venture into the dreamed of but unrealized land of war, eclipsed the sorrow of parting.'[95] When Charles May finally received definite orders to move, however, he noted that interest, rather than excitement, was the chief sentiment: 'interest in what the work will be really like, how we shall manage and how much we shall learn. This eagerness to learn is the predominant note among the officers who are one and all keen to get au fait with their job.'[96] Such sentiments predict the growth of professionalism within the officer corps, a development which was to have a profound impact on the experiences of junior officers, and which is discussed in more detail in the next chapter.

3

Active Service and Professional Skills

When the new officer finally received orders to head abroad he typically found that travelling to France and then to his unit or sector of the front was a protracted and uncomfortable process. The journey to Southampton was usually straightforward enough, although mishaps could occur – one of Lionel Sotheby's letters notes a train accident at Ilford in December 1914 which cost the lives of 70 people. It was at the port that young officers took their first major step towards their new life on active service. For many this would have been the first journey abroad they had undertaken and very likely an unsettling move into the unknown. For one thing, with the exception of those unfortunate enough to have witnessed a Zeppelin raid or naval bombardment of some coastal town, it was the first time that the new officer was placing himself in the firing line, exposed to enemy action. Sotheby himself was particularly conscious of the threats to shipping: 'I suppose the papers will say as of yore "It is very unfortunate, but as it will have no material effect on the war we must look these things in the face, as they must happen." All very well, but when many ships go like this, What then, & we cross to-night.'[1]

Some voyages were comparatively swift and comfortable, others very much the reverse. Seasickness was common, brought on by nerves and the rough sea, as were delays caused by the weather and the threat of enemy mines or U-boats.[2] P.J. Campbell took two days and three nights to make the crossing to Le Havre, his passage slowed by concerns about mines. Somehow, despite the unpleasant conditions onboard, he recalled an undimmed spirit: 'we had carried our valises up to the top deck and unrolled them as close as we could put them. The wind was cold on deck, but our affection kept us warm and neither of us would have wished to be anywhere else. We were setting out together, knights in shining armour, on the Great Adventure. Lying under the stars, watching the lights of England slip away behind us I had no thought of fear in my heart in spite of the unknown that lay ahead.'[3] It is not ridiculous to suppose, given the romantic imaginings of many young officers, that such a sentiment was not confined to Campbell and his party, but it seems unlikely that this feeling predominated amongst officers on troop ships, certainly in the later years of the war. Things did not necessarily improve once the ship had docked. Owen Buckmaster enjoyed a calm passage, but on landing at Boulogne had to spend the night in a tent with only grass underneath him.[4] Discomforts of this sort were a foretaste of what awaited them, although some officers would have been used to life under canvas from their training in Britain.

From the port of disembarkation an officer would typically have proceeded by train, a mode of transport which was notoriously slow. It once took Eugene Crombie 29 hours to complete a journey, apparently a particularly severe occurrence as it merited a mention in one of his letters. He was at least 'pretty comfortable considering – first-class carriages with only six Officers in ours.' This was an improvement on an earlier leg of the journey, when he found the company of a group of drunken Australian officers less than congenial.[5] Occasionally there were alternatives to the train. Alfred Chater recalled the comparatively luxury of a red London bus for part of the journey.[6] Eventually it was necessary to proceed on foot which, as Gerald Burgoyne noted, could be exhausting: 'Arrived at Bailleul where we detrained. A guide met us who seemed uncertain about the way. Over awful cobble stones we marched 6 miles to Locre; there I heard the 2nd Battalion were in the trenches, and I was sent a further 2½ miles to some huts at West Outre. Arrived there in the dusk, fagged out all of us.'[7]

The officer's destination and any interim stopping points on the way would be determined by his status and the nature of the unit to which he was attached, as well as the phase of the war. Officers whose troops were already in the line somewhere probably proceeded straight there. Others would have to accompany their men through one of the army's rest camps (which were in use continuously from August 1914) or the base depot established by each division as it arrived in France. Most divisional infantry base depots eventually concentrated at Étaples, home of the notorious Bull Ring training ground.[8]

John Brown cannot have been alone in finding it 'dreary work waiting here', or Desmond Young in deeming it 'stagnant waters'.[9] Both had already been in action, but even the uninitiated chafed at the delay. Though not popular in Army circles, those who went through Étaples and similar establishments almost certainly benefited from the additional time spent absorbing both the military culture and the details of their business. Over time, increasingly sophisticated techniques were employed to impart greater realism to training.[10] In January 1917 Edwin Vaughan was particularly impressed by new techniques designed to give a flavour of trench warfare. He and his colleagues occupied a position which was then bombarded with simulated artillery fire. Required to take cover to avoid these training rounds (which still created fairly powerful explosions), they were then attacked by instructors using more pyrotechnics.[11] Vaughan's side inevitably came off worst but he appreciated the value of such demonstrations.

By making it this far and experiencing training of this type the newly-commissioned officer was definitely changed and set apart from the civilian existence he had left behind. However, going abroad and making one's way up to the depots was still only an intermediate step. Wearying and uncomfortable it may have been, but it could not in itself establish a young man as a soldier in his own estimation. Officers commissioned into infantry regiments consequently remained eager to get to the trenches, just as artillery officers (for example) presumably looked forward to joining their batteries. There was a natural expectation that status would be conferred by making the transition from trainee to practitioner. In the case of infantry officers, this perception seems to have been heightened by an appreciation of the iconic nature of the front line. Stephen Hewett awaited that great moment of self-definition when he would join the ranks of trench fighters with enthusiasm and excitement: 'I am rather keen on getting through with my first tour in the trenches. It is that really which makes one, and doubtless others, feel in oneself the difference between a man who has "*been there*" and one who has not.'[12] This distinction, the separation of trench warriors from other soldiers as much as from civilians, expressed more than inter-service rivalry. Although, as Dan Todman has noted, many varied occupations were presented during wartime as making a vital contribution to the national effort, the role of trench fighter rapidly became iconic, both to a generation of newly-commissioned young officers and the wider British public.[13] Trench fighting was a commonplace of military tactics and engineering long before the First World War as a traditional component of siege warfare, and the Crimean War, American Civil War and Boer War all witnessed this type of fighting.[14] Nevertheless, the trench network that developed on the Western Front was arguably unprecedented.[15] It contrasted dramatically with expectations of a war of movement, gave the campaign an easily-understood structure and was rich with prurient details.[16] Fighting in these trenches was rapidly established in both the civilian and military mind as *the* totemic British experience of the conflict. Front-line service was 'proper' soldiering.

Many other contributions seemed diminished in contrast, even though they were vital to the success of military operations. The Army Service Corps needed officers but to a man like Paul Jones, prevented from joining the infantry by his poor eyesight, it could never compare to the contribution that he wished to make. According to the memoir published by his family:

> From time to time he heard voices from the trenches calling him. He was always contrasting his lot with the hardships that were being patiently endured in the front line by, as he would say, "better men than myself." He received his promotion to lieutenant in the spring of 1916. His pleasure at that step upward was soon dashed by his appointment to a Supply Column. This "grocery work," as he characterised it, was most distasteful to him; he thought of throwing up his commission and trying to enlist as a private.[17]

For Jones, to be denied access to the world of the trenches and the opportunity to be a member of the front-line fighting team was to break with all the gentlemanly virtues of teamwork, loyalty and self-sacrifice. It was also emasculating, since the man who was not initiated into trench warfare was denied a warrior status which was defined as much by the public as the military.

Officers, many of whom did not lack motivation to achieve the exalted status of trench combatant, consequently risked having their contributions deemed invalid by society more widely if they did not operate right in the front line. They faced this prospect even if they did endure significant danger or discomfort in the performance of their duties, as George Adams discovered to his chagrin:

> We have great excitement getting up to the Trenches, we have to go up the Old Railway Cutting and this part is swept by Rifle Fire and it is thrilling to hear them whizzing by you and you can generally tell when one is close you can feel the wind from it. It is just like running the gauntlet. I had to go down the line 3 times with a Ration party last Sunday night and it was so hot that we had to lie down for a few minutes while the burst of fire lasted and things calmed down a bit ... Ah, it's a thrilling time going to fetch the Rations or [Royal Engineer] stores up at night. And then folks have the cheek to ask you when you go home on leave, if you are at the front and say 'of course you're not in the firing line are you.' You say, Oh, no, only at these places in our line we are only 15 yards away from the Huns. It makes the officers from here feel very sick I can tell you and disgusted with the people at home.[18]

George Adams served with the 6th Battalion South Staffordshire Regiment. Born in 1888, he reached the rank of captain and died in October 1918. (Imperial War Museum)

The communication trenches experienced by Adams and his men were doubtless much more dangerous than the numerous sections of the line which were so quiet at different times during the war as to be almost dormant. 'Front-line' trenches varied substantially in security and comfort. Nevertheless, they seemed to merge into a single idealised theatre in matters of definition and perception, arguably not unreasonably, since unit rotations would have given most combatants experience of a range of tactical environments.[19] Only a few other occupations of the First World War – for example, engaging in quasi-chivalric jousts in the Royal Flying Corps – could provide a similarly satisfying and widely-recognised identity.

For this reason, many young infantry officers clearly looked forward to going into the trenches, at least for the first time. The mysterious world of the line also stimulated their curiosity. Closer contact with experienced soldiers might dampen their enthusiasm but, paradoxically, conversations with people who regarded the trenches as normal might actually make them seem more unreal. Edwin Vaughan, both when at Étaples and immediately behind the lines preparing to go into the trenches for the first time, was particularly struck by the disparity between his own nervousness and the relaxed attitude of those around him who were already experienced: 'Very hard to imagine it,' he wrote during training, 'for no one seems to worry and "going up" is treated like going into mess or on parade.'[20] Contacts of this sort were nevertheless starting to develop that necessary aspect of soldierly identity – the ability to regard the trenches as unremarkable. Other experiences in the vicinity of the line may also have tempered their enthusiasm and challenged their assumptions. Douglas Bell, who eventually took a commission in the Queen's Own Cameron Highlanders, first experienced the front line as a private in the London Rifle Brigade. Before going into the trenches for the first time he witnessed the return from the line of a number of filthy, bedraggled men. They were not a formed unit, but came straggling back on their own or in little groups. Clearly exhausted, some had even lost their weapons. Bell and his colleagues were shocked by the sight.[21] If this episode threatened his morale at such a sensitive moment, he was at least able to assume that their dishevelled appearance was connected to some unusual occurrence, and that they were in some way therefore outside soldiering norms. It would have been much more frightening if he had thought this was the normal condition of soldiers returning from the front line.

Many were naturally apprehensive when the time came to go into the trenches themselves, and their fears could be realised well before arriving in the front line. As George Adams discovered, simply getting up to the trenches could entail significant difficulties and danger. The uninitiated soldiers would quickly start to see the sights and experience the smells, slide or stick in the mud, and squeeze past the various human and other obstructions they encountered. Raymond Hepper's initial experience was clearly challenging, even if his letter seemingly makes light of it: 'The communication trench is safely negotiated, a difficult task in the dark as one slips off the narrow track or duck boards into the water beneath and wet feet are the cheerful result.'[22] It took a while to acclimatise to this subterranean labyrinth. Andrew Buxton, like Hepper, was especially struck by the difficulties of moving about: 'You can have no idea of the difficulty of keeping direction and getting a proper idea of the lie of the land and of trenches in the maze that masses of trenches, dug-outs, communication trenches appear when you first get into them.'[23] First impressions of the front line itself would depend substantially on the nature of the front at that point. Lt. Wilbert Spencer was clearly in a particularly unpleasant spot in December 1914: 'I wonder how many people realize what Hell the trenches can be. No shelter from rain or cold. Mud in some places right over one's knees, nearly always over one's ankles.'[24]

In more favourable circumstances officers' writings often reveal them to be curious, interested, often excited at the prospect of entering into something so vast, so momentous, so unfamiliar and invested with so much personal significance – and not necessarily focused on such sombre subjects as the prospect of their own death. Gilbert Talbot admitted that 'everybody's nerves were a little on edge as we went, being entirely new to the business.' The business was made much easier by the presence of experienced colleagues who could defuse the tension by projecting a sense of normality: 'We were accompanied by a nice officer of the Terriers, to whom we were to be attached, but who talked in a cool way of it all that was bred partly of genuine familiarity and partly of a desire to impress us. And it was both interesting and exciting to hear the rifle fire grow louder as we approached and to watch the lights of the flares that both sides send up all night. I must honestly say that before we started, and when we got there I felt surprisingly unfrightened, and much more curious than anything else.'[25]

Similarly positive sentiments can be found in many letters and diaries. Graham Greenwell, who admittedly published his diary in 1935 as a riposte to the anti-war literature of the inter-war period, wrote that 'it is all so delightfully fresh after England that the unpleasant side of it does not strike me, though all my friends have been trying to instil into me the gospel of "frightfulness."'[26] Sam Paget called his first trip 'two most interesting days and nights'.[27] 'Didn't feel any fear; rather interesting' was Robert Hamilton's first comment on trench experience.[28] In Billie Nevill's opinion, 'The trenches are the greatest fun, & I'm longing for our next trip'.[29] 'The most novel of any twenty four hours of my life', wrote Ralph Bickersteth before adding, in an interesting observation on the potentially dire apprehensions of the uninitiated, 'but first I must tell you how every single thing is absolutely entirely the opposite of what I expected in every single detail'.[30]

Some historians like Robert Wohl have criticised the use of this sort of upbeat language to describe front line experiences, arguing that it is inevitably a distortion of true emotions.[31] It would be wrong, however, to disregard such sentiments simply because they conflict with modern perceptions of those wartime conditions. It is inherently difficult to interpret these sources, making due allowances for individual characteristics and the cultural influences (particularly the standardisation of gentlemanly language noted in Chapter 1) which might well distort written accounts. Even so, it is not totally incredible that they can be taken at face value to some extent, given the mystery and expectation surrounding the trenches and the contrast with the orderly Edwardian world (and therefore interesting novelty) which they represented. Although many soldiers continued to write in the most candid terms, some may have adopted or eventually developed languages designed to protect loved ones from reality, but to suppose that front-line service yielded no experiences which could be described positively assumes a standard level of horror which was clearly not apparent. As Hew Strachan and John Bourne have both pointed out, the system of trench warfare developed in order to *prevent* casualties and *reduce* the awfulness of industrial war.[32] British monthly casualties during the open warfare of August 1918 were approximately 50 per cent higher than those suffered a year earlier at the height of the Third Battle of Ypres.[33] One of the reasons the war was able to continue as it did was because trenches protected men from the awesome firepower of modern weapons. They may not have been pleasant, but life within them was not insupportable.

Getting to the trenches was a significant milestone in the development of an infantry officer's soldierly identity, but that goal was rapidly superseded by others. Douglas Gillespie noticed that a group of territorial soldiers under his instruction were anxious to experience some form of action as quickly as possible: 'I think they would all have liked to be sentries, or go out for patrols in front of the wire; this morning they were all squibbing off their rifles, just for the pleasure of writing home to say they had had a shot at a German, and they were far too excited to go to sleep.' In other words, they were keen to start constructing easily-understood narratives in which they were acting in appropriately 'soldierly' ways – most simply expressed by acts of aggression. Shooting at the enemy, even pointlessly, validated the new soldier both in his own eyes and those of the civilian population, defining him as a combatant rather than an observer. At this stage, soldiering was active and exciting. 'Their enthusiasm will soon wear off, I'm afraid,' added Gillespie, 'but it's quite refreshing to see it.'[34]

The transition would continue into new phases as initiated soldiers learned that they would have to endure patiently, with potentially little excitement and perhaps no actual sighting of a German for many months, no matter how eagerly awaited.[35] Billie Nevill was 'simply dying to see these curious blighters. I hope they'll show their noses a bit, but they are such rabbits, we may not see a 'pickle haube' for days yet.'[36] This in itself took some getting used to. 'It gives you an uncanny feeling,' wrote Christopher Stone, 'knowing that there are hundreds and thousands of men hidden under the ground, eyeing each other perhaps furtively: not a soul showing above ground.'[37] There must have been plenty of unfortunate Tommies and officers who never saw their enemies, falling victim to a sniper's bullet or a shell before they had the opportunity to see the people opposite for themselves. Nevertheless, by simply discharging a weapon – even in the absence of a target – the individual was able to represent himself as a complete soldier, having been present in the front lines and participated in action, if only of a limited sort.

Coming under fire was potentially a daily occurrence anywhere in the vicinity of the front line, either from direct or indirect fire. Many soldiers seem to have reacted positively to their first shell, providing the bombardment was not too intense or effective.[38] It was another form of initiation. Clifford Platt was a short distance from the lines in Albert in early December 1915, shortly before going into the front line:

> And then our first shell! How we enjoyed it! What a joke we thought it! And how sadly disillusioned we all are now some 8 months later! We were just getting into bed … when Pss-s-h… thump! A "dud" had hit the next house! We ran to the window, threw it open and anxiously awaited the arrival of the next laughing. Ps---s----h – it seemed a great while in the air to us waiting there – crump! No "dud" this time but further away from us. And so to bed, highly pleased with our new word "crump".[39]

Like aggressive action, these experiences also had the power to turn civilians in uniform into combatants in their own estimations and those of other people. The tendency to make light of a first experience of the threat from shell fire is also common. 'Contrary to expectations I did not feel frightened, only greatly interested!!' wrote Brian Lawrence after witnessing his first shell. 'Five minutes after this I heard a similar noise, but it was all whistle and no screech, again the cloud of earth and stones shot into the air about 350 yards beyond me and there was a much louder explosion. A shell had passed over us and hit a dug-out used as a mess by some Australians. I believe four men were killed and two badly wounded. I still felt interested rather than frightened; one felt excited, like a spectator at a theatre watching a thrilling drama. It seemed impossible that we were part and parcel of the show and that we might be hit ourselves. I experienced an entirely detached feeling.'[40] Having come under shell fire for the first time, James Dunn noticed that 'since no one was hit, the men began to make merry with one another on the subject.'[41] In part this seems to reflect what would now be called 'avoidance humour', which is discussed further in Chapter 5.[42] It also seems likely that this casual dismissal of a very real threat derived from a lack of experience of the true nature of that threat and the novice soldier's wish to assert a confident military persona, both publicly and to himself. Of course, many soldiers came to develop an intense fear of shells once they had lived with them for some time. This might make humour all the more necessary. 'I never realised before I came out how dreadful shell fire is,' wrote Wilbert Spencer to his mother in February 1915. 'Very few people did. But we all keep cheery and joke about them. It's the only way to keep going out here.'[43]

Whatever the immediate reaction to new experiences, officers only became acclimatised to their new working environment over time. Billie Nevill found that he adjusted to the challenge of movement in such a potentially treacherous environment in a couple of weeks: 'Today I've about found my "trench-legs"! It's extraordinary how clumsy one is at first. You see these comm trenches are very rarely more than 3 feet wide, & the floor has drains, gutters, gratings, catch-pits, etc. You simply bump into the wall every time. Now this morning I noticed quite a difference, I can swing round corners at full walking pace without knocking at all. It's quite an art'.[44]

Ease of movement was very different to an ability to cope with living and working in such conditions for protracted periods of time. It was undoubtedly completely different to anything they could have experienced in civilian life, and they were arguably disadvantaged by their comfortable upbringings. Correlli Barnett and others have argued that the working classes were able to adapt to trench conditions by virtue of their habitually uncomfortable living conditions and because many of the unpleasant aspects of war were not entirely dissimilar to their experiences of civilian life.[45] Any implication that the middle and upper classes fared substantially less well overall is refuted, however, by the evidence of officers like Stephen Hewett. In March 1916 he described to his mother the 'great endless ditch across a blasted plain', the 'little holes with deep flights of steps which lead down to long holes or cellars hacked out of chalk', and the 'labyrinth of mud, which cakes us from hands to feet'. Despite this 'Rembrantesque' setting, he declared that 'the discomforts of trench-life are not insupportable and not an uninteresting experience.'[46] One week after his initial introduction to the trenches, Douglas Gillespie wrote: 'Everything in this life gets to seem so natural that after the first few days I wonder what there can be to say.'[47] 'I am writing this letter to you,' wrote Bernard Long to his sister Ethel after only a few days' trench experience, 'in a dug-out in the front line with my feet in a foot of water so you see we get used to anything.'[48] Given the circumstances, they had little choice but to adapt quickly and make the best of it, although for some the trenches never lost a macabre strangeness. 'I had an awful idea the other day as I walked along a particularly sinuous and bloody communications trench, that I had got lost in the bowels of the earth and was slowly exploring the entire length of that great creatures intestines,' confided Arthur Parry in a letter to a friend in June 1916.[49] As well as conjuring an image of an alien landscape, his choice of metaphor neatly summarised the more unpalatable realities of prolonged human occupation.

Occupation of a dug-out (where available) was one of the privileges enjoyed by officers in the line and would usually have saved them from enduring the very worst of the prevailing conditions. The quality of these structures varied enormously, however, and is a frequent subject of officer letters and diaries. Many lieutenants and captains seem rapidly to have become connoisseurs, grading each different dwelling according to criteria such as spaciousness, dryness, furnishings and the degree of protection afforded. At best, a dug-out might have contained a number of rooms with separate sleeping

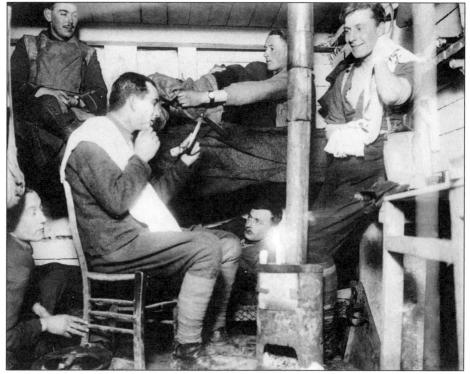

Life in a dug-out near Roclincourt, January 1918. (Imperial War Museum Q 10623)

and living quarters, beds, chairs and tables, and room for personal items such as the gramophone. It would also protect the occupants against all but a direct hit by a high explosive shell. Eugene Crombie was particularly taken with a capacious specimen in a support line:

> The Company H.Q. dug-out only lacks electric light to equal any drawing-room! You enter at the bottom of a 40-foot shaft by a real front door (doubtless taken from a cottage) and the room is about 7 feet high, 8 broad and 25 long. There are four wire beds at one end, and at the other a nice table, chairs, benches, shelves, pegs, and all sorts of luxuries. The walls are timbered, and are hung with pictures, mostly Punch Cartoons, and there are bookshelves containing the well-thumbed literary offal of generations of occupants. To complete the ideal home, you have a wooden partition and communicating door to the kitchen![50]

What constituted the very worst type of dug-out depended on the preferences of the individual officer. Some were little better than small tunnels in which a man just had room to lie down, but in which he certainly couldn't sit upright. Others were barely even proof against the splinters from shrapnel shells.

As Crombie's description shows, officers usually sought to customise their accommodation, even in the most dangerous settings. Bertram Medley found that a few homely touches could improve even the humbler residences:

I found a nice dugout, just a hole cut out in the side of the trench (furthest from the Germans); a row of sandbags and door draped with a ground-sheet in front, wallpaper and carpets of sacking, roof of corrugated iron with beams across, and two shelves – one long and narrow, another small and broad; on this last one all things for keeping clean (though, as clean water is very scarce, this may be hard), on the other a candle, jam and sugar, my books (Browning, Keats, Anthony and Cleopatra, King Lear), and, last but best of all, a jam tim full of roses which I brought from the Chateau in my haversack to feast my eyes upon and to help to disperse the disgusting smell of trench warfare. There is a Madame Ravary and a William Allan, some lovely deep red ones and light pink ones – in fact, every colour; and in my pale blue jam tin who could wish a brighter ornament.[51]

This ability to create a personalised space which defied some of the harshness of war was generally denied to the other ranks, who often had to do the best they could with holes cut in the sides of the trenches, and with their overcoats or waterproof sheets. All ranks might derive a similar benefit, however, from the presence of domesticated animals. Douglas Bell was amazed in April 1915 to find himself sharing a trench with an affectionate cat, despite the frequent shelling all the occupants endured.[52] Of course, officers were more likely than their men to be able to make special arrangements to keep a pet with them.

Despite certain home comforts (or substitutes), officers undoubtedly had to lower their standards of hygiene in such an environment. When Stephen Hewett did detail the most challenging aspects of trench life he listed lack of sleep first but followed this with 'the difficulties of washing, and the prevalence of smell, flies, rats and parasites' rather than any threat from the Germans.[53] Stories of disgusting encounters with lice and rats are incredibly numerous in accounts of life on the Western Front; a dog might be particularly useful for dealing with the latter. Montague Moore of the Hampshire Regiment boasted that his battalion had an animal 'that has killed at least 1,000 rats in 5 months, not bad going. He catches quite a number in No Man's Land at night. I expect Boche wonders what is happening, because he always lets everyone know where he is.'[54]

As well as co-habiting with unsavoury vermin, officers also had to get used to habits which, at home, would have been considered quite ill-mannered. Civilised norms, however, receded quickly in the face of discomfort and squalor. 'It is quite amazing', thought Hewett, 'how one gets accustomed to things one would have made a huge fuss about at home. For example my neighbour at table has just upset his chop on the floor, has picked it up, and is eating it with added relish.'[55] This decline in standards brought with it a remarkable revelation. In what must have been a moment of startling emancipation, young men such as Brian Lawrence, whose upbringing had previously fenced them round with all manner of personal restrictions, discovered how easily they could cope with previously unimaginable privations: 'I was always brought up to believe that if one got wet through and did not change into dry clothes at once one died shortly afterwards of some terrible complaint or survived for a few painful years at Harrogate or some other anti-rheumatic spa. We were wet through for four days and nights, dried slightly in the dug-out from time to time, so that the steam came off us in clouds, of course, but were soon afterwards just as wet again. We all agreed afterwards, that we had none of us felt better in our lives, so that's one folly the war has exploded at any rate.'[56]

❧

Even allowing for differences in their training regimes, it appears as though most officers appreciated on reaching the front line that they had a great deal to learn about their duties. This was most apparent when officers began to join units which had already served in the trenches. Edwin Vaughan left school in 1915 but did not go to France until January 1917. Going into a forward position in February 1917 clearly challenged his self-conception: 'When we had been out of the line, I had despised these officers and NCOs and criticised the men, but now I realised that I was the most useless object in the Company. Immediately on entry, they had quietly melted away and taken up their duties, already keenly alert and capable, and here I was, still confused, wondering and fearful.'[57] This was clearly quite humbling. At different times during the war, however, newly-trained officers might lack more than ready familiarity with their duties. Much of what they had been taught might be hopelessly unsuited to modern trench warfare. Consequently their training might have to be superseded quickly by more appropriate methods which others had developed through operational experience. Theories and 'best practice' did not always survive long in the combat zone. As Victor Germains notes, it was all very well teaching New Army officers about the relative merits of placing trenches on forward or reverse slopes, but nugatory if the local topography did not give them a choice.[58]

New officers therefore completed their transition from uninitiated soldier to capable fighter in the trenches by developing their tactical skills and learning the difference between theoretical and practical knowledge. Realising that trench warfare could best be taught by practical experience, the army routinely placed fresh units in quiet stretches of the line under the instruction of practised troops.[59] Old hands were at pains to stress the importance of being a quick learner. Henry Ogle's first experience of the combat zone was in the company of regulars of the Durham Light Infantry. His instructors began with a sobering lesson, pointing out that a man could not afford to make a mistake, whether it was one's first time or not. They warned of the dangers of exposing oneself by looking over the parapet, of simply staying out of cover for any period of time, of volunteering to do something without fully understanding what the job required. There were then practical lessons on cleanliness, food, trench maintenance, and the best ways in which to balance being useful and productive and resting.[60]

Ogle was with his unit of similarly uninitiated Warwickshire territorials and could therefore learn his business alongside them under the tutelage – expressly laid on for them – of regular NCOs and senior soldiers. Young officers joining their battalions in the line for the first time, in contrast, relied heavily on the example of fellow officers and senior NCOs for unofficial instruction. Geoffrey Fildes was inspecting his section of the front line one morning and observed a sergeant reprimanding a man for allowing a fire to smoke with the warning: 'You'll be getting something worse than smoke if Fritz sees that'. 'My education in trench lore was merely commencing,' he noted afterwards.[61] As this account implies, it was scarcely possible for the individual to become a practised trench warrior after a short stint in the front lines. Even those who were more formally instructed by regulars appear to have appreciated the degree to which they were still uninitiated. After undergoing training in the forward trenches Guy Chapman realised that there was much that he still didn't know: 'We bade our instructors good-bye ...

our term of finishing school over, nominally trained soldiers. I tried to reckon up what we had learned. It was very little. We could put up wire, keep ourselves clean. We knew something about ration parties and other fatigues, and we had learned to build sandbags into a wall which looked strong, a seductive art, too seductive, as we were soon to learn.'[62]

The transition to fully competent soldier was complicated further by the constant alteration and evolution of strategies and tactics, especially when the fighting finally became more mobile towards the end of the war. The story of the British Army on the Western Front was one of improvisation and hard-won experience, especially during 1914 and 1915. Historians such as Paddy Griffith and Gary Sheffield have recently charted the development of the new British armies from these amateurish and unsophisticated beginnings through to the emergence by 1918 of skilled and highly successful fighting units.[63] Once junior officers had learned their business they were in an excellent position to appraise and refine their techniques and tactics. Robert Mackay served with the Argyll and Sutherland Highlanders from September 1916. His diary entry for 7 August 1918 recorded many lessons learned on the Soissons front, ranging from comments about camouflage and concealment to 'some odd points about ammunition and its supply in the field. Ditto re food and water.'[64]

There was also increasing official emphasis on the platoon – commanded by a junior officer – as the chief tactical unit. Robert Graves, teaching at an Officer Cadet Battalion in Oxford, regarded the Army text-book S.S. 143, or *Instructions for the training of Platoons for offensive action, 1917*, as a particularly key document in the development of the new doctrine.[65] Officers at the front clearly had a professional interest in keeping abreast of new developments and learning new techniques. They did not, however, always seem to appreciate this training. Raymond Asquith described a Brigade Field Day in September 1916 designed to teach 'all the newest and most elaborate methods of capturing German trenches with the minimum of casualties. It involved getting up at 5 a.m. but in other respects was funny enough. The "creeping barrage" i.e. the curtain of shell fire which moves on about 50 yards in front of the advancing infantry, was represented by drummers. The spectacle of the whole four battalions moving in lines across the cornfields at a funeral pace headed by a line of rolling drums, produced the effect of some absurd religious ceremony conducted by a tribe of Maoris rather than a brigade of Guards in the attack.'[66] His humorous tone suggests he may have been less than impressed. Edmund Blunden, admittedly writing well after the event, said that he found training in new tactical methods pretty boring.[67]

Others seem to have been more interested in and impressed by tactical developments. Alfred Pollard, a self-styled "fire-eater", seems to have been impressed by the co-ordination of artillery and infantry: 'Gone were the days when we ran across No Man's Land as fast as we could. The creeping barrage had been introduced and an attack was now a scientific performance worked out to a time-table. We had nine minutes in which to cover four hundred yards. We could take our time and preserve a perfect line.'[68] Andrew Buxton, learning the duties of a staff captain in January 1916, wrote that 'In all the vileness of war, there is a wonderful fascination in tactics to adopt, and in new inventions or improvements.'[69] Captain James Neville, having just taken part in an attack in November 1917, reported that 'The whole affair shows a vast improvement in our mode of attack, generalship, and staff work.'[70] Snippets of this sort indicate that many officers were aware of the changes taking place around them and that they appreciated the developing sophistication of their methods, in some cases taking a professional pride in their increased skill.

❧

Practical experience also taught officers to be wary of the more predictable threats which arose from the unprecedented scale of static trench warfare. Each separate location had its own vulnerabilities. Numerous and highly localised unwritten rules abounded in the vicinity of the front line, demarcating safer paths and practices for the initiated. Knowing where to duck one's head in a support trench, for example, could mean the difference between life and death. James Neville, for example, knew that a particular junction was shelled at five minutes to every hour. On one occasion, however, distracted by a party of sappers, he was still there at 10.55 p.m.: 'The next thing that I knew was that I was sprawling full length on the ground, just clear of the pieces of frozen earth that were falling all round. I felt myself all over, thinking I must be dead, picked up my tin hat and ran round the corner. There was not a graze on me. The explosion came from a whizzbang, which burst on the parados immediately behind my head. I saw the shell crater, the next morning. How it missed my head, Heaven only knows. Of course I never heard it coming; you never do hear the one that hits you. That shell must have arrived punctually at 10.55!'[71] Vital knowledge of the sort acquired by Neville had to be learned quickly, either through observation or imparted by colleagues, if an officer wished to increase his chances of survival. Concentration remained essential.

Part of the transformation from civilian to officer was appreciating that efforts to maintain a fighting capability were scarcely less important than the fighting itself. The officer's paternalistic concern for the welfare of the troops, a subject which will be covered in more detail in Chapter 7, played a significant part in ensuring that they were ready for action. The officer and his men also had to maintain the fabric of the trenches and complete regular logistical functions to enable them to survive there. Michael Roper argues that these different tasks ensured that soldiers 'were more deeply involved in domestic work than they had ever been before the war' and that this bridged the gap between the home and the line.[72] It should also be noted that responsibility for large numbers of men also ensured that officers had to become proficient administrators, whether as platoon or company commanders. Challenges could arise in the most unexpected quarters. Gilbert Nobbs was less than delighted when given the challenge of cutting up and distributing 3,534 rations among 1,178 officers and men on Rouen station: 'Have you ever had such a problem as that? If not, then avoid it if it ever comes your way.'[73] Harassed officers also quickly understood that administration generated a huge amount of paperwork, especially once they had started to make their way up through the ranks.[74] Leslie Peppiatt had much to say on the subject as part of a detailed description of his duties in February 1918: 'A Company Commander is, of course, more or less hedged round with returns which have to be rendered – casualty reports, situation reports, returns of numbers of socks sent down to be washed, indents for trench stores, reports of work carried out, strength returns, intelligence reports, salvage reports, patrol reports etc. There is a list of returns hanging on the wall of my dug-out as I write. Some are due at 2.30 am – some at 8.30 am – some at 12 noon – some at 3 pm, some at 6 pm – some at 8 pm and one at 9 pm – so there you are. In the meantime (provided of course you aren't on duty and have nothing else to do) you can go to sleep.'[75] Montie Carlisle complained that there were so many different pieces of paper to deal with that he never seemed to have any time free, the job consequently proving extremely tiring.[76] An officer with experience of white-collar employment would very likely recognise aspects of the processes, his duties therefore also bridging the gap between the trench and the office.

The potentially exasperating nature of much of the bureaucratic effort and its perceived tendency to distract from more pressing matters was immortalised in one of Captain Bruce Bairnsfather's satirical cartoons, 'The Things that Matter'. Colonel Fitz-Shrapnel's bulging eyes and raised eyebrows testify eloquently to the strength of his feeling on being asked about jam stocks while he is under bombardment.[77] Many requests for information were, of course, entirely legitimate and enabled staff officers and higher formations to organise and operate the vast structures under their control. Gary Sheffield has also justified 'the much-derided obsession of the staff with apparent trivialities' by highlighting the importance of a 'bureaucracy of paternalism' in ensuring that even temporary officers were taking adequate care of their charges.[78] In any case, efficient officers learned how to make the best of the system. Leslie Peppiatt qualified his list of tasks by noting that 'the rendering of these returns isn't really a very serious matter. A good many of them can be prepared beforehand and sent in whilst one slumbers provided no change in the situation has occurred in the meantime.'[79]

Junior officers were initially only responsible for a platoon, but they also had to learn that they automatically had roles to play within the context of their company or even battalion. The officer corps faced high levels of occupational instability.[80] Varying levels of available manpower could substantially increase the burden placed on subalterns. Many were catapulted without warning into positions of seniority to replace officers unfortunately killed or incapacitated – the 'grim and unceasing automaticity' of promotion, as one writer called it – with a knock-on effect spreading the impact of such changes throughout the chain of command.[81] Other factors increased this level of volatility, although usually on a more temporary basis, ensuring that junior officers held a variety of posts for a short period of time while they awaited the return of the usual incumbents. It was, of course, entirely standard for juniors to take command while their superiors went away on leave or detached duty.[82] As fighting techniques and inter-arm operability developed, officers were also despatched to undergo short placements with the artillery or Royal Flying Corps in an attempt to promote cross-unit understanding and co-operation. John Nettleton was quick to appreciate the advantage of such a system:

> During this summer, the Army had one of its brain-waves and decided that a certain number of people should be attached, for short periods, to other arms, so that each could learn something about the other fellow's point of view. It was a good idea, in general, that one half should see how the other half lived, but the particular aspect that appealed to me was that it produced additional opportunities of getting short spells out of the line. It gave me two or three days with an 8 inch howitzer battery and a whole week with the Flying Corps.

This exchange to the artillery also usefully demonstrated to Nettleton that, 'though they did not get shelled as frequently as the PBI [poor bloody infantry], when they did, it was with heavy stuff,' which doubtless did wonders for the PBI's appreciation of the

The Things that Matter.

Scene: Loos, during the September offensive.

Colonel Fitz-Shrapnel receives the following message from "G.H.Q.":—
"Please let us know, as soon as possible, the number of tins of raspberry jam issued to you last Friday."

'The Things That Matter', Bruce Bairnsfather. (Copyright Barbara Bruce Littlejohn) gunners' contribution.[83] Captain Arthur Gibbs was also clearly glad of the opportunity to take a break from infantry routine and see how the other half lived: 'Upjohn came up this morning and took over the company. I am going off for 8 days, the day after tomorrow, to be attached to the Artillery, to see how things are done there. I applied to go and am looking forward to it, as long as Fritz doesn't start his counter battery work.'[84]

Officers were also frequently taken away from their front-line duties to attend the numerous courses which were put on at various camps dotted across the back areas of the British military zone. These courses were intended to equip them with new skills such as sniping or machine gunnery, to refresh their knowledge of infantry work and to bring them up to date with the latest tactical developments.[85] They could not take the place of full formation training, as experienced by Raymond Asquith or Edmund Blunden, but they could enhance capabilities by providing units with additional specialist knowledge. They were also useful for giving tired or stressed officers a rest from front-line work.[86] Leslie Peppiatt was delighted to be sent away for Lewis Gun instruction in July 1918: 'I can see that the "Battle of Le Touquet" will be quite a pleasant business. The School is in huts and everything seems remarkably comfortable and pleasant … This afternoon I wandered down with Newsome to the sea and bathed and sat and read. It was a perfectly glorious afternoon – an afternoon which made one long to be in the sea. I came across a description of Heaven in one of Charles Service Poems – "just a place where one can rest – and forget". Here one can certainly rest to a certain extent and it's possible in some measure to forget the scenes being enacted just a short journey away – the screaming shells, the noisome trench, the bleeding mangled form on the stretcher and all the sights and sounds of the war.'[87] Guy Chapman's battalion had an even more altruistic purpose in choosing their nominees, reportedly seeking to protect 'one of our baby officers' by sending him on all available training opportunities. In the normal course of things, however, these programmes were often unpopular because of the disruption they caused.[88] Frank Warren was less than delighted to be posted to a course at the Second Army School in November 1917 as it would mean being separated from the Company work which he was enjoying.[89] Other officers like Charles May questioned their utility: 'The courses are a strange feature of Army life. Some are excellent, indeed all are good – for men in need of them. But so often it happens that men are sent for instruction in most elementary stuff, stuff they knew well years ago. It seems quite unbusinesslike, quite like the Army.'[90]

In addition to questioning the value of these periods of supplementary training, officers sometimes complained that they were actually counterproductive, removing commanders from their men and imposing a greater burden of work on those who were left behind. Reginald Cockburn was appalled by the number of officers removed temporarily from battalion duties: 'They go to Platoon Commanders' "courses", Company Commanders' "courses", Infantry "courses", Bombing "courses", Bullet and Bayonet "courses", Lewis Gun "courses", Sniping and Scouting "courses", Aeroplane "courses", and a hundred stupid courses. They are taken away in such numbers and so often that they never get to know, or have the chance to train and look after their men. They are taken away when they are most needed to be with their men. And at these courses, they learn nothing that they find useful to them afterwards and which they get the opportunity to tell others, that they could not far more profitably learn with the Battalion. The best training a Platoon Commander can have is to be with his platoon.'[91]

Officers apparently referred to the malign influence of the 'Hidden Hand' – a reference to a popular contemporary myth that the British war effort was being sabotaged by secretive pro-German influences.[92]

As Cockburn was so acutely aware, any eventuality which depleted a company's pool of officers would increase the workload of those left behind. Illness was a significant problem, especially during the influenza epidemic of 1918.[93] It was also sometimes a source of envy. 'One of us managed to slip a kidney the other day and is now in England and likely to remain there some time,' wrote Edgar Matthews in October 1915. 'We are all wondering where our kidneys are now, but we must all have got hold of the wrong place, because no-one has had any luck yet. I'm afraid mine have been put in rather too carefully.'[94] When circumstances conspired to remove several colleagues at once, the junior officer could find the weight of his burden very substantially increased, as Graham Greenwell discovered when had to cope with several simultaneous absences:

> Poor Freddie Grisewood went down with a temperature of 105° yesterday and has gone to hospital: Deacon also has departed on account of eye trouble, so we have no Adjutant. The Second-in-Command has gone, and as four or five officers are on leave we are very short-handed.[95]

These problems were exacerbated if companies lacked a full complement of officers to begin with, as they frequently did. In Nettleton's experience, 'we never had as many as five officers to a company as far as I can remember. It was more usually two or three … In theory, there should have always been at least one officer on duty in the front line. But numbers were so short that often this was not physically possible. Much of the time we were down to the Company Commander and two subalterns in C Company and, on occasions, to only one. When this happened, the front line just had to be left when things were quiet, because even subalterns have to eat and sleep sometimes. That was when the worst moments occurred.'[96] Leslie Peppiatt also appreciated the increased strain of trench duty on a depleted officer pool: 'if a Company has only two or three Officers, front line work is very trying – more trying for the Officers than for anyone else in the Company as (apart from the responsibility) the Officers have to do duty all the time whereas the men are sometimes in close Company support at Company H.Qs.'[97] On 6 March 1916 Frank Wollocombe complained in a letter to his mother that 'since Feb 5 Pearce and I are the only Subalterns in the Company now, which leaves a lot of work to be done'. He reported that he had been taken down from the trenches because of illness, blaming it on his lengthy stint in the line and giving some indication of the vicious cycle of over-work in which many officers found themselves.[98] If being short-staffed was not bad enough, it should be remembered that those officers who were available were not necessarily sufficiently experienced or capable of carrying out their work unassisted, still further increasing the pressure on their colleagues. This was certainly a perception of some more experienced officers, such as Charles Dudley-Ward: 'We have sufficient old soldiers here now who know the ropes and whom we can trust, a thing newcomers don't understand. If it were not so the running of the army would be impossible.'[99]

Despite having to absorb so many skills and so much information, the initial trench education of junior officers usually appears to have been completed impressively quickly. Naturally there were 'dud' officers who never got to grips with their job. The number of these reaching the front line probably fell after the establishment of the OCB system, which could weed out the obviously unsuitable.[100] For those who did make it through, there were various ways in which to remove them from sensitive posts. Military policy actually required rapid 'veteranisation' since inexperienced troops were frequently sent into the line to learn from relatively inexperienced officers. Subalterns compelled to adopt the mantle of 'old stagers' for the benefit of new arrivals did not find themselves wanting even if they themselves had relatively little experience of their own. If anything, these informal training jobs demonstrated their own development. As Sam Paget commented in September 1915: 'We have been having officers attached to us for instruction the last day or two – so we feel quite the old campaigners.'[101] This episode occurred less than a month after his first induction into the trenches.

Although trench work became normal enough within a short space of time, it was only a part of the soldier's life on the Western Front. Battalions holding a section of the line would rotate their companies through the forward trenches, reserve lines and rest. Longer periods away from the trenches might be due to battalion rotations, formation moves or troop concentrations in preparation for a large-scale assault. Troops consequently moved regularly between trenches and accommodation in the rear. Many letters bear the heading 'In Billets', reflecting both the greater opportunity for writing and the writer's natural wish to convey this reassuring news to his audience.

Billets offered the promise of greater security and comfort, although they did not necessarily deliver either. 'Shell-fire in the front line is expected, and one is prepared for it', remarked Francis Hitchcock of the Leinster Regiment in June 1915, 'but shell-fire in billets is most unpleasant.'[102] After a tour of the trenches, especially in the bad weather and mud which was all too common, even the simplest comforts were rapturously received and the prospect of leaving the line often elicited expressions of relief. 'I really enjoyed this last spell in the trenches,' wrote Douglas Gillespie from the safety of a rear area in April 1915, 'but it is always nice to get back into billets, after sleeping in one's clothes and boots for five days and nights.'[103] The prospect of catching up on some sleep was certainly welcomed, given the deprivation which was a routine feature of trench life. Jack Oughtred complained of only getting six hours sleep in three nights in January 1916, remarking that this was 'the only thing that really gets at you.'[104] The officer would also have a chance to acquire clean and dry clothes, and wash themselves. Sam Paget enthused about the prospect of a hot bath: 'It sounds ordinary enough but have you ever tried going two months without one – and living in a sewer for the greater part of the time! It makes a difference.'[105] Christopher Stone was similarly moved by the respite: 'the first night out of the trenches is always delicious: and this time we have struck good quarters in a spacious house. I had a bath before dinner which was heavenly – you've no idea how delicious – & then a good dinner'.[106] Leslie Peppiatt tried to explain the effects of even the simplest comforts to an audience back in Britain: 'I cannot lay too much stress on the fact that out here all comfort and discomfort is comparative. That is to say that if one has been spending 12 days in muddy trenches and stuffy, dirty and unhealthy dug-outs and cellars without having one's clothes off, a night's rest in a sleeping suit and blankets (even if the blankets are on the floor of a barn or shed) is comfort. The men of course do not have valises to sleep in but they have blankets and dry huts or billets, fire, good food, baths and clean clothes. I know it all sounds very ordinary but if I could convey any real idea of the discomforts which they put up with in the Line, it would also be understood how these modest arrangements for their comfort are appreciated.'[107] The focus on basic arrangements of food and shelter is a further reminder of the domestic effort constantly required of officers.

Not only were comfort and discomfort comparative, but so were the qualities of different billets. As with the sections of the line they occupied, or the dug-outs in which they crouched and worked, billets on the Western Front were nothing if not varied. James Neville wrote in the most complimentary terms about the village of Camblain-Chatelaine: 'My billet is heavenly and so comfortable that I almost imagine myself at home when I wake up in the early morning. We are having a most awfully good time, like a pre-war holiday, and it is good to be alive and enjoy it all.'[108] In contrast, Oliver Lyttelton was disgusted at one time to find himself in 'the worst billets out of the line that I have ever struck. The filth left behind by the troops is inconceivable and would make the Germans buck up if they could see it. However we are gradually getting it clean'.[109] The most comfortable were generally those furthest away from the firing line. Sometimes arrangements were well established; at other times officers had to make the best of whatever the locality had to offer. When Graham Greenwell arrived in Arquèves in July 1916 he was able to find accommodation for his Company in barns. On turning his attention to the question of officer billets, 'I succeeded after a lot of hunting round in persuading an old girl to take in my three officers and myself in one small but well-furnished room with one bed in it.'[110] This was not an uncommon arrangement, officers often being compelled to arrange their own (and often their charges') accommodation through a process of negotiation, their domestic arrangements frequently encroaching on those of the local populace. J.R. Monsell found just how sensitive a matter this could be on one occasion in July 1915:

> My corporal who looks after the horse troughs erected by the [Royal Engineers and] not to be used by civilians, was badly smacked by a strapping wench who wanted to fill her pail – I had to go and preserve the Entente Cordiale. A sullenly drunk Frenchman lay down in the bed of an Officer and refused to budge – had to turn him out; also with an eye to E. Cordiale, tenderly as it was his own house, this at 11 at night![111]

Establishing a working relationship with the locals was therefore another important skill that the junior officer had to master in short order. This was not always an easy task. Charles May was upset, after eight nights in the line, to encounter a particularly difficult host:

> Madame apparently does not like us, an antipathy evidently shared by her father. Madame turned up last night, abused Bunting, flung our valises out in the mud and then smashed chairs, tables, windows and the door. Quite a New Cut Saturday night affair I believe. And really most unpleasant for us all. And to crown it, this morning le père rolled up, called us "les cochons Anglais" and nailed up the side door. Dearly would I have liked to have taken him by the ear and kicked his bottom

down the street. But one mustn't do that. We soldier in a friendly country and we must respect the rights of the inhabitants – even, I suppose, to the extent of allowing them to fling one's kit in the filth of their midden. It is, of course, only the wretched peasantry who behave in so unseemly a manner and I doubt not but what our own lower classes would do the same or worse to a French army fighting in England. It is not the true French, no more than it would be the real English, who behave like this. Pig blood will always come out, runs it in the veins of English, French, Spaniard or Basuto.[112]

Keeping on positive terms could be made particularly difficult by numerous disputes which arose, particularly concerning property which had been destroyed or damaged. In some cases the Army seems to have taken these issues somewhat too seriously, given the circumstances of war. Paul Jones recounted an episode in which engineers had felt it necessary to reinforce the trenchworks they were building with some doors from the nearby ruined houses:

… the village was little better than a dust-heap, yet a solemn and portentous court of inquiry was held on those doors: we were justified in taking them, and should payment be made for them to the old inhabitants or their representatives? Eventually it was decided that, as the doors were taken to help to make trenches, they might be considered as destroyed by a *fait de guerre*, which, I believe, corresponds to an "act of God" in the civil courts, and payment ought not therefore to be made for the doors. It was, however, pointed out that if the said doors had been used to make a road, not a trench, they would not be *faits de guerre*, and in such case payment would have had to be made to the Mayor of the destroyed commune![113]

At other times it would be hard to deny that a district's temporary military residents might have a case to answer. Edgar Matthews sat on a court of inquiry tasked with discovering the reasons for the death of seven cows and a goat: 'Some private with an inquisitive soul had given the cows army biscuits to see what would happen. The result was that they became "gonflé" [swollen] and then died.' Like Jones, Matthews clearly considered the effort involved in such cases to be disproportionate: 'We had to take sheets of evidence from the owner and his friend and then sheets more from various members of the B.E.F. The idea of an antique major – with one foot in the grave – an elderly captain – with a bald head, and myself solemnly enquiring into the demise of seven cows and a goat filled me with joy, and at times I had to turn away and laugh silently.'[114]

Junior officers generally seem to have sympathised with their hosts, and recognised the part they themselves had to play in ensuring good relations. 'To have an alien army quartered on you is annoying, to say the least of it,' acknowledged John Nettleton. 'Yet reasonably decent behaviour by the soldiers brings an immediate response from the civilians, in France, as in other countries, and the response is accurately proportioned to the conduct that calls it forth.'[115] Alfred Sansom had a similar opinion: 'The peasants are much the same all over this part of France, cold and suspicious at first till they know you, then warm-hearted and ready to do all they can for you as soon as they have been treated with a little courtesy and tact.'[116] As Chapter 6 will explore in more detail, so much of the officers' duties revolved around this sort of stakeholder management. This was not, however, a purely transactional relationship, as Sansom and Nettleton indicate. The relative comfort of billets and the importance of their contribution to morale were too significant, and some officers clearly found some of the acquaintances emotionally nourishing. Sam Paget's letters describe a friendship with a housekeeper and her 10-year-old daughter who would enquire, when next the company came back from the trenches, after 'le jeune capitaine'.[117] Just as James Neville delighted in the particularly homey nature of his Camblain-Chatelaine billet, so it is not hard to imagine men of his and Paget's age briefly finding substitute families amongst whom they could experience some comfort. In both cases, the recreation of something which was strongly emotionally resonant of a pre-war civilian life provided a special refuge from the world of the front line. No wonder men like Hitchcock found the intrusion of shell fire so distasteful.

Rear areas were usually a more comfortable alternative to the stresses of trench life, affording more opportunity for relaxation and entertainment (a subject which will be covered in more detail in Chapter 8). Many officers, however, did not particularly enjoy their time out of the line. Units at rest were regularly used as labour, which for the officer meant tedious and tiring work supervising his men. 'At present we are in billets … but it is nearly as bad as the trenches,' complained Clifford Platt. 'The fatigues are terrible'.[118] It sometimes felt as though anything was preferable to the interminable boredom and work which was the lot of soldiers out of the line: 'It's not much of a job being in Brigade Reserve as we are now,' wrote Malcolm Davidson, 'as you have endless digging parties and parties carrying stores up to the trenches – all night and most of the day.'[119] These ambivalent attitudes are understandable when one considers that there was no guaranteed escape from boredom or, indeed, danger, as many realised. Artillery and (as the war progressed) aeroplanes could make life in billets quite as hazardous as life in a dug-out. What most infantrymen understood relatively quickly was that, for them, there were genuinely few easy options on the Western Front. Raymond Asquith considered that there was 'more novelty and excitement about the trenches themselves than any other part of the show, but I should still be discontented if I were made to stay in them for a month on end instead of coming out and doing these bloody fatigues'.[120]

Since there might be comparatively little to commend rear areas, many officers were content to be in the trenches, usually because this enabled them to satisfy their eagerness to fulfil their culturally designated combat roles. As Charles May noted, 'when one is in them one feels that, more or less, one is doing one's job.'[121] It should, of course, be remembered, that front-line experiences differed dramatically depending on the sector, the time of year, and the strategies pursued. Not even Graham Greenwell, who claimed to have enjoyed the war overall, much enjoyed serving on the Somme amongst 'the most ghastly surroundings'.[122] Frequently, however, trench life was a matter of pure routine and quite tolerable. James Neville felt able to write that he was 'very well off in this part of the line, and have nothing to complain about really.'[123] Stephen Hewett was similarly contented: 'It is a fine life, this, on the whole, and so far well within the limits of endurance'.[124]

⁊⭑

Once an infantry officer began performing his duties in the field, his career could follow various different paths depending on factors including length of service, wounds, illness, transfers and promotions. It should not be forgotten that the Western Front was not the only theatre in which British soldiers were engaged. Operations in Gallipoli, Salonica, Italy, Russia and Mesopotamia all diverted troops away from the Western Front and, consequently, beyond the scope of this book. Greenwell fought in France and Flanders until posted to Italy in November 1917.[125] On the Western Front, the infantry dominated the British military effort to the extent that it was not unknown for soldiers from other arms to be posted into it.[126] The system did allow some movement in other directions. A frequent accusation levelled against the British Army in the First World War is that thousands of young officers were squandered in the ranks of the infantry, where their talents were largely wasted. The creation and development of various new and emerging weapons such as tanks and aircraft did, however, create numerous openings.[127] Officers were able to follow their interests and inclinations to some extent, or could at least try to. Douglas Bell volunteered for the Royal Flying Corps when the opportunity presented itself because he was fed up with life in the trenches and fancied a change.[128] Paul Jones was able to transfer from the ASC to the Tank Corps, finally achieving the combat role he craved.

The army actively sought some men with special skills to perform specific functions, although without ever implementing much in the way of a formal and thorough system of talent management.[129] For example, following the use of poison gas by the Germans at Ypres in 1915, the War Office quickly began to assemble a force capable of countering and utilising the new weapon. In order to obtain a cadre of chemists to advise field units concerning chemical defence Sir Alfred Keogh, the rector of Imperial College and director-general of the Royal Army Medical Corps, selected a group of 21 soldiers ranking from captain to private, all of whom had chemistry degrees.[130] Subsequently, when the army wanted to expand the ranks of the mysteriously titled Special Brigade of the Royal Engineers, it sought out more trained chemists, despite the fact that the work consisted mainly of manual labour manoeuvring, installing and discharging cylinders.[131] While attempting to make more effective use of available human resources in these ways the army still had to contend with ingrained prejudices against non-traditional military roles, which took a while to break down. Commanding officers could be as unsympathetic to requests for specialists and applications for alternative employment as they had once been to those seeking commissions from the ranks.

A small but still significant number of British officers did find themselves employed in more than one field during their war service, judging by the experiences of Winchester College alumni. 1,193 pupils entered the school between September 1901 and April 1913. Of these, forty-nine per cent went to war as infantrymen. Approximately six per cent of these subsequently transferred to the Royal Flying Corps, Royal Naval Air Service or (when formed) Royal Air Force. Nearly a further three per cent transferred to the Tank Corps or the Royal Engineers, reflecting the opportunities created by the establishment of the former and the fifteenfold increase in the size of the latter.[132] A handful seem to have joined various intelligence departments and one went to the Royal Laboratory at Woolwich.[133] Nearly 10 per cent, therefore, eventually found employment in more specialised units. Pupils from Winchester and other prestigious public schools may have had the advantage over colleagues from other backgrounds in enjoying either the education or the social contacts necessary to change position more easily, but it seems quite possible that this distribution would be matched by the alumni of many other schools.

The statistics do, however, confirm the impression created by a survey of personal writings. Most officers who joined the infantry remained there, although this did not mean that their lives were unvaried. Infantry officers had to be extremely flexible and capable of dealing with a wide range of situations. As they became increasingly experienced and senior, extra duties frequently devolved on them, however unfamiliar they may initially have been. Greenwell was delighted to be instructed 'to act as Transport Officer in Gibson's absence on leave for eight days, so I am now temporarily a mounted officer in charge of seventy horses.'[134] Clifford Platt thought almost any specialism was better than simply being a platoon commander, 'the rottenest job in the world'. He advocated trench mortars, brigade machine guns or even the position of 'regimental anarchist', a common and unflattering allusion to a bombing officer.[135] Other officers like Robert Mackay disliked being shifted about: 'Have now been signalling officer 5 times, Adjutant once, platoon officer 4 or 5 times, and Corps Dropping Officer. Also Billetting Officer, Intelligence Officer, Interpreter, and Road-maker, etc. Expect I will get used to this in time.'[136] These are only a selection of the jobs or functions which junior infantry officers were called upon to perform. Sitting on a court martial or court of inquiry was another relatively common occurrence which only took an officer away from his usual company duties temporarily. Other jobs might remove an officer from the vicinity of the combat zone altogether whilst remaining under the aegis of the infantry. Substantial numbers of instructors were required for the numerous courses and training establishments which sprang up both in Britain and on the continent. Sam Paget was posted to the Fourth Army School as an instructor in 1916. Robert Graves ended up as an Officer Cadet Battalion instructor because he applied for the job following his sojourn in an Oxford hospital.[137]

The varied careers of an infantry officer: Sam Paget (fourth from left, front standing row) at Fourth Army School ... (Private archive)

... and as a staff officer (rear rank, centre). (Private archive)

Opportunities for staff postings or career openings frequently presented themselves. The rapid expansion of the army created a large number of senior command appointments, all of which needed to be supported. Simultaneously, pre-war systems regulating the selection, appointment and promotion of staff officers largely broke down under the pressures of the campaign. At first, posts were filled quickly by experienced regimental officers, while commanders on the continent took on inexperienced officers who could learn on the job. A more uniform system of selection and training was instigated in April 1916.[138] Even so, young officers had to be prepared for the unexpected, as vacancies were apt to arise at short notice. This was Desmond Young's experience within moments of reporting for duty with Brigadier-General Kennedy 'for further instruction in staff duties', and finding the Brigade Staff at tea in a small hut on the edge of a trench:

> ... an odd shell, trundling over in the quiet of the December afternoon, burst on or in the hut. When the smoke and fumes cleared, the General and I were untouched, the rest were dead or dying. My British warm was covered with blood. Kid Kennedy pulled himself together first. As men came running and the others were carried out of the wreckage of the hut, he turned to me: 'You seem to be now my only staff officer,' he said. 'You'd better take on Brigade Major.'[139]

Once again, the officer's response to such challenges was often stoical. As William Fraser noted when facing the possibility of moving to another division to take up a post as Brigade Major, 'One just takes the job that comes along and tries to do it.'[140] Class and social contacts, however, remained potentially important determinants of the distribution of desirable appointments. A staff job was engineered for Edward Tennant, the eldest son of Lord Glenconner, by friends for his pregnant mother's sake.[141]

Staff officers are a controversial presence in the *dramatis personae* of the British Army on the Western Front. Many commentators have condemned them, along with the generals they served, as the donkeys who sent tens of thousands to their deaths, shirking their patriotic duty in comfortable billets behind the lines. Fighting officers during the war were often vitriolic in their criticisms.[142] There is, moreover, a perception that, while nobody much cared for the life, the army was held together on the Western Front by a refusal on the part of ordinary soldiers to leave their comrades doing the dirty work while they slipped away to safer and easier jobs elsewhere. It is not difficult to find these sorts of views expressed in officers' writings, especially those produced after the war.[143] John Nettleton stated in his memoir that 'you had to carry on as long as you were fit, however much you disliked it'. A 'legitimate excuse' for escape could be welcomed without shame or dishonour, but for Nettleton this meant nothing short of physical disablement.[144] Lieutenant E.W. Stoneham, an artilleryman, similarly told interviewers that he would have felt that taking a post at brigade headquarters was in some way a betrayal of his soldiers. Though tempted to go to safer employment, he decided that he had to stay with them.[145]

This idea of not breaking faith is bound up with participants' different perceptions of wartime activities. As Janet Watson has argued, professional soldiers were inclined to think of the war as work for which they had been trained whereas volunteers were more idealistic and interpreted their activities as service.[146] This perspective placed special emphasis on the importance of serving in a particular context and observing the correct codes of conduct; in other words serving where the perceived need was greatest (in the trenches) and maintaining solidarity with fellow volunteers. However, as previous extracts have already indicated, many temporary officers *did* accept safer jobs away from the front line. Some took these postings simply because they were ordered to do so; others more actively sought them out.

Their willingness to do so was often a reflection of the ongoing transition from civilian to soldier and the growth of a more professional mentality. Young officers were not likely to be inherently well-disposed towards the staff; the natural initial response of the enthusiastic volunteer was to denigrate all but front-line activities in the teeth arms. They were also likely to be influenced by the perspectives expressed by Nettleton and Stoneham. These views, however, were eroded as they developed professional skills. Subalterns could not avoid paperwork, as they had an important role to play in maintaining the administration of the army. They also had to become proficient in a wide range of skills to function effectively as infantrymen. Through this work they gained a greater understanding of the whole range of military duties which they needed to master if they were to be competent soldiers. These experiences enabled them to develop a more sympathetic appreciation of the contribution elements like command headquarters were making. It also helped them develop a more professional military persona, as did greater exposure to regular army practices and viewpoints. In Desmond Young's case it was the experience of seeing Brigadier-General Roland Boys Bradford – 25 years old, decorated with the VC and the MC – in action which 'put the whole business in a new perspective. It was not some desperate adventure, some ghastly gauntlet to run, with death inevitable at the end, but a job to be done as efficiently as possible.'[147]

Norman Taylor was born in 1895. During the war he won the MC and rose to the rank of Captain. He was killed in the German offensive of March 1918. (Imperial War Museum)

When young officers were posted to staff appointments or received more training in administrative functions this increased the rate of their professionalization, further changing their views of the nature of the work and those who were carrying out these duties. Desmond Young admitted that he learned 'a great deal about the administrative side of the Army', not to mention its 'inner workings', when posted to General Sir Horace Smith-Dorrien's headquarters.[148] He may have been referring to a new-found understanding of the relative influence and power exercised by the different branches found within a headquarters. Stephen Foot certainly felt he had learned something along these lines: 'the useful bit of information I had gleaned was that the branch of the General Staff that really matters is that which is in control of "Operations." What they say goes. If I ever got on the Staff of the Army, it would be on the "Operations" side.'[149] This greater understanding made it easier to find personal validation in a staff posting. The experience of any administrative work, whether at platoon, company or staff level, might also alter the relationship between the officer, the war and the army. Young officers were encouraged to adopt a more professional attitude, in the sense that they became more sensitive to the traditional structure of an army career and the benefits which might accrue from broader experience of army business. As their horizons became wider some became increasingly willing to leave the trenches in search of more favourable employment elsewhere.

Thoughts of self-preservation undoubtedly lay behind some of these efforts. Norman Taylor, a territorial officer in the 1/21st Battalion London Regiment, was emphatically anxious to escape from the trenches, possibly because of a morbid preoccupation with the life expectancy of subalterns in his position which was revealed in a series of letters to his father, the first dated 5 March 1916:

> We shall be celebrating the anniversary of our landing in France in about 10 days. It is rather a record for infantry subalterns. There are only 3 other subalterns in this battalion who came out in March 1914 and have been with us all the time and even so this battalion has more original officers still out here than any other in the division … I am tired to death of the monotony of this life – it was all very well for about 6 or even 9 months, but a year is a bit much – I should be very glad if you could get me a better job. The point is that it is only by asking and pushing oneself forward (or being pushed) that one ever gets anything in the army – if I knew anybody in high quarters I'd write to him every week regularly until he got so tired of me (that) he gave me something to keep me quiet.[150]

A week later he wrote in a similar vein: 'I want to get well away from the danger zone because I consider I've risked my life quite enough and have been very lucky in coming through a year untouched. Also I've no desire to be knocked out and it's tempting Providence to stay up the line longer than absolutely necessary (don't think that I'm 'nervy' because I should not be allowed to be here if I was).'[151]

Taylor was anxious to dispel any suggestion that he was suffering from fear, an admission which for many would have been emasculating and shameful. Officers were expected to set an example by not showing any signs that they were afraid, a psychological challenge which will be examined in more detail in Chapter 4. For those who were struggling with the nature of trench fighting, a staff appointment or other duties away from the line, whether actively sought or not, could be a great relief, especially if it resolved the tension between fear and a sense of duty by removing the officer's responsibility for his own employment. Other officers saw a move as a way of circumventing local difficulties associated with their employment and prospects, especially when hopes of promotion were frustrated. Arthur Gibbs, finding his chances of advancement blocked within his battalion, wished to move to 'a staff job in Division, Corps, or Army' because he did not 'fancy hanging on here for another 3, or 6 months, or even a year, and still being an ensign'. He was not even particularly concerned about whether or not the job was 'out here'.[152] Similarly, Jack Oughtred commented that he might get a soft job somewhere only after losing command of his company to a more senior captain.[153]

Other officers had more long-term aspirations. Those who were naturally ambitious sought promotions and plum jobs in the same way that, had they been in civilian life, they would have pursued status and career advantage. The public-school system had taught pupils like Alec Waugh to judge their progress according to the different stages reached on the road to seniority: 'If he were one day to get into the Fifteen, he should by his sixteenth birthday have got his house cap. Everything was mapped out. The rungs of the ladder were labelled. Colt's Cap, House Cap, Seconds, Firsts, Fourth Form, Fifth Form, Sixth.'[154] Transplanted into the military, this habit manifested itself in a greater readiness to pursue opportunities for personal advancement, particularly encouraged within the careerist atmosphere of an elite battalion. More generally, as young officers became more professional they came increasingly to understand that staff work away from the lines could play an important role in career advancement. Regular officers were already familiar with the connection between seniority and bureaucratic work and could directly advise their juniors. John Nettleton's CO pressed him to take a staff job 'and from a regular's point of view, a job on the staff, even a very junior one, was a good step for a young officer to take if he got the chance. It brought him under the direct notice of the higher authorities and might lead to all sorts of opportunities for extra-regimental advancement.'[155] Nettleton declined the position because he was 'only a "temporary gentleman" and had no intention of staying in the army a day longer than [he] had to'.[156] Many volunteers, having joined up hoping simply to see action before the end of a short war, were presumably similarly unconcerned about any longer-term military prospects, at least initially. These men were overlooking the fact that there might be a direct relationship between their wartime achievements and their post-war prospects back in civilian life. Others realised that their future interests could best be served by taking advantage of flexible wartime conditions. Oliver Lyttelton was not interested in a military career but believed that he would be 'a more eligible business man as a reputable member of staff than a regimental field officer.' This view, which was also influenced by a recognition of the risks he was running, underpinned his interest in January 1917 in the staff officer post for which he was recommended by his CO: 'It is not really that I am tired but I think too long at every job, I have been 18 months at this, is a mistake especially if one wants to get on … And I don't see if I pop the parapet how I can avoid a bit of lead somewhere again, and you can't rely on them through the arm.'[157]

Plenty of officers who had only joined up during the war did decide that they wished to stay in the army afterwards. Many young officers had volunteered straight from school or university. Without wives, children or civilian jobs awaiting their return, they regarded the prospect of demobilisation from the only adult way of life they had ever really known with disfavour. A proportion probably belonged to that group who would have been attracted to the life of the professional soldier in any case. Clearly the often unpleasant nature of active service did not dissuade others from contemplating a military career. Those who did think about soldiering as a long-term profession were understandably willing to exploit any openings which enhanced their prospects. Rapid personal advancement during the war, when such a thing was possible, was vitally important if an officer was to secure favourable terms of service afterwards. If missed, the frequent opportunities for promotion which were created by the hostilities could not be recovered once peace returned, the fluid wartime hierarchy solidified and vacancies – particularly for active command appointments – dried up. Montie Carlisle, who left Cambridge two years before the outbreak of war, thought that his ability to have a satisfying military career after the war would depend on either being a battalion commander or getting a good job on the staff during the war.[158]

Ambitions, or at least a desire not to fall behind or waste opportunities, also spurred some young officers with temporary or territorial commissions to seek to change to regular terms. Some, Janet Watson argues, were able to use the opportunity presented by the war to obtain this status which they would never have been able to afford in peacetime.[159] Coming from a wealthy family, Sam Paget would have had no such concern. He was more interested in his prospects when he wrote to his mother in September 1915 about swapping his temporary commission for a regular one: 'I see from the Times that if we take one we get seniority from the date of gazetting, and we have just been issued with the necessary forms. What I feel about it is that if there is conscription or a large standing Army after the war, and if it will then be one's duty to serve, one will have the seniority. Whereas if I found I didn't want to go on I could send in my papers in the ordinary course. It seems as if a lot of us would be wanted to go on and I rather think at present that I should like to.'[160] While Paget seemed ambivalent about a military career, Carlisle was clear that he wanted to avoid returning to work at the Baltic Exchange, where he was employed between 1912 and 1914. When he had got his own permanent commission in August 1916 he had told his wife he was very pleased because it meant he could banish the prospect of having to go back to a financial career.[161] Many young men went to war because it seemed like a more exciting and satisfying prospect than the jobs they would leave behind; even the hardships of the Western Front failed to persuade some that they should return to their former occupations. Subsequently, certain cohorts within the officer corps fully adopted a military identity and therefore thought more like professional soldiers in such matters, their ambitions potentially providing the mechanism whereby these new personas were nurtured.

The development of a more professional attitude and commensurate careerism, even if ultimately self-serving, was not entirely divorced from the moral universe described by Nettleton and Stoneham. It remained largely unacceptable to break faith with one's comrades in the trenches or the battle zone entirely, and many staff roles were still sufficiently dangerous and close to the front to persuade officers that they were not, in fact, having a 'cushy' time after all. The moral dilemma for each career-minded individual was the degree to which disloyalty was justifiable and how to excuse that unfaithfulness. For example, escape to 'Blighty' was unacceptable to Taylor:

> I could not myself accept or try to obtain a job in England – simply and obviously to get away from fighting. It's too bare-faced and really does not seem quite the game to leave all one's friends here ... On the other hand any job which would be a step up for me as a soldier and an advancement to my career, although it took me back out of the immediate danger-zone (in France of course) – I should have no hesitation in doing all I could to get it.[162]

There were, however, numerous ways in which a safer job could be justified, at least in the eyes of the individual. Interestingly, Taylor argued that he was 'far too valuable an officer to be wasted and risked as an ordinary infantry subaltern any longer – with my experience I deserve something better'.[163] Overlooking the obvious fact that experienced officers were needed for trench warfare, this could be interpreted as a further expression of the development of a more professional attitude. Taylor's own interest in a lengthy military career, despite his evident concern for his safety, is apparent in his consistent interest in obtaining a permanent commission. His comment suggests that some officers came to regard trench warfare as a comparatively basic form of employment which could therefore safely be undertaken by the militarily inexperienced. An alternative justification is provided by Arthur Gibbs who candidly wrote 'Now that I have been out here a year, I feel as if I were entitled to get "a job" somewhere'.[164] Ironically, service in the trenches had enabled him to discharge his moral obligations to his fellows rather than creating a new or strengthened commitment. Both Taylor and Gibbs came to regard trench service as an essentially finite duty, which was either outgrown or discharged over time. A similar sentiment may be discernable in Lyttelton's thoughts about staff appointments and the wisdom (or otherwise) of staying too long in any one type of employment. Clearly this view wasn't universal within the officer corps, although its appearance in cases such as these is an interesting counterpoint to the traditional history which stresses the importance of primary group solidarity and doing one's duty by one's comrades, and an interesting footnote to the familiar narrative of officer disillusionment.

Richard Holmes, building on a comment of Martin Middlebrook's, has considered the limits of a soldier's endurance, arguing that he will continue to fight until such time that he considers he has done sufficient and can justifiably stop.[165] In saying this, however, he is clearly referring to the moment during *combat* when the individual soldier decides to *surrender*. In the writings of some of these officers a very different phenomenon can be discerned: officers, often stimulated by rapidly-acquired professional attitudes, deciding that they have 'done their bit' as far as a particular type of service is concerned. Whilst this would not necessarily make any practical difference in the military system, since soldiers are not free agents able to move between jobs and postings at will, it raises interesting questions about combat motivation and the experiences of a citizen army in a modern war which are applicable to wider studies of warfare in the 20th Century.

4

Violence and Fear in the Trenches

Officers could learn a great deal about their jobs and the nature of trench warfare in an impressively short time, but the process of acclimatisation to conditions on the Western Front normally took place over a lengthier period. The process of becoming a soldier did not end on setting foot in the trenches or witnessing a shell fall for the first time. While these were formative in some respects, certainly in the conscious impact they were likely to have had on the individual, the real emotional transition could begin only when the individual was confronted on a daily basis by the routine realities of life in the front line. This process can be broken down into four separate areas: coping with regularly coming under fire, rather than being only temporarily exposed to danger; dealing with fear; learning to kill; and becoming accustomed to the routine presence of death. Each of these represents a hurdle that had to be overcome before the new soldier could consider himself successfully acclimatised, although they were not necessarily obstacles which had to be tackled separately.

Becoming an experienced inhabitant of the trenches and growing used to the danger inherent in that environment may have been a substantial challenge. When starting his trench career Lieutenant Edwin Vaughan was initially 'windier' than some of his contemporaries (judging by their – admittedly perhaps less candid – accounts quoted in Chapter 3). He found it difficult not to dwell morbidly on what lay ahead of him, despite witnessing the nonchalance of his more experienced colleagues. Several brief visits to the line did nothing to calm him, and stories of particular incidents began to have a more damaging effect. He 'saw horrible pictures of myself lying dead in a shattered trench, or helplessly bleeding to death in a shell-hole, with no power to call for help.'[1] When required to spend a longer period of time in the trenches several days later, these imaginings were still potent. He describes standing on his own, contemplating the scene at night and feeling the terror stealing over him as he contemplated his circumstances: 'the mud, the smell of earth, the ragged sandbags, the gruesome litter numbed my brain; a cold fear chilled my spine and set my teeth chattering. I stood shaking and gazing horrified into the darkness, thinking: "this is *war*! And I am in the firing line!"'[2] In his agitated state he then mistook an old coat hanging on the side of the trench for a furtive enemy. Clearly starting at shadows at this stage, it is interesting to note that he was apparently more perturbed by his imaginings, constructed from his impressions about active service and trench life, than by his first sight of a dead body the following day.[3] He quickly seemed to find that the reality was less terrible (or more easily endured) than he had feared. Other officers, however, may have found the reverse occurring – that the trench environment into which they initially seemed to fit without difficulty began playing on their nerves from quite an early stage, fuelled by their inexperience once the initial sense of novelty had worn off. When James Dunn's men joked with one another about their first experience of shell-fire (as noted in Chapter 3), they may have been able to do so because an isolated experience of danger (as it then was) was less likely to produce significant mental strain. Active service in the front line required an acceptance that a heightened level of danger was hereafter to be a defining characteristic of life – a very different psychological challenge.

Nevertheless, according to the evidence of their diaries and letters, officers often were able to adapt extremely well. 2nd Lt. Bertram Medley of the Highland Light Infantry went up the line for the first time on 5 May 1915. Two days later he wrote in his diary: 'I feel at peace. Isn't it strange how, even with the shells pounding outside, one can so soon begin to forget that trenches have ever been dug or bombs have ever been thrown?'[4] It might seem surprising that trench-fighters could sincerely find themselves comparatively at ease in a short space of time, quickly feeling, in the words of Lt. Lancelot Spicer of the King's Own Yorkshire Light Infantry in October 1915, 'just as safe here as one does at home'.[5] Too often the Western Front is depicted as being incessantly lethal, made up of trenches which were thigh deep in mud at all points, with rain and shells falling constantly. In reality, many young officers would have found themselves regularly entrusted with relatively quiet sectors of line, occupying well-constructed and therefore comparatively safe trenches. (Spicer himself was actually not one of those fortunate enough to have an easy initiation, having been pitched straight away into the Battle of Loos; perhaps it is no wonder routine trench duty seemed safe by comparison.)

Officers' immediate reactions to the line have already been discussed in Chapter 3, but perceptions of danger cannot be entirely divorced from surrounding factors, especially in a strange environment. Young officers were reasonably well placed to prevent the inherent strangeness of the trenches from augmenting their fears. They had received some measure of military training, and had been living under military regulations and conditions for some months before reaching them. The military lifestyle itself, and an accompanying degree of privation, could therefore be well embedded already. When they went to the line they were usually accompanied by troops, either in their own units or, if the unit as a whole were inexperienced, provided by the military authorities, who could show them how to operate and whose very demeanour might be expected to have exerted a calming influence. Although ever-present, danger was not always considerable. Firing was sporadic in many areas, and much that did occur presented no threat, but officers could not initially know this or, if they did understand it rationally, prevent themselves from reacting instinctively to sudden sounds or explosions. It took time for them to begin both to distinguish between different types of threat and to master any involuntary responses. 2nd Lt. Stephen Hewett of the Royal Warwickshire Regiment described a 'purely physical fear of the noisy things' in a letter to his mother in March 1916 but explained that 'one gets over the feeling with a very little practice.' By this stage he was able to distinguish between these shocks and 'a mere bullet-sound' which 'has no terrors'.[6]

The ability to differentiate between different threats raises some interesting questions about their potential impact. William Moore, in his study of morale and capital punishment in the First World War, has commented on the way soldiers were often frightened of some threats but not others, comparing the phenomenon to widespread and familiar phobias. Moore's essential point is that no one threat was inevitably psychologically devastating.[7] This observation seems to conflict with Andy Simpson's conclusion that soldiers were more usually afraid of shells than of rifles or machine guns.[8] Shelling certainly could present a serious psychological problem for many officers.[9]

Moreover, like the trenches, it acquired a totemic status – illustrated by reactions to first experiences of shell-fire discussed in Chapter 3 – which ranked only behind that of the trenches themselves and the experience of 'going over the top'. There was good reason both for the fear and the perception; shells caused more British casualties than any other weapon and generated intense psychological strain, as the eminent physician Charles Moran understood. Having served in the war as medical officer to the 1st Battalion Royal Fusiliers, rising to the rank of Major and winning the Military Cross, he wrote a study of men and morale, *The Anatomy of Courage*, which cited shell-fire as having a particular impact on the nerves of a man who was not fully prepared for the awful effects that these weapons might have on his body and consequently on his conceptions of sacrifice.[10] Gilbert Talbot simply described it as 'beastly.'[11]

Regular heavy bombardments could produce their own transition, wearing down a soldier's endurance. Michael Roper has written of a 'nameless dread', an intense terror that soldiers could experience and which was often associated with bombardment.[12] Despite this numerous accounts suggest that, like other weapons, in some cases it could indeed lose its psychological potency. The novelist Alec Dawson published a set of letters from the front anonymously in 1916, in one of which he seemed to suggest that the stimulus provided by shell-fire out-weighed sensations of fear.[13]

Although reporting that nobody seemed immune to the effects of shellfire, Thomas Heald of the Cheshire Regiment admitted in 1915 that 'It is quite alright if one has something to do. You don't notice it if you have not time to think. The great thing is to keep a real grip on yourself and not to give way to it. … I think it must be the bang that upsets one's moral equilibrium.'[14] Knowledge and experience clearly helped, starting with the ability to recognise distinctive noises and characteristics of the different types of shell.[15] Heald himself also understood that attempts to escape from the area under shell-fire were likely to be counterproductive, placing him in more danger than staying put. Soldiers might later develop the useful ability to predict where a shell would land. The reassurance this provided enabled Graham Greenwell, although accepting that living under shell-fire for prolonged periods was likely to wear a man down, to be generally dismissive. Like Heald, however, he also stressed the importance of keeping one's mind occupied at such times: 'Once you know where the things are going, or rather that they aren't directed against your particular spot, you cease to take any interest'.[16] According to John Nettleton, artillerymen developed this *sang-froid* to a fine art, never moving 'unless the thing dropped practically into their laps':

> On the other hand, I have taken a party of artillerymen up to forward positions and had them ducking and spreading all over the place under machine-gun fire, although the bullets were going miles over our heads. Which merely serves to show that the Devil you know is less terrifying than the Devil you don't know and that you can come to terms with anything.[17]

The location and the phase of the war were both potentially significant. When Desmond Young returned to the Western Front in 1917 after an absence of a couple of years it was his impression that the intensification of shelling had made life much grimmer for the infantry.[18] Nevertheless, the writings of officers like Heald and Greenwell suggest that artillery did not occupy a uniquely terrifying position in the arsenal of the Western Front. Some soldiers were clearly able to acclimatise even to this threat. It is interesting, moreover, that shells have largely been demoted within modern conceptions of the First World War. The difficulty of rendering convincing special effects within a production budget may be more important than the cultural dominance of any particular viewpoint, but films and television programmes generally feature them only as a sporadic presence, if they feature at all. *Blackadder Goes Forth* contains only a handful of references to shelling and at no point are the cast actually under shell-fire.

Nowadays machine-guns probably enjoy the popular pre-eminence which Simpson and others have historically applied to shells. Many depictions of the conflict – including the finale of *Blackadder Goes Forth*, described by Adrian Gregory as 'the definitive image of the First World War for a generation' – focus on the moment of the doomed charge towards their lethal barrels.[19] In fact, letters and diaries seem to suggest that officers were not particularly concerned about them – probably because machine guns were not usually a major threat to those in trenches, and accounts of attacks across No Man's Land are relatively rare. No doubt they loomed larger in the minds of those contemplating taking part in an assault. Some regarded direct rifle fire as similarly insignificant. Lt. Leslie Hill of the 6th London Rifles, for example, largely dismissed this threat less than a month after first deploying up the line, casually commenting that 'you do not seem to take much notice of [it].' He seemed more concerned about shells, rifle grenades and trench mortars.[20] In contrast, 2nd Lt. Ralph Bickersteth of the 7th Battalion Leeds Rifles, West Yorkshire Regiment, assessing matters from his trench in April 1915, thought that, 'as far as I can see, if one is careful, it is pure bad luck being hit, as it is impossible really and only a stray bullet could hit one.'[21]

Bickersteth's letter suggests that his perception of risk was based at least in part on his appreciation of the weapon's apparent combat effectiveness in a given tactical scenario, an important reminder both that snipers were a real threat on the Western Front and that officers generally learned quite quickly about the vulnerable points in their positions. Officers did not always, however, have such rational reasons for fearing or disliking a particular type of threat. Bertram Medley told his mother that 'The rifle bullet is what I hate the most' but this was not because of the risk he believed it posed. Instead it was because 'it is aimed at a definite man and it always seems in itself anxious to bury itself in a man, hitting the ground, when it misses its mark, with a kind of baffled wheeze.'[22] This perception of the agency behind the attack is interesting, especially because of the way in which Medley anthropomorphises certain weapons. He did 'not much mind shrapnel after a while: it comes along with a kind of apologetic purr, unlike a Jack Johnson with its loud triumphant shout, or the rifle bullet with its decisive ping.' Nicknaming heavy shells after the famous heavyweight boxer was common throughout the army.

Medley's statement that he was 'infinitely more afraid of bombs, trench mortars and grenades than of shells' was echoed by numerous other officers.[23] Many developed a particular distaste for trench mortars, especially the notorious *Minenwerfer* – the standard German light trench mortar.[24] Douglas Gillespie revealed how these weapons could prey on troops' minds when recounting an exchange of fire that took place in June 1915. The German artillery 'put more than thirty shells over our heads, and into the trenches on our left. They also showered rifle-grenades on us, to which we replied in kind, and for a while there was quite a battle with turnips, sausages, rifle-grenades, and shells all flying through the air, and bursting round about.' Fortunately nobody in Gillespie's company was hit, but for some time afterwards they 'all had a sausage eye, and kept looking up anxiously when a swallow passed the trees, and in the evening when three or four large bats came out, I kept on seeing them past the corner of my spectacles, and looking round anxiously for cover.'[25] There is, however, no accounting for taste. According to his diary, 2nd Lt. Alan Clapham quite enjoyed the experience of coming under fire from these 'sausages'![26] Since these projectiles were visible during their relatively lengthy flight it was possible to run away from them – presumably hence the potential for a certain sort of enjoyment. A similar perspective is provided by Lt. Lionel Sotheby, who also reacted positively to the presence of danger in the line and claimed that 'the bullets have quite an exhilarating effect on me, keeping my spirits up and the shells are quite interesting to watch burst when they are more than 30 yards away.'[27] Assuming statements of this sort should not be dismissed as bravado, accounts of this nature reveal the extent to which soldiers became habituated to their strange subterranean world, accepting dangers which would be quite intolerable to the average civilian, but by a personalised and uncertain process.

The war was characterised by the development of new technologies and weapons and naturally the reactions of soldiers to different perils could therefore depend on the period of the war and the prevalence of the threat. Many weapons, most notably shells, were present throughout and did not change substantially in character. If technological improvements made them more effective it is unlikely that those on the receiving end particularly noticed. In the case of gas warfare, however, there were distinct phases. The first large-scale gas attack on the Western Front occurred on 22 April 1915, when the Germans used chlorine gas at Ypres. The incident sparked outrage, although both sides subsequently developed extensive chemical warfare programs.[28] The sight of men dying from gas poisoning was horrific; Jack Oughtred called it the most horrible thing he had ever seen.[29] Initially, it was much feared by troops who were facing a weapon with relatively unknown properties, and could cause collective panic.[30] However, it appears that within a few months, as its use became more common and effective countermeasures were developed, both its capacity to shock and its tactical effectiveness were diminished.[31] Charles May was distinctly unimpressed in November 1915:

> We had our first dose of gas this afternoon – and are somewhat disappointed. It is not at all exciting. One merely pulls on a helmet, which smells abominably and which causes an otherwise decent battalion to at once assume the aspect of horrible ogres near which it would be criminal to bring any highly-strung infant, and walks solemnly through a house filled with a yellowish atmosphere. There is nothing in it and this fearsome 'gas', which has been held up as our bête noire these months past and which previously we have not been able to think of with that perfect equanimity so desirable in a solder, assumes on close contact merely the proportions of a beastly nuisance. And that mainly because it necessitates one confining one's manly headpiece within an unbecoming and smelly flannel bag.[32]

As its use became more common and more effective countermeasures were developed, it appears as though many officers became remarkably blasé. Christopher Stone, bombarded with gas shells in April 1917, wrote that 'I am too stupid or not stupid enough to put on my helmet, and prefer the risk of being poisoned to the discomfort of wearing the damned thing.'[33] In fact, for much of the war gas appears to have been regarded as an irritant rather than a terrifying weapon. Raymond Asquith's account of a gas attack certainly suggests impatience: 'we all had to put on our gas helmets and stumble about spitting and slobbering and swearing and looking like the Wolf in *Little Red Riding Hood*.'[34] However, when chemical warfare escalated dramatically in 1918 with the perfection of delivery techniques including Livens projectors and gas shells, it arguably became a greater psychological threat than shelling. The German offensive of March 1918, spearheaded by enormous quantities of mustard gas, caused a 'gas crisis' as seven thousand British soldiers a week poured into field hospitals suffering from shock.[35]

Whilst some officers were able to face certain weapons with more equanimity than others, dealing with fear remained a daily challenge, the magnitude of which depended on the individual. One of the greatest fears – that of being thought a coward – has been well noted by historians and was an anxiety that weighed especially heavily on officers because of the expectations placed on them by their class upbringing and the grave responsibilities with which they were charged.[36] The 'stiff upper lip' and traditional English reserve inculcated by public schools have been derided by many over the years, but a controlled deportment (if achieved) was clearly valuable to officers who had to inspire courage in others and were anxious to avoid showing fear themselves. Douglas Wimberley, who was educated at Wellington and served with the Cameron Highlanders, recognised in his memoir that his school had 'taught me how to keep the semblance of a stiff upper lip in public when inwardly I felt in a very different frame of mind'.[37] The wartime army chaplain Maurice Ponsonby recalled 'very well' an episode in a reserve trench in front of Cambrin: 'The Huns put up a mine, and then started rapid fire. The men near me were standing on the fire-step and getting very excited, when the Company Commander came out of his dug-out in his shirt sleeves and said in a drawly voice, "Well, well, someone's got the wind up this afternoon." The effect was quite electrical; everyone became perfectly calm and collected.' Ponsonby concluded that 'the callous indifference of the public-school manner has its values in war.'[38]

Naturally the stiff upper lip could not entirely negate the fear of being wounded or killed; in fact, the expression is meaningless if it is not an acknowledgement that the fear remains, but is being suppressed in some way. What cannot be deduced from primary sources is whether the observed 'indifference' is genuine or an affectation. It is quite possible that it was real. Officers – like all soldiers – developed complex and varied responses to the diverse conditions and challenges of the Western Front, and the prospect of death or injury is no exception. The prospect of death presented particularly complicated psychological problems, which will be discussed fully in Chapter 11. Wounding was not necessarily less complicated, being potentially more immediately distressing in actuality and consequently also in prospect. Charles Stormont Gibbs found that his expectations about the nature of combat injuries were far removed from reality. 'Like most people,' he wrote in his memoir, 'I had not fully realised before that the horror of war is wounds, not death. I had thought of people being killed perhaps, if they weren't lucky enough to get a nice little wound first. I had never imagined, even remotely, what a man looks like with a wound in the stomach. Here for the first time I was brought up against a sickening horror of war.'[39] This realisation has been identified by Richard Holmes as a common occurrence. In a study ranging across 20th Century warfare he argues that serious injuries are more distressing to soldiers than dead bodies, and that seeing someone who has been mutilated or disabled changes the nature of a man's fear. Performance anxiety – the fear of failing a test of courage – is replaced by the dread of a life-altering and permanent wound.[40] Holmes' analysis suggests that the first occasion on which serious physical trauma was witnessed was a formative and transitional moment to rank alongside entering the trenches and coming under fire. Initially, as Gibbs illustrates, they had little idea of what to expect but experience wrought a significant change. The attitude of junior officers towards wounding subsequently evolved as the transition from civilian to soldier progressed. As with many other aspects of the transition, this was not necessarily a journey with a single direction of travel. While veterans might be more afraid of being wounded than newly-initiated soldiers, habituation to risk could overcome the caution which might be considered a normal accompaniment to these fears. Stephen Hewett was surprised to note 'how hardened the old stagers become, so that after a year or more they get caught at last by the most flagrant lack of precautions'.[41]

If this seems unusual, it should be remembered both that soldiers became accustomed to a range of environmental factors, of which heightened danger was only one, and also that injury was never an entirely unappealing prospect for the soldier on the Western Front. The dread of serious wounds developed alongside an appreciation that relatively minor injuries which were nevertheless sufficiently serious to require transportation back to the United Kingdom provided release from trenches and military duties. These so-called 'Blighty ones' were eagerly desired because they provided an escape from the front but carried absolutely no moral stigma. So appealing was this prospect that soldiers were sometimes known to mutilate themselves surreptitiously to achieve the desired effect.[42] An anonymous glossary of trench terminology sardonically acknowledged this possibility with its definition of a 'Blighty' wound: 'This is obtained by mutual co-operation with a hostile party or parties unknown. It is the aim of the receiver to gain his objective without exposing his "main body".'[43]

The letters and diaries of junior officers suggest that they reached this conclusion remarkably quickly, if not always for the same reasons. In May 1915, shortly after going up the line for the first time, Bertram Medley wrote about passing a dressing station: 'a constant stream of stretcher bearers came to it, carrying those who had suffered in last night's fighting, but all pity for them was swallowed up in a great envy, for a wound is the best way of getting leave from this horror.'[44] It seems clear that he is describing a 'Blighty'. However, this comment is not like the numerous allusions to these types of wound found so frequently in contemporary accounts. Two notes jar in particular: the suppression of pity, and the assumption about the severity of wounds. The two are linked; if the wounds are not serious, what need is there to feel much pity? If they are, the unfortunate casualty can hardly be said to have got leave. It seems likely that this is a reflection of Medley's own naivety and lack of experience; his own revulsion at the war seems to be uppermost in his mind, causing him to ascribe fortunate escape rather too hastily. Douglas Gillespie, also writing in early 1915 shortly after entering the trenches for the first time, was similarly quick to swap pity for envy, although he was a little more cautious about the circumstances: 'Somehow, one doesn't feel very sorry for a man who gets hit, not dangerously, with a dressing station handy, and a doctor to attend to him at once; for even if he feels the pain for a week or two, that's nothing much in the long run.' Rather than concentrate on the 'horror', as Medley does, Gillespie instead immediately focuses on a simple desire which the war prevents him from fulfilling: 'I wish I could see Hopetoun park on one of these sunny days – last year I had such a short spring holiday, and then the weather at Rhuveag was as bad as it could be, until the day I had to go away.'[45]

Both Gillespie and Medley contrast life on active service with the pleasant world they have left behind in a manner which was presumably entirely typical of newly-initiated soldiers. This is not yet, however, the socialised discourse familiar from numerous sources such as Jack Oughtred, who described casually how an officer wounded through the arm in November 1916 received a 'really beautiful blighty'.[46] While variation of this sort may always be a product of individual characteristics, rather than any sort of trend, a possible explanation is that the development of the detached, almost ironic stance on such wounds was part of the wider transition from civilian to soldier which required time to take full effect. Oughtred joined the army in May 1915. By the time he used the term in his letter he had therefore had much longer than Gillespie or Medley to establish both the outlook and the tone. Graham Greenwell's letters start in October 1914, and he first went into the trenches in May 1915. In March 1917 he described his adjutant as a 'lucky dog' because he had got a compound fracture in his arm from a bullet.[47] Comments like Oughtred's and Greenwell's suggest that 'Blighty' wounds were afforded a talismanic and slightly unreal status – hence their feigned lack of seriousness – which elevated them into a part of the superstition and fatalism which was a recognised phenomenon associated with trench warfare. This was a developed, not an instinctive response. There is a sense in which Medley and Gillespie, on the other hand, were reacting in a more intuitive fashion.

However, there is perhaps a stronger case that the contrast reflects the development of the concept and its socialisation over time, and consequently the speed with which young officers could absorb it, rather than its adoption being a function of time served. Neither Medley nor Gillespie used the term, which suggests that it may not even have been in such common usage in the first half of 1915, but thereafter it became deeply engrained in the military culture of the Western Front and a familiar part of the narrative of the war. Given the frequency with which it was soon being used, it is possible that new officers simply adopted it in order to hasten both their acceptance and their creation of a new identity as group members, or that they were reflecting the phenomenon witnessed by the French observer André Gide who, on visiting a medical station at Braffye was surprised to hear survivors describing their experiences using the very clichés contained in newspaper reports of the battle.[48] This might suggest that it was only a figure of speech, but it clearly had some deeper significance. If a wound was imagined to be a positive occurrence, it made it easier to face the prospect of one's own suffering, and young officers readily conformed to the prevailing paradigm.

※

In addition to mastering any fears relating to their own safety, officers also had to grow accustomed to the horrors of the trenches if they were to endure and carry out their duties. There were two reasons for this. First, officers needed to maintain their own psychological well-being. In the words of an anonymous officer, 'One must learn to be callous – or else break down.'[49] Secondly, it also served a vital practical function. Officers had a responsibility to their men which required them to maintain their composure. As the same anonymous officer remarked:

> What can one say to a man who appeals to his officer with sickly face and shaky voice, because the front of his tunic and his trousers are drenched with the blood and smeared with fragments of the brains of a man he has been bearing down the trench on a stretcher? 'Wipe it off with this' – an empty sand-bag – meets the case, for the uses of a sand-bag are many, and to be callous is the only safe course when dealing with a man whose face is pale and whose voice is unsteady.[50]

This account suggests that callousness could be a choice, a selected response to a particular set of circumstances. However, if an officer was to maintain his standing in the eyes of his troops and provide an emotional mainstay in the long-term, it was essential that he genuinely become hardened to some extent. The psychological pressure to maintain only a façade of insensitivity despite feelings to the contrary would be self-defeating over time. This view was shared by the young officer Stephen Hewett, who noted that 'if one did not quickly lose one's first sensibility one would have to knuckle under and come home.'[51]

No soldier can afford to be too squeamish or sensitive, but the Western Front made the need to develop an emotional carapace especially pressing since death, in the words of Theodore Cameron Wilson of the 10th Battalion Sherwood Foresters, was 'everywhere. You have to walk through it, and under it and over it and past it.'[52] It could strike anywhere throughout the armed forces, even in areas well away from the front line. The historian Denis Winter was told by his father that he saw a man shot by accident in the stomach when a round was ignited by the heat of a burning brazier.[53] The battlefields were obviously particularly lethal and, at some stage, many trench soldiers had to live cheek-by-jowl with their fallen comrades, even if they did not witness the deaths of those around them directly.

Death had hitherto been a relative stranger to these young public-school and university-educated men. By the Edwardian era, falling levels of infant mortality and improved healthcare had rendered bereavement a much less common occurrence.[54] For Desmond Young's generation, 'the impact of violence … was something new. With the exception of a platoon of miners, I do not suppose that any of my contemporaries in the battalion had seen a man die a violent death. We were not even accustomed to the suddenness and squalor of "death on the road". The wars of the past were so remote that they seemed no more real than "Westerns."'[55] After 1914, however, violent death became all too familiar and many officers struggled to cope with it. After moving from the King's Own Scottish Borderers to the Highland Light Infantry, Medley ended up sharing quarters with a doctor, which he described as 'gruesome work':

> Even as I have been writing some of this, a man was brought in groaning and sighing, shot by one of our own men while cleaning a rifle, as if there were not too many tragedies in the world already. … While I sit reading in my room a life is being sighed out in the next, a piece of transparent sacking alone between the two rooms: yet even that cold, inanimate thing lying so near does not make one realize all the hatefulness of war. We buried him this afternoon. Just a hurriedly

dug grave, just a few of the most wonderful words ever spoken, the shovelling on of earth and the reverent laying of a bunch of lowers, and for most the remembrance of Pte. Jamieson is wiped away. So little it takes for one of God's creatures to pass to Him that loves him.[56]

Medley was clearly deeply affected by this and through his diary entry he seems to be struggling to comprehend quite how dramatically his world has changed. It is perhaps also significant that this was the scene of an accidental death, the unnecessary nature of the incident heightened the sense of tragedy and waste.

Growing accustomed to this feature of the war was surely one of the most difficult parts of the young officer's transition. Adjustment generally took place over a longer period of time than the process of acclimatisation to trench life since most officers were spared the very worst conditions and only intermittently occupied sections of line which saw particularly hard fighting. The sheer scale of death might be hidden for a while, although the first sight of a corpse or casualty could still be extremely upsetting. At a very early stage in his military career James Neville 'saw a boot sticking out of the ground. I kicked it and then saw a piece of khaki puttee attached. It gave me rather a nasty turn.'[57] It became easier to cope with such sights over time. As veteran Richard Hawkins recalled, 'The most extraordinary thing about being in the trenches was how you came simply to accept death.'[58] Some even claimed never to have had a problem. Edwin Vaughan, in so doing, was taken aback by his own reaction. When confronted with a corpse for the first time he admitted that he 'was surprised' that it did not distress him.[59] Vaughan, however, as has already been noted in this chapter, had other psychological challenges to overcome, suggesting that a period of acclimatisation was the norm, even if the circumstance to which the officer had to grow accustomed varied.

No doubt most soldiers were rather more affected by the sight of death, but those who did not fail entirely to adapt to its near continual presence seem to have made the change remarkably quickly. Brian Lawrence reported the case 'of a young subaltern who had never seen a dead body when he went to the front, and the first time he saw a man killed in his platoon he felt sick and faint and had to go and lie down. Four months later he was hit in the arm, and while waiting to be conducted back to the dressing station, he piled up three dead bodies at the entrance of his dug-out and used them as a seat in the sun, while he smoked cigarettes and cracked jokes with his friends.'[60] Approximately one month after first entering the line Jack Oughtred was working in close proximity to a number of men killed by snipers: 'Very unpleasant believe me. But it is a most remarkable thing how soon one forgets. Very callous I suppose but without any doubt it is just as well.'[61] Less than two months after travelling to France, Stephen Hewett witnessed the death of a man whose face had been 'horribly smashed in by a bullet': 'This being my first casualty I was severely shaken; but one has to get callous both in mind and body, and one does: and an hour's sleep revived me.'[62] Despite being badly shaken by his earliest interaction with the debris of war, James Neville soon became hardened. Fourteen months after his first traumatic experience he was able to describe this harrowing encounter with the crew of a disabled tank without any noticeable distress:

The officer's face was completely raw, all the skin off his forehead and face hung like an icicle from the tip of his nose, while the skin of his jaw and chin encircled his neck in a grey fold, like an Elizabethan ruff. His hands were raw too, and he gave me the impression of having been lathered in blood. Wounded men came crawling up to our posts, too, beseeching us to carry them back to the main Albert road on our stretchers; these pitiful requests had to be refused, because our stretcher-bearers were already doing the work of four times their number. One man with a shattered ankle crawled up to me and asked me to get him taken back. When I told him that it was impossible, he started off dragging his ankle, and said he would get back to Albert as he was, rather than be taken prisoner. The pluck of the man![63]

It is striking that his extended account contains few clues as to his personal reaction, and his tone is businesslike throughout.

Some soldiers did fail to become emotionally hardened. Douglas Wimberley remembered 'so well my laughter at Stewart retching at the dead bodies – I was used to them, but he never seemed to get so.'[64] Arthur Adam seems to have been a similar case. On his first tour of the front line he witnessed the aftermath of a bout of shelling which he struggled to cope with. One man had been killed and two wounded, including Captain Sindall who 'was knocked up pretty badly ... I won't go into details, but clearing up ... was to say the least disagreeable, and I don't somehow like that sort of thing much. I felt utterly helpless, but I think the next time it occurs I shall be more likely to be able to help properly.' Two weeks later, his distaste for the infantry's lot was still apparent. He preferred the gunners who 'on the whole [have] less of the mess to clear up.' Ten months later, he wrote: 'I lost a man the other day – the first since I have had the company, and I am afraid I have gone very soft-hearted; he was a boy of about 17 and one I loved very much.' Although, in his own opinion he had grown callous, he was still highly vulnerable to this sort of emotional trauma and so continued to suffer throughout his period of service. As he himself admitted, 'I find it a very strange feeling, living always as it might be in the presence of death; quiet though this part is, there is always a leakage, both of officers and men, and the strain in the trenches is continuous.'[65] Officers like Adam were distinctly disadvantaged, although the transition, if made, was not a one-way process. Graham Greenwell may have been able to write relatively dispassionately within four months about headless and limbless corpses despite the deeply shocking death of a good friend within four days of his arrival in the trenches. Even he was shaken by the apocalyptic battlefield of the Somme.

Arthur Adam was quite unapologetic about the emotional strain produced by the suffering of his men, and this admission highlights an interesting facet of this element of transition. Although officers appreciated that they needed to become emotionally hardened they often lamented the fact or seemed embarrassed about it. Lionel Sotheby was prepared to claim that being in the line 'amuses me intensely, as one becomes totally callous of the dead and death that are around you' but he also felt compelled to caveat this: 'Horrible to say this is the truth.'[66] It seems that any degree of desensitisation was regarded as an affront to their humanity and civilisation. The change from civilian to soldier was regretted, even if it was not resisted. The idea that they might become totally hardened seems to have been almost painful to them. Billie Nevill described how he and his colleagues 'found the skeleton of a German in his equipment, in the wood where we were digging. Rather gruesome, but I'm afraid I've been cured of squeamishness by now at unpleasant sights, *not to callousness of course* [my italics].'[67] His hasty disclaimer seems to reveal how uncomfortable he felt about the change he had witnessed in himself. Regret seems to have been a gentlemanly reflex to these most uncivilised circumstances. Young officers understood the reality of their situation, but they wanted to retain their humanity in the eyes of their families who were typically the recipients of these writings. These difficulties were intensified when they were called upon to take lives.

Duty obliged officers to add to the lethality of their environment and, by killing fellow human beings, to cross a significant line separating law-abiding civilians and soldiers. There were many different reactions to this imperative. Many found it strange to begin with. Even Julian Grenfell, who had enthusiastically embraced a military career with the Royal Dragoons in 1910 and was soon likening his work to hunting dangerous animals, was unsettled at first. Like many of his generation, he had been brought up under strict instructions to be extremely careful with firearms and not to point them at other people, even in jest.[68] Strange or not, it was very common, however, for soldiers to seek to assert their aggressive character as soon as possible by shooting at the enemy (as Chapter 3 notes). This was part of their entry into the world of the trenches and their construction of a military identity, but in many cases it was probably also a reflection of a tendency, highlighted by Joanna Bourke, for those with the least experience of fighting and most separation from the front line to express the greatest hatred of the enemy.[69]

The most bellicose anti-Germany rhetoric was indeed generally expressed by the very young and inexperienced. It often seems to have been prompted by naïve ideas about the nature of war and killing; a failure to comprehend the true nature of soldiering. As part of the transition from civilian to soldier the officer gained experience and attitudes were usually tempered. Views on killing and the enemy became more complicated. Edward Tennant's letters provided a good example of this shift. His early missives from the front contain several bloodthirsty references to the Germans. On September 15th 1915, he described being out on a wiring party:

> It is rather fun making these entanglements and imagining the Germans coming along in the dark and falling over these things and starting to shout; whereupon you immediately send up a flare (which lasts ten seconds) and turn a machine gun on to them as they struggle in the wire. It sounds cruel, but it is War.[70]

The next day, apologising to a friend for the dull nature of his letter, he promised to 'write a better screed' once he had 'a few grim notches on the butt of my revolver, and a captured Junker or two in tow!' By 17 January 1916, however, after months of fighting and a spell in hospital, his tone is strikingly different: 'I think I shot a German the other day; if I did, God rest his soul.'[71] This is the first time he gives any indication in his letters that he thinks somebody is dead at his hand, and he appears shocked.

While Tennant's discomfort may have been caused by simple revulsion at the reality of his deed (the prospect of which had once been so appealing), it is equally possible that by this time the enemy had been humanised in his estimation by longer experience of active service. There is copious evidence that many soldiers did develop respect and even admiration for their opponents, and in attributing positive qualities to them they can only have rendered them more understandable, making the necessity of fighting them more morally complex. In doing so, they were demonstrating another aspect of the transition from civilians to soldiers, developing a form of trans-national community which Janet Watson identifies as a particular characteristic of pre-war professional soldiers: 'Regular soldiers often exhibited a powerful respect for other professional soldiers, friend or foe. They described themselves as a fraternity of men whose work was war, and they could respect and admire each other when that work was performed well.'[72] Watson sees regulars separated from volunteers by different views on patriotism and professionalism. This is a key distinction at the early stages of the formation of a volunteer's soldierly identity, but the regulars' perspective was not exclusively their own. The development, if only to a limited extent, of comparable sentiments amongst volunteer junior officers provides further evidence of their ongoing professionalization (at least of attitude) and the growth of their military selves. It is also an indication of a diminution of their civilian selves, for it was amongst the civilian population that the most venomous anti-German sentiment was typically found. As Frederick Keeling commented in December 1914: 'I believe the loathsome, vitriolic hatred of the Germans is confined to journalists and civilian intellectuals. I doubt if it exists among the men who have got to face the bullets.'[73]

This did not mean, however, that some officers did not nurse their own deep enmities, or that others were not prone to passionate outbursts against the enemy.[74] A spark of hatred might be prompted by a particular sight or story which kindled the writer's anger and disgust at what he perceived to be German barbarism. Adrian Gregory argues that the British public were largely convinced at a very early stage of the war both that Germany was responsible and 'that there was something tangibly wrong' with the way she was conducting it.[75] Enemy action which seemed to confirm this might consequently strike a chord with officers, provoking strong feelings. 'How pleased the Germans will be that they have sunk the *Lusitania*!' fumed Douglas Gillespie in May 1915. 'It's no use protesting against them now, except with the bayonet; their leaders must have lost their heads in their rage, and I think it's a sort of just judgement for their gospel of hate.'[76] Junior officers were also as prone as other sectors of the population at times to having their ire inflamed by propaganda and rumours of atrocities. 'Isn't that corpse-factory business disgusting?' wrote Christopher Stone, referring to the story (probably fabricated by British intelligence) that the Germans were rendering corpses on an industrial scale to extract various products: 'One can hardly believe it.'[77] In fairness to Stone, this particular story was widely circulated and believed, as were the accounts of crucifixions of Allied soldiers. Geoffrey Fildes recounts the fate a Canadian sergeant as fact in his memoir when it was probably mythical.[78] (He may, admittedly, have had propagandist motives of his own.)

It is difficult to say whether greater knowledge of and respect for the enemy generally reduced this susceptibility. Some officers were clearly sceptical about accounts, recognising the disparities between press and other reports on the one hand and their own personal experiences and more nuanced view of the enemy on the other. A visit to an old church still standing despite its obvious utility as an observation post prompted Lionel Sotheby to observe that 'I think it proves that the Germans do not make a habit of bombarding churches, and that perhaps the papers exaggerate too much when they talk of the Germans' so-called "atrocities." After all it is very easy for a shell to strike a church by mistake and to cause so much damage as to lead one to expect many shells had fallen.'[79] Then again, when the reported atrocity concerned something outside the officer's direct experience, like the *Kadaveranstalt* or crucifixions, there was inherently more chance of credulity, even without the distorting effects of the propaganda machine. Overall, it seems likely that the growth of experience and a more professional attitude did shape officers' perspectives, but that these factors and the varied speeds of personal transitions created more of a spectrum of outlooks than might have been found in the pre-war regular population.

A more direct desire to avenge fallen comrades could also be a powerful motivation to kill, as Lionel Sotheby himself found following an unsuccessful attack by the Black Watch on Aubers Ridge in May 1915:

> On returning I find myself in charge of a Company of 25 men instead of 200. …
> We lost over 500 men. I feel a changed person at present and unable to laugh or
> smile at anything, feeling almost in a dream. Next time the Germans will get it.
> Given a chance with wire down and at close quarters, they will be slaughtered, and
> I feel quite mad at it, and long for a decent smash at them.[80]

Jack Oughtred similarly emphasised the importance of retribution: 'I personally accounted for 5 Huns – Thank God. I never did a better day's work. I have avenged someone.'[81] Unlike Sotheby, however, he does not seem to be thinking of retaliating for the deaths of people specifically known to him. Given British presumptions about the guilt of the German nation, he perhaps did not need to connect their now-forfeit lives to any specific losses, although it seems more likely that he was thinking of the many deaths he had either witnessed by this stage in his career or was aware of from amongst his circle of acquaintances. As Chapter 11 will argue, a sense of belonging to a community and of having an obligation to them was a powerful motivation and emotional support for junior officers.

While an officer might nurture an undifferentiated hostility towards the enemy, this could falter if he observed the enemy displaying more varied characteristics which similarly helped to humanise them. Gillespie, for example, wrote letters on successive days which presented the Germans in very different lights. In the first, produced on 6 March 1915, he was struck by the desolation of the town in which he was billeted and wrote that 'when I see these ruins and the light of the burning farms at night, I wish with all my heart that they were German houses, and German farms.' The next day, however, he reported that 'The Germans near here behaved very well when they were in billets, and paid for everything. One is glad to know it.'[82]

Reconciling various different perceptions like this could have been difficult. One technique adopted by Gillespie himself seems to have been dividing the enemy into categories. He could admit that Saxons had 'some sport in them' but was prejudiced against Bavarians, largely because of the reported contents of a letter which he believed had been taken from a dead body. This episode provides another interesting example of the ways in which popular perceptions of the enemy were manipulated and distorted throughout the war, the more interesting for the fact that Gillespie eschewed any temptation to equate 'Bavarian' automatically with German. The Bavarian who wrote the supposed letter in question had apparently boasted about killing civilians: '"You will thus have a charming souvenir of a German warrior who has been right through the war from the very beginning, and has shot and bayoneted many Frenchmen, and also bayoneted many women. Dear Grete Maier, in five minutes, I bayoneted seven women and four young girls in the fighting at Batovile; my captain told me to shoot them, but I bayoneted the rabble of swine instead.'" It doesn't apparently seem at all strange to Gillespie that this Bavarian should have placed so much emphasis on his misogynistic violence. He simply states that 'That's the sort of man whom I yet hope to see on the end of our bayonets.'[83] Germans could only be respected if they conformed to what an officer believed were British standards.

Whether or not they actively hated the Germans, few officers ever expressed any doubts about the necessity of killing them in order to achieve their goal. Gillespie himself thought that 'There's just a bit too much sitting still, and not firing at the Germans because it will only make them fire back; but we should always fire when there is any target, and take jolly good care to aim straighter; it's the only way to end the war'.[84] This pragmatic attitude did not necessarily, however, make killing any easier and different individuals reacted in different ways to the imperative to kill. Range lessened the difficulty, as did the adoption of uniforms, especially the steel helmets which robbed the combatants of distinct individual appearances and humanity.[85] However, even after months of trench service, the prospect of personalising killing could still be shocking: 'I have seen enough of horrors,' wrote Andrew Buxton of the Rifle Brigade, 'but mercifully have not had the very worst one … of having to shoot a man, or men, point-blank.' He was not opposed to killing as such, but found it difficult to regard it as anything other than a sad necessity. 'What does one say when these things are reported?' he asked rhetorically in November 1915, the things in question being the success his men have enjoyed in sniping some of the enemy. 'I suppose, "That's splendid," but I cannot get further than "Is that so?"'[86]

Having killed, some were conscious of crossing over a threshold, of a loss of their civilised status which corresponded to the regret that many felt on realising that they had grown callous.[87] Alan Hanbury-Sparrow, who took a regular commission shortly before the war started, analysed the point in his memoir *The Land-Locked Lake*, published in 1932:

> It is only the next day that you realise that the real nobility and spirit of the war has been lost to you. For you have killed a man, and through so doing have coarsened and degraded something in yourself. At first you don't speak about it, or else you say you think you missed also with the second shot, but later on you find yourself bragging that you got one. But this stage is not reached till many moons have passed, for it takes time for the germs of decay to accumulate.[88]

Ironically, it was the inability to become totally degraded which reinforced the sense of one's own degradation. Hanbury-Sparrow's regret seems fuelled by a sense of empathy with his victim – identified by the German neurophysician Dr R. Steiner as a major cause of psychoneurotic illness, and potentially the culmination of any process of humanisation of the enemy.[89] The sudden development of empathy had a significant impact on Charles May. He initially showed aggressive tendencies and enjoyed sniping, describing it in December 1916 as 'exciting work': 'In fact one must curb the tendency lest it should become a fascination.'[90] In February 1916, however, he was shown a bible discovered on the body of a dead German, at which point the scale of the personal tragedy which lay behind each death was brought vividly home to him:

It was a kind of children's testament, filled with gaudy prints and the Story told more in the nature of a series of short tales. On the fly-leaf was the name Hermann Stampa, I think, and over this in a child's hand-writing the word 'Dada'. War is very sad. Poor devil, I suppose he had a wife and kiddie somewhere filled with pride for the daddy who was a soldier and now stricken down with grief for the daddy who is 'missing.' It brings things home to one to come upon a little human touch like that. It makes one feel that it would be well if Kaisers and ambitious, place-seeking politicians and other such who make wars could be stricken down and peaceful, home-loving, ordinary men be left to live their lives in peace and in the sunshine of the love of wife and children. Perhaps the man may have been quite a blackguard or just a hateful, bullying, swaggering Prussian and, as such, something to loathe and detest. I do not know. All I am conscious of is that somewhere in his Fatherland there is a little child who called him 'Dada'. I have a little baby too.[91]

This was clearly a profoundly moving experience. The pre-war professional soldier, brought up to regard his opponent as a kind of brother and therefore human, might have been better able to reconcile these personal tensions with the need to perform his function, although Hanbury-Sparrow's words suggest that this could still present a significant challenge. It was certainly hard for the citizen-soldier.

A range of studies as well as numerous letters and diaries suggest that it was common for soldiers to feel guilty about taking life. A sense of shame might be so profound that it endured into their post-war lives.[92] Faced with such an intense challenge to their soldierly and moral identities, soldiers made various attempts to 're-conceptualise' killing in order to legitimise aggressive behaviour. Jack Oughtred sought to reassure his girlfriend that his five victims were killed during 'fair fighting', appealing to a chivalric concept familiar to the Edwardians in order to assert a continued civilised status.[93] Another technique, Joanna Bourke argues, was to transfer responsibility for the killing to the authority directing the war, abnegating any sense of personal liability and thereby reducing whatever feelings of guilt or distress might arise.[94] This did not necessarily require reference to any specific command hierarchy. Malcolm Davidson clearly found his experience of killing traumatic, but attempted to justify himself with reference to his function within the military machine in the most general sense:

I shot my first Hun this last time we were in. My part of the trench was only about 40 yards from theirs, and this fellow was hammering in stakes in front in the early dawn – so I put a bullet into him. Felt such a brute afterwards, as he probably loathed the whole show just as much as I do, and it was very cold blooded – he gave such a dismal howl – however I suppose we're here to kill each other: it's all very deplorable.[95]

Davidson's ability to empathise on some level with his quarry contributes to his sense of unease but also provides some justification. He seems to be apologising, both to his victim and to his *civilian* audience, for his 'deplorable' action, but cites the ultimate sanction for violence – kill or be killed – whilst also proffering his personal anguish as a form of penance and proof that he retains pre-war sensibilities. By embracing guilt in this way, men could demonstrate that they had retained a 'civilised' morality, had not become totally debased and were capable of rehabilitation and reintegration.

When Davidson talked about the necessity to kill he was describing the circumstances of the Western Front – the *order* of things and his purpose within it – rather than orders from a superior officer. The physical manifestation of authority in the form of the military hierarchy was also potentially important, since instructors placed great importance upon instantaneous obedience to direct orders to kill. If soldiers were expected to respond immediately, even reflexively, then they could not themselves be blamed. This thinking has two negative implications for officers. In the first place, it probably placed the defence beyond the reach of many officers. They had to obey orders from their commanders, but these orders were typically different to those issued to their men. They were more strategic in nature, and junior officers were responsible for translating a battle plan into tactical reality, directing the fire of their troops. Their actions were altogether more measured and consequential. They didn't just obey orders; they interpreted them, turning intent into the lethal application of force.

Secondly, Bourke suggests that this method of transferring the ordinary soldiers' responsibility (and potentially their collective guilt) to their officers may possibly have caused the officers more moral suffering.[96] If this was the case, it is difficult to know how an officer could have been expected to have reacted. Leaving aside some form of psychological collapse such as shell-shock – which could be caused by such a range of factors such as nervous tension or the pressure of responsibility that it would be difficult to isolate 'collective guilt' in particular – the logical response would have been some form of avoidance, using their localised influence to restrict the violence carried out by the men under their command. Truces are known to have been a feature of life on the Western Front at different times and in different places. Tony Ashworth's theory of 'live and let live' places particular emphasis on this method by which front-line soldiers could reassert some control over their lives.[97] However, it seems unlikely that a strategy of non-aggression could have been anything more than a temporary means of avoiding a feeling of culpability. Ultimately, an officer who refused to provide the right sort of leadership would have placed himself in a very difficult position. Moreover, examples indicating officer reluctance to sanction aggression can frequently be explained with reference to tactical realities and a desire to avoid provoking some form of retaliation. Such thinking is not immediately redolent of a guilt-stricken conscience.

Alternatively, officers might have sought to lessen their sense of guilt by refusing to commit violent acts themselves. In this way they might have been able to construct a more robust defence that they, like their men, were only following orders rather than personally violating a moral code. There are certainly many examples in letters and diaries of officers eschewing opportunities to be aggressive. John Keegan notes that many amateur and some regular officers, at least in the early stages, shrank from taking lives.[98] It is difficult, however, to cite *guilt*, rather than squeamishness, principle or some other factor, as the main cause.

Those who did not shrink from violence did not have to use the language of guilt to bolster their emotional stability. Rather than focusing on negative connotations many officers – especially those who might be described as 'fire-eaters' – instead re-conceptualised their lethal work by translating their military activities into the language of sport and hunting.[99] James Neville described a morning's work in the lines as 'great fun shooting at human rabbits!'[100] This sort of dehumanisation of the enemy potentially lessened the guilt associated with killing while also emphasising the pleasurable aspects of the activity. The analogy did not even require violence; Douglas Bell's unit had prepared a hidden vantage point concealed beneath an abandoned piece of rolling stock. It was designed for use by a sniper, but Bell seemed to find it more useful simply for observation. He described watching the enemy through a telescope, the magnification allowing him to see them operating out of cover behind their lines. More interesting, probably, than a view into the opposing trench line – a world he could almost certainly have imagined without difficulty – this was a perspective on an entirely different reality: German-occupied France. For Bell, however, it was simply the ability to see his quarry after fighting an invisible foe for so long which excited him, reminding him of the moment in a deer hunt when his target was seen at a distance.[101]

As Bell's experience suggests, many officers had first-hand experience of pastoral or hunting lifestyles on which to draw. Sassoon was famously involved with field sports, publishing his *Memoirs of a Fox-Hunting Man* in 1928. Sam Paget went shooting when on leave in October 1916. A picture in his family's 'War Scrapbook' shows him holding a shotgun.[102] In the early months of the war it was possible to participate in these pursuits whilst on active service. Caroline Dakers has highlighted the popularity of various types of shooting and hunting and the lengths to which the upper classes were prepared to go to maintain their traditional hobbies, including transporting hunting packs out to France.[103] The illustrator J.R. Monsell described a day's sport catching rabbits with falcons whilst in France in the summer of 1915.[104] Some officers without pre-war experience of hunting may well have been initiated into these practices by friends, but the window

Sam Paget on leave, October 1916. (Private archive)

of opportunity was short-lived as both hunting and shooting in France were banned in 1915, curbing (but presumably not entirely curtailing) the practices.[105]

Those without any practical experience were not excluded, however, from using the same terminology and mentality to rationalise their military duties. Michael Adams has described how the language of hunting appeared in earlier wars; it was also a mainstay of popular literature, especially the type of 'morally-improving' fiction aimed at schoolboys.[106] The public-school culture was steeped in these concepts, to the extent that by the Edwardian era there was a widespread belief that hunting was a good training for war.[107] This meant that a young officer could imagine that his soldierly activities were comparable in some way to the exploits of the hunting field.

Casting the enemy as game complimented the even more widespread practice of reducing them to a mass of faceless 'Boche' in letters and diaries. This technique for depersonalising the enemy was available to all, and apparently became second nature, a point which seems to have struck Arthur Gibbs mid-way through writing a letter to his mother in March 1916. 'On reading through the last two paragraphs,' he wrote, 'I see that I said the "Boche", and perhaps you have noticed that I have never used the word "German" when referring to the enemy. The word "German" seems to be absolutely taboo out here, as being much too good a term to apply to the people that we are fighting.' Gibbs continued, his explanation suggesting that the convention was impressed on soldiers within a short time of their arrival. This would make it an important element of the transition both in the sense that it was part of establishing the right character in company with other soldiers, and because it automatically moulded attitudes towards a central part of the war: the opposition. He said that 'no one uses the word out here and after I had been here for less than a day I never mentioned the word "German". We always call then Huns or Boche and the men usually call them Fritz or Aillimans (pronounced the same way as Ellimans!) – the last obviously being from the French.'[108] This vocabulary may not have been standard across the British Army, but it is interesting that Gibbs should have noticed a distinction between the words used by the officers and the other ranks, especially since there is more of an element of personality in both 'Fritz' and 'Aillimans', the one being a Christian name and the other a typically British mangling of a foreign term. The Reverend Thomas Wentworth Pym noticed the same thing: 'With the officers the attitude varies; but in their mouths the German is rarely described as "Fritz" – the Christian name – but usually as "the Hun" or "the Boche." This again is partly conventional; it's not exactly good form to stand up for the Boche, especially if the speaker or any one else present is known to have lost a brother or father at German hands. In part, too, such a designation is an attempt, by artificial means, to stimulate keenness in the speaker or others for a business that nobody likes, which however, to be brought to a successful issue, must be carried on with enthusiasm.'[109]

Both terminologies – of hunting and national stereotyping – effectively dehumanised the enemy, simultaneously forestalling the psychological problems associated with empathy which Charles May experienced when he discovered the dead German's bible, by protecting men from the real consequences of their actions, and setting them up, by creating the potential for a shocking revelation. Coping strategies were potentially, therefore, also a source of vulnerability. None, Joanna Bourke argues, could enable the soldier to avoid guilt entirely and it would, in any case, have been undesirable for them to have done so; an ability to feel remorse was important because men knew that that was how they should react.[110] Guilt was, on some levels, reassuring. It is interesting that men who had been steeped in a culture that stressed vigour and a warrior spirit should apparently have required this emotional turmoil, and that guilt – perhaps thanks to the romantic rather than businesslike manner in which war was portrayed – was almost a necessary adjunct to the work of national salvation to which they were called. The internalisation and reconciliation of that guilt must consequently have been for many a particularly challenging element of the transition from civilian to soldier.

5

Responsibility and Personal Growth

As Guy Chapman sat in a headquarters dug-out waiting for zero hour he listened to the noises made by the pigeons in their baskets and watched runners drinking tea. Some of his colleagues were asleep; others were making their final preparations. Chapman addressed a question to the wireless mechanic crouching in a corner:

> "Is your machine ready?" I asked. "Not yet," he answered. "Get on with it, then." I sat down and my head began to nod. Suddenly I heard the colonel's voice say: "Have you got your connection yet?" "No." "Why not?" "They're shelling." I listened. The guns had switched away from our quarter. "Go and put it right," said the colonel. The man hesitated and glared. Smith sat up straight. "If you don't go at once, I'll have you thrown out by the runners. You should have been in touch an hour ago." The man stumbled clumsily into the darkness. Three minutes later there was a blinding crash over our heads. The candles swept out. From the door came a careless voice: "They've got that wireless cove all right, and blown his aerial to shivers."[1]

This episode probably was not unusual, but it serves as a reminder that officers had to cope with the knowledge that their orders could kill their own men as effectively as if they had pulled the trigger themselves. It was not just the enemy which was to blame; when accepting commissions, young officers also had to come to terms rapidly with the responsibilities of command.

This was potentially a significant and unfamiliar burden. Arthur Adam's letters show clearly how the stress caused by his duties could weigh officers down: 'It is sometimes a little overpowering to think that a small mistake on your part may mean several lives lost.'[2] It was not, however, just their own lives or those of a few of their men which had to be considered; the stakes were potentially much higher. Clearly this could come as a shock, especially for those who might barely have left adolescence. James Neville, although eventually a highly capable and decorated officer, struggled initially when unexpectedly compelled to take responsibility in a delicate tactical situation: 'Billy's departure left me in command of the Company to carry out a rearguard action and a retirement later. I was taken by surprise, and had the wind up badly that I should make a mess of it.' At this stage in his career, taking charge at what seemed a critical juncture was an intimidating test: 'The responsibility of that rearguard was the worst part of it, and the knowledge that if I floated, one hundred men's lives would be on my head.'[3]

Despite the potentially daunting nature of the challenge, many young officers seem to have been remarkably assured on first taking up taxing duties on active service. Bertram Medley seems to have been ready to stamp his authority on his platoon from an early stage. This speech was made a week after crossing to France:

You had got plain commands from your Company and Platoon Officers that no lights were to be shown and no noise made. At an exceedingly critical time in our march I went round my platoon and found not only a great many men talking but ten or twelve men smoking cigarettes. … It is not for you to decide when it is safe for you to smoke: it is for your Officers, and, by disobeying your Officers then, you were risking the lives of not only yourselves but of your platoon and battalion.[4]

This confidence was part of the bequest of the public-school system. Pupils were encouraged – both actively by exhortation and systems like prefectorial governance, and by the schools' concentration of the higher end of the social strata – to see themselves as leaders. Their poise must, however, have been challenged by the nature of the Western Front, where conditions created particular tensions. Shelling or sniper fire could dispense death without warning. More problematically for a commander, the threat of more concerted enemy action was ever present, as James Neville knew only too well: 'We had to "stand-to" all Friday night, expecting a raid by the Boche. As I leant up against the parapet in the front line waiting, waiting and waiting, my thoughts wandered back to those divine days at home; in front of us, the night was waning to a grey dawn. It really is wretched having to wait all night on the *qui vive* for a raid. It really is the hell of a strain'.[5] The reference to all-night vigils is a reminder that trench life was largely nocturnal, and that there were only limited opportunities to sleep during the day.

Fortunately, while it undoubtedly added to the stress under which an officer was placed, responsibility actually helped many men to overcome their fear or nerves and discharge their duties.[6] Jack Oughtred confessed in February 1916 that 'when I am by myself up at the line I am an awful coward. Thank Heaven that when I am with men leading or directing them I am as right as rain. I cannot account for it, I suppose it's because one cannot be anything else but calm when you feel the men are watching you.'[7] Captain Tom Adlam of the 7th Battalion Bedfordshire & Hertfordshire Regiment said after the war that he was surprised to win the VC because 'when it gets going, you remember you're in charge of a group of men, and we were taught we had to be an example to them. So you lost your sense of fear thinking about other people.'[8] Over time, it also seems that the process of personal hardening dulled some of the worst pressures of responsibility. This may seem contradictory, given the officer's concern for the well-being of his men, both on a professional and personal level (a subject which will receive further attention in Chapter 7). Guy Chapman's experience with the unfortunate wireless technician and the reactions of his fellow officers point, however, to a recalibration of a sense of tragedy and guilt. While the man's death was cause for regret, the reactions of those present suggest that none of them was seen to be personally culpable. In fact, Chapman's colleague Smith seemed inclined to blame the victim himself: '"If he'd done it when you told him, he'd be alive now," he said to me.'[9] Soldiering in wartime is, of course, an inherently dangerous occupation and commanders cannot be considered liable for all casualties, but the sort of resignation exhibited by Smith seems particularly to reflect the lethality of the environment on the Western Front. As officers developed a greater understanding of the awful ordinariness of death (an idea which will be explored further in Chapter 10), it changed their perceptions of their own agency and duties. Blame was shifted away from them, absorbed by the impersonal violent forces that held sway over the line.

John Nettleton was inclined to attribute his own ability to handle his responsibilities to the fact that he had no alternative other than to meet them head on: 'You coped with the situation in front of you because you had to. There was no one else to do so and if you couldn't cope, the consequences were staring you in the face and there was no safety in hiding your head in the sand and refusing to face them. Therefore you learnt and learnt fast.'[10] Faced with this reality, and influenced by an inevitable process of acclimatisation, it was natural that officers who initially lacked confidence became more comfortable with their circumstances over time. Officers might even be conscious of the process taking place. Captain Norman Taylor wrote to his father in March 1916 saying that 'The thing that this army life has done for me is, as you can see, to give me a tremendous opinion of myself and self-confidence – a thing which I entirely lacked a year or 18 months ago.'[11] Medley was especially pleased to notice that after a while he no longer regarded a sergeant as 'almost a sacred being'.[12] Stephen Hewett, who joined up in 1915 but did not reach the trenches until early 1916, was struck by the differences he noted after spending a few months at the Front. On 19 June 1916 he wrote to his mother that he was 'losing the dread of responsibility, of having to control men and things, of having to act; and most remarkable of all, I am beginning to lose the fear of Persons, of Generals, Commanding Officers, and all critical superiors. I feel ten times the man I was. I think I am ten times as fit, and have yet to meet the strain which is too much for me.'[13] He was particularly conscious of the importance of the relationship with his men, and in this area too he was pleased with the position he had achieved: 'I have got to know all my men well. I know that I have authority, and though I could never inspire the affection and devotion which every officer and man in this Company feels for our Commander, Captain Bryson, I do not think I lack their respect.'[14] For Hewett, a comparatively short period of time in the trenches achieved more than months of training and preparation in Britain. The transition had to begin in earnest once he was overseas.

Rapid personal development of this sort might have needed to have taken place in the context of a much swifter assumption of responsibility than would have been possible within the pre-war regular army, making it all the more challenging. The platoon commander was in charge of about 40 men. The company commander, officially a major or a captain, had command of four platoons.[15] In the Edwardian army, a regular platoon officer might have to wait four or five years for this promotion. Due to heavy casualties Edward Tennant, having joined the army aged seventeen, became an eighteen-year-old company commander. He described the circumstances in a letter to his mother in September 1915:

> The Battalion took Hill 70 last night, but as all 2nds in command of companies were left behind (in case of heavy casualties) I did not go into action, but remained about 2½ miles from Hill 70, among our big guns which kept up a continual bombardment. I ought to be very thankful I did not go into action as out of 18 officers 11 are now *hors de combat*, though I believe only one or at most 2 to be dead. The Commanding Officer (Hamilton) is recovering from a gas-shell, Myles Ponsonby (Major), and George Houston-Boswall are both badly wounded. Two more are slightly gassed. Alan Tompson is dead – he was a charming fellow. My captain, Flick, has a bullet through the arm, and is for England all right. This leaves

me in the responsible position of Company Commander. I pray God I may fill it with honour during the future engagements.[16]

Interestingly, not many months previously one of his direct contemporaries, Harold Mellersh, had experienced a similar effect at school: 'The big increase in school-leavers caused by the war had had the result of rapid promotion in the school hierarchy for those left behind. In the first of the two terms that had still to run I was a House-prefect and, in the second, school prefect and head of the House. I was thus an important person.'[17]

Some officers preferred to avoid greater responsibility, at least in terms of unit command. Lionel Crouch thought company work would be too restrictive, preferring the idea of 'a roving commission to saunter around where I like.'[18] G.M. McGowan was pleased to be employed in the communication trenches, 'for I'm even more my own boss than I was when a platoon commander.'[19] Others, like Tennant, seemed apprehensive when required to take on more challenging duties. 'I've been given a great company to command', Arthur Parry wrote to a friend. '– me, ye gods.'[20] Graham Greenwell found himself in the same position in June 1916. While clearly aware that his advancement was precocious, he did not display the same trepidation. A comparison is difficult without more information about the relationship the two men had with their respective correspondents, but Greenwell nevertheless seemed to remain impressively nonchalant:

This morning the new Colonel had a talk with me; he said that I was very young, but that he had himself once commanded a company when he was the same age, though not on active service. Thank God the responsibility doesn't worry me and seems to give me a new interest in life; but it may be rather a trying ordeal at first.[21]

In fact, in due course he became so self-assured as a commander that he became frustrated at his lack of autonomy and the control which superiors tried to exert over him: 'Personally I *will* not take instructions from the man behind once the show has been launched,' he asserted in April 1917. 'It is fatal and has been proved to be so hundreds of times. The man on the spot must have power to decide.'[22]

In addition to greater confidence, responsibility also promoted a personal process of maturation. In some cases, seniority within the hierarchies of various educational or training establishments had masked the fact that, in reality, many young officers still had a lot of growing up to do, and entry into the tough military world, coinciding with an inevitable reassignment to the bottom of the pile, could be quite shocking. John Merton discovered this when, as a newly commissioned pre-war regular, a dispute with his captain led to the cancellation of leave on his twentieth birthday. He was appalled to learn that, had he explained matters to his superior, he would have been reprieved:

Joy, darling, I am sure that you have never experienced the awful indignity – to imagine yourself a martyr to injustice and cruelty one moment, and to find the next that instead you are simply a silly little fool! I was twenty on that day. A year before I had been a senior at Sandhurst; two years before I had been captain of my House at school, and my word had been law to fifty smaller boys; and yet just at that very moment, to which I had always looked forward as being a definite dividing mark from boyish days, I found a lump rising in my throat, almost a tear in my eyes, as I manfully tried to gulp out, "Oh, it doesn't matter a bit."[23]

Merton's experience is a reminder that twenty remains a young age, and yet, as Graham Greenwell commented:

For the first time, you were really in command of a couple of hundred men – four platoons – perhaps four or five officers under you, in my case sometimes they were older. You ran your own show. You were in command not merely of the fighting side, but the domestic side of it, the economic side, the human side and everything else. To have that responsibility at twenty is a tremendous spur and achievement.[24]

Although not a commissioned officer at the time, Alfred Pollard provides an interesting list of the experiences which he recognised had had such a profound and formative effect on him:

Up to now I had merely been a boy playing with realities. The rebuff to my proposal of marriage; the experience of my wound; but mostly the knowledge that I could successfully lead men in action, had turned me into a man. I had had my preparation. I knew what responsibility entailed.[25]

In cases where there are no explicit testimonies about maturation there is often still much that can be gleaned from primary sources. Although it is by no means a common feature of diaries and letters from this period, it is often possible to witness the development of a more mature outlook and attitude on the part of the individual, forcefully reminding a modern reader of the vast chasm between the relatively carefree life of a young member of the upper classes and the dangerous and arduous life of a subaltern or captain on the Western Front. This is inevitably a subjective assessment.

Further complications arise from the wide variation in the quality of source material. A lengthy diary or series of letters is not, in itself, a guarantee that interesting insights about the author can be extracted. So much depends on the audience of the writings, the temperament of the writer, his personal circumstances and his fluency. Many correspondents were content to provide a limited amount of news and some anecdotes, without making the sorts of comments or observations which really illuminate deeper feelings about the war. A change in tone or style is, however, normally relatively easy to detect. Extracts from Sam Paget's letters illustrate the point. On 8 March 1914, aged 18, he was in the Winchester College Sickhouse addressing 'a malignant blister on the heel which I wanted to get thoroughly cured':

I was on 'Continent Room' for a whole day with two juniors ... and managed to keep them amused and conversational the whole time ... there is a real pleasure for me in talking to people who take a vivid interest in what one says and are not blasé: moreover it is certainly a great help to get to know about people one would not naturally converse with: it was rather a feather in my cap that one of the small boys petitioned to be allowed up later in order to profit by my company ...[26]

A few years after this photograph was taken Sam Paget, like many others of his generation, had to shoulder the burden of leadership. (Private archive)

The fact that he was prepared to spend two days in bed curing a minor ailment presumably at the expense of his academic work suggests a questionable sense of priorities. Moreover, while his status as 'Prefect of Hall' – effectively Head Boy, in an age when such things were more significant than they are now – meant he was something of a local celebrity, his attitude towards the younger boys seems somewhat condescending. Within two years he had grown into a level-headed and mature officer, as this description of an accidental shooting by a sentry illustrates:

> One's attitude towards the man who lost his head and shot is a hard one: he is quite in a state of collapse and I kept someone with him all the time as I really feared he would take his own life: the men do their best to cheer him up and I have done mine: we have no right to withhold forgiveness.[27]

His balanced and sensitive handling of this affair suggests that Paget had matured immensely in the intervening years. The experience of being in the army, which he joined immediately on the outbreak of the war, and serving in the trenches must have had a similarly profound impact on many of his generation.

Responsibility did weigh heavily on thousands of subalterns, but not so heavily as to prevent them from finding escape and pleasure in the humorous incidents afforded by wartime soldiering. A sense of fun survived and its retention was vitally important in maintaining morale in the face of mud, blood and danger.[28] Like their men, officers – even relatively senior ones – enjoyed a good joke.[29] Officialdom was no bar to the determined humorist. William Villiers noticed a comedian at work in a divisional report in January 1917:

> '11pm-12 midnight. Machine guns, Lewis Guns, Stokes, 18-prs & rifles fired a few rounds rapid by way of New Year's Greeting & bugles were blown. There was little reply though some Germans shouted back. 12.15am War was resumed'. I don't know who the wag is but suspect our Brigade Major.[30]

One of the most famous expressions of First World War humour was the *Wipers Times*, perhaps the best known of the many trench journals. John Ivelaw-Chapman surmises that it was primarily aimed at young officers, given the extent to which the content matches their worldview and cultural influences.[31] They were also more likely to possess the education and opportunity to produce material, not to mention a possible background writing pieces for school magazines.

Their humour was also expressed in acts of youthful exuberance. Some of these were entirely benign, if not perhaps best calculated to maintain the dignity of the officer corps in the eyes of the men. One morning in October 1915 Graham Greenwell and his colleagues had 'a grand apple fight in the orchard where the Transport is, and the men were regaled with the sight of six officers all pelting each other.'[32] Such acts of tom-foolery helped release pent up excitement and tension. Other pranks were much more explicitly military, utilising the tools of the officer's trade. Robert Hamilton's diary entry for 27 August 1915 is a curious mix of the prosaic and the startling: 'Very hot day. Finished parade at 4 o'clock, too fagged to do anything. Just slacked. Very short note from L. Leave talked a lot about. Ragged in bedroom, and let bomb off under Castle's bed.'[33] His laconic style unfortunately didn't allow for any further elaboration. He was admittedly working as a bombing instructor at the time. James Neville similarly utilised explosives, describing the dramatic consequences in one of his letters:

> Yesterday we played a trick on the Doctor, McTurk, who was standing in front of the fire holding forth at great length. "Shiny" Horley got hold of a Verey light cartridge which we cut open outside the mess. We then extracted the magnesium and powder, and I put the empty cartridge in my pocket. Unaware of a plot, the Doctor was still gassing when we returned. "Shiny" took cover behind the folding doors which divide the long mess room and which were half open, while I walked up to the fire which was practically out and, quite nonchalantly, dropped the cartridge into it and made for safety behind the doors!
>
> There was a loud explosion and clouds of embers and the grate were blown into the room and McTurk was enveloped in dust. For a second he was almost invisible. Then, roaring like a bull and spitting fury, he took up a book and hurled it at me just before I could reach cover. It was a good shot and caught me on the left ear with the point of the cover![34]

Nobody appears to have been hurt in this particular incident, although Neville admits that the explosive force produced by a Verey light cap took him by surprise. Even so, it is striking that he and Hamilton should have felt so comfortable using such devices

Soldiers could develop a very casual attitude towards the lethal tools of their trade.
Here four men of the Royal Army Ordnance Corps can be seen playing cards on a
pile of trench mortar ammunition, July 1916. (Imperial War Museum Q 1375)

in this manner. Episodes like these indicate the extent to which junior officers became comfortable within a military environment and recalibrated their perceptions of risk.

More surprising still, given the frequently tragic nature of life on the Western Front, are the instances in which officers mimicked combat situations in the vicinity of the front line in order to play on their colleagues' nerves and derive amusement from frightening them. Having discovered a cache of German stick-bombs, Edwin Vaughan then proceeded to amuse himself by dropping fuses into the ventilation shaft of a dugout to make the occupants think they were being shelled. His fellow officers mistook the first comparatively feeble report for a dud shell, expressing relief that such a close hit should have failed to detonate. After six more of Vaughan's 'shells', the mood changed: 'I heard Johnny say in a puzzled tone, "They can't *all* be duds." Then I pictured Ewing's horrified face as he yelled "They're GAS! Can ye no smell them?"' At this point Vaughan decided that the episode had gone far enough.[35] About a week later he tried to repeat the performance on Anstey, another of his colleagues, but was rapidly found out. The two then decided to amuse themselves by throwing live bombs into a shell hole. Still armed with his 'patent fizzers', Vaughan could not resist one further attempt at a practical joke, dropping one behind Anstey and shouting a warning: 'Poor Anstey, white as death, bounded a couple of yards and dropped flat with his face between his hands pressed into the wet earth. As the fuse fizzled out, I shrieked with laughter and raced for the trench, followed by Anstey who had jumped up with his face muddy and his clothes wet. Roaring with rage he pursued me round bays and traverses past the astonished troops.'[36] Charles May similarly could not resist a joke at the expense of colleagues distracted by experiments with a new trench mortar:

> I came upon it unseen and found Thelmerdine and Oldham gazing anxiously over the top to see where the missives dropped. Everyone was at a tension – trench mortars are impartial in their destructiveness. I took a handful of snow, rolled a ball and threw it at Oldham, at the same time yelling 'Mortar.' It grazed the back of his neck and hit Thelmerdine's head and you never saw two more scared officers in your life. Thelmerdine fell off the step and Oldham leapt a foot in the air. Both swore most horribly. I was sorry afterwards. I know it would have put my heart in my mouth had I been the victim.[37]

A very irreverent spirit was clearly at work, although at least May recognised that such amusements were extremely cruel.

Such episodes are reminiscent of the grim humour exhibited by troops who shook hands with skeletons or combed the hair of corpses.[38] Cosmo Clark explained the practice to his parents:

> Father asks in his letter why it is the dangers or rather the various killing schemes of the Boche are always referred to in a joking manner. It's the only way to look upon these things. Often, when deep down in your heart you have a terrible fear of them, you can pass it off and get over it quickly by joking about it. If it wasn't for the light-hearted way in which the British army take these things, half of 'em would be sent home with 'nerves'.[39]

Humour was the soldier's weapon against the oppressive anxieties of the front line. As has been seen in Chapter 3 in relation to experiences of shell fire, it enabled them to re-contextualise their experiences, achieving a form of mastery over them by refusing to acknowledge their true nature. How this was done, and for what purpose, depended on the situation and an officer's own state of mind. It might be the spontaneous result of nervous tension, a forced response to a persistent dread, or a habit of mind born of long desensitisation.

Alternatively, examples of officers fooling about may be indicative of an *immaturity* which, paradoxically, went hand-in-hand with the maturity required to command men in action. Eliot Crawshay-Williams analysed this connection between warfare and childishness in his 1918 publication *Leaves from an Officer's Notebook*. Soldiers, he wrote 'have all the animal joy in existence, the heartiness, and the simplicity, which characterize the healthy schoolboy; and they have also his semi-contempt for what he considers over-mentality, and for a devotion to the softer or more serious aspects of human affairs ... so long as military life exists at all, it will possess fundamental characteristics which must infallibly develop the schoolboy vein.'[40]

Many appreciated that the war was extremely serious, but at the same time farcical, even slightly juvenile, especially for those experiencing the tactical reality of a trench deadlock. Arthur Pick told his parents that 'we often think what silly fools we all are to be stuck in a ditch in the middle of a field, with other fools about 200 yds away doing the same thing, and neither side very anxious to visit the other.[41] Small wonder, then, that a sense of the ridiculous should be evident from time to time in their actions, especially since life as officers placed young men in situations in which they were relatively unfettered and able to indulge their humorous whims. They had also been conditioned to indulge in bouts of high-spirited activity by their experiences of public school or university; the practice was carried over into the military world, where some regimental messes also had a tradition of rather rowdier and somewhat ritualised behaviour intended to instil the appropriate spirit and comradeship.[42] Such practices apparently survived into wartime. Philip Maddison, the hero of Henry Williamson's semi-autobiographical *A Fox Under My Cloak* witnessed similar exploits in a mess in Britain:

> Two officers were blindfolded, and lay on the floor, rolled newspapers in their right hands, and holding each other's left hand. One cried, 'Who goes there?' the other replied 'Kruger!' and then had to move his head away from where he had spoken, or be sloshed by the rolled newspaper.[43]

Paul Kruger was the leader of the Boers during the Second Boer War of 1899-1902. Although a fictionalised example, a regiment like Maddison's could well have had experience of that campaign, games of this sort potentially preserving that heritage in the collective memory as effectively as any battle honour and thereby helping to forge a distinctive unit identity. There was also a precedent for the malicious antics described by Vaughan and May. According to Henry's son Richard, one particular incident in a house in Newmarket ended with Williamson's clothes and furniture being thrown out of the window in a fashion reminiscent of public-school or university 'ragging'.[44] When abroad, these instincts found their outlets in more militaristic and, in some cases, even macabre pranks.

Humour and high spirits helped defuse stressful situations, providing some mental relief for soldiers under stress. For most officers, family and friends back in the United Kingdom provided another important psychological prop, as well as a crucial link to their pre-war civilian life. Some historians have argued that there was a gulf between the home front and the front line, and the soldier's life in the trenches may indeed have been far beyond the experiences of most civilians. Their sense of separation is certainly revealed in many of their domestic habits and attempts to create surrogate families and homely quarters when on active service (noted in Chapter 3). They were not, however, shut off entirely from their loved ones, either logistically or in terms of experience.[45] The parties could communicate with comparative ease. The Western Front was both close to the British Isles and largely static, enabling the creation and maintenance of dependable and comparatively swift lines of communication, something the military authorities consistently regarded as a priority. Further distinctive characteristics of the British experience of the war in Europe ensured that there would be substantial levels of interaction between men at the front and their families and friends back home. The Western Front's scale and attritional character (coupled with a perceived existential threat to the homeland) led to the creation of a mass citizen army. As Chapter 8 will discuss in more detail, many networks of friends and even family travelled across to France and Flanders as a result. While this had a clear impact on the society of the front line,

A British officer writing a letter on the Western Front, May 1917. Letters were a vital link to family and a pre-war civilian identity. (Imperial War Museum Q 5242)

it was a further factor ensuring that familiar contacts were not inherently pushed to the margins. More importantly, however, many of those who went off to serve did so with the clear idea that this was an aberration from civilian life, rather than the beginnings of a military career. This meant that their civilian identities were less subordinated to new military characters than they might otherwise have been.

Letters home, as Jessica Meyer has argued, were a crucial link to these older civilian personalities.[46] Through them soldiers asserted the continuing existence of their civilised, domesticated selves, as well as sharing their experiences (to greater or lesser extents) with their audience back home. Both of these elements bridged the gap created by active service, overturning any notion that the man had been changed beyond recognition and enabling those left behind to gain some understanding of his present circumstances. The sheer volume of surviving material, written both to and from the trenches, demonstrates the importance of these linkages. Men communicated through letters, diaries written to provide news in instalments, or service postcards designed to provide contact and reassurance at even the busiest times. The topics covered, sentiments expressed and styles employed are as numerous as the correspondents themselves.

Unsurprisingly, many letters are fundamentally about love and concern for loved ones. Sometimes this is forthright, intimate and passionate, particularly when writing to lovers. 'It is a strange world', mused Charles May in a diary apparently written for his wife. 'Here I am in the midst of men, of work and dirt and close to fire and steel and sudden death. My heart should be fired with martial ardour, I should have no thought for anything but the fighting I am paid for but instead my whole being is filled to the exclusion of all else with the thought of you, dear heart, of our darling baby and of the happiness which has been ours.'[47] Even where sentiments of this sort are not explicit, the fact of communication is inclusive and affectionate, the family asserting itself and its continuing importance within the military world of the Western Front.

The duty of correspondence often (but not always) devolved to mothers or sisters, the acceptable custodians, in Edwardian culture, of the more tender aspects of family life. For many officers and their families the habit of regular correspondence was well-established from earlier days, when young boys at public school were similarly the regular recipients of letters and parcels from fond mothers and other relatives. Michael Roper sees these previous experiences as setting the emotional terms for wartime separation, and there are indeed many similarities between letters from boarding school and from the front line, in some cases written mere months apart.[48] Parental perceptions of the enduring childlike status of their offspring probably heightened the sense of loss felt by many bereaved mothers and fathers. In this way, seemingly innocuous habits of communication could possess their own dangers.

Letters from family members to serving soldiers have not survived in such large numbers, which is unsurprising given the conditions into which they were sent, but the replies often testify (both explicitly and in terms of their own frequency) to the regularity and importance of the communication. Lt. J.A. Talbot clearly appreciated receiving mail from a number of correspondents: 'Madge is awfully nice about writing, and also Robin. I had eight letters to-day, the first I have had for ages. I feel quite bucked with life now!'[49] In contrast, Jack Oughtred clearly felt the loss when he did not get any for days at a time.[50] While letters from home clearly could have an important impact on the morale of the man at the front, officers also understood that they themselves had a duty to those back in Britain. One of the most important functions of a letter from the Western Front was simply to acknowledge the family's concern and provide frequent reassurance. Those back home were well aware of the risks; letters were required frequently if family and friends were not to get anxious and mistake a lack of communication for tragedy. The writer also had to take into account the audience's likely knowledge of the terrible conditions at the front, whether conveyed by the media, acquaintances or the officer himself, hence the numerous soothing comments about 'bearing up'. The number of letters, and the length and detail of many, also demonstrates the hunger of those at home for news and information. Letters may typically have been addressed to one or two people, but many will have found a wider audience. When Sam Paget wrote a short note to his brother Paul in August 1915 he concluded with the line 'I won't write more as I know you get the benefit (?) [sic] of my letters to the family.'[51] In making the fullest possible use of these communications within a family or circle of friends, relatives could overcome physical separation to some extent and help keep the soldier more integrated within the old networks. Some officers can also be seen actively trying to prop up morale through their letters. 'Your letter seems a little bit sad, dearest, but cheer up!' wrote Eugene Crombie to his mother.[52] Such examples often play on the contrast between the civilian's lot and the plight of the soldier, which is usually downplayed. When Dennis Neilson-Terry commiserated with his mother about her experience of an air-raid in late 1915 he dismissed the risks he himself was running in comparison with her experience, saying 'we're out here to put up with horror and fear so that all of you at home can have honourable peace & comfort.'[53] Through rhetorical devices of this sort the officer could continue to assert a moral presence within the family while simultaneously providing reassurance.

The civilian and military worlds often came together again temporarily when officers went on leave. Rare indeed was the soldier who did not look forward to some time away from his military duties, and its frequency (or otherwise) was a common cause for dissatisfaction. Anticipation of leave was such that officers like John Nettleton noticed a peculiar effect amongst his colleagues: 'Men who stood up to all sorts of horrors in the line behaved like frightened rabbits when they were going on leave. It was a well-understood phenomenon and nobody thought the worse of you for it.'[54] Many officers looked forward eagerly to time away from the front, to the comforts and companionship of home life. It is not hard to discern the excitement in Sam Paget's letter announcing his imminent return in November 1915, along with the superstition noted by Nettleton:

> Do you believe in anything bringing bad luck – or in not counting some chickens before they are hatched – no? All right then. Please send all available clothes (civilian) to Webb Miles to be cleaned and pressed and returned to you without fail on the 20th: this should include a suit of clothes, morning coat and trousers and mess clothes. Then you will sit down and expect me home somewhere about breakfast time on Sunday 21st. I believe one gets into W'loo (not Victoria) somewhere about 6 a.m.: so that if there's anything left of me after the crossing I shall roll up in time for breakfast on Sunday – when I trust there will be real sausages, bacon and battered eggs[55] for breakfast – not to say porridge and kidneys and kippers and 'anything else that is pleasant to drink'.
>
> I must have nearly £100 in the bank by now – so lets go the whole hog and enjoy ourselves 'regardless': when I come home on leave from the Slough they please to call trenches nowadays I don't come to invest my hard earned Savings in warloan – not half!
>
> I suppose you'll be able to get Paul up from school all right for the week or some part of it – it would be a great shame otherwise but we should have to motor down there and see him if not. Still he must come up.[56]

Paget was clearly interested in devouring as civilian an experience as possible, hence his insistence on non-military attire, home comforts and the special presence of family, including his brother Paul. Inevitably, however, as with all matters involving family, attitudes towards spending time together could vary substantially. Edgar Matthews was not enthusiastic about the prospect of a reunion in December 1915:

> I don't know what to do about the leave question – to begin with leave is very slow in coming and I am beginning to be afraid I shall miss it altogether. Then once home I shall be rather in clutches of family.
>
> Were it not for the fact that two other officers in my battalion live in my village I could creep up to Cambridge on arrival in England, and not report at family headquarters till a day later – Then I must put in one night in London. But under the circumstances it is all rather difficult – and the most difficult thing is the getting of leave.[57]

It is not clear why Matthews should have been reluctant to go back to his family. His language and the fact that he had only served for a few months in France by the time he wrote this letter suggest some antipathy that predates the war. In this respect, as in others, the war might have very little impact on intra-family dynamics.

Other men found that they were distanced from their relatives by their experiences, or by the atmosphere they found back in Britain. Some of the bitterest letters of the war were written by men returning from a disillusioning time of leave.[58] It was after periods in the United Kingdom that officers were most apt to complain about the attitudes of their fellow countrymen, and to compare the privation and dangers of the trenches with the bright lights and carefree existence they thought they witnessed back home. They were angered by the comparison between their privations and the apparent comforts enjoyed by those who were, in their view, failing in their patriotic duty. They were also frustrated by the way new laws and regulations reinforced their status as soldiers, further separating them from the civilian experiences for which they yearned and which they felt was their right, either simply because they were themselves citizens or because they felt entitled as a result of their service. 'It strikes me, from what you tell me in your letters and what I read in the papers, that, what with all the restrictions placed on officers in England, we are really better off out here,' complained Lieutenant Geoffrey Holt in December 1916. 'It seems that one can't feed, dress, or do anything else one likes in England now'.[59] There was, in essence, a tension between the officer's expectation of leave and the reality, which was not simply a product of the separation of civilian and military experience. Leave was so ardently awaited as a relief from the hardships of active service that officers were under self-induced pressure to make the best possible use of it, whatever that might mean, or at least to avoid wasting it. The apparent emphasis placed by Sam Paget on enjoyment was not always shared, however; some felt that their leave somehow had to transcend mere holiday after such trials. 2nd Lt. Kenneth Macardle seems to have felt the need to elevate his time away from the trenches in some way:

> There are only nine days of leave after a hundred of war. A hundred of discomfort and hard work, plain, necessary food, stupid necessary work. A hundred days and nights of uneventful dullness or of wearying strain; a hundred days and nights of 'keeping cheerful' where everybody else is doing it too; of being nice to everybody where everybody is being nice to you – just because friction or a grouch would make a strained position quite intolerable; a hundred days and nights of pretending you don't mind dirt and discomfort and are quite used to being killed; – and then nine days and nights of leave. Surely they should be something more than a holiday full of comfort and pleasure![60]

The respite would always end, no matter how fervently an officer might wish that it would not. Returning for duty was a time of mixed emotions for many officers. It could be a positive experience. Some were only too glad to get away from a country they were no longer sure they recognised, while others were relieved to be back with their men. Many, however, were dejected at being plunged once again into the world of the Western Front. 'The first few days are always a bit depressing after leave,' admitted Christopher Stone in a letter to his wife, 'and my leave was so absolutely perfect that anything would be an anticlimax after it.'[61] In various ways leave consequently had the potential to be a double-edged sword. A return to the civilian world could be nourishing or it could reinforce the very sense of otherness – the creation of a military identity at the expense of its peacetime precursor – which many officers sought to overcome through their maintenance of close family contacts.

Physical separation inevitably defined the relationships between soldiers and civilians, but for many young officers it was not unprecedented. As Michael Roper notes, those who had been educated at a public school could already have had a decade of experience away from the family.[62] Separation from relatives at this time in their lives was still, however, highly significant for many. Personal development and conduct was significantly affected by the removal of young officers from any parental or educational authority. The officers' code was admittedly restrictive, requiring quite exacting standards of public behaviour, but it was not rigid and in any case categorised the officer as an adult rather than an adolescent, automatically assuming certain freedoms. There were some prohibitions but offences were usually a matter of degree. Many behaviours were acceptable, provided certain lines were not crossed.[63] This was probably a looser rein than that to which most were accustomed. Officers also quickly learnt what John Nettleton described as the army's first rule – 'Thou shalt not be found out'.[64] Consequently, subalterns and captains, many of whom were comparatively fresh from school or university or were living away from home for the first time, were presented with a range of opportunities while also enjoying greater personal freedom to sample them. Lieutenant Stuart Cloete appreciated this change: 'The umbilical cord was finally severed. That it had been replaced by an iron chain of army discipline meant nothing to me. I could accept that much more easily; indeed I embraced it.'[65] There were many rites of passage to be negotiated and men of Cloete's generation and circumstances now had to steer their course outside the traditional family or social context.

Their companions on this new road may have been entirely unfamiliar. Army life inevitably entailed living cheek-by-jowl with men from many different walks of life and for some this was a dramatic shock. Those who experienced the greatest distress in the early years of the war were almost certainly those more sensitive and sheltered members of the middle- and upper-classes who enlisted rather than taking a commission, whether out of impatience, group loyalty or an ideological imperative. Some who had been brought up in particularly refined circumstances or had very delicate sensibilities could not cope with the realities of sharing their everyday lives with strangers, whether it was the loss of privacy, the requirement to share cutlery or crockery, or the basic sanitary arrangements.[66] Others could not adjust to the behaviour and discourse of their fellow soldiers. It is difficult to say how many men serving in the BEF were affected by such problems of personal revulsion, but it seems likely that this would have undermined the solidarity and comradeship that has generally been ascribed to them. Joanna Bourke has stressed the difficulties that could be faced, noting that some men found 'to their disgust that the "drunkenness & language & gambling" were having an effect on them, and they eschewed all friendships as a consequence. Many men did not "fit in", and were lonely.'[67] A commission might come as a blessing to a suffering ranker, although the man who had not attended a public school might still be alarmed at some of the practices and personal habits of his fellow officers.

As the war progressed the social composition of the officer corps altered. Officer cadets could increasingly find that they were training alongside men from very different backgrounds. Basil Willey was, by his own account, the product of a very sheltered, religious home and had never been away to boarding school. Aged seventeen in 1914, he joined his school OTC before progressing to an OCB in July 1916:

> More fearful to me than bullets or shells or sudden death was the experience of being snatched away from what I now know to have been a way of life exceptional in its Christian innocence and unworldliness and plunged straight into what then seemed to me a sink of all iniquities. In the cadet battalion I was one of only a very few who had come straight from school; nearly all the others had seen active service as privates or N.C.O.'s in France or elsewhere and had done well enough to be recommended for commissions. Never having had the normal brutality, and worldliness, I was aghast at the sort of men these seemed and at the things they said and thought and did.[68]

In mid-1916 some of these men training for commissions would have come from lower class backgrounds but a large number would have been those with public-school educations who had initially volunteered for service in the ranks. For a man like Willey, however, the social mix was still uncomfortable. Whilst training in Cambridge he could at least shield himself to a degree in the privacy of his own room. The life of an officer on active service, however, was intensely communal, and was particularly trying for him:

> Privacy ceased to exist, and my fellow officers, as well as the men of my platoon (nearly all of them Yorkshiremen), were at first as strange to me as foreigners. They spoke an alien dialect, and when I could understand what they said, it was generally bawdy. Long winter evenings spent huddled with them in billets or dugouts, they smoking and drinking and playing cards and telling dirty stories, and I trying to read a serious book as though I were at home – these things at first nearly broke me down.[69]

Willey's experience suggests that the communal life of a public school or a university provided valuable lessons in the art of accommodating oneself to one's colleagues. Had he been educated at a boarding school away from the influences of a sheltered home he might have learnt, as Douglas Wimberley claimed he did, how to associate with different people: 'Wellington gave me my first lesson in how to mix with every type of character and how to hold my own.'[70] This view was widely shared amongst the public-school fraternity.[71] The self-styled 'headmaster soldier' Harry Sackville Lawson, admittedly not the most impartial commentator, wrote to his son in October 1917 with a parable about 'winning spurs':

> Once upon a time in English history there was a prince fighting in an English Army commanded by his Daddy. Everybody wanted to help the prince when he was fighting the enemy's seasoned warriors, but his Daddy said, "No, let the boy win his own spurs." So they left him alone; and afterwards he fought with great prowess against the enemy and swamped them. That is the sort of thing that happens in schools. Boys have to walk on their own legs, and make their own friends, and establish their own reputation, in the place which seems to be quite complete

without them. Sometimes it is like fitting a new piece into a puzzle picture which looks as if it were already complete and finished. But this sort of picture is really not complete and finished. There is always room for other pieces and fresh colour comes into it; no picture can ever be quite perfect. When you have been a little while at school in the big new world you will find a place of your own in the picture which will grow more and more beautiful, complete and perfect according as you and others wish it.[72]

Joining the officer corps clearly required similar adjustments, even if it was much more apparent in wartime that the individual's contribution was desired. Those young men who had gained experience of fitting themselves into an established order had an advantage, which was compounded by the striking social and cultural similarities between the educational and military institutions. Ironically, those who had the right cultural grounding arguably did not need such an ability to be socially malleable, but those who lacked either or both were certainly disadvantaged.

The fact that Willey eschewed the habits of his comrades clearly placed him outside the mainstream. Only a minority of soldiers were teetotal and such abstemious behaviour was relatively alien within the military culture. Social drinking had been a traditional pre-war feature of officers' social lives.[73] The vast majority of men who became officers after August 1914 would have had pre-war experience of it, even if they had only just left public school (where opportunities were limited but not unknown).[74] Many habits were developed at university. Douglas Wimberley recalled that, at Cambridge, gentlemen 'might or indeed should drink wine or spirits at meals, or after dinner in our rooms, but to enter a bar was for me, or any of my friends, most certainly not the custom.'[75] Alcohol acted as Desmond Young's social passport at Oxford; the hospitality he could offer after being supplied with an extensive range of bottles by his father quickly winning over his fellow students: 'Before they moved on I had several invitations to dinner within the next few days, had agreed to play football, of both varieties, and was involved in various other college activities of which I knew nothing.' He apparently became a member of a fairly rowdy set:

> There was plenty of public drunkenness, with soda-water siphons exploding in the quad like shells and lump sugar flying about like bullets. In Hall, the practice of "sconcing" resulted in many people trying to swallow more beer than the human stomach can contain. (One could send a "sconce" or pint mug of ale to anyone in Hall who seemed to be making himself conspicuous. If the sconce could drain it at one draft, without drawing breath, the sconcer had to pay for it. The origin of the word – and the practice – is obscure, but it dates back to the 16th century.) Yet there was no secret drinking and no case of alcoholism that I remember. Public opinion would have been very strongly against anyone suspected of becoming fuddled in the solitude of his own rooms. Drinking was a purely social custom.[76]

Many an officer's relationship with alcohol changed on active service. In France drinking became functional as well as sociable.[77] For a start, it could mask some of the less pleasant aspects of the environment. Bernard Long wrote to his sister requesting 'a small metal flask to hold brandy in it as it is jolly necessary to burn horrible smells and tastes out of your mouth.'[78] It might also be a psychological prop or palliative against frayed nerves, a truth recognised in the regular issue of a rum ration. Francis Hitchcock was disconcerted to hear a rumour in November 1915 'that it was the intention of the Higher Command to stop the rum issue and give hot coffee in lieu. Fortunately nothing materialised and we all breathed in peace once more.'[79]

Officers valued it as much as the men. Christopher Stone claimed that 'about 50 per cent of officers, probably more, cannot keep going even in normal trench warfare without alcohol of some sort: and in a fight we all need it.'[80] Many officers would have drunk in moderation in the line, but drunkenness on duty was emphatically frowned upon. At other times, however, some officers clearly relied on the relief that intoxification could provide. Alan Hanbury-Sparrow was clear that 'strong drink saved you. For the very evening you got out of the line and into security, you first took a couple of pills to clear your stomach of the gas, and then went to the tent of another C.O. who had been with the division just about as long as yourself. There, quite deliberately, you sat down in his company to get tight, for sleep, a night of dead leaden sleep, was what you had to have.'[81] Many officers concealed the extent to which they were dependent on alcohol, both to hide their fear and because of the social taboos to which Desmond Young referred.

Some did take a principled stance against excess. Douglas Gillespie believed abstention might be a necessary sacrifice: 'it makes one very sad to see a drunk out here. Why can't we do as the Russians are doing, for the war at any rate? I like French wines myself, but I'd be glad to give them up.'[82] This is, however, a fairly isolated call. Drink simply became an everyday part of life on the Western Front. It is impossible to say how many officers became the type of alcoholic immortalised by R.C. Sherriff's Captain Stanhope in *Journey's End*. Approximately 30 per cent of all courts-martial on officers at home and abroad were for drunkenness.[83] Robert Graves was aware of several fellow officers who were heavily dependent on spirits and were only saved, in his view, by being invalided out or sent back to the UK for some other reason.[84] However, junior officers clearly did not all become dipsomaniacs.

While alcohol was at least a familiar part of Edwardian life, newly-commissioned young officers, especially those who had only just left school or university, could be almost entirely ignorant about sexual matters and consequently ill-prepared to face the associated temptations and dangers. A spirit of Victorian prudery continued to hold sway within the Edwardian education system. Schools did not take much initiative. Neither did Victorian parents, 99 per cent of whom, claimed one Rugby doctor, sent their sons away to boarding school ignorant of sexual matters.[85] As far as the public schools were concerned, the onset of puberty was to be managed through that mainstay of Edwardian education, games.[86] There was virtually no provision of sex education. In 1918 Martin Browne published *A Dream of Youth* – 'An Etonian's Reply to *The Loom of Youth*', Alec Waugh's controversial semi-autobiographical novel of 1917. Browne wrote: 'I do not think more than ten per cent of us have it properly explained to us, even by the time we leave school, how we were born, and what our Mother's body is like.'[87] This deficiency was exacerbated by an almost total segregation of the sexes. Douglas Wimberley admitted that at Wellington 'we hardly saw a female from beginning to end of term, and the few we did see were all old enough to be our parents, or indeed grandparents.'[88] Not that Stuart Cloete, a pupil at Lancing College, noticed 'any tremendous emotional upheaval with the onset of puberty': 'I do not think we were even fully aware of what had taken place. We now had erections, wet dreams and some boys masturbated secretly, terrified of being caught, beaten and possibly expelled. Masturbation, we were told, led to lunacy and blindness. This we doubted. My father had told me not to touch myself and I didn't. Not till the war.'[89] This last line is telling. Even university men, however, were unlikely to have had much experience of the opposite sex. As Desmond Young noted, 'Womanizing' in Oxford was definitely not 'done':

> The famous Patience and Mabel, who nightly paraded the High Street under the watchful eyes of the proctors, must have had their patrons but few would have cared to boast of having enjoyed their favours. At the same time those who went too often, or indeed at all, to London in term time were viewed with disapprobation. Female undergraduates were tightly controlled and hardly seen except at lectures. In any case they were safe, for public opinion still resented their presence. Oxford, it was felt, was a monastic institution in which they were out of place.[90]

Consequently, as Peter Parker notes, 'a young man going to the Front straight from university might be in as woeful a state of ignorance as a boy just out of school.'[91]

Realising that many men would have their first sexual experiences during the war, the military did provide some sex education in the form of lectures.[92] Young officers could benefit from the experience of their colleagues. The same had potentially been true of university, although Douglas Wimberley had participated in conversations about sex at Cambridge and admitted that 'few of us can have had the least idea about what we were talking.'[93] Youthful officers were not always in any better position to acquire information. Harold Mellersh recalled that sex was the usual topic of conversation – 'sex and the regrettable lack of experience of it on the part of some of those present.'[94] There was, however, an increased possibility that there might be men present who had been initiated into the secret; such men were consequently questioned extensively since knowledge of this kind was a valuable commodity.[95] This provides an interesting counterpoint to those constructions of wartime manliness which emphasise gradations of combat initiation and experience, suggesting that this knowledge could even be seen as more significant than fighting status in defining masculinity.

Artillery officer P.J. Campbell's experience supports this interpretation. In his autobiography *In the Cannon's Mouth*, published in 1979, he recounted a conversation in which a new arrival called Pearson, who was an uninitiated combatant, having never been under shellfire, broke a taboo by confessing openly to feeling afraid. Pearson 'said he wasn't going to do anything more than he had to or put his nose outside a dug-out if he could help it.' He is described as being 'as much of a newcomer' as Campbell. According to certain conceptions of masculinity, Pearson is 'unmanly', first because he is not yet an initiated combatant and, secondly, because he openly challenges certain masculine ideals. However, 'Josh' – as the newcomer was soon known by all – was quickly integrated into the group whilst Campbell continued to struggle to be accepted. The key difference between the two of them was that Josh was married and Campbell understood that 'all the others were sure he would have something to tell them.' 'I knew as little about life as I still knew about the War. Josh knew about life, the others all knew about the War, they were men.'[96] A further interesting feature of this source is that Josh's experience of *married life* is potentially more important than simply his experience of *sex.* Even though the questions are still essentially sexual in nature, they explore issues of intimacy and the challenges – particularly reproductive – of a protracted relationship. The husband is credited with extra knowledge of women and sexual matters and hence masculinity.

Increased knowledge did not necessarily translate into action. As Bourke notes, non-marital sexual intercourse was more acceptable to regular soldiers than civilian recruits and many ex-civilians found that they could not adopt the regular's attitude.[97] Harold Mellersh, who entered the army direct from school and later found himself the presumed object of a woman's intentions in Saltburn, East Yorkshire, blamed 'the power of tradition. I had not been brought up to the idea that soldiers must automatically and unquestioningly want to have sexual relations with any female available. I did not like this particular woman, and so my desires were not in the least inflamed.'[98] Men who were already sexually active could struggle to deal with the privation caused either by lack of opportunity or this sort of aversion to casual relationships; Cyril Dennys knew one captain 'getting on in age' who applied for and obtained special leave, boldly stating that the reason for his application was 'sexual starvation'.[99] In contrast, young men who were largely ignorant of women and had been conditioned by public-school life not to mind their absence presumably remained relatively unconcerned. Many more were not bold enough to make the attempt or actively refused to participate in the kind of sexual antics indulged in by their colleagues. In Stuart Cloete's case, this was mainly due to a dislike of prostitutes, rather than any lack of hormonal drive:

> Sex was pressing me hard and I began to masturbate regularly. I was not going to touch the kind of whores who were available and even refused Paris leave because I was afraid – shy of the better-class prostitutes.[100]

Consequently, despite an increased knowledge of sexual matters, men could find that the war actually delayed their sexual maturity.[101] Robert Graves memoir suggests revulsion at what he seems to have considered to be the sordid sexuality of the army. His stated reason for abstinence was his wish to avoid getting infected.[102] Female companionship and sexual intercourse were certainly potentially hazardous, and not just in terms of personal health. Naïve young officers were tempting targets for the unscrupulous. Mrs C.S. Peel, reviewing national wartime life from the vantage point of the late 1920s, described how some 'were victimized by women, known in criminal argot as "crows," who took them to dance clubs and when they were drunk lured them on to some other place for a game of cards, with such financial results as may be imagined. Drink was sold after hours at preposterous prices in these so-called clubs, and many were the charges of theft and blackmail made to the Provost Marshall in Rochester Row, Westminster, by victims of harpies of the underworld.'[103] Potentially more seriously, by 1918 an officer who contracted venereal disease might be required to resign his commission, in which case he would immediately have been conscripted and forced back into service as a private.[104]

Some officers simply missed female companionship. 'Much as I like most of my brother officers – and I do like most of them very much,' wrote Lancelot Spicer. 'One gets dreadfully tired of eternally seeing people in trousers, and those khaki!'[105] Others, however, did not miss it at all and might, in any case, have found that it seemed strange and unwelcome in comparison to that of their own gender. This was, to some extent, a function of their upbringing. Martin Stephen argues that aspects of Edwardian culture promoted close male relationships; in particular those who had attended public schools had been exposed to a culture in which secluded maleness and a focus on athleticism made alumni more conscious of homosexuality.[106] The Western Front replicated some of these conditions. Some young officers may have found its overwhelming maleness and the emphasis on bodily health, physicality, and leadership – not unlike that found on the sports field – created a similar atmosphere. Paul Fussell has also pointed out that close-knit male bonds were unsurprisingly produced by the emotional pressures of soldiering.[107]

It is possible that certain feelings were awakened, even if these stopped some way short of full and understood homosexual impulses. Certainly many sources exhibit homoerotic characteristics. These are quite often platonic rather than explicitly sexual. Clearly some officers went to war in the full knowledge that they were gay, and others came to the realisation while serving. Many remained abstinent. One officer admitted that he was attracted to 'an adorable telephonist, who is alone with me now on this desolate hilltop where I observe. A terrible temptation – when the days get longer one has to sleep up at the ghastly places. But I have no courage.'[108] Some were bolder, and active relationships were far from unknown. Raymond Asquith once defended a fellow officer who was charged with '"homosexuality", as these over-educated soldiers persist in misnaming these elementary departures from the strict letters of "Infantry Training 1914".'[109] Between 1914 and 1919 22 officers and 270 other ranks were court-martialled for 'indecency' with another man.[110] This seems a low number, given the size of the army and the normal incidence of homosexuality within populations. Even if abstinence dramatically reduced the incidence of active gay relationships, we may infer that superiors turned blind eyes or used disciplinary procedures which stopped short of formal courts-martial. Lovers may also generally have been successful in avoiding detection. Legal action was, nevertheless, an additional danger associated with the development of an intimate relationship and doubtless the source of considerable psychological pressure for some, placing an extra burden on officers already dealing with almost continual bereavement as contemporaries and colleagues died around them.

6

Working Relationships and Seniority

Officers undergoing the transition from civilian to soldier had to learn how to live up to their responsibilities and acquire the confidence needed to command. This personal growth had to be matched by the development of the inter-personal skills needed to be a fully capable soldier. Good relations between company commanders and their platoon officers were essential since many routine administrative decisions within infantry companies were taken informally by the small clique of company officers.[1] The same was true at battalion level. Furthermore, these units contained numerous figures, ranging from the cooks to the Colonel, who all had a role to play in maintaining the life and effectiveness of the whole. Some had formal authority invested in them. Others were important figures and held considerable effective power over their colleagues because they controlled certain key services. An officer's commander might determine such matters as tasks and leave prospects, but a figure like the quartermaster was equally significant on a day to day basis because he controlled the transportation of baggage – and could therefore have a material affect on the officer's ability to make himself comfortable if he chose to do so. John Nettleton saw his QM, Captain J.H. Alldridge, 'throw an officer's valise off into the mud because it weighed more than the regulation 35lbs. The owner had been unwise enough to cross swords with the QM on some other matter and, then and there, he had to jettison so much of his kit as would bring his valise down to 35lbs'.[2]

Consequently, as an important part of their transition, inexperienced soldiers needed to identify the possessors of both formal and informal (but no less effective) powers and learn how to optimise their relationships. This was not necessarily a skill which could be mastered quickly, not least because the period of acceptance could be substantially dictated by the more senior figures. As Nettleton found, the lowlier members of the officer hierarchy had to accept that they would not be allowed to forget their junior status for some time. Alldridge apparently 'regarded junior officers as unlicked cubs, who sometimes had to be disciplined for their own good. And when this happened, it was no good trying to argue with him. He knew King's Regulations backwards and forward and inside out and was absolutely sure of his ground. It was better to take your medicine with what grace you could summon up.' On the other hand, Alldridge's assistance could be invaluable, if obtained. The unfortunate Nettleton, having had his revolver and holster, ammunition pouch and compass stolen, was dismayed that the QM seemed reluctant to replace them for him at government expense. Some little while afterwards, however, replacements mysteriously appeared: 'if you did not do anything to get in his bad books, Alldridge was a very good friend and I think he enjoyed playing fairy godfather to young officers.'[3]

The infrequency of acrimonious reports in a large number of primary sources and the successes of British infantry battalions throughout the war suggest that these inter-personal matters were generally well managed (or did not, at least, create worse problems than might be expected in comparable groupings). Chris McCarthy notes that it was possible by 1918 to plan and launch operations extremely quickly as commanders at brigade and battalion level issued verbal orders and consulted with their subordinates.[4] The success of such a system depended on trust and good relationships within units.

When personal antipathies of any kind arose, however, they could at the very least make life uncomfortable. First impressions might be extremely important, and officers arriving in a unit for the first time could be met by very different receptions.[5] Some were unfortunate enough to encounter entrenched peace-time prejudices, especially at the beginning of the war. Thomas Pratt was gazetted as Second Lieutenant to the 4th Duke of Wellington's Regiment in September 1914. Joining his battalion in camp near Grimsby, he and his fellow novices found themselves less than welcome:

> Throughout all the period at Riby Park we were haunted by the feeling of not being wanted and we were frequently snubbed and did not at any time there feel at all at home amongst the older officers. I found out later that this Battalion, which was recruited from Halifax and district, was run by a clique of families of the district and that many of them had sent in the names of brothers and relatives hoping to have them gazetted to the Battalion. When we were sent before these names came through they resented the fact strongly. This was their Battalion – what right had these unknown men to come into it?[6]

Prejudices of this kind tended to break down over time, although units and messes continued to form cliques which might be inimical to newcomers. As the war progressed, the shift from a predominantly volunteer army to a conscripted force created a further source of tension between new arrivals and those with experience. Charles Dudley-Ward explained in 1916 how he and his colleagues became wary of new officers, whose history (or avoidance) of front-line service was likely to act as an important determinant: 'One gets very clannish, old hands herd together and look on new men with suspicion asking how it is they have only just come out and so on. It is natural I suppose.'[7]

Moreover some units, especially self-consciously elite battalions, retained distinctive customs which might be daunting to outsiders. Since the system for postings was relatively fluid it was not unusual for an officer to be reassigned to a new battalion to replace battle casualties or fill vacancies, and at this point the young officer might have to adjust to a very different culture. Bernard Long discovered that a regular battalion, even after three years of war, might have rigid rules of conduct or appearance. Commissioned into the 16th (Service) Battalion West Yorkshire Regiment in January 1916, he was wounded in Givenchy in September of that year. On returning to France in July 1917 he was selected to join the 2nd, a regular battalion. Long was very sensible of the honour (though apparently a little concerned about the expense) and quickly appreciated the difference in tone: 'The 2nd is a very swanky battn I tell you,' he wrote to his sister Ethel, 'and the discipline is awfully strict for the men while we have to be awfully particular about our dress. I don't like it so much as the 16th but it isn't so bad really.' To his mother he complained that 'there's too much of the peace time about its special ways of wearing puttees, steel helmets, equipment etc. It gets on your nerves. Also officers must have all sorts of fancy compasses etc. which I don't intend to get. I don't fancy I shall like being here very long. But it's no good grumbling I suppose.'[8] Robert Graves similarly struggled with the attitudes of members of the regular army. On one occasion he was reprimanded and given extra saluting drill because a more senior officer had deliberately engineered a mild breach of King's Regulations on Graves' part. Graves was prepared to acknowledge that there was nothing personal in such actions, which instead reflected a desire to improve soldierly standards, but it can hardly have improved the atmosphere in the officers' mess.[9]

Although relations between officers within the same battalion or company were often fraternal, serious difficulties could arise if personal antipathies between junior and superior officers developed and festered.[10] Charles May was dismayed to find that his commander was a 'bully and [a] cad', and realised that this was not the sort of man 'whom we would look up to and follow.'[11] These problems were exacerbated when favouritism and rivalries entered into the equation. Cosmo Clark evidently disliked his colonel and, by extension, some of his colleagues because of the man's effect on the social networks in the battalion:

The CO of the 6th is the fattest man I have ever seen, though he is only 4'8" high. He is a mean, despicable little swine who everybody hates. I say everybody but this is a mistake, because there is a little clique in the mess of about two captains and a dozen or more subalterns who crawl around the old boy and stand him drinks and applaud when he is playing billiards. I've never in all my life known of such a state of affairs in a mess.[12]

Whilst such situations were doubtless bad for morale, they could also have a more direct impact on operational effectiveness. Eventually the particular fault-line described by Clark split wide open, leaving the remaining officers to pick up the pieces and cope with an increased workload:

The colonel (who you know I have no love for) has made a terrible and awful mess of things in our [company]. Bradley and Tooze who are both fine officers and men, he has long had a spite against, and has at last succeeded in getting them sent home. They go either today or tomorrow and I might add they go home without a stain on their character as soldiers or gentlemen. More I cannot say but will explain in detail when I get home on leave. This leaves me at present second-in-command to a [company] of 200 men and Oxenbould (who is an excellent chap but quite young – 20 years) in command. I only hope this state of affairs won't last long and I don't think it will. Anyway all I can do is my level best and hope for a little leave before long.[13]

Lancelot Spicer had a similar problem with his own battalion commanding officer, Colonel Lynch, whom he called 'an utter scoundrel, and extraordinarily underhand.' Again, the problem eventually boiled over and the junior officers took sides – as they did in Clark's battalion – in a dispute between the unit's two most senior officers:

What basically brought matters to a head is that the 2nd-in-Command of the battalion has gone sick. During his temporary absence the C.O. has promoted one of his personal friends, a fellow called Capt. Stephenson from 2nd-in-Command of a Company to 2nd-in-Command of the battalion, thereby passing over all the Company Commanders, including Griffen, a piece of extraordinary impertinence, but unfortunately General Routine Orders give him authority to do so if he wants, and also he has got the sanction of the Brigadier to this appointment. The Brigadier, unfortunately, though quite a nice man in himself, is absolutely under the thumb of Lynch – why I don't quite understand. Griffen naturally protested, and at any rate had the satisfaction of telling the C.O. precisely what he thought of him. But it didn't do any good.

Spicer's association with one of the parties in this dispute clearly affected his relationship with his colonel. Other officers in the company were in a similar situation. Spicer thought he saw an opportunity to escape the uncomfortable situation when a chit came round asking for officers for Balloon Observation work. In total, three officers submitted their names. That Saturday evening Colonel Lynch called all the officers together:

He told us that he was now addressing the officers of 'D' Company (my company). He then stated the facts as to our applying for this balloon job, and said that in the first place it showed that we were insubordinate and mutinous, and secondly it showed cowardice. This latter charge he dwelt on for some time. He said that I had disgraced my birth and breeding by not holding Griffen back from coming and complaining to him. He could understand Griffen doing it alone, but when I was there it was disgraceful that I should not have stopped him.

Lynch warmed to his theme, clearly taking the view that any attempt to move away from battalion work was a betrayal of the fighting men:

The fact that we were applying for a job out of the firing line showed cowardice. He hoped that if we got the job we should cut off our present buttons and wear leather ones. He did not know what badges we should wear, but he hoped it would be the white feather. It was also impossible for him to trust such officers – if he gave the order for 'D' Company to advance, they might quite possibly refuse. All this and a great deal more he said before the whole of the officers of the battalion. He then told us, without allowing us to say a word, that in consequence of this action he would stop our leave for the present cycle of officers, and would send us all to different companies.[14]

This was a quite stunning public rebuke, after which he and Spicer had 'a pretty straight talk'. There did not seem to be any immediate resolution, but the problem was solved within six weeks when Lynch and many other officers were killed on the Somme.

In the midst of a great patriotic struggle, as many wished to portray it at the time, it is not surprising that some observers wished to play down the impact of these ordinary human frictions. Could pettiness and antagonism really survive amongst the brotherhood of the trenches? Lt-Col. Alan Hanbury-Sparrow thought not, castigating *Journey's End* in the early 1930s as 'wrong as a picture of the war, for the knowledge of the not-self that we felt, but did not know, prohibited hatred either towards each other or towards the enemy. All the antipathy that the war engendered was turned towards the careerists of the staff, the base, and the trade unions.'[15] Fighting officers' relationships with these types may not always have been good, but inevitably there were also personal antipathies within their own community. In some cases, these were driven by snobbery. While training in Colchester in October 1914 Sam Paget commented that 'Some of the subs are exceedingly nice – including Nielsen, late of [Winchester College boarding house] Freddie's – I don't know if you knew him: but some are too deadly for words – and obviously were not educated at Winchester or Eton! But then one needn't have any dealings with them – so it doesn't matter.'[16] The reality of army life, however, was that formerly sheltered individuals like Paget, brought up within a fairly rigid caste system, could not hope to avoid colleagues they found distasteful in perpetuity and could ill afford to let prejudices affect their ability to co-operate with them.

More striking intolerance is evident in Edwin Vaughan's diary, a veritable catalogue of personal dislikes and grievances. A first meeting with his company commander was inauspicious: 'He is very small and quite inefficient, though full of bounce and bluff.'[17] Vaughan noted that he disliked and despised him. Although later revising his opinion somewhat, he still had no higher opinion of his abilities and declared that he 'continues to grate on my nerves.'[18] Another officer was criticised because 'both his character and his appearance are thoroughly spoiled by drink.'[19] 2nd Lieutenant Frank Wollocombe frequently refers to an anonymous officer whom he disliked intensely, apparently both personally and on account of his incompetence. This man was apparently no more successful with his other colleagues: 'X____ was terribly told off by the RE Captain today for leaving his men bunched up in the back of the Tambour, the most unsafe place of all – and rushing for a dug out himself – and several other little tricks. I wish a crump would drop on him.'[20] Eventually Wollocombe 'told X____ at some length what [he] thought of him.'[21] Wilbert Spencer knew a similar case in the Wiltshire Regiment in February 1915: 'Our other subaltern (we only have two now) is not at all nice. No one in the battalion likes him. He seems such an absolute outsider. I do my very best to be decent to him but he continually annoys everyone. Thank Heaven I am senior to him. He comes from another regiment and thinks too much of himself, making himself generally unpopular.'[22]

Unsurprisingly, men who failed to harmonise with their colleagues, perhaps acquiring a reputation for being difficult or unreliable, could damage their prospects and the informal cliques on which so many routine decisions depended. Possibly because of his prickly demeanour, Vaughan's relations with different colleagues deteriorated. Eventually, after a misunderstanding about a working party, he was hauled up in front of his commanding officer and accused of being absent from parade. His history of antisocial behaviour and inability to blend in during his time with the battalion was deployed against him: '"You fall foul of Brigade the first time you report to them; you make a fool of yourself when you are sent up to find your company HQ, and now you slink away from your work."' The CO made it abundantly clear that this catalogue of misdemeanours was likely to affect Vaughan's prospects for promotion and that his conduct could ultimately result in his being ordered back to England in disgrace.[23]

The predominantly smooth operation of the system of command and control could be ensured, however, by a flexible arrangement of postings and transfers. As Vaughan's account suggests, those officers who were manifestly unfit for active service or simply a nuisance could be quietly dispatched to other duties. Well-connected officers could wield very substantial power over their colleagues and subordinates, especially if they had a good knowledge of the army's inner workings. Desmond Young saw at first hand how effectively one Commanding Officer dealt with 'a very tiresome and argumentative ASC officer':

> Colonel Beadon got on the 'blower' to the War Office and asked to speak to the Quartermaster General, Travers-Clarke. 'Do me a favour, Travers, will you?' he asked. 'Post Major X to Mesopotamia.' I was on duty in the office the next morning when the posting order came through.[24]

The hierarchy's power over the individual could be used in still more brutal ways if officers did not meet a required standard. Guy Chapman's colonel dealt firmly with two problem officers described by Chapman as a 'fainéant' and an 'incompetent': 'Both appeared before the divisional commander. There was no court-martial. Their commissions were removed on his report and they left us to be drafted into the ranks at the base. It may have been cruel; but it was necessary. The lives of others depended on it.'[25]

This system could also be used in a much more benign way. A 'failed' or shell-shocked officer could be protected rather than punished or marginalised. Ben Shephard, examining the psychological challenges facing First World War soldiers in *The War of Nerves*, suggested that a common educational background often encouraged this. Officers, reluctant to let down one of their own, would be as sympathetic as possible in their treatment of men who in other contexts might have been condemned as cowards.[26] They were even assisted in this by the terminology applied by the establishment to shell-shock when experienced by officers: neurasthenia. This categorised the symptoms as an illness, something for which the officer himself could not be held personally responsible. Through various contacts Robert Graves was able to manipulate the system to assist his friend Siegfried Sassoon following the latter's outspoken protest against the war, Sassoon's treatment as a psychological invalid protecting him from punishment.[27] The fluidity of the officer corps also ensured that genuine personality clashes could often be resolved to the satisfaction of all parties. It was frequently possible for an unhappy officer to obtain a transfer to another section. This was especially easy to effect at times when the Army was seeking men for new or developing services or, according to Sir Basil Liddell Hart, amidst the disordered circumstances of the early years of the war. He recalled meeting many officers in 1915 who had simply moved themselves to a more congenial posting and managed to get these changes ratified.[28]

While this sort of adjustment might have been possible at various times, officers generally could not circumvent the constraints imposed by an official hierarchy, a system which could have a very profound effect on their careers and relationships with other officers. This is an obvious point, but it is perhaps worth noting that the young men who took commissions in the early months of the war straight from school or university probably could not have fully appreciated just how important the chain of command was and how much influence it would have over their lives. Their prior experience of comparable hierarchies would, of course, have given many an instinctive understanding. At school, they had been hedged in by numerous trifling regulations designed to reflect gradations of seniority, wearing of particular caps or ties or gaining the privilege of leaving certain buttons undone.[29] Surprisingly similar trivialities could apply in the army – for instance, orders in Graves' Royal Welch Fusiliers battalion prevented his colleague Robertson, though a former Parliamentary candidate in his early forties, from enjoying a whiskey and soda in the mess because he was classed as a young officer[30] – but the most important effects of official seniority in the army were on pay, job prospects and prestige.

Promotion, either substantive or to temporary or acting ranks, was therefore of great interest to many junior officers. As has already been discussed in Chapter 3, some were ambitious or had developed the habit of trying to climb any career ladder that presented itself, but there were other reasons too. Different challenges at a higher level could be rewarding in their own right – as indicated by Douglas Gillespie's comment 'I quite enjoy commanding the company.'[31] Alternatively, there was the pride which made it difficult to contemplate losing a position of seniority even if, as in the case of Arthur Pick, it placed him under some strain. 'I am finding it rather trying to have a Company', he told his parents in July 1917, 'and I don't know whether they will leave me in charge, as the C.O. seems to think I am too young. If they do take me off it now, after letting me have it for so long and putting me in charge of it for a show, I shall try and get away from the Battalion altogether, although I don't want to do that after having always been with it.'[32]

Inevitably, the system could not always satisfy these many competing hopes and ambitions. The speed of promotion, as in the pre-war army, varied from regiment to regiment. Moreover, the distinction between an officer's substantive rank within his regiment and any acting or temporary rank assumed to fill a specific appointment, sometimes away from that regiment, could create particular tensions. Performance at a higher level than one's actual rank was commonplace, as many officers had to take command of formations to replace battle casualties or colleagues posted to other duties. This created an expectation of substantive promotion, but the system often lagged behind the reality. Many subalterns consequently found themselves waiting impatiently for substantive rank to accompany their newly-elevated status. 'I'm not daring to think much about a Captaincy yet', Arthur Gibbs wrote to his mother in April 1917, 'but I suppose it ought to come through eventually. I think I am entitled to it after having the Company for a month.'[33] Even though he left Oxford early in the war to take a commission, it is possible that Gibbs' sense of entitlement reflected a civilian's sense of how the military system, a by-word for order, should operate. If that were the case, it is ironic that he was able to satisfy his wish because of flexibility in the system a few months later. 'I've got my 3rd star at last, I'm glad to say', he told his mother in July. 'I don't know when it will be gazetted but I have got permission from the major-general to wear my 3 stars. I only heard an hour or two ago, but I have put it up at once, of course.'[34]

Unfortunately, non-substantive promotions easily gained could be as easily lost. Acting or temporary ranks which accompanied specific duties would be relinquished if the post was given up or a more senior or qualified officer removed the need for an interim appointment.[35] The arrival of a regular captain prevented Jack Oughtred from retaining company command: 'Had he not done so I should have kept it and had the glory of 3 pips – the Adjutant assured me of this.'[36] Clearly this was a frustrating occurrence. Even harder for the individual officer to reconcile, a transfer to another unit or an upgrade to a permanent commission might cause him to lose his rank and status altogether, perhaps being reduced, despite months of experience, to a lowly 2nd lieutenant and subordinated to the latest batch of young officers fresh from England. When Robert Graves rejoined the 2nd Battalion Royal Welch Fusiliers he was disappointed not to have received a warmer welcome, but soon discovered why. One of his colleagues who had been dispatched to France before him had managed to obtain a regular commission. Consequently he was only a second lieutenant while Graves arrived with the rank of lieutenant. It was this disparity which was creating the ill feeling.[37] Douglas Bell found himself in a comparable position to Graves' companion, losing status when he received the permanent commission for which he had applied after about a year serving as a temporary officer. He was similarly peeved to find himself subordinated to uninitiated younger men.[38]

The problem of relative seniority also arose in the case of officers who had remained in England while other members of their battalions were posted abroad. The general level of seniority usually increased within the pool of officers left at home because they did not suffer battle casualties and also benefited from the accelerated promotion which might accompany the formation and training of new units. On reaching France, they leapt straight over the heads of officers who were officially their juniors but who might already have experienced months of active service. As Charles May rather tartly observed, 'I veritably believe that if half of us here got home and played to the gallery a bit we'd be colonels in a month with fresh battalions to mould.'[39] This sort of cynicism might be combined with more barbed comments about the merits and character of the officers in question.

With so much potential for animosity, it is hardly surprising that officers posted to France might find their situations uncomfortable. Geoffrey Dugdale was rather disconcerted, when sent to the front for the first time having already reached the rank of full lieutenant, to discover that his company's platoon commanders were 2nd lieutenants despite being veteran trench fighters. Though they were not unpleasant towards him, he clearly received a cooler welcome than he would have liked, reflecting their resentment of the fact that he was their superior despite his lack of practical experience.[40] In cases like this other officers might be reduced in rank as a result of a new arrival. J.R. Monsell, who lost out in this way, suffered additionally following a decision to rationalise the establishment allowed in his battalion:

> The Army, God bless it, is a mysterious institution. By a benevolent decree it has just issued I find myself a Lieutenant again! They have very kindly arranged … that there shall be 2 Cols 4 Majs + 16 Capts all genuine + real, instead of 1 Col 2 Majors + 8 Captains divided between the 1st + 2nd Battns, the other Cols etc being Temporary Rank. It sounds very nice in theory but in practice – take our Rgt. The 1st Battn came out at Xmas 1914. Only two of the original officers are left. The 2nd Battn sat tight at home – all its Officers are left. It puts a premium on squatting at home. … The oddest result of things is that fellows who were subalterns under me out here are now senior to me … It's a little bewildering but God bless the War Office say I.[41]

A degree of instability within the hierarchy's structure was, consequently, an innate obstacle with which all junior officers had to contend.

Especially galling was the loss of rank as a result of being wounded, which many officers considered grossly unfair. Arthur Pick became a full lieutenant in August 1917 but had been serving as an acting captain since July. Mildly gassed in May 1918, he was evidently disgusted, on returning to the battalion two months later, at his treatment: 'By the way don't forget in future that I am a Lieut. I have paid the penalty of being a battle casualty by losing my rank.'[42] Arthur Gibbs's cherished third star was similarly lost after he was wounded in April 1918, his indignation increased by the cumbersome system of official gazetting: 'Thus one is rewarded by a grateful war office ... What a life.'[43] His colonel was clearly sympathetic, allowing him to wear three stars.[44] The episode is a reminder that these issues of seniority could create significant problems for battalion commanders, anxious to maintain morale amongst their officers and to ensure that the most efficient men occupied the most important command appointments. The extent to which this man-management (and the complexities of the system) could occupy an officer's time and energies is illustrated by a series of entries in the diary of Lieutenant-Colonel W.H. Matthews, commanding 1/20th Battalion London Regiment:

21/4/17

Sent in application for Dolphin to be re-gazetted acting Major & 2i/c & Reede acting Capt. both having appeared in the gazette as relinquishing the ranks owing to readjustments of seniority list on the 3 Battn. of the 20th Regt. Being made for purposes of seniority in regiment. Have kept back report on Fitz.G. until [Dolphin] clearly entitled to be reappointed 2i/c although at the moment Fitz.G. is senior to him. The readjustment of seniority has in these & several other cases worked very hard on individual officers. Service at the front & the consequent casualties counting for nothing but working for the permanent promotion of officers who stayed at home & ran no such risks.

22/4/17

Drew up report on Fitz.G. applying for his employment away from Battn. as I did not consider him fit to command Coy in field. Had unpleasant ½ hour with him when I read him the report before sending it to Brigade – Parker present at interview – Thank goodness it is over. I hate those kind of interviews they are quite the most unpleasant part of a C.O's job.

19/5/17

Arranged with [Brigadier] that if Dolphin not well enough to come up this time FitzG shall be left behind Reede act 2 i/c and Hewitt take Reede's Coy. Damned nuisance having the "Dud" officer about and to think he has been swanking at home for 2 years having a very easy time, getting promotion over the heads of good fellows out here, whom he lords it over when they go home sick or wounded, and then when at last he is pushed out here he turns out to be what nearly everyone knew him to be – a "washout".[45]

For some, the irritation caused by the vagaries of the promotion system was more explicitly connected with financial matters. Richard Holmes has noted that the common reversion to second lieutenant – with commensurate loss of pay – was a considerable disincentive to many temporary officers contemplating a regular commission.[46] Financial calculations were similarly important when other changes in rank occurred, especially in circumstances of considerable flux. Jack Oughtred described his life in his battalion in July 1917 as 'extremely varied', there being some confusion even as to whether he was a 1st or 2nd Lieutenant. By August, however, the situation had been resolved – not to his satisfaction: 'By the way in the Gazette of July 26th I relinquish the rank of Lieutenant – have to refund 1/- per day from January 17th 1917 – £9.16.0 altogether. Rather rotten, isn't it, but it's no use grumbling. I ought to get my promotion from the 4th [East Yorkshire] any time now and that will be permanent.'[47] This misfortune then seems to have preyed on his mind, his feelings about the requirement to refund his bank becoming entwined with his hopes for promotion. On 8 September he wrote about the possibility of becoming a full Lieutenant, and couldn't resist referring to the financial implications: 'I expect to get a second pip shortly. My name has been forwarded. I hope that it will be permanent this time. I am tired of refunding money to Cox and Co.'[48]

On 3 November he wrote: 'I have just received a chit from the Adjutant containing news about the contents of which I am sure, darling, you will rejoice with me. I am now a Captain – s'nice, isn't it – especially with my M.C. at the end. What a swank I am getting, ain't I? Anyway the 5/- a day is a sure thing now.'[49] Although he also wrote of the 'great honour' of company command in the 1st Battalion, it is interesting that he should pick out the increase in pay, and that he should continue to do so in subsequent letters. On 4 November he wrote that 'I get 18/- per diem now so I get £328.10.0 in a year. It's not too bad. I ought to save a lot of it. I'll soon finish paying off that War Loan anyway.' On 13 November he agreed that 'It is as you say very nice to have a Company of one's own. But you know what pleases me most is the extra pay.'[50] Not that things went smoothly from this point, as Oughtred explained later in the month: 'I seem to have been done in over my promotion to Lieutenant as Cox & Co. inform me that they have credited my account with £4.2.0 instead of £20- odd. I have written to them tonight again on this subject. Rather a swiz, I think, as I refunded £16 in July last. However, my Captain's pay ought to be coming along soon, which will soon make up for that. But I don't believe in losing any money in this show. For what one does in "Pushes" and that kind of thing you get little enough.'[51]

It is always difficult to extrapolate judgements about junior officers as a group from an inevitably narrow evidence base, but an examination of the different themes contained within Oughtred's letters suggests that he was probably far from alone in his attitude towards pay. As Chapter 3 has discussed, careerism was not uncommon within the ranks of junior officers, and it is perfectly natural that concerns about seniority, employment and prospects should be reflected in a desire to ensure that they were receiving the appropriate salary. While it may not sit with an image of heroic subalterns selflessly sacrificing all for King and Country, it is understandable that men should not have wished to forego the pay which they felt they had so thoroughly earned through their exposure to discomfort and danger. Oughtred tartly suggests that the state owes him rather more than he receives for his efforts; others would doubtless have agreed with Captain Blaikie, a character in John Hay Beith's *The First Hundred Thousand* (a fictionalised narrative serialised under the pseudonym 'Ian Hay' in 1915 and apparently widely read in the UK), who complained that 'The farther away you remove the British soldier from the risk of personal injury, the higher you pay him.'[52] It is hardly surprising, given such perceptions, that the trench fighter should have been concerned about getting his proper entitlement.

There were other, more selfless reasons for this interest. In October 1917 Oughtred went on leave and got engaged; his anxieties about pay and his comments about saving need to be seen in this context. It was clearly important for him to prepare for his future married life. Many officers must have been in a similar position, looking forward to the end of their years of military service (either with or without romantic attachments) and trying to ensure that they did not lose out financially while in uniform. Others will have had more immediate concerns about their domestic responsibilities, the wives and families they had left behind. It seems likely that they would have been particularly influenced by concerns about the impact on their dependents of their death or disablement. Soldiering was, ultimately, a job of work. Even if many officers (especially volunteers) would not have thought of it in quite such mundane terms, their interest in their terms and conditions indicates the extent to which they did adopt the mindset of a professional soldier.

Oughtred's problems with promotions never seemed to abate. Correspondence on the subject was passing between his battalion and division as late as October 1918, with the unfortunate Oughtred once again contemplating having to refund the difference between a Lieutenant's and a Captain's pay.[53] War Office officials did eventually realise that problems relating to promotions were a major cause of grievances within the officer corps, but a 1917 Committee on Promotion, chaired by Winston Churchill, noted that 'the military authorities have been constantly redressing anomalies and making improvements in the system of promotion. Many of the complaints which might have been justified a year ago are now groundless, and much of the work which seemed to be comprised in our reference has already been accomplished.' The committee did, however, consider 'the immediate loss of acting rank whenever an officer is wounded or invalided home' to be the most noticeable and substantial ground for complaint:

> There is no doubt that this is considered to be a hardship. His friends and neighbours, not fully appreciating the conditions under which acting rank is granted and held, find it difficult to realise why the loss of rank has occurred, and why an officer, good enough to be captain at the front, should become a lieutenant or second lieutenant when invalided home. The officer himself, when posted on recovery to a depot or to a home serving battalion, often finds himself junior in regimental rank to others of his own age and standing who have neither his experience in command nor service at the front.

It is especially interesting that an official body of this sort should have recognised the importance to the individual of the wider social implications of his officer status, bracketing rank alongside such significant experiences as trench service and being under fire as important cultural determinants of success and self-validation. Both non-professional soldiers and their civilian acquaintances required unambiguous distinctions and gradations which could be used to interpret an individual's period of service. Regular soldiers may have been more used to the vagaries of the system, but even they may have fallen foul of the peculiarly fluid wartime system. The committee addressed these problems by recommending that acting rank be retained on home service, although pay could only accompany a duty actually being discharged. It also proposed 'that acting rank should be freely accorded to the officers who are actually bearing the burden of command' and that promotion from the probationary rank of 2nd lieutenant should occur after a definite period of time.[54] This interval was eventually set at 18 months' commissioned service.[55]

※

Considerations of seniority were important for individuals but inevitably also shaped dynamics within the wider officer community which, by its nature, imposed different statuses on disparate individuals who, in other walks of life, might have been ranked very differently. The junior officer corps was never composed entirely of very young men. The popular enthusiasm that drove volunteering in 1914 and early 1915 was not confined to those only just out of school and university. Andrew Buxton reached his 35th birthday just as Europe's armies began mobilising, making his way promptly thereafter into the Rifle Brigade by way of the Cambridge OTC. Before the war he had been Local Director of the Westminster Branch of Barclays Bank.[56] Christopher Stone rushed to enlist as a private in Kitchener's Army in September 1914, taking a commission the following March at the age of 32. The introduction of conscription in 1916 then guaranteed that the age profile of the officer corps would be quite broad for the rest of the war.

This presented younger officers with particular challenges. Older civilians, often with families and distinguished careers in civilian life, were a very different proposition to the older regular officers who were secure in their permanent commissions and veteran status. Questions of relative seniority might be especially important to these older men serving as junior officers. On volunteering, many were suddenly reduced to the same status as the youths fresh out of school and it was not always easy to co-exist harmoniously. Lieutenant Osborne, Sherriff's former schoolmaster in *Journey's End*, fortunately soldiers extremely contentedly alongside his company commander, Captain Stanhope, recognising the younger man's abilities as a commander. There must have been numerous Osbornes in the British Expeditionary Force. Stone himself clearly considered relative ranks to be largely unimportant, claiming that he didn't really care about promotion 'because I've seen far too much of the life out here to put any value at all on the rank or decorations … the important thing is to do your work decently and not to be a pusher. In this odd profession the ideal is the fact and the pusher is never thought much of. If I live to the end of the war and all my friends are killed I may get all sorts of promotion; but I'm not looking forward to it with much keenness, je t'assure.'[57] Age and youth, however, did not always coexist so easily.

Not unnaturally, older men might object to being subordinated to officers who were younger than them, often by some margin. While age differentials were a significant and obvious factor in creating tensions, however, the experience of Douglas Wimberley at Sandhurst in the early months of the war suggests that competing civilian and military identities could ensure that a more complex process of self-imaging and self-definition was at work, potentially rendering different groups incompatible even when the age gap itself was not considerable. Wimberley arrived from Cambridge for a short wartime course in December 1914. His companions, about a hundred other undergraduates from various universities, but mainly from Oxford and Cambridge, were dismayed to find that the Cadet Under-Officers had gone straight from school to Sandhurst before the war. These 'seniors' had reached their exalted status rather more quickly than usual by replacing those cadets who had been hastily commissioned almost immediately at the start of the war. The newcomers, clearly retaining a sense of seniority based on their civilian attainments, were disinclined to accept the hierarchical claims of the established cadets and their military identity. This quickly generated ill feeling:

> There were many curious rules and customs at Sandhurst, mainly devised to keep the recruit cadets in their place and to uphold the authority of the Under Officers and N.C.O.s. What ensued was interesting to watch, as the University 'Bloods', who fancied themselves, regarded the existing Cadet NCOs as mere schoolboys. Rules such as the custom that no first term cadet might read a morning newspaper in the ante room until the seniors were done with it, infuriated them. For some weeks considerable bickering arose, the young pre-War regular cadets invoking the rules of custom and discipline on their side, the University 'Blues' loftily regarding the N.C.O.s, several years younger than they were, as mere boys.[58]

Such apparently capricious and pointless distinctions irked men who, in civilian life, were not bound by such petty rules. These different markers of seniority were not themselves important, but they provide a clear challenge to the residual civilian identity of newly-commissioned officers and any sense of superiority based on it. Doubtless some held their tongues and soldiered on, resenting the system even as they accepted that they had a role within it. Others eventually adopted the mindset that originally offended them so much, accepting the military approach even where it seemed to clash with central elements of a former civilian identity. Interestingly, the Officer Instructors at Sandhurst solved their problem by promoting this transition. They made all the 'Blues' into Lance Corporals, thereby co-opting them into the hierarchy which sponsored these artificial gradations. Soon, Wimberley observed, these former recalcitrants 'were enforcing old customs quite as zealously as ever before.'[59] The creation of a soldierly identity in the minds of civilians was apparently assisted by the provision of easily comprehensible roles and military structures. Since virtually all new officers would have had some experience of hierarchy and restriction, coping with those encountered in the army was perhaps more dependent on the extent to which the individual officer found himself transplanted either up or down the pecking order.

Most military institutions and units of the First World War were not like Sandhurst – with its quasi-public-school system of privileges – or hide-bound messes like that of the Royal Welch Fusiliers, where Robert Graves' colleague Robertson had such difficulty getting a whiskey and soda. Such quibbles therefore tend not to be particularly prominent in wartime sources, but there is still plenty of evidence of friction generated by age differentials or, perhaps more properly, conflicting perceptions of seniority and entitlement. In October 1916 William Villiers (born January 1897) had to cope with a new subaltern whom he found 'rather awful': 'He is 35 years old & I think rather resents having a boy of 19 in command of the [company] and no wonder too, but I am senior by

Charles Dudley-Ward served with the 16th (County of London) Battalion, The London Regiment and the Welsh Guards. He survived the war, reaching the rank of major. Born in 1879, he was older than many of his fellow junior officers and often had a different perspective on the war. (Imperial War Museum)

gazette & have been out 4 months longer than him.'[60] Villiers' challenge was to justify his position of authority in the face of this new competitor. Writing (coincidentally) less than a fortnight later, Graham Greenwell (born April 1896) was faced with a different dilemma – how to accommodate a newly-arrived former schoolmaster in his forties without creating exactly the same sort of problems: 'it is a little difficult. I have four platoon commanders already, all good fellows, and with one exception quite young. He will have to be supernumerary to one of them. I can't put him with a boy half his age, though I am myself young enough to be his son. Poor old man, I expect he will soon find his way back to England.'[61] The war was often a young man's game, partly because younger men were more likely to be unattached and came under more sustained social and cultural pressures to volunteer in the early stages. Those that survived were therefore veterans by the time conscription brought older men into the war in large numbers.

Charles Dudley-Ward (born 1879) was on the other side of the age divide and likewise observed the conflicts that could arise. He was commissioned into the London Regiment in November 1914, but transferred to the 1st Battalion Welsh Guards in 1915. Here he found his older colleagues inclined to be irritated by a younger member of the mess:

Young Crawford Wood ... is irrepressible, cheeky, talkative and silly. He is quite a boy, only twenty and suffers from the assurance of youth. ... He is always "bucking" against Allen and speaks to him in an insolent, cocksure way. Allen is unfortunately not a strong Captain but he is a man of 34 and has been in the army before. He is the same too with Luxmore Ball who is about my age. Both Allen and Ball have spoken to me about him today. It is one of the difficulties of the army that subalterns are now of all ages up to forty and frequently the older ones are junior to the younger so that it is hard for the older men if they are treated like young boys from school and the younger ones are apt to get frightfully cheeky by reason of their senior position in the regiment. The situation requires common sense rather than army custom.[62]

He was similarly aggrieved at the treatment meted out by more senior officers and the military hierarchy: 'Whenever the staff has nothing in particular to do it delights in bullying junior officers forgetting that owing to the peculiar conditions of this war they are not all young men. I am afraid our ideas on war are absurd – it is still looked upon as a kind of sport and the army as a school for young gentlemen.'[63] Men who had made careers for themselves in business or the professions can hardly have appreciated having their wisdom and life experiences set aside and being reduced in status quite so dramatically. It seems hardly surprising that this should have soured relations between the likes of Dudley-Ward and the military as a whole. Having seen much more of life than a young man straight out of public school they had a much better idea that there existed an alternative to the prescribed army method. Consequently they were often less willing cheerfully just to accept the workings of the military machine.

This was particularly noticeable when an experienced mind encountered a military problem being tackled in an apparently illogical fashion. Stephen Foot was in his late twenties when the war began and had worked for four years with an oil company in Mexico, Kuala Lumpur and Singapore. During the course of a remarkable military career, he successfully completed projects including the construction of concrete-reinforced defensive strong-points and the re-fitting and re-starting of timber mills in the St. Pol district. The best indication of the potential clash between the military and the business brain, however, is found in a conversation Foot had following a lecture in early 1916 about the Battle of Loos in which the speaker had detailed the method by which water had been carried in petrol tins to the front line. 'Coming away from the lecture I met my friend General Furse ... He asked me what I thought about the lecture. "Well, sir," I replied, "it reminded me of the British Museum for quite another reason." "What was that?" he asked. "Because they keep the Egyptian mummies there," I broke out; "the methods employed seemed to me to be equally archaic. In civil life," I went on, "if it is necessary to move a quantity of water from one place to another a couple of miles away, we should not employ hundreds of men to carry it in petrol tins." "What would you do?" asked the General. "We should employ fifty men for one night in laying a small pipe-line, and then we should push the water through it with a pump."'[64]

Foot was a Royal Engineer officer. Given his specialism and background he understandably had a more technical approach to such matters than either Furse (late Royal Artillery) or Lieutenant-General Sir Edwin Alderson (late Royal West Kent Regiment), who chaired the lecture and 'spoke in terms of admiration' about the practices derided by Foot as archaic.[65] He was able to persuade Furse to adopt his proposed alternative system in preparation for the Somme battle. His attitude was mirrored by similarly-experienced infantry officers frustrated at the tyranny of the army mentality, albeit not always with the same success. Fresh from Oxford, Desmond Young of the King's Royal Rifle Corps made a daring start by procuring files and a card index system for regimental papers and a modern typewriter, overcoming his colonel's initial suspicions.[66] Later on in his career, tired of the frequent carrying parties required to bring up water, he proposed installing a one-inch water-pipe in the sloping embankment which carried the Menin Road. He put this idea to his Colonel, who forwarded it to Brigade with a recommendation, but the plan was firmly rebuffed by the higher authorities: '"Captain Young was to desist from making such fantastic proposals and try to remember that we were soldiers in Flanders, not plumbers in London." I have often wondered what was the expenditure in lives, energy, sweat and curses before, a year or two later, the sappers laid a water-pipe under the Menin Road. When my father sent me out a line-throwing gun and I was able to lay telephone lines without having to make my signallers crawl across the open in daylight, I prudently kept the innovation to myself.'[67]

Charles May, born 1889, similarly complained that the skills which civilians had brought into the military were being overlooked. 'I cannot help but both see and feel that there is a vast wastage in this army of ours,' he wrote in December 1915. 'Not, I mean, of materials or stores – for the distribution of such things is wonderfully organized – but of men and brains. Initiative is asked for, but woe to the man who displays it. Opinions are sometimes sought – but apparently with the sole idea of making an opportunity for the airing of some higher grade's scheme, already settled in his own mind. So that one feels – and somewhat resents it – that there is humbug about and that one is being looked upon as more or less of a fool. One does not like being thought a fool, even though one has no claim to genius. If I were alone in this I might be thought that unutterable thing – a man with a grievance. But I am not alone. All our officers feel as I do. And when thirty active business brains feel like that surely it were but foolishness to deny justification. We came out here to fight, not heroically or in the heat of passion, but just to do our little bit like Englishmen should. We did not expect to be satiated with red-tape and buckram or have our brains cramped into a hidebound receptacle of blank banality which those of a lad could fill.'[68]

At the highest levels of command the army did entrust important tasks to civilians with specific expertise. Sir Eric Geddes's appointment to the British Expeditionary Force in December 1916 as Director-General of Transport is a case in point;[69] he had extensive experience of transport and logistic systems from his pre-war work with railway companies in North America and India, as well as with North-Eastern Railway. Moreover, officers in the field can be seen to have played an important role through their tactical innovations in the development of the British Army into a sophisticated modern force over the course of the war. It would be difficult, however, to say whether officers like May could ever be satisfied that the apparent wastage of resources throughout the army was rectified. Such a complaint seems born of the conflict between military and civilian mentalities within the army which could never be entirely resolved, thanks to the steady process by which more and more civilians were brought into uniformed service over the course of the war. Moreover, it was not unique to older officers. If some found their sense of only soldiering temporarily enhanced by lost status and frustrations with military inflexibility, it does not seem to have sapped their willingness to continue to work within the system. The tensions between different generations of officers likewise could not always be overcome easily, but do not seem to have been any worse for the officer corps than numerous other sources of friction. Charles Dudley-Ward summed up the choice: 'To go through this war in comfort one must cut out all military ambition, or if you have such ambition you must also have the patience of Job, and a skin like a rhinocerous.'[70]

Relations between officers of different units or branches of the army were further modulated by military culture and prejudices. At the start of the war professional soldiers were inclined to adopt a somewhat dismissive attitude towards the territorial and New Armies because of a perceived lack of professionalism.[71] Regular battalions also enjoyed the prestige derived from illustrious histories and heritage. Their status as a distinct elite was challenged by the war. As Richard Holmes has argued, the distinctions between the different types of Army units were eroded, the fate of any given unit's identity depending to a large extent on its good fortune (or otherwise) in avoiding shattering casualties – but unit characteristics were seldom entirely swept away, as officers like Bernard Long might find when required to move from one tribe to another.[72] Gary Sheffield credits the ability of many regular battalions to maintain a strong professional identity in part to continuity of command: 'Regular officers tended to be appointed to command Regular units, which also seem to have received many, if not most, of the wartime products of Sandhurst. In addition, temporary officers posted to Regular units generally quickly absorbed the ethos of their regiment. Surviving prewar Regular and Special Reservist rankers would also pass on the traditions of the unit.'[73] Young officers recognised this enduring prestige, and it was partly for this reason that some applied for permanent commissions. Douglas Wimberley basked in the reflected glory while a cadet at Sandhurst: '[We] were immensely proud that we were now in the Regular and not the Territorial or Kitchener's Army. We took considerable delight in "throwing" our smartest salutes … if we saw an officer in uniform with medals, that we considered to belong, also, to the Regular Army. Then if we saw a callow young man, dressed as a subaltern in Kitchener's Army, or the Territorials, we merely gave him a supercilious look, provided no member of the Sandhurst staff was about!'[74] Membership of a regular unit was a source of great satisfaction for officers such as Edward Tennant, who joined the Grenadier Guards at the start of the war, serving with them until his death in September 1916. In his last letter to his mother he wrote vividly of the feelings he had for his unit: 'The pride of being in such a great regiment! The thought that all the old men, "late Grenadier Guards," who sit in the London Clubs, are thinking and hoping about what we are doing here! I have never been prouder of anything, except your love for me, than I am of being a Grenadier.'[75] (As a product of the public schools, Tennant was probably in the habit of placing institutions on a pedestal; Viscount Buckmaster, expressing a sentiment which would almost certainly have been appropriated by the alumni of any large educational institution of the period, commented that 'It may be that, under the surface, all Public Schools are like each other, but to the Wykehamist there can never be but one school'.[76])

This sense of belonging could clearly provide a powerful boost to morale, as could an awareness of the obligations conferred by this status. 'Within our collective assembly there was something at stake that mattered exceedingly,' recalled Geoffrey Fildes of the Coldstream Guards: 'the good name bequeathed us by our predecessors.'[77] Such a sentiment was presumably not exclusive to the Guards; wherever it was found, a strong regimental attachment would have played its part in maintaining fighting spirit. It was not always easy, however, to be a regular, especially if a young man held a temporary rather than a permanent commission. Professional soldiers might apparently have mixed feelings about fresh arrivals, especially since the standard of new entrant could be so variable.[78] John Nettleton received a fairly cool reception on joining the 2nd Battalion Rifle Brigade: '[We] were the first "temporary gentlemen" the battalion had had to absorb and I fear we were a bit of a shock to them. All their officers had been through Sandhurst and had had proper training before they took up their commissions and they did not understand how people could be sent to them to do an officer's job who had not been trained at all.'[79] The only solution to this state of affairs was a period of re-training with the new unit, although situations like this must have become less and less common as the war progressed and the number of pre-war professional soldiers diminished.

The proud bearing of regulars was often reflected in overt criticisms of the practices and habits of their colleagues in the Territorial and New Armies. It is difficult to say whether this was largely a product of institutionalised snobbery or whether it was a genuine and accurate critique. Raymond Asquith's comments from within the ranks of the Grenadier Guards in December 1915 certainly suggest a condescending attitude:

> I had an officer of the Welsh Fusiliers and half a platoon of his men attached to me for purposes of instruction. He was a well-meaning little fellow, but a thorough-faced snitcher and I found his society irksome, as I daresay he did mine. His men were absurd and pathetic and made me more than ever glad that I chose a good regiment to fight with. They were little black spectacled dwarfs with no knowledge, no discipline, no experience, no digestion, and a surplus of nerves and vocabulary.[80]

Writing to Lady Diana Manners about the same period, he was similarly candid:

> We had a Welsh regiment attached to us last time for instruction, tiny little tots, utterly unfit for anything more strenuous than a children's ball. They would pull a couple of sandbags out of the parapet and nest in the crevice like swallows under the eaves. One asked oneself if Kitchener was serious.[81]

He had no better report to make in August 1916: 'I am not favourably impressed by what I have seen of the [Kitchener] armies in this part of the line. I daresay they go ahead all right in an attack, but they are horribly nervous under the ordinary conditions of trench warfare'.[82] His opinion of the New Armies generally seems to have been shared by Norman Taylor, a territorial with the 1st Battalion, 1st Surrey Rifles, London Regiment:

> [We] are still behind the line & crowded out with Kitchener's army who are, I'm sorry to say, a bit above themselves & will insist on enquiring in hissing sibilant whispers as we go past on the march whether we have ever been in action. We content ourselves with the time honoured reply – "Well, Dada, what did you etc – ?" "Kitchener's lads" as they roguishly style themselves are rather a ragtime crew

& not such a howling success as the papers make out; there have been one or two scandals lately.[83]

Territorials typically liked to regard themselves as superior, although both they and Kitchener troops were, for the first few years of the war, expressing the same voluntary enthusiasm. Ralph Bickersteth, a territorial officer in the 7th Battalion Leeds Rifles, thought that his organisation was making quite a name for itself on active service: 'The Territorials seem to have made a pretty good impression out here – in fact they say the smartest. Certainly we have got nothing but praise so far.'[84] They did not always impress. Gilbert Talbot of the Rifle Brigade was moved to criticise them by the condition of a recently vacated and filthy barn: 'This all shows that the discipline of some of the Terrier Battalions who preceded us is in these ways bad.'[85]

There was, however, apparently little or no deep-seated animosity between regular and non-regular units. The most typical expressions of intra-service irritation came, as in Talbot's case, after some specific minor incident in which one unit had annoyed another. As a general rule the infantry stuck together and turned its animosity outwards towards those sections of the population and the armed forces which seemed more deserving of disapprobation. Some ideas about attitudes (particularly those of the rank and file) towards groups like senior officers and the staff have lodged within the popular memory and imagination of the Great War. They bear re-examination, however, from the specific perspective of junior officers.

7

Superiors and Subordinates, Colleagues and Class

Trench soldiers of the Western Front are commonly thought to have hated and resented senior officers and the staff. The First World War has become a byword not just for military incompetence but also for the sacrifice of men who were all too well aware that their leaders were sending them to their deaths. There is some truth in this picture. It is certainly the case that many soldiers criticised commanders and their supporting staff in their letters or diaries, while numerous further criticisms were made after the war. It must also be admitted that these generals and administrators were not always competent, despite innovations and developments in the field of staff work, as in so many others.[1]

The trench fighter's apparent antipathy towards officers seems, however, to have been steadily exaggerated over recent decades, expanding to include almost any commander more senior than his own platoon or company commander. The accusation of self-preservation and callousness has extended steadily down the ranks, until even field officers are as vulnerable in the public mind as the most senior general. Where are the majors or lieutenant-colonels in *Blackadder Goes Forth*? In William Boyd's 1999 film *The Trench* a CO makes one appearance in his battalion's trench, accompanied by an official film crew as if to emphasise the notion that only the most exceptional circumstances could have persuaded him to come this far forward. Required to deliver a rousing address on the eve of the ill-fated Somme offensive, he assures his men that, following the British bombardment, they will be able to go over the top armed with walking sticks. As he wishes them good luck and encourages them to win medals for the battalion, a voice from the anonymity of the ranks makes a caustic remark about the fact that the CO won't himself be participating. The colonel concurs, reinforcing the popular misconception that even field officers were effectively removed from the danger zone. In fact, many battalion commanders did advance into No Man's Land on 1 July 1916 and on numerous other occasions. Martin Middlebrook describes Lieutenant-Colonel Reginald Bastard leading the last company of his battalion into heavy fighting on that very day.[2]

Whatever the relationship between rankers and lieutenant-colonels, subalterns were extremely unlikely to take a uniformly negative view of their COs. The Colonel was perhaps the dominant presence in the young officer's life, establishing the tone and standard of battalion life, wielding tremendous influence over careers, and operating closely alongside the company commanders who were frequently newly-elevated lieutenants (and therefore needed more support and guidance than would usually have been the case). It is no wonder that this important figure should have a closer relationship with, and therefore be better understood by, one of his sixteen platoon or four company commanders than one of approximately a thousand men directly under his command.[3]

He might be in a position to shield his battalion from certain duties, something that his junior officers might have been in a better position to appreciate than privates. He could also help officers with problems within the battalion, including tricky situations created by personal rivalries and tensions. When Geoffrey Dugdale found that his presence as an uninitiated trench fighter but superior lieutenant was creating a difficult situation in D Company 6th Battalion King's Shropshire Light Infantry, he raised the matter with his CO, who promptly managed to set things to rights.[4]

Thanks to these sorts of skills, relationships between colonels and junior officers were sometimes very special, the more senior officer nurturing, admonishing, encouraging, supporting and directing those under his command. Clearly the relationship was not always good, but some undoubtedly found it immensely important. Alfred Pollard said that his commander, Colonel Boyle, was the man whose opinion he valued above all others. Boyle had occasion to reproach his subordinate, but it is clear from Pollard's recollection of the incident that the Colonel only went up in his esteem by seeking simultaneously to restore his junior's morale, leaving him with a determination to prove himself afresh.[5] The analogy of a housemaster, headmaster or tutor and his pupil seems particularly apt in such cases. The relationship is even reminiscent of a father and son, particularly in the way Pollard seeks validation. Desmond Young also recognised this, noting that 'no son ever stood more in awe of a Victorian parent than we did of Colonel Chaplin … It was not so much that we were afraid of him, though we were; it was that we were afraid of being found wanting and perhaps sent away.'[6] On transferring to the command of Colonel Rowland Feilding, the author of *War Letters to a Wife, France and Flanders, 1915-1919*, 'one glance was sufficient to show me that I was in the presence of another Colonel Chaplin.' Feilding's demeanour unsurprisingly had a similarly stiffening effect on Young: 'For it is one of the paradoxes of war that even the naturally timid are more frightened of being found wanting by such a man than ever they are of being killed.'[7]

At first sight, the attitudes of junior officers to their colleagues on the staff were much closer to those expressed in the disillusioned poems of Siegfried Sassoon and others, which have since become so strongly embedded in the popular understanding of the war. Young officers were indeed frequently critical of staff work at all levels. In Billy Congreve's diary there is an entirely typical outburst against the staff, prompted by an incident in which a group of twenty wounded men had been left in a ruined building rather than properly cared for. All but one had died. Congreve placed the blame on wider failings by the staff.[8]

Robert Hamilton was similarly angry at the perceived inability of administrators: 'Appalling road selected by our very incompetent staff. Transport stuck. … Got to Houchin 8.30. Dark. No billets. Men have to sleep in an open field. Stupid beastly slackness on part of disgraceful staff. They ought to be shot.'[9] Compounding instances of failure were episodes which reinforced the impression in the minds of the infantry that staff officers were aloof and uncaring. Something as relatively trifling as traffic problems on the roads prompted Douglas Gillespie to complain in April 1915 that the staff 'in their motors are a great trouble to the humble infantry.'[10] Small issues of this sort could rapidly become emblematic of more profound divisions.

One frequent and specific complaint was that staff officers had very little idea about the practicalities of infantry officer work. John Hay Beith's fictionalised narrative introduced readers to the bad staff officer, the 'Hyde', prone to inflicting arduous and unreasonable tasks on his subordinates, or interfering in the appropriate conduct of affairs.[11] Beith's more experienced protagonists know how to deal with such an encumbrance. Recognising that a staff colonel's orders were totally impracticable, Captain Blaikie instructs his young subalterns in the art of 'managing' staff officers: 'When given an impossible job by a Brass Hat, salute smartly, turn about, and go and wait round a corner for five minutes. Then come back and do the job in a proper manner.'[12] Leslie Peppiatt's diary entry for 19 March 1918 suggests that the potential problem of impossible or unfeasible tasking persisted for most of the war:

> A rather amusing order came round this afternoon to the effect that men who had been in strong gas should change their clothing before going into dugouts. What a splendid idea – but where will one obtain the change? Perhaps they will have a quantity of spare clothing handed over as trench stores on each relief – or possibly Atkins will have to hump a spare suit up to the trenches with him. Truly the mind of the Staff Officer is fearfully and wonderfully made![13]

The overall impression might be that staff officers were nuisances whose follies were only barely tolerated. These accusations became rather more biting when relating specifically to trench work, given the location's totemic importance and the apparent reluctance of staff officers to hazard themselves in it. As Andrew Buxton commented bitterly, 'It is inexplicable to me how Staff jobs are given to men with no trench experience. The absence of that experience is continuously obvious.'[14]

On closer inspection, however, attitudes within the officer corps towards the staff are rather richer and more varied. Staff officers faced a perennial difficulty – that their failures were always more apparent than their numerous quiet successes – but their efforts did not pass entirely unnoticed. Beith himself was careful to balance his denunciation of the 'Hyde' with a tribute to 'Brass Hat Jekyll – officer and gentleman; and, to the eternal credit of the British Army, be it said that he abounds in this well-conducted campaign.'[15] Although voiced by a fictional character in a relatively early phase of the war, such an appreciation for the efforts of the staff was not confined to the pages of literature, and many officers appreciated that valuable work was usually done extremely efficiently. Looking back in late 1918 on nearly eight months' service in France, Peppiatt's reservations did not prevent him from expressing admiration for the staff's performance overall: 'Often there seems to be an insufficient cohesion between the general staff and administrative staff work, frequently orders are given which are all but impossible to carry out solely for the reason that those who issue them are not sufficiently in touch with the actual situation on the spot; often it seems that comfortable jobs and praise and reward go one way whilst discomfort and danger go the other; many seem to be following after favour and personal advancement rather than the general good – but in spite of all, and above all, one is very deeply impressed with the wonderful smoothness with which on the whole the gigantic machinery works. Especially is this so in the present advance when guns and ammunition, supplies and equipment have followed on as fast as the troops could move.'[16]

Usually, as with Peppiatt, it was only on reflection that officers realised the staff deserved congratulation. Only rarely might an officer offer an immediate comment on an impressive feat accomplished. Beith does provide one such example, possibly rooted in his own direct experience:

> The main body travelled here by one route, the transport, horses, and other details by another. The main body duly landed, and were conveyed to the rendezvous – a distant railway junction in Northern France. There they sat down to await the arrival of the train containing the other party; which had left England many hours before them, had landed at a different port, and had not been seen or heard of since.

> They had to wait exactly ten minutes!

> "Some Staff – what?" as the Adjutant observed, as the train lumbered into view.[17]

It is, perhaps, telling that these words should be put into the mouth of the adjutant, the battalion's senior administrator and perhaps, therefore, the most finely attuned to the nature of the challenges which had been overcome to deliver this feat of logistics. As Chapter 3 has noted, however, all officers had to learn the art of administration to some extent to fulfil their everyday platoon and company duties. Many found themselves filling adjutant appointments with little prior experience or on a temporary basis between periods of platoon or company command. It was this steady growth of military knowledge and administrative experience which made it impossible for junior officers to adopt the sort of universally baleful attitude towards the staff which is the staple of modern caricature.

In so far as it is possible to generalise, attitudes were influenced by degrees of seniority and the size of formations to which staff officers were attached. It appears as though the absolute summits of the military hierarchy were as far from the thoughts of most junior officers as they were from privates. Arthur Behrend thought that most generals were essentially remote figures, and that this shielded them to some extent from criticism. His only real impression of his Commander-in-Chief was that Sir Douglas Haig looked smart and soldierly on his horse, and gave the impression of being a competent general.[18] His experience with a commander somewhat more closely connected to him suggests that, individually, senior generals could acquire reputations for particular qualities and skills. Behrend reported that General Sir Herbert Plumer had a good reputation for looking after the men under his command in the Second Army and was therefore generally considered to be a good leader. He particularly praised Plumer's conduct of the Battle of Messines, in which he participated.[19]

Writing long after the event, Behrend suggests that high-ranking officers were seldom subjects of informed debates and criticism. Comments about senior generals are certainly rare in the writings of junior officers and, moreover, were almost certainly subject to the usual standardisation of expression. Douglas Gillespie suggests that statements made by officers concerning superiors should not necessarily be taken at face value, the soldiers' culture having thrown up a particular mode of discourse with which to discuss very senior officers:

> Here, of course, we talk of our generals as small boys do of their schoolmasters. They may be secretly respected or admired, but, to hear us talk, you would suppose

they were all nervous, excitable old gentlemen, doddering with age, hopelessly incompetent, and utterly ignorant of what a trench looks like, and even of the way to fire a rifle. All of which is not perhaps strictly true.[20]

Moreover, it was well understood that many of the various miseries inflicted on the infantry were nothing to do with the senior commanders but almost entirely the fault of lower-level staff officers. Graham Greenwell, though critical of the staff, appreciated that there was a big difference between the overall direction of the Army and the implementing of everyday administrative tasks:

Fortunately they get the right men now in command, which makes a lot of difference and they are now constantly sending people home. But it's among the lower grades that we lack the qualities so much in evidence on the German side.[21]

On the whole, generals within the more rarefied echelons of the army were too far removed to provide a satisfactory or effective focus for resentment or anger. Alan Hanbury-Sparrow, his division 'shattered', may have felt a 'dull fury … against Gough and the gilded staff of the Fifth Army ' but found himself unsure when confronted with the figure of Haig:

Yet such was the power of Sir Douglas's demeanour that as your eyes followed him round the three-sided square of the division you began to have doubts of the rightness of your judgment about his general. But when you looked at the depleted battalions and thought how all these lives had been fruitlessly lost, your mood changed again. You didn't know what to think. You wobbled, mistrustful of Gough and mistrustful of your own judgment.[22]

These beings operated on a different plane, one which could not easily be comprehended by more junior officers with more parochial concerns.

Moving down the pecking order, the attitudes of junior and field officers towards the Staff seem fairly consistently divided, with brigade staffs on one side and corps or army staffs on the other. Divisional staffs occupy an uncomfortable middle-ground, but were often placed beyond the pale with the higher formations. Staff officers from the more senior headquarters were frequently the epitome of faceless *apparatchiks* as far as the trench soldier was concerned, as remote and unknowable as the most senior generals. Infantry officers (particularly junior ones) had little contact with them, did not understand their ways or their work and were unlikely to appreciate their contribution very much. The charges against them can be placed into two groups. First, they might be considered to be selfishly concerned with their own comfort and safety, ignoring the hardships of life in the line. Desmond Young noted how Colonel Feilding did not hesitate to take guilty parties to task:

Lille, however, was much too comfortable for the common soldiery. We continued our march through the city and out the other side into slums, while the divisional and corps staff moved in to enjoy the amenities, including Leslie Henson's revue. Colonel Feilding did not approve of this treatment of the fighting troops. Dining at

Corps H.Q., he was offered a whisky and soda on arrival. 'But you have no whisky,' said he. 'Oh, yes, Colonel,' replied the unwary A.D.C., 'we have plenty.' 'You must be mistaken,' said Colonel Feilding. 'You cannot have. The fighting troops have had none for the last fortnight or more.' As he then tackled the Corps Commander himself, the atmosphere at the dinner table became icy.[23]

Secondly, it was these higher formations which tended to commit the sorts of offences lamented by Peppiatt and Buxton – those of adding to the infantryman's burden with schemes seemingly divorced from realities on the ground. This professional incompatibility was a source of much frustration to junior officers. For most of them, the intrusion of the higher formations was probably an immutable and unfathomable feature of military life. Experiencing their (sometimes unwelcome) commands through the filter of more proximate staffs, particularly brigade headquarters, they can have had little understanding of either the structures or the strategic perspective of a corps or army headquarters. Even those who did know them better might be unimpressed. Guy Chapman was able to base his critique on personal experience within a Corps headquarters. He argued that these 'monstrous tumours swelling with supernumerary officers and self-importance' had outgrown their useful establishments and become much too insular, blaming the rotation of units between different corps or armies: 'A Corps staff which had been well dug-in for a year on a quiet front, resembled nothing so much as the menial hierarchy of a ducal palace – with the duke away.' Since they never developed a close relationship with the formations under their command, 'they had come to regard them as persons to be employed but not encouraged.'[24]

Divisional staff officers have frequently been ranked alongside their much-criticised colleagues in corps or army headquarters. Douglas Bell's experience in October 1915 provides evidence for the accusation that they were remote and resented. His brigade had just come through a difficult operation and Bell, who had just returned from spending a few months in England, was shocked on rejoining his battalion to find them exhausted and the number of their officers significantly reduced. Taking command of what remained of one company, he was immediately pitched into detailed planning for another assault. Amidst the work of reorganisation and ongoing trench duties, he was overwhelmed by the quantity of detailed orders emanating from the staff. More seriously, he thought that the plans were almost certainly going to lead to the failure of the operation, given his experience of the tactical realities. Bell raised the matter with his CO, to no avail. He was informed that the orders had come down from the divisional headquarters. Bell noted in his diary that such matters should have been left to either the battalion or brigade commander who understood the conditions, unlike (as he saw it) the staff in the higher formation. He later reported that the operation, in which he himself was wounded, had failed entirely.[25]

Divisional staffs were not, however, so far removed from battalions as to make good relations impossible. Guy Chapman (perhaps because he spent quite a lot of time serving on the staff) was sufficiently well-disposed towards them to defend them alongside their colleagues at brigade level:

It is unfair to make fun of brigade and divisional staffs, of all those sorely-tried and overworked officers, who, from having been happy thoughtless subalterns and company commanders, were suddenly thrust by the fortune of war into positions where they were called upon to perform superhuman feats of imagination and tact, of rapid thinking and quick acting ...[26]

Field officers without his experience may not have shared this view, but divisional staffs were probably the lowest headquarters formation which still received widespread opprobrium.

Brigade staffs were an entirely different proposition, not least because they were much more directly concerned with an infantry unit's daily business. Brigade staff officers themselves had much closer associations with front-line infantry battalions than more senior staff-officers. Many had recently been promoted from within the ranks of a battalion and personal contact was much more frequent. These staff officers certainly knew what front-line conditions were like.[27] Erstwhile colleagues in the battalions were well aware of this, as they saw them on a regular basis or had served alongside them. As Gordon Corrigan notes, a better acquaintance with brigade staff officers dissipated antipathies which were often artificial in any case.[28] The knowledge that these staff officers probably had what the infantryman would regard as real familiarity with fighting was extremely important in developing confidence. As Charles May commented, 'Thank heaven that some of our Staff know from personal experience what it is like to have hot iron flying about their ears.'[29] Chapman, describing his first posting to the brigade staff, wrote in his memoir that: 'Both the general and the brigade major came from the same battalion of the H.L.I., and had served through the Retreat and First Ypres together. They were of that superb type, the best kind of regimental officers, devoid of personal ambition. They knew all the miseries which can afflict men in the field.'[30]

The closeness of this contact may have influenced the many officers who were attracted to jobs in brigade headquarters. In the climate of quick promotions and in the context of rapidly-developing professionalism and careerism, a job of this sort was both achievable and desirable. The life of a staff officer at brigade level was undoubtedly often both difficult and dangerous.[31] It is possible that this had its own attractions for officers who might otherwise have felt guilty about finding a soft billet away from their fighting troops. Moreover, brigade service seemed to some to be definitely preferable to service with higher formations. Guy Chapman certainly had clear views on the subject. The future Prime Minister Anthony Eden seems to have shared these opinions. Writing after the war about his desire to get a job on the staff, he noted that the appointment of brigade major always seemed particularly attractive to him, as it compared favourably both to the work of an adjutant and life in the more senior levels of the command hierarchy. He argued that a brigade headquarters was sufficiently large to give officers satisfying professional opportunities, but was not so remote from the fighting units that it became out of touch.[32] Walter Guinness took a similar view despite working alongside the irascible Brigadier-General Hugh Keppel Bethell. He too highlighted the fact that no staff officer from higher than a brigade headquarters ever seemed to be seen in the vicinity of the front line, his comments suggesting that an ability to stay in touch with the fighting troops was valued amongst officers who were presumably mindful of the presentational risks they were running in accepting any form of service away from the front lines.[33]

The brigade commander himself similarly benefited from the fact that a brigade (comprising four battalions until the winter of 1917-18, at which time it was reduced to three) was sufficiently small for him to be relatively well known and to take a close interest in his sections of the line. As Peter Simkins has noted, brigadier-generals typically had to live and operate in close proximity to the soldiers under their command, working closely with their subordinates. They were frequently to be found in and even beyond the trenches. Modern prejudices against châteaux generals are further disproved by the number of decorations received by brigadier-generals (and, for that matter, brigade majors and staff captains) for bravery. Their jobs entailed a high degree of paternalistic care, especially when out of the line. Moreover, many would have been battalion commanders only a short time before and still only had the substantive rank of regimental officers. They knew what it meant to soldier in the line.[34] Clearly they were not an uncommon sight, even if this did not make them significantly less remote and imposing to the average private.

Brigadier-generals might therefore be judged much more on their merits and, thanks to these different factors, be a relatively popular figure within the constellation of 'red tabs'. By appearing under fire or in the lines they secured their standing in the eyes of subordinates. Charles May was particularly impressed, both by the meeting and by the new brigadier's reputation:

> The new Brigadier was round this morning and I was introduced to him. He is a topping chap, a soldier both in appearance and being and one feels glad to have him in command at very first sight. 'C' Company tell a tale about him which even though malicious joy is apparent in the telling, is nevertheless quite true. I should hesitate to say that the C.O. has wind up. Certainly however he is extremely cautious. At 69 Street, which is sniped occasionally, he said to the General, "I do not think I should go down there, sir. It is dangerous." "Oh," said the General, "well there is no need for us all to go. You stay here if you will, but I want to go and see the men."[35]

Although episodes of this kind endeared brigade commanders to their men, they sometimes proved fatal. The expressions of sorrow in the letters of men like Captain Arthur Gibbs reinforce the impression that a close bond might form between the officers of a brigade staff and their subordinates in the battalions:

> We had a great loss a little time back, our Brigadier was killed. He was a splendid man and everyone liked him immensely. He was a very good looking man with white hair, which he had had since he was about 30. When he was about my age he had grey hair and was known as Pa, a name which stuck to him ever since. He was very popular among the men too. He was round the trenches nearly every day and was certainly not one of these behind-the-liner red-tabs, whom everyone hates so out here. He was always immaculately dressed and wonderfully clean, even in the front-line trenches. He usually had on lemon gloves, a shining belt, beautifully cut breeches with white strappings – he was the admiration of all.[36]

Born in 1895, Arthur Gibbs was educated at Eton and Oxford. He served with the
Welsh Guards, winning the MC and surviving the war. (Imperial War Museum)

This did not, of course, mean that brigadier-generals or their staff officers were
universally popular. Even when there was no personal animus or disdain (as there
certainly could have been, not least judging by inter-officer relations in other parts of
the hierarchy), friction might be created when independently-minded officers thought
themselves pestered by the higher formations. Corps and, to a lesser extent, divisional
headquarters may have been the source of frustratingly irrelevant directions but it was
those headquarters more intimately associated with the work of a company which
might really intrude into the business of the junior officer. Greater understanding and
respect there might be, but a brigade HQ was also potentially more of a nuisance as
well, especially if located nearby. It was this proximity which prompted Dudley-Ward
to complain about the section of line he held in July 1916: 'I dislike this line immensely.
Everyone lives too close – the battalion staff, the Brigade, all those sort of people are
practically next door and they send for you and ask questions!'[37]

However, even when criticisms are levelled against them, the complainant often
seems to be making general accusations about a *type* rather than an individual with
whom he is well acquainted. *Other units* were encumbered with bad staff officers rather
than one's own. This appears to be another subject area which developed its own mode
of generalised discourse. Charles May, for example, criticised the selection of young staff
officers, deciding that nepotism, a public-school education and an ingratiating manner
appeared to be the chief essentials. He was, however, anxious to point out that this
was not the case in his own brigade: 'I speak generally, of course. Our own Brigade
is a pleasurable exception to the above, the Brigadier, Major and Staff Captain are all
topping officers, radiating authority and knowing their job, but there are hundreds of

others less fortunate than we are'.[38] This kind of praise for usually reviled staff officers, although seldom heard in modern popular representations, chimes with broader historiographical developments. Richard Holmes, calling for the rehabilitation of the staff officer's reputation, has praised their bravery and dedication and argued that, if they were not always as competent as they should have been, they did at least appreciate the importance of doing a good job and understand the circumstances in which their colleagues were fighting.[39] Junior officers certainly did not condemn them out of hand.

Similar factors governed the relationship between fighting officers and their colleagues in other arms, especially the non-combatant ones. The degree to which an officer who was not serving in a fighting unit could be accepted as an equal (assuming he was not already an acquaintance) depended largely on the degree of separation from the danger zone and the degree to which they helped or hindered the daily existence of the soldiers. Engineers enjoyed a somewhat ambivalent relationship with the infantry. On the one hand, sappers were responsible for many of the arduous tasks with which the infantry were saddled, both in and out of the trenches. Moreover, officers like James Neville clearly regarded them more as rear-echelon shirkers than fellow trench warriors. Relating a tale of a lucky escape from a shell burst in December 1917, he spoke of his 'amazement at seeing Sappers in the front line, let alone going to do a job of work in No Man's Land ... My escape was almost as miraculous as the sight of a Sapper wiring party!'[40] (His comments are not entirely defused by a sense that the rhetorical flourish potentially indicates mere teasing.) Despite Neville's scorn, however, and as this extract indicates, Royal Engineers were frequently in dangerous situations and shared many of the same hardships as the infantry. Charles Douie's memoir suggests that, whatever may have been said, there was a degree of understanding between the two groups:

> In public the infantry reviled the sappers day and night; in private they extended an admiration, no greater than was due, to a body of men who never enjoyed a period of even nominal 'rest' out of the line, who endured many of the dangers and discomforts of the infantryman's life, yet were denied the occasional moment of exultation which was his compensation and reward.[41]

It is much rarer to encounter sympathetic comments or recollections relating to those personnel who worked mainly in the rear areas. Officers working in logistical and supply capacities, for example with the Army Service Corps (ASC), are most frequently mentioned in letters or diaries when they have in some way exasperated the infantryman. Captain Arthur Gibbs was marching with his company down 'one of those long, straight roads with very chalky dust on it': 'Several absolute beasts of ASC officers came tearing along in their motors and raising an enormous cloud of dust. I spent a lot of my time stopping them and cursing them like anything. I told them that we had already marched 16 miles, and had another 10 to do, and if they couldn't use a little more consideration, they were hardly fit to be called officers, and certainly not gentlemen. I really was angry. One hates the ASC at nearly all times, the more especially when one is slogging down a dusty road, and they pass in rather a nice Vauxhall or Sunbeam.'[42]

Such apparent thoughtlessness and inconsiderate behaviour was always going to raise hackles. As with staff officers, the relatively mundane could be taken as evidence of more general failings. Dislike of these non-combatants seems to have cultivated a sense of superiority in some officers. 2nd Lt. Alistair Milligan sneered at the 'soft time' being had by ASC officers and explained to his mother how unfitted one had proved when posted to his company: 'he growsed straight on for a fortnight and then went sick and home. He was well off too as he had a bed practically every night, as we were never near the trenches. Some lads!'[43] It is ironic that officers like Milligan should have regarded ASC officers as inherently incapable, while still lamenting their failure to match his own contribution. Such remarks seem to reflect a sense of tribal solidarity rather than a balanced assessment. Even a posting to rear echelon elements prompted little diminution of antipathy. When Rod Swayne was sent to a Railway Company he complained that they were having too easy a time: 'We do ourselves very well here & have pate de foie gras as savoury; a nice fire & a good shed. It gives you an insight into what a cushy time the [Line of Communication] troops have, as the ASC & RE Railway Troops are better off still. It makes me wild to think that they get credit for being at war. No one on the L of C ought to dare to say he is on active service.'[44] As ever, trench fighters were sensitive to any suggestion that others could legitimately claim to be emulating their efforts and sacrifice.

A more serious charge levelled at these other trade groups was that they were deliberately ducking responsibilities which were being discharged by trench fighters at great personal cost. Milligans's brief acquaintance may be given the benefit of the doubt, unlike the ASC subaltern who made Robert Hamilton 'beastly sick' when he 'talked of dodging duty with gusto.'[45] Had Hamilton's acquaintance been in some way medically ineligible for the infantry like Paul Jones then that would potentially have cast him in a very different light. In the absence of any mitigating circumstances, however, his behaviour was always likely to provoke a reaction in a trench fighter. Such conduct was unacceptable to front-line soldiers, whether or not the offender belonged to an organisation like the ASC or an infantry unit, many of whose officers were seconded to (or actively sought, as discussed in Chapter 3) supposedly safe duties away from their regiments. Gibbs was amused by the revenge taken by a fellow officer on some of the most egregious shirkers late in the war:

> I wonder if you have heard of the list of Sturmtruppen which I am told is going the round of the Club in London now. I believe Crawley de Crespigny may have originated the idea. He got a list out for the Grenadiers. To be a member of the Sturmtruppens it is essential to have been in the Army since the beginning of the war, and never to have been in the trenches with one's regiment: in other words, to have a real soft job for the whole of the war …It has caused no ordinary flutter, I believe.[46]

Those who purposefully avoided the toughest duty were regularly censured. At the same time, this did not turn into a blanket condemnation of officers not employed on regimental duties. Clearly, being in a non-combatant job at any given time was not, in itself, a serious offence, although it might still attract some degree of opprobrium. Junior officers were themselves quite prepared to take – even to seek out – safer and more comfortable jobs at different stages in their careers. Many were therefore prepared to recognise the difference between the officer who had, in some way, done his bit and the one who had not. Judging by Gilbert Nobbs' description of the Railway Transport

Officer (RTO) – 'an individual who is prominent in the memory of all those of us who have passed up the line' – the distinction was usually obvious:

> There is the one who has earned his job at the Front by hard work. He has been through the thick of the fighting, and after months in the trenches has been sent back to act as RTO at the railhead or the base, to give him a well-earned rest beyond the sound of the guns. We have no unpleasant memories of him. He is a man; he is human; he treats you as a comrade; he is helpful and considerate. And you can spot such men in a moment.
>
> But RTO No.2 carries no sign on his features. He has never heard the sound of guns, and never intends to if he can help it. Look back upon the time when you left the base, and you find him prominent in your memory. When you are huddled up in your dug-out, how you wish he could be transferred to you for a tour of duty in the trenches.[47]

It is probably a disservice to many to suggest that only ex-trench fighters could deal efficiently and sympathetically with the needs of troops in transit. It is similarly difficult to know just how common it was for officers to think well of a colleague like an RTO. Efficient and helpful officers were less likely to attract comment, favourable or otherwise, while those who made mistakes were roundly criticised. Nevertheless, as when assessing members of the staff, junior officers were capable of distinguishing between 'Jekylls' and 'Hydes'.

What they could not always do was shake off the irritations caused by shared membership of a single system. Fighting men may have been in a very different line of work to RTOs, ASC officers or a host of others, but combatants and administrators were all members of the same military hierarchy and their comparative ranks were still a matter of interest and envy. Infantry officers were perhaps especially prone to resenting the career advancement and promotion available to men who were, in their view, failing to make as great a contribution to the war effort as them because they were not in a combat unit. In March 1917 Alistair Milligan complained to his mother: 'I don't know why Ronald is being made a Captain. He hasn't been in the ASC much longer than I have been in the Army and I am still plodding along as a 2nd Lt.'[48] The vagaries of promotion within a company or battalion were a source of much annoyance to officers throughout the war. Given Milligan's views, however, on the competence of ASC officers compared to the infantry (and his juxtaposition of 'the ASC' and 'the Army', as if the one were not properly a part of the other), this must have been a particularly bitter pill to swallow.

The officers of the army chaplaincy were officially non-combatants as well, but were clearly different from other types. Their specialised vocation separated them from the rest of the officer corps. While they did hold commissions, they were instructed to discourage officers and men from addressing them by any rank.[49] Their promotions could not be construed as coming at the expense of others. Many did spend significant amounts of time near the front line, although the military system sometimes prevented them from doing so, thereby undermining their ability to empathise and connect with the troops.[50]

Neither the dog-collar nor the lack of a weapon seems to have been particularly significant to junior officers. In the first instance, chaplains were simply another member of their own peer group. Lt. Clifford Platt was clearly pleased to learn that there was somebody else in the vicinity who had gone to his old college: 'the Brigade chaplain, we discovered, is a Corpus man, whom G.B. Smith knew, and of whom I had heard. It really is extraordinary how you run into people everywhere.'[51] Chaplains were not, after all, distinct from the generations which volunteered in 1914 and 1915. They were the relatives and friends of men who joined up to fight, and were subject to almost exactly the same imperatives to serve (and be seen to serve) as their peers. When Maurice Ponsonby applied to the Chaplain-General for a commission in November 1914 he was asked why he wanted it. He answered in a way which, apart from the explicitly religious elements, was probably indistinguishable from thousands of those applying for commissions: 'I don't like being thought a shirker; I might even get a white feather on my black coat. I don't like to think myself a shirker. I don't like being out of it in anything; I am fond of excitement. It is a fine chance of studying human nature. I should like to know more of myself, how I should behave when I am "up against it." It seems dreadful to be living in ease, safety and comfort when others are suffering so much. I should like to try to ease some of the sufferers. I should like to try to cheer the men on in their struggle by some message from God, and so perhaps do some service for my Master.'[52]

On a social level, chaplains might well be a welcome addition to an officer's circle of acquaintances, but it is harder to determine how beneficial they were on a professional or spiritual level. For some like Alan Hanbury-Sparrow, religion failed to supply the philosophical answers they craved: 'Instead it shirked the bombardment of intellect by rushing to the funk hole of Faith, from which periodically the chaplain's head would peep out to proclaim: "God moves in a mysterious way" or "His ways are inscrutable" – Truisms that blocked the way to Truths that both instinct and intellect urged were discoverable.'[53] Many other officers were unquestionably religious and frequently wrote in religious idioms. Personal faith could and did survive the Western Front, but attempts to link the teachings of the Church and the war aims of the military produced contradictions which some officers found uncomfortable. Douglas Gillespie complained that 'when a cleric says 'Please God, the Germans will take it in the neck,' he makes me wriggle in my chair, and feel uncomfortable all down my back'.[54]

Officers did not have to share Gillespie's apparent distaste for militaristic religion to take a negative view of the army's efforts to maintain religious standards. Charles Dudley-Ward seems to have regarded the chaplaincy simply as a nuisance: 'Our stupid parson has gone away with a fever and so we have not been plagued with a church parade today.'[55] John Nettleton was more charitable, but no more enthusiastic:

> It was here that a new padre joined us. We did not have a padre all the time; they came and went. I think I can remember four during the time I was with the RB. Most of them were not bad fellows in their way, but they all seemed to me entirely useless. I may be hopelessly prejudiced and they may have been of use to somebody. All I can say is that it didn't come to my attention.[56]

A few were more understanding, if not more willing to privilege the role of religion in military life. Christopher Stone noted that his new chaplain seemed 'a decent sort of fellow' but 'has yet to learn the discouraging fact that the army always moves on Sundays in preference to any other day of the week'.[57]

The officer corps contained numerous different tribes and gradations which shaped relations and moulded unit or cohort identities. In certain cases, the price of this group cohesion was the generation of antipathies between different ranks, trades or generations. Dramatic changes in the class composition of the officer corps over the course of the war produced further challenges to harmonious relations.[58] While it was not unknown for rankers to take commissions before the war, in 1913 these men made up only about two per cent of the total intake. Gary Sheffield argues that the creation of Kitchener's New Armies almost immediately began to broaden the social base of the officer corps and notes that, on demobilisation, over a third of officers were from working or lower middle class backgrounds.[59] By 1916 the War Office, recognising that a social gap would exist between those officers commissioned from public schools and those commissioned from the ranks with lower-class backgrounds, had instituted crash-courses in the social manners, outlook and attitude considered necessary and commensurate with command and traditional military ideals.[60]

Apparently socially-mixed officer candidates were able to train together comfortably enough. Gilbert Hall, who trained with the Artists Rifles Cadet Training Battalion in Romford in 1917, told interviewers that he recalled no tensions between men from different backgrounds when training.[61] Despite the best efforts of military educators, however, tensions still arose between officers from different backgrounds on active service. According to Victor Wallace Germains, writing in 1930 about the Kitchener Armies, 'there were many New Army officers and Territorial officers who, whilst brave men and capable leaders, could not reach to the social standards of the pre-war Regular officers.'[62] Many officers clearly resented the social dilution of their ranks. Some officers were content just to air their grievances in their correspondence. Captain Arthur Pick complained in July 1917 that 'Judging from the type of officer we are receiving now-a-days, anybody can get a commission, whether they have had a decent education or not'.[63] Lieutenant Geoffrey Holt, writing in January 1918, commented that 'It is very funny about Watson. Fancy his getting a commission. It is wonderful what they are descending to in these days.'[64] Others quarrelled as personalities clashed and class conflicts erupted. James Neville encountered 'a most temporary gentleman':

> He got on to the subject of Eton and started running down the traditions and dress, etc. I choked him off by saying that traditions make a school just as they make a regiment. He replied by making remarks about the 52nd's traditions which made my blood boil, and I fear I was rather rude. A man like that gives himself away badly, because he shows at once that he has not got the spirit of his regiment, or he would not run down another better than his own. Heaven help the Army if chaps of his kidney are going to be its officers of the future.[65]

The army could inculcate a certain attitude, but it couldn't entirely replicate years of class upbringing. Arguments like this, though relatively rare in primary sources, were presumably not uncommon. Episodes of this sort may not have been particularly significant, except that they reinforced in the minds of some public-school-educated officers doubts about the suitability of the latest additions to their ranks. Memoirs suggest that many never fully lost these prejudices. Charles Stormont Gibbs described an officer who joined from public school sixth form 'and carried the *Iliad* about with him. What a magnificent type of man compared with the officers we got later from secondary schools or from the ranks.'[66]

Strong and enduring class prejudices naturally also shaped relations between officers and their men. Although there were important variations and changes in the demographic composition of both the ranks and the officer corps during the course of the war, officer-man relations were essentially those of the upper and lower classes, especially in the earlier years. British officers, whatever their background, were expected to conform to standards of behaviour which were largely arbitrated by the upper classes while the British soldier, John Bourne suggests, 'was essentially the British working-man in uniform'.[67] Many officers had decided views about the qualities of the 'lower orders'. For example, Douglas Gillespie, writing in May 1915, seemed to credit his men with limited understanding: 'Most of them, I think, respect me enough to obey orders, but I don't think many of them like me, for many of them haven't been soldiering long enough to understand that an officer doesn't give punishment out of spite.'[68] He had himself only been in the army since September 1914 and on the Western Front since February 1915. Officers were also particularly prone to adopting a condescending tone when writing about their experiences censoring letters. Ralph Bickersteth described this activity as 'screamingly funny, but very boring after a bit. The men say very funny things indeed.'[69] Graham Greenwell performed this duty when acting as Orderly Officer: 'It is a weary job, but occasionally amusing, as you may imagine. Most of the men have been wounded or gassed and their efforts to spell the names of the scenes of their accidents are distinctly original.'[70]

Although sometimes giving rise to this sort of disparaging tone, continuity of social conventions actually helped both sides understand their roles. The social fabric of the trenches, Gerard DeGroot has argued, was as strong as the British social fabric which it mirrored and was reinforced by strong cultural notions about the characters and roles of officers.[71] Peter Parker has noted the importance of both sides satisfying long-standing expectations; soldiers required their officers to be gentlemen and to behave accordingly.[72] In addition to a certain bearing and style, this manifested itself most particularly in the officers' concern for their charges, which played a vital role in the maintenance of the British Army's fighting capabilities. This care is widely known as 'paternalism' (although Michael Roper advances an impressive argument that 'maternalism' would be a more appropriate description of their emotional and practical role, as well as a better characterisation of their power relative to a more distant command hierarchy).[73] Junior officers worked hard to ensure their men got their rations, were adequately accommodated and maintained adequate standards of hygiene, a focus on domesticity which underpins Roper's argument.[74] If these mundane duties are perhaps sometimes less evident in the writings of the officers themselves, the following extract from the war diary of Leslie Peppiatt provides some explanation: 'I am afraid I have said so much in my notes of what the Officers do and don't do (and incidentally what the Officers eat and drink) that I may have given the impression that the Officer's comfort is all important. Of course it isn't. I have said perhaps more about the Officers' lives than the Men's because my notes are more or less a personal diary and record of my own doings.'[75] The same is likely to be true for many chroniclers of the period. It does not mean these duties were insignificant to them on a daily basis.

The strong feelings which many officers developed for their charges derived from of this outlook, although they also reflected a romantic ideal of the relationship between leaders and led. Lionel Sotheby had a personal attachment to his platoon which made him reluctant to leave: 'I have no wish to be anything than a second Lieutenant out here – one is part of the men themselves then, and that is what I like.'[76] In addition to the daily duties and domesticities, officers frequently sought to do some acts of kindness to improve the lives of their men further. In the early stages of the war, when commissions and private wealth were more highly correlated, officers were often prepared to provide additional comforts for their men at their own expense (something many officers commissioned from 1916 onwards simply could not afford to do).[77] Some focused on practical requirements. One officer procured 150 pairs of socks from well-wishers in the UK, emphasising to his mother the importance of daily foot-care.[78]

Others wanted to bring some extra entertainment or cheer into their men's lives. Lt. Brian Lawrence distributed a bottle of port and one of brandy to each platoon in his Company at Christmas: 'strictly against all regulations, of course, but still I think it marked the occasion in a fitting manner, and did no harm.'[79] In 1915 Sam Paget and his fellow officers in D Company 8th (Service) Battalion, the Norfolk Regiment, exerted substantial efforts to arrange a Christmas party for the entire company. They procured sausages, plum puddings, cigars, cigarettes, turkeys and beer: 'all went well until Christmas eve when we were still 7 turkeys short. We were determined that there should be no hitch and so we bought half a pig. Needless to say the 7 tardy turkeys turned up on Christmas morning – however nothing daunted we turned our pig into the 2nd course.'[80] Paget also solicited the help of his family when he discovered while censoring letters that a man in his company asked his mother not to send any sort of Christmas parcel because he knew she could not afford it:

Can anything be done? Could you send a really good parcel to him – a plum pudding or a cake or something. His mother lives at 56 High House, Neatishead – I don't know if you would know anyone in that part of the world who would look up Mrs. Grimes at that address and see if they are really in a bad way. He is the most splendid boy and a thorough good Norfolk one – Perhaps Granny might like the job of sending him something.[81]

Brought up a Norfolk man himself, Paget clearly has a lot of affection for his men, revealed especially when he writes fondly about enjoying their distinctive accents or reading their particular idioms. He came from a wealthy family; his father was, at this time, the Bishop of Stepney, living at Sidestrand Hall, Cromer, and also keeping an address in London. Serving alongside members of a community with which he seems to have felt a great affinity appears to have stimulated Paget's paternalism. His efforts to enlist the help of his family suggest that they were likewise familiar with a role in supporting deserving locals.

Many other young men would not have had the benefit of such a clear transposition of familiar and evocative social models. It was nevertheless expected that a paternalistic attitude would come naturally to the products of the public schools. One of the criticisms made of 'temporary gentlemen' by traditionalists was that they would lack some of the necessary attributes which public-school-educated men were assumed to possess. Major R.T. Rees, a public-school master with a temporary commission, acknowledged that the new type of officer could learn his business eventually, but still regarded him as somewhat inferior. He complained that these new men were initially the cause of some anxiety, although it is unclear whether he meant this in an operational context or in the sense that their superiors did not believe they would have the right attributes. Certainly he thought they did not have the same qualities of leadership which he associated with the products of the public schools.[82]

That system – as a particular facet of Edwardian society more generally – certainly promulgated and reinforced many of the class conceptions which shaped officer-man relations, giving pupils a clear sense of their place in the order of things. They can also, however, be seen as providing useful preparation for the dramatic change in status which schoolboys experienced on joining the army. Gary Sheffield has suggested that sport – which was such a mainstay of a public-school education – played a key role in helping the ex-schoolboy 'to avoid stress caused by "role ambiguity" on joining his unit by helping the newcomer to make sense of that situation by relating it to a familiar experience. The young officer, faced by his platoon for the first time, was able to fall back on his experience in a sporting team.'[83] He was also able to benefit from the public-schoolboy's familiarity with power relationships. For decades the public schools had entrusted seniors with authority and responsibility, emulating the system devised by Thomas Arnold at Rugby. Had such a system not been in place, the Reverend Henry Cadwallader Adams argued in his 1878 book about Winchester College, it would effectively have developed of its own accord anyway:

> … whether boys may, or may not, be fit to be trusted with power, [nobody] can prevent power from being entrusted to them, and power, too, of a kind which it is not easy to resist or counteract. Look at the boys at any school. There will be some, whose bodily strength makes them the masters of the others. There will be some, whose keen wit, or daring spirit, enables them to lead the rest whithersoever they will. There will be some, whose good temper, skill in school-games, command of money, or the like, make them the idols of their schoolmates. All these things are power, real power, if that word means anything.[84]

Arnold's system was intended to curb these endemic, automatic and frequently deleterious power relationships which developed amongst pupils.[85] It was not uncontroversial, but it did make it highly likely that a public-schoolboy would have experienced a system in which authority was wielded by people remarkably similar to himself, and that he himself, had he stayed in the institution long enough, would have had quite real power some years before being commissioned into the armed forces. As a caveat, as Alec Waugh noted, many public-schoolboys never became prefects.[86] However, even those who never reached that exalted status had an easily understandable model with which to interpret the power structures found within infantry units.

In comparison to the senior military hierarchy or even the remaining officers of the regular army – the 'teachers' – volunteer officers, who had comparatively little experience, effectively represented the prefects. Alfred Pollard and Colonel Boyle provide a particularly clear illustration.[87] This was also a familiar contemporary literary allusion. As Peter Buitenhuis has noted, John Hay Beith's *The First Hundred Thousand* adopts a tone similar to Kipling's *Stalky & Co.*, apparently transplanting the public-school fiction genre into a wartime context in which various military personages assumed the mantles of headmasters or senior boys.[88] This was not a new development. Some Boer War poems cast officers in the role of idealised prefects.[89] Kipling's short story *The brushwood boy* (1898) describes a young subaltern likening a fresh private to a 'dazed and sulky junior of the upper school' and equating the colonel to his 'old Head in England'.[90]

First World War officers like Lancelot Spicer, a Rugbeian, can consequently be seen to have been on familiar ground, working in semi-autonomy beneath the power of the 'master' and responsible for soldiers who were apparently comparable (in their eyes) to a house of unruly boys. 'For the last fortnight we really have had a pretty easy time' he wrote in November 1915, 'but one can never have a real holiday here because one always has the men to look after, and they do take a lot of looking after. They really are such a helpless lot of babes!'[91] Leslie Peppiatt noted in his war diary that 'One does appreciate out here the Officer's part as a leader. Properly led by a man in whom they have confidence, these men I believe would go almost anywhere and do almost anything within the bounds of their ability – but with no leader they would I believe be like helpless children.'[92] References like this to the incapacity of the men in the ranks are common.[93] At the same time, however, the officer's sense of his own superiority was potentially an illusion when viewed by the keen eye of the professional. The prefect, after all, is not himself the finished article. The Etonian Billy Congreve, with the benefit of several years' pre-war service, could recognise the shortcomings and underlying immaturity of his less experienced wartime colleagues. To him, the new type of officer and NCO both were childlike in some respects, requiring particular cajoling and direction if they were not to lose their interest or motivation.[94]

Like prefects, the young officers can be seen as trying to maintain a mask of authority to distance themselves from their charges, whether they were really so dissimilar or not. Even if the new officers were less fully developed than they might have imagined, another element of the public-school experience which could benefit them was an understanding of the relationship between seniority and social intimacy. Douglas Bell temporarily served in the ranks of the London Rifle Brigade, a 'class corps'. On being promoted he remarked on both the importance and the difficulty of establishing a new rank persona with old acquaintances. Although celebrating with his former mess-mates, he took pains to point out that he was henceforth to be addressed by his proper title, not in any more casual or familiar fashion. His experience as a school prefect had provided a clear precedent. He understood that his new authority would be undermined by over-familiarity.[95]

In addition to rendering command roles more familiar, prefectorial experience could provide even more practical benefits. Whether in school or the army, different authorities had to avoid coming into conflict if their power was not to be diluted by clashes. Even the frequently rather tactless Edwin Vaughan realised at an early stage that he had to temper his use of authority and not undermine the position of any of his military colleagues who had different standards or methods. Shortly after joining Lieutenant Hatwell's company on active service he was taken aback by apparent ill-discipline amongst the NCOs. On one occasion he decided to challenge one of the sergeants about it, only to receive the response: '"Why, Sir! It's always done up here." I wanted to say "Well it won't be if I'm on parade," but it would have been subversive of Hatwell's authority so I had to let it pass.'[96] Senior schoolboys almost certainly had experience of moderating their use of authority so as not to clash with fellow prefects, head boys, or teachers, and could subsequently avoid problems when they became officers. Sam Paget was responsible for discipline when, in his final year at Winchester, he was the head of his boarding house. Senior prefects each had a younger boy, known as a 'writer', to perform certain chores for them. One such junior was found to have neglected the prefects' fire, presenting Paget with a dilemma:

> Now stokers used always till quite lately to be beaten for letting out the fire and in this case it had apparently occurred twice in one day. But I always think that offences which only cause inconvenience are so much less important than those which start from insubordination or worse … So when Macdonell asked me if he … should beat the boy I said No. He immediately jumped to the conclusion that it was 'favouritism' on my part – because not unnaturally my writer and I are very good friends & on terms of closer intimacy than is possible in the case of most juniors – and he subsequently gave my writer 150 Greek lines … entirely vindictive; … so I immediately by an 'ex cathedra' utterance commuted it to 100 Latin lines … it was difficult to do so without on the one hand convicting myself of biased judgment or on the other casting a slur upon Macdonell's justice – which must be applied in principle even though it is faulty in practice: or finally without giving my writer the idea that he is a sort of privileged person who cannot be punished without my intervening as a sort of 'deus ex machina' on his behalf: I told him pretty plainly that I should do the same for anybody under the circumstances! Needless to say it perforce caused no little unpleasantness.[97]

Probably unusually, Paget enjoyed sufficiently autocratic powers to have been able to act as he saw fit, but he still had to consider the consequences. In other words, young subalterns who had attended public schools and had similar experiences to Paget's did not need to make much of a transition in order to cope emotionally with their new roles as disciplinarians and leaders within a hierarchy which allowed them some autonomy, but only so much.

❧

While public schools could provide some subalterns with useful training for command roles, leadership remained a difficult and subtle challenge. Being an effective commander and leader required officers to demonstrate a special and largely unquantifiable set of skills across a range of competences. What worked for one personality might not work for another. The 'self-help' books which proliferated during the war could provide some answers. 'Always be particularly careful to avoid sarcasm in dealing with your subordinates' warned *A General's Letters To His Son*. 'A good telling off often does a man good, but sarcasm invariably leaves a bad taste in his mouth. Do everything in your power to check domineering and bullying, but at the same time be careful to uphold authority.'[98] Bullying was generally seen as the antithesis of the 'gentlemanly conduct' so prized within the officer corps, but more importantly the General identifies the difficult balancing act required of a new officer. Either excessive leniency or strictness could undermine his position.

Achieving an effective style of command was made harder by the lack of a proper grounding in the ways of the military. Officers had to learn the true nature of their authority and understand that the black and white contents of the rule book actually concealed a complicated spectrum of greys. It took a while for Douglas Wimberley to realise that it might be counterproductive to follow the military code punctiliously at all times: 'I remember on one occasion ordering Sergeant Souter to rub his feet in front of me, as by the letter of the law an officer was supposed to see the feet of all his command rubbed, with anti-frost bite grease every 24 hours – that annoyed him very much. I would never think of giving an order like that now, but young subalterns are often strict when they should stretch a point, and slack when they should be firm.'[99] The lesson was that the definition of undesirable behaviour could not be taken verbatim from King's Regulations, since many actions could be judged benign or harmful depending on the nature of the unit or the context. It is interesting that an ex-schoolboy should have been deficient in the matter of bending (or breaking) rules, apparently either being extremely conscientious or becoming over-awed by the prescripts of the military machine. He was probably also displaying a lack of that confidence in his own position which would develop over time. In Wimberley's case the ramifications were relatively mild. The importance of mundane issues like footcare should not be underestimated, but an officer's status gave him powers the use of which might have more much dramatic consequences. An inexperienced Guy Chapman and colleague were prepared to sentence a man to death for being drunk in the trenches, having not yet gained any understanding that they also had the power to show leniency. Although horrified at the prospect, they took their cues unquestioningly from the Manual of Military Law.[100]

Once they understood how the system worked, officers had to decide – potentially at an early stage, if they were not to lose the trust and respect of their men – how to position themselves relative to their men and the expectations of the military hierarchy with regards to discipline. Their tendency to develop strong bonds with their troops has already been noted. They witnessed the sufferings of the ordinary soldiers and it is not surprising that the reaction of many officers when faced with men on a charge should be pity. 'The whole of this morning I was sitting on a court-martial' wrote James Neville in August 1918. 'I loathe it; I feel so sorry for the poor devils accused.'[101] Faced with a system which could exact harsh penalties for even minor offences, many consequently rejected excessively rigid controls and defended their men from the impersonal military system.[102]

Many of those with life experience outside of educational institutions would naturally have recognised the importance of using judgement in such situations, and have had the opportunity to develop broadly applicable leadership or management skills before joining the army. Thousands more with public-school backgrounds had practical experience of performing exactly this judicial role, working within the bounds of the rules and what would be considered 'fair', and were therefore able to draw on this tradition in making their transition from civilian to officer. The dilemma faced by Sam Paget at Winchester College when dealing with the unfortunate stoker is a case in point, particular since the 'writer' in question had a particular link to him and, consequently, a claim on his paternalistic protection. The Etonian officer Lionel Sotheby was prepared to bend rules in a similar fashion to Paget, upholding principle whilst looking after the well-being of his men:

> McWilliams has just brought me a crime made out against 3 of my men, who put into town this afternoon & were accused of pocketing a bottle of wine. I am sorry for the men as to be confined in a train for 48 hours is no joke, and I am prepared to be lenient, as we are at the end of the journey. If we were going to have another long stop like this, I should make an example of them, to stop it occurring again, but as we shall be at the front in the morning, & as I know what it is for a man to start badly with a crime against him, I will let them off.[103]

In both cases it is significant that the person exercising their judgement was conscious of the likely impact of their actions within the community of which they were themselves members.

While novice army officers would have faced problems of this kind in any age, the work of First World War subalterns was further complicated by the wide variety of men that might be contained in their units. After August 1914 no officer, regular or volunteer, could safely assume that the soldiers under his command conformed to any expectations or stereotypes. The rush to the colours, haphazard expansion of the army and, as seen in Chapter 2, the voluntary enlistment of men who would more usually have become officers, had created platoons and battalions which were, on the whole, better educated than ever before. 'The British soldier of to-day impresses by virtue of his intelligence,' wrote J. Golder Burns, who served as a chaplain. 'You may speak to a stretcher-bearer and enquire what he does in civil life, and be told that he is a chartered accountant. In an officers' mess you may find waiting at table a banker and a solicitor.[104] One of Captain Charles May's sergeants, a 'distinctive character' who opted to enlist, was 'a Don of Balliol, a lecturer at the London Varsity': 'It is no doubt fine to think of but it is also "an economical waste" … Months ago I tried to get him to take a commission but he had views of his own and I doubt not but that he is as happy where he is. He talks French fluently and is already great friends with the villagers.'[105] From 1916 many more middle-class men were brought into the ranks by conscription. The Military Service Acts changed the relationship between the Other Ranks and the Army by bringing in men who might not otherwise have thought of serving. This led to a diminution of the voluntary spirit which had hitherto defined the army and increased emphasis on the idea that the war was work and an imposition. This placed the British officer in an unfamiliar position, unlike his German counterpart, for whom conscription was a well-established part of national life.

Opinion within the officer corps was divided over whether or not the characteristics of the volunteers made leadership at junior levels easier. It probably made it more important for officers to be aware of the different characteristics of different units, and to adjust their style of leadership and command accordingly. Charles Dudley-Ward was particularly struck in November 1915 by the contrast between the men of the newly-formed Welsh Guards and his former territorial colleagues in the 16th (County of London) Battalion (Queen's Westminster Rifles), recognising that he had needed to adapt to get the best out of them: 'I have learnt that one must be much harder with these men than with Territorials. They are not the hard soldiers of the old army and have not the conscientiousness of the better educated. The truth is that the 2nd Batt. of the Westminsters were very good. I noticed that the 1st was not nearly so tough last spring and now with this lot they are a rougher, stronger type but want a stricter discipline which would have seemed brutal with Territorials of the Westminster class. They are very quick to take advantage of kindness, mistaking it for weakness. Men are very interesting.'[106]

Overall, in so far as it is possible to generalise, most officers appear to have agreed with Dudley-Ward and appreciated the value of well-educated and intelligent recruits, especially once their energies were focused on a particular task. Unfortunately, it was not always a simple matter to turn them into what the army would regard as properly trained soldiers because the obedience which is such an essential part of the military system was alien to many of them.[107] Having volunteered to serve their country, they often responded badly to orders if they did not understand the point of them. The prevailing culture in a Kitchener battalion was potentially, therefore, very different to that found in a unit of the Edwardian army and might be inimical to attempts by any young officer, himself largely inexperienced, to inculcate other standards. Middle-class rankers were more inclined to complain about the officer-man relationship than their working-class counterparts, being frequently less easily convinced that soldiers should be deferential in return for a paternalistic style of leadership.

Charles Douie left Rugby 'before the due time' to take a temporary commission in the Dorsetshire Regiment. He concluded that the regular army subaltern had a far easier job than his New Army counterpart: 'The former came to a regiment of trained and disciplined soldiers, with high traditions. His authority was never open to question. He was supported by the experience of good non-commissioned officers; ... there were senior officers able at all times to advise ... The New Army subaltern was thrown much more on his own resources. His senior officers had often as little experience of war as himself; his non-commissioned officers were chosen at the shortest of notice by methods of trial and error. His men came from every walk of life, wholly without military traditions and frankly scornful of discipline. In so far as they had any respect for his personal qualities, they were amenable to his authority.'[108] Robert Hamilton found that he had a specific problem with a platoon whose members, having been educated together at Goldsmiths and trained under an officer who was himself an old Goldsmiths student, were not properly subordinated to military hierarchy and discipline. Though Hamilton was inclined to be dismissive of their education ('You know that cussed education that leaves them half stranded on decency's shore') he found that it was at odds with his attempts to command:

> I was introduced to a platoon of chaps who had got into the habit of running the war and damning the powers that be for inferior schemes of strategy and discipline. The sort of chap that says "discipline is absolutely necessary for success, but do they think we're damn fools enough to spend an hour each day polishing already clean bayonets?" So that, as I told you, I spent many weeks damning them, and snarled

at everybody, and told them collectively in so many words that they were the worst platoon I'd ever seen, and not a patch on the one I'd come from, who were small boys, and I hoped they weren't a sample of the rest of the battalion, and moreover I had no intention of associating myself with such a lot of untidy, dirty slackers, and if they couldn't make a pretence of looking like soldiers, I'd have the platoon split up among the battalion and wash them out entirely. This was a shock to them.[109]

Commanding soldiers who were more one's social and educational equals could clearly present a difficult challenge. Charles Jacomb, writing from the ranker's perspective, corroborated this by providing an insight into the mentality of an educated platoon:

These men by their very life have proved that they can and do conform to all rules of decency and good conduct, or otherwise how could they have supported their families? And to submit them to a system which in effect robs them of all feeling of self-respect or reliance, makes them labour without respite on useless and soul-deadening tasks, and compels them to kow-tow to men placed by accident above them – often men whom in civilian life they would probably not be able to employ in any useful capacity – is scarcely the best way to preserve the enthusiasm that caused them to volunteer.

He additionally commented that 'the sight of a man of thirty-five or forty, who in civilian life is the father of a large family, and perhaps either the owner of, or holding a responsible position in, an important business, being compelled most deferentially to salute a little whipper-snapper of a boy of perhaps eighteen or nineteen, who has no practical knowledge of the world, or any education to speak of, is simply laughable.'[110]

A public-school education did not necessarily provide the young officer with much preparation for this, since seniority in those institutions was largely defined by longevity, and this natural order was seldom if ever upset. The older man in the ranks was also less likely than an older but more junior officer to be mollified by a young officer's greater experience of trench fighting. An older but inexperienced officer was lagging professionally behind his younger initiated counterpart, who at least had a claim to seniority as a result. The older officer could hope to catch up once he had gained some experience, whereas the ranker might seem trapped in an immutable and unfair situation. As a source of grievance – mirroring the problems caused by age differentials within the officer corps, but with the differential in status transformed into a wide gulf – the inversion of the natural and culturally-sanctioned hierarchy must have been relatively widespread and would potentially have added substantially to the difficulty of moulding New Army or conscripted units. Those who came from more comfortable backgrounds were also more likely to resent officers' privileges, particularly if they themselves had been passed over for a commission.[111]

Robert Hamilton was able to use harsh treatment to galvanise his platoon, carefully modulating his behaviour towards them to provide encouragement and reward without relaxing the pressure on them to conform: 'I was able yesterday to compliment them on some traverses they were building and to unbend a bit, and after my previous sternness they got quite sunny. The first thing is to get them into a groove of doing things smartly and well, and without "intelligent" thinking of orders before they obey them; then I can attend to their souls, which, as you say, if it doesn't uplift theirs, it will mine.'[112] The transition from civilian to soldier was, of course, equally being undertaken by the men in this platoon, something Hamilton clearly recognised. He at least had the advantage of an education which was comparable to any of his men's. There was always the possibility, however, that a subaltern or captain might be in command of men who were *more* (rather than *as*) educated and intelligent than he was, especially as the war drew on and the army relaxed its attitudes towards the awarding of commissions. Educated rankers such as Jacomb were amused to discover the various shortcomings, as they perceived them, of their officers:

> The lectures, whilst being very tedious for the most part, were not altogether devoid of humour, and gave me the opportunity of noting down one or two rather amusing mispronunciations, which threw an interesting side light on the standard of education possessed by some of our superiors. For instance, I was utterly bewildered one day when an Officer made use of a word which he pronounced as 'făcsĭmīl,' and was convulsed with laughter when I realised, a moment or two later, that he had intended to say 'facsimile.' On another occasion the same Officer told us that a certain thing would be a most 'hēēnious' offence.[113]

This man was not necessarily any less competent than one who did not speak in this way, but men like Jacomb were clearly capable of showing the educated man's snobbery as well as his erudition. Judgement having been passed, it might take a long time to remove the negative impression. This applied to working-class men as much as enlisted members of the middle classes. The Other Ranks expected officers to behave in a certain way, and any tell-tale signs that a man was not entirely up to the standard laid by convention and class preconceptions could be damaging.

The change in the army's character post-1916 is not reflected strongly in the letters and diaries of junior officers, perhaps because they did not get much of a chance to experience the differences. In many cases the young officers of 1914-1915 were either progressing through their military careers, maybe taking staff posts or other jobs away from platoon and company work, or sadly had been killed or wounded. The shift to a conscript army did not, however, create a radically different dynamic. As Ilana Bet-El argues, the army saw the conscripts as unwilling: 'Unwillingness was a trait identified in schoolchildren – and it was in this way that the army treated the conscripts'; the rankers, however, saw the war as a job and only responded to aspects of military discipline which related to their fighting capabilities.[114] Although this seems to imply a significant shift, it should be remembered both that volunteers in the ranks were often regarded by officers as 'childish' and that military discipline could not be applied indiscriminately to them either, albeit for different reasons.

The techniques and characteristics required for successful junior leadership consequently remained relatively unchanged throughout the war. The Army's efforts to homogenise the subaltern product despite changes in the human raw materials helped, as did the fact that from 1916 most newly-commissioned officers had already served in the ranks, and therefore knew more about the character and condition of the men they were to command.[115] Officers could generally win the support and trust of their men if they were competent, while bravery could wipe out any number of social disadvantages. Conversely, those who did not live up to the standards of courageous leadership, gentlemanly deportment and paternalistic care expected by their men would be failures.[116] Many subalterns wanted to be liked; some had to learn that it was better to be respected, but both were valuable.

8

Sociability and its Significance

Victorian and Edwardian regiments provided their officers with a surrogate family, and it was vitally important that the members of these self-contained units could live and work together harmoniously. Socialising was consequently an integral part of pre-war military life. Over the course of the 19th Century the natural sociable energies of thousands of young officers were steadily channelled in ways which could enhance unit effectiveness and cohesion. The mess provided the focal point and became a repository of much regimental and battalion tradition. The importance attached by the Edwardian army to this establishment and the bonding process it provided was clearly reflected in Major Earle's 1914 report on commissioning NCOs which noted that 'the mess stands for much.'[1] Of course it was also important that good personal skills extended beyond the regimental family. In a system which relied for many routine decisions on the harmonious relations between commanders at all levels, such skills could make a vital contribution to the Army's operational capabilities.

During the war it was similarly important that officers should be able to cope with being constantly in each other's company. As Harold Mellersh noted, 'The members of this little community would be constantly close together, very much on top of one another and reacting upon one another, crudely so at times.'[2] The size and composition of that community could change frequently, the alterations depending on a unit's strength at any given time. This inevitably affected the group dynamic, and officers had their preferences accordingly. Some favoured smaller, more intimate company messes whilst others preferred battalion or regimental arrangements, recognising that in these larger groups there was less likelihood of friction.[3] Charles Dudley-Ward belonged to the latter camp:

> Men cannot live together in threes and fours, under trying conditions, without squabbling over trivialities. There is nothing in particular to talk about, no one to see from the outside world, no where to go to when you are up in the line, consequently if it is possible you should see as many people as you can. And it must be better for the officers of the whole battalion to meet than for the two or three in each company to coop themselves up.[4]

Whatever their size, different messes could adopt widely varying practices. The extent of that variation would not always be apparent to officers with no previous experience of Army institutions, but would be impressed on them in the event of a transfer. This was Bertram Medley's experience when he moved from a volunteer battalion to the Highland Light Infantry: 'The system of feeding is also wonderful ... whether we are in the trenches or not, we are sent up practically anything we can desire to eat or drink.' Clearly this particular regiment also had a very different attitude towards social activities: 'A great deal here is subordinated to the food question. In the [King's Own Scottish Borderers] we stood to arms at 9 o'clock and dined about 9.30: here we say to the Company-Sergeant-Major "Stand to", and in a lordly fashion continue our dinner.'[5]

The location of the mess and the availability of food and drink (which will be discussed in Chapter 9) played a vital part in determining the style and comfort which could be enjoyed, as did heritage and aspiration. Many traditionally-minded battalions managed to keep up appearances while on active service, placing greater emphasis on social practices than New Army equivalents. The more class-conscious units of the Territorial Army might also maintain highly formalised messing arrangements, attempting to substitute this ersatz class for a status which would always be denied them. This did not always go down well with less class-conscious officers, who regarded it as an unnecessary imposition. 'There was much etiquette observed in Mess' observed Thomas Pratt of the territorial 4th Duke of Wellington's Regiment, 'probably more than in a regular Battalion, as Territorials were always a little too anxious about their prestige.'[6] Jack Oughtred, serving with a territorial battalion of the East Yorkshire Regiment, was similarly vexed when a new CO tried to instigate a more formal regime: 'He has insisted on etiquette at Mess and all that pertains to it. If you remember that little book I once brought over on that subject some time ago you will know fully what I mean. The waiters to be dressed in white suits, wines served round every night and toasts drunk etc. One cannot rise from the table until he gives the sign or until the coffee has arrived. Rather like being at school again. When he speaks to you, one feels queer inside I guess you will comprenez what I mean. To quote someone else the CO is "it".'[7] It would be wrong, however, to ascribe the more demanding codes to conceit. Some officers were simply reflecting an ingrained sense of Edwardian propriety, believing that certain levels of hospitality befitted the dignity of their regiment or battalion. In this they were encouraged by self-help pamphlets, usually written by regulars in an effort to provide guidance to 'temporary gentlemen', which encouraged the preservation of practices which closely reflected Edwardian social mores.[8] Moreover, many officers had been brought up to believe that the status of gentleman carried with it various obligations, particularly in matters of protocol and hospitality.[9] A colleague of Charles Dudley-Ward's, inspired by 'thoughts of glorious peacetime soldiering', lobbied a mess meeting in December 1916 for 'beer, cigarettes, port wine, delicacies from Fortnum etc. His argument is that when a man comes in to the mess one should be able to offer him something whereas we have nothing.' There was, however, a price, as Dudley-Ward readily appreciated, noting in his journal that 'at other messes in our brigade where this sort of hospitality is dispensed the bill amounts to £30 a month and with us £40 a year.' The liberal officer 'half carried the day', causing Dudley-Ward to ponder both the likely increase in expense and also the likelihood of waste once practical considerations such as transport were brought to bear: 'A move will mean the sacrifice of all the port and stores we have.'[10] Whatever a unit's aspirations, logistics were always an important limiting factor. It is likely that practicalities of this sort, not to mention changes in the social composition of the officer corps and the declining influence of pre-war regulars, caused a general erosion in standards over the course of the war.

Such decisions about the running of mess affairs were typically taken by a committee headed by the mess president. By choosing to retain this arrangement, units would have helped preserve messing as an essentially communal activity despite the strains of modern warfare. This officer had to be sufficiently efficient to ensure the smooth running of mess business. In a highly class-conscious community, it was also important that he should be 'the right sort' and that he should not, in other words lower the tone or otherwise transgress against social standards. Where so mandated, the mess president was the arbiter of politeness, presiding over dinner, granting permission for early departures, and possessing authority over the admittance of guests.[11] With influence over company, budgets and arrangements, much depended on him. An uninterested officer could dramatically affect the quality of the fare. Graham Greenwell handed control over to another officer and was vexed by the change in arrangements: 'Since I gave up the Mess Presidency we have fed like Gadarene swine on ration beef and tinned fruit without alteration.'[12] For this reason some officers preferred to keep control themselves. Captain Edgar Matthews insisted on running his own company mess so that he could try 'to eke out an unpleasant existence by feeding on tinned asparagus, and turtle soup made from squares supplied by Harrods and Fortnum and Mason.'[13]

Alternative social venues could be found in the messes of other units. Officers typically placed a high value on hospitality and prided themselves, as Dudley-Ward's journal demonstrates, on the warmth of their welcome. This was the result of long-standing army custom as well as gentlemanly codes of behaviour. Before the war, some peripatetic staff officers had depended for their messing on being welcomed by nearby battalions.[14] In the inevitably rather disordered circumstances of active service it was common for officers to move between messes in a similar fashion. In some cases, long-standing connections between units could convey special privileges in one another's messes and these historical associations were often absorbed into the character of New Army units. Robert Graves heard of a regular major of the Royal Fusiliers ordering a drink in the mess of the 19th (Bantam) Battalion of the Royal Welch Fusiliers in order to test the historical associations between the two regiments dating back to the Peninsula War. Despite being a New Army battalion, the 19th had copied its regular counterparts by acknowledging that, thanks to an agreement following the Battle of Albuera, Royal Fusiliers and Royal Welch Fusiliers were honorary members of one another's messes in perpetuity.[15]

Other possible locations for relaxation and comfort were too numerous to detail. Associations such as the YMCA established hostels in France and Britain.[16] Soldiers on the Somme visited Amiens whilst those in the Salient went to Poperinghe.[17] Oliver Lyttelton and James Neville both described enjoying Paris leave.[18] Lancelot Spicer was delighted to go to Paris-Plage for a bathing holiday.[19] On leave in Britain, there were restaurants, hotels and the homes of family and friends. London was full of social venues, although its character was changed over the course of the war by increasing restrictions on opening hours and the consumption of spirits.[20]

An officer's choice of relaxation might be as varied as the settings in which this activity took place. Reading was one of the most common pastimes of the Great War, providing solace in even the toughest circumstances.[21] Harold Macmillan read Aeschylus's *Prometheus* while sheltering, wounded, in a shell-hole.[22] Books were requested from home and also supplied by organisations such as the YMCA.[23] Inevitably, as Lt. Arthur Preston White of the 1st Battalion Northamptonshire Regiment remarked, there were 'many objections to carting about a free library with one'. Given limited availability it was always likely that dog-eared volumes might circulate round an entire mess, but officers like White still thought it important 'to make some choice of a little book that will always

Reading could enable soldiers to escape briefly from the realities
of the Western Front. (Imperial War Museum Q 4370)

be fairly fresh and readable.' 'I've got a Shakespeare … and I always carry about a pocket edition of the Golden Treasury … Major Cantley has Marcus Aurelius's Meditations, the doctor has the Pickwick Papers. Chacun a son goût – what?'[24] Newspapers were also popular. White himself favoured *Punch*, *The Passing Show* and *London Opinion*. William Villiers requested *The Sketch* and *The Spectator*.[25] This seemingly common preference for weekly periodicals rather than daily newspapers was explained by Captain Leslie Holt: 'We get no time for reading the paper each day so that would keep us informed as to the doings at home.'[26]

Those who sought some sort of creative outlet could write or draw. British officers on the Western Front are almost synonymous with poetry, usually of a doomy and disillusioned kind. In reality, poetry was put to many different uses by men from various classes, so common was it as a mode of expression and a form of entertainment. Many of those who appear in this book seem either to have dabbled themselves or to have appreciated a good verse, whatever its source. In October 1915 Sam Paget sent home a poem written by one of his corporals 'on rumours emanating from our servants.'[27] There can be little doubt either that many officers approached their letters or diaries with serious literary intent as well as simply seeking to keep in touch with family and friends, a point borne out by the publication of so many memoirs and accounts of the war in subsequent years. There are also plentiful examples of sketches and drawings done by officers, seemingly just for the aesthetic pleasure provided.

Smoking was another common activity, fuelled by a rapid expansion in the habit in pre-war Britain, where tobacco consumption had increased fourfold since the turn

A sketch by Sam Paget, May 1917. (Private archive)

of the century.[28] The government recognised the importance to morale of the supply of cigarettes to the armed forces, introducing a new contracting system and inviting firms to tender for the supply to the military.[29] Firms such as Wills were soon producing large quantities of 'contract' cigarettes and tobaccos for the BEF. Soldiers were given a weekly issue of up to thirty cigarettes, many branded with colourful names like Trumpeter or 'Arf a Mo's', in addition to the more familiar (and more highly regarded) Player's or Woodbines.[30] Officers, like their men, could certainly be great smokers. At the time of his death in September 1916 Raymond Asquith was carrying a cigarette case (tortoiseshell, damaged), a leather cigar case, three cigars, a tobacco pouch, a pipe, and a further tin of cigars.[31] Officers were encouraged in their habits by a medical establishment which was not yet encumbered by a modern appreciation of the health implications and happy to promote the psychological benefits.[32]

Less solitary entertainments and diversions were also available. A Wykehamist wrote in 1916 that he managed 'to keep quite amused by going to the "Follies" the theatre got up by the 4th Divisional Staff which is excellent.'[33] Sam Paget's company contained a number of musical men and frequently staged concerts. Activities of this sort could take place in barns or other humble billets; on occasions when Paget's men took to the stage of the local 'Labour Hall' it did not always answer so well: 'the fact of the stage is in itself enough to chill the performance. It is much better if your singers simply stand up in their place!'[34] Paget was not above performing himself, apparently favouring the works of Gilbert & Sullivan. The musical setting clearly provided an opportunity to behave in a more familiar fashion with his men without feeling that he was undermining his status as an officer.

Various parlour games could usually be catered for. Useful for simply whiling away the hours, they could also provide distractions at difficult times. Xavier Marcel Boulestin, who served in the French army as an interpreter to the British forces before becoming a famous chef and restaurateur, told a friend that 'I have done nothing of any interest except playing bridge (and sticking to it) under heavy bombardment'.[35] Kennard Bliss, a forward observation officer in the Royal Field Artillery, preferred chess and wrote of playing 'in an interval between two of our frequent and exasperating bombardments.'[36] These pastimes were not, of course, the exclusive preserve of officers. In order to satisfy the incessant demand for playing cards, dominoes, draughts, and jigsaw puzzles, the War Library started a Games Department.[37] Many of these pastimes might have been essentially familiar to the soldiers of the Napoleonic Wars, but technology was considerably more advanced by 1914 and officers (then as now) used its latest forms on active service. By 1914 easily portable gramophones were available and many billets, dug-outs and messes were eventually equipped with one. Andrew Buxton of the Rifle Brigade recalled a 'rare good evening' in October 1916 'within 300 yards of the Bosch', his gramophone 'going well' having been brought up earlier with the rations by his quartermaster sergeant.[38] Significant numbers of records found their way to British forces abroad during the course of the war.[39] Gramophones became extremely popular with men such as Christopher Stone. The device provided the soundtrack to his letter writing in January 1917. He remarked that 'the gramophone is going as usual ... I can't think how we got on in the old days without one.' Admitting to 'voracious and catholic tastes', Stone – who eventually found fame as the founder and editor, with brother-in-law Compton Mackenzie, of *The Gramophone* magazine and as Britain's first radio

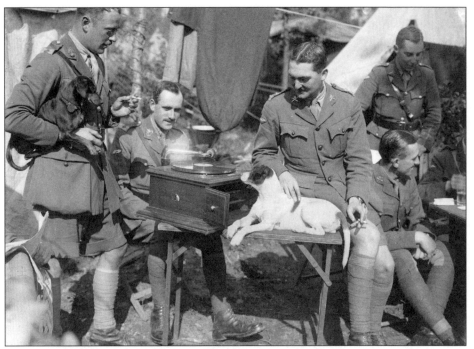

The gramophone was popular amongst British officers all over the Western Front. These tank officers are in a camp behind the lines at Poperinghe, September 1917. (Imperial War Museum Q 2897)

These artillery officers are using their gramophone in more primitive conditions outside their dug-out near Carnoy Valley, July 1916. (Imperial War Museum Q 4006)

disc-jockey in the 1920s – was clearly an aficionado but, as with reading material, 'we all have different tastes, the Colonel's running to waltzes and soft gentle things, Adams to baritone songs, the Doctor to banjo and ragtime'.[40] Presumably partly as a result, his battalion acquired an extensive record library:

> No one went on leave without bringing back records, we ordered a good many by post, and we never had the heart to get rid of any; but on the contrary we 'made' a large pile of rather indifferent ones which some other battalion had been forced to dump in a billet that we took over. The Decca was a serious addition to the load of the mess cart, but it was not long before we acquired a signalling pannier – in ordinary language a large clothes basket – which carried gramophone and records with discretion ...[41]

By bringing discs back with them from leave, officers could ensure that the latest material was available and could therefore share directly in the cultural life of the home front.[42] Over the course of the war, Peter Martland argues, servicemen came to prefer straight popular selections to patriotic numbers.[43] Market forces therefore inhibited the gramophone's use as a propaganda tool. For those on active service, however, music was not solely about entertainment; Nick Hiley argues that it played as important a role in the emotional and cultural lives of soldiers as it would have done had they been back at home.[44] The fact that it was literally the same music, more or less tracking the changing trends in the UK market, probably increased this resonance as well as providing an emotionally sustaining sense of continuity. Then as now, it may not have been without its pitfalls as a social instrument; Robert Graves witnessed the bad temper that could be caused by the conflicting tastes of senior officers.[45] Nevertheless music in all its forms clearly retained tremendous power to make officers feel more comfortable. Those who were themselves musical could find great solace in an opportunity to reconnect with their hobby, as Paget's enjoyment of company concerts demonstrated. 'I have found two pianos in different billets since we have been out,' wrote Malcolm Davidson, 'and they have been great reliefs.'[46] The importance of these continuities is perhaps most evident when officers have cause to lament the lack of them, as Davidson did several months later, having 'only touched a piano twice in the last 3 months.'[47]

Sport and physical exercise provided another important form of social relaxation and a further link to a pre-war civilian existence. *Troop Morale and Popular Culture*, John Fuller's study of the war and working-class culture, has stressed the role which officers played in promoting games amongst the rank and file.[48] Clearly they also enjoyed these activities themselves for their own sake. Many had been enthusiastic sportsmen at school and relished the opportunity to continue playing cricket, football and rugby. As with music, it could also provide an opportunity for officers to bond with their men, or at least show a lighter and perhaps more likeable side of their personality. 'Men love an officer who enters into their sports with them,' noted Major-General Pilcher in his published collection of *A General's Letters to His Son*.[49] Those who enjoyed riding were often able to take advantage of the availability of horses on the Western Front. 'I get a jolly good gallop round nearly everyday in billet on the captain's horse and occasionally a bit of jumping,' wrote Wilbert Spencer, 'but not much.'[50] The difficulty of enjoying any equine activity more elaborate than simple riding seems to have similarly affected James Neville, who complained at Cambrin in July 1917 that 'We have not had much opportunity of playing polo lately owing to this continual front-line work.'[51]

The number of officers who would have been interested in such pastimes almost certainly fell during the course of the war as the correlation between officer status and private means fell and more men were recruited from non-traditional backgrounds, but the link between officer status and luxurious living (of a sort) remained constant. Throughout the war officers on the Western Front were able to keep quite well supplied with food and drink purchased locally or transported from Britain, the cost of which was usually either covered by the officer himself or by parents anxious to promote his wellbeing. The often elaborate patterns of consumption, which will be discussed in more detail in Chapter 9, were valued in their own right for their gastronomic pleasures and the extent to which they made life on active service easier and more enjoyable.

Higher living standards were, however, only an adjunct to the real business of socialising. It was the ability to be sociable, rather than the circumstances of a mess, which bound officers together and enabled them to live more easily alongside one another. It also provided officers with an important element of continuity with their pre-war lives. Those who had been educated in the public-school system and grown up in genteel Edwardian society preserved, as best they could, customs and habits which they had enjoyed during peacetime. Although it is comparatively rare to find a series of wartime letters which stretch back into an officer's adolescence, those that are available (along with various published memoirs and autobiographies) often refer to the Edwardian public-schoolboy's habit of regularly dining and socialising with friends, colleagues and superiors. Sam Paget enjoyed a busy social life in his final summer at Winchester, calling on friends in other boarding houses in the manner of a true socialite:

> I am going to tea with John Lascelles and Ian Matheson – & it is always a nice compliment to be asked to tea in another house, and then to supper with Durell where I gather I shall again meet John Lascelles, who is a most charming person – always issuing sweeping invitations to come and stay – for Goodwood in July, for pheasants in October – hunting (in whatever month one does hunt in!) ...[52]

Things continued in a similar vein at university, where many undergraduates ran up heavy debts socialising. Gilbert Talbot, who had enjoyed a busy social life at Oxford University, explicitly connected the familiar atmosphere on certain occasions on active service with his life as a student: 'We hung the tent, which is open on three sides, with wild roses from the hedges, and discovered that we'd got some eggs, cherries, strawberries, and three bottles of champagne! We made an awful noise, and somehow it felt quite like Oxford.'[53] Those who had not been to university might find that the sociable nature of the officer corps made it a valuable educational substitute, an opportunity to negotiate the rites of passage and build the social networks which the war might otherwise have denied them.

On the Western Front opportunities presented themselves on a frequent basis for social activities which went beyond the ordinary habits of the mess. In October 1916 Greenwell commented that he was 'making use of my excellent billet to entertain every night', and that there were always 'eight or nine to dinner.' He noted that he was being joined by the CO, the adjutant and 'a great friend from the Bucks, Captain Reid.'[54] Convivial companions were always an essential ingredient. Fortunately, there was usually a ready supply. William Cairnes, commenting in 1900 on army society, noted that officers willingly welcomed strangers to their mess 'provided, that is to say, they are good fellows and what we English call "clubbable".'[55] This trait was the very essence of broader Edwardian upper-class social conditioning and lay at the heart of a system buttressed by various entry criteria designed to ensure that only 'the right sort' – those with the proper manners and background – were accepted within the circle to begin with. It was this elitism which prompted so many middle-class families to devote significant resources to obtaining a certain style of education for their children.

The social 'passport' which such a system provided was very real and very effective. Its physical manifestation was the 'old school tie.' Acknowledging that this symbol was often mocked by foreigners, Stuart Cloete pointed out that 'to the Englishman the tie seems a very good idea. By it you can recognize men who were at your school, or in your regiment, and if you do not actually know them you are still likely to have mutual friends.'[56] Equally, you knew that you shared various other points of reference, possibly also attitude and outlook. It was this confidence in the likelihood of compatibility which was important since it enabled young men constantly to enlarge their circle of acquaintances through chance meetings. Paget, for example, struck up a friendship with an Etonian cricketer when a member of the Winchester team in the summer of 1914:

We had great fun at the supper in Hall on Saturday night – the two XI's together: they certainly are an extraordinarily nice set of men and we made the best of friends: in fact I am probably going to stay with George Rawstone – the captain – next holidays: which ought to be great fun.[57]

Ex-public-school men on the Western Front needed no encouragement to act in a similar fashion. It is relatively rare for a diarist or letter-writer to mention meeting a disagreeable acquaintance from within the privileged circle (although this may reflect a sense of reserve or manners). Thanks to widespread 'clubbability', anybody with a claim to friendship could be welcomed almost unquestioningly. 'I suppose you don't know any amusing person in the neighbourhood of GHQ,' Edgar Matthews enquired of his friend Edward J. Dent, a Cambridge musicologist who maintained a regular correspondence with numerous acquaintances during the war; 'now that I am so close there I should like a little entertainment.'[58] While answering a chance inquiry about a lost dog in April 1916, Kennard Bliss made a pleasant discovery:

I happened to mention Madingly and he said "I suppose you were from Kings." I said "And you of course from Trinity." It turned out that he was Ryder, whom I remember by name as being a friend of my friends. … He was very charming and mannered in a most unmistakeable way – one of the Fletcher's crèche (a word he used of course) whose Bach was worse than their bite. It is quite delightful meeting one of those 'pleasant creatures' again.[59]

Ryder may not have been known personally to Bliss when they were at Cambridge, but this proved to be no barrier, especially given his possession of characteristics which so readily enabled Bliss to place him socially. Any pre-existing connection seems to have acted as – or held out the possibility of – a passport into an officer's social set. The added pressures of wartime placed further obligations on men to be welcoming to brother officers.

Thanks to the relatively cosmopolitan nature of the various educational institutions, social connections were not always limited to the British or Dominion armies. The ties between Geoffrey Dugdale and his Gallic colleagues were surely strengthened by a chance meeting with a French officer who, it transpired, had been at Christ Church, Oxford at exactly the same time that Dugdale had been at Hertford College.[60] For Arthur Pick, the French were almost synonymous with entertaining, even taking it to surprising lengths: 'It is said that a French staff officer visited one Company Hqrs dug-out one night, and found the German officers having dinner with them. The Germans were most annoyed when he refused to allow them to go back to their own lines, as it had become a habit with them.'[61] This episode is more surprising because Pick was writing in October 1916. Truces and fraternisation were not unknown throughout the war, but genuinely cordial relations between British and German combatants became more unusual over time. Janet Watson argues that it was the vestiges of the British professional soldiers' traditional respect for fellow soldiers which made the famous 1914 Christmas truce possible, something which would have been very largely eroded by 1916 because of the influx of volunteers and then conscripted men.[62] Either the old traditions survived in the French army or the Germans happened to find themselves opposite particularly sociable enemies in this case.

It was not just the combatants' attitudes to socialising with each other which was changed by the war. The unprecedented nature of the Western Front shaped the dynamics of wartime sociability in certain ways. First, it provided extra lubrication for the mechanics of socialising. As 2nd Lt. Bertram Medley found, 'one gets on well here with people one would never get on with in any other place.'[63] As has been seen in Chapter 6, there were still frictions and antagonisms, but these were potentially rarer than they might have been in other circumstances. Certainly some officers thought so.

Secondly, thanks to a dramatic increase in the size of the officer corps and the choices made in its selection, the war created an unusually large pool of possible acquaintances. In particular, once significant numbers of young officers began to arrive on the Western Front, existing social networks could effectively be transplanted in their entirety and it became increasingly possible to fall back on these rather than relying on the creation of newer ones. Fundamentally, this was beneficial. As Peter Parker notes, the presence of school-friends was certainly a comfort and it is extraordinary how frequently individuals ran into old friends they might not have seen since school.[64] The letters and diaries of the junior members of the officer corps overflow with references to meetings, especially if they had recently attended a major public school or university. Lionel Sotheby found that a wide circle of acquaintances had moved to France:

> Heaps of Etonians arriving ... Amongst the 60th Rifles I met Fowler awfully nice fellow whom I knew at Eton. He was at Well's. There was also Sherlock of Somerville's & Hordein of Churchill's also at Eton. Hordein I knew very well, we went through the school together, & I like him immensely. Last of all! But wait a minute. A draft of the Black Watch 56 men with McFarlane, Murdock, & Haldane as officers arrived. Haldane is a nephew of the Chancellor Lord Haldane & was a captain of the school at Eton being in college.[65]

Arthur Gibbs was similarly thankful to find the place 'swarming with Etonians who are my contemporaries, and I run against them everywhere.'[66] William Villiers described the community of Wykehamists he met as 'quite a colony'.[67] Gilbert Talbot, a fellow Wykehamist, kept in touch with his brother Neville and, through him, various other Oxford friends:

> I had managed to get a message to Neville, who I knew was just north, and after I had spent an abortive afternoon riding in search of him, the next day he rode over and had luncheon with us. He was well and fairly cheerful, and found a great many friends from Oxford and elsewhere in my Brigade: Billy Grenfell, Henry Bowlby, Geoffrey Colman and so on.[68]

Talbot's diary and the plaintive testimony of innumerable war memorials serve as reminders that many members of the same family saw service, often in relatively close proximity, further expanding an officer's social network. The effect of this transplanting, however, was not to limit sociability – a possible outcome that might be expected if it was made easier for individuals to satisfy their sociable impulses through contact with familiar faces – but to augment its affects. When two officers reconnected or forged a new friendship both tended to widen their social circle by co-opting that of the other, or at least acquiring a fresh set of potential acquaintances and contacts.

Schools and universities played an important role in assisting the creation and maintenance of social networks throughout the war, often through the practice of publishing special lists of alumni and old members serving in the armed forces. From an organisation's point of view, this was an act of pride and patriotism, and a way of demonstrating how successful it had been in instilling the 'correct' attitude towards national interests and foreign policy. For the serving officer, these lists served the extremely useful practical purpose of keeping Old Boys informed of the whereabouts and employment of their various acquaintances. Officers such as Villiers frequently wrote home requesting up-to-date lists. 'Please send the War Roll', he asked his mother in June 1916, 'as it will be so useful out here to see what Wykehamists are in units that I may come across.'[69] The correspondence of John 'Trant' Bramston, Winchester College housemaster and compiler of the Wykehamical War Service Roll, reveals the close interest serving officers took in such publications. Even before Trant's product was available, Alan Ferguson was writing to him requesting that he 'get Wells [the school bookshop] to send me one of the Wykehamist War Rolls when they come out.'[70] Officers wrote expressing thanks or supplying corrections or updates. Laurence Booth, who was commissioned into the Royal Field Artillery in 1912 shortly after leaving Winchester, wrote during the war to tell Trant that he had just received the Wykehamist War Service Roll two or three days before. He thought it 'very interesting and must have cost you an awful lot of trouble and now I am going to make more by saying that my Battery is the 110th and not the 69th. Hogg of College is 110th also.'[71] Periodically updated and reissued, these lists remained popular to the end of the war. Trant published a fifth edition of the Winchester War Roll in July 1918 and received a note of thanks in August 1918 from Frederic Luttman-Johnson, a captain in the 19th Hussars who had left the school the same year as Booth: 'I want to tell you how very much I, and all Wykehamists, appreciate and thank you for your work in getting this book out. It is the only way in which I can keep in touch with my many friends who are now so scattered.'[72] Whilst Wykehamical doings are well-documented, other institutions should not be ignored. In January 1916, Arthur Gibbs thanked his mother for forwarding the Brasenose College, Oxford list.[73]

Figures like Trant had strong personal reasons for providing this level of support to serving alumni. Trant himself was a housemaster, after whom one of Winchester's boarding houses is both named and nicknamed to this day and who maintained extensive correspondence with the young men he had known at the school. Institutionally, these establishments thrived on the concept of community. The 'old school tie' was physically an item of clothing but also a fortuitous linguistic accident, the ties between the individual, his fellow former pupils and the school (and university, although to a lesser extent) seen as carrying great significance. These community bonds underpinned the 'clubbability' of young officers and were reinforced during the war by the schools' other regular publications such as magazines. Writing his last letter in February 1917 2nd Lt. William Mills of the Royal Field Artillery described 'feeling very Wykehamical at the moment', his sentiments partly prompted by the arrival of the latest copy of *The Wykehamist* – 'rather a good one.' This feeling was compounded by an edition of *Land*

and Water which 'has two very good things mentioning the place, and describing it so well, it must have been written by a Wykehamist ... It made me quite home-sick to compare that lovely place with this – well, "abomination of desolation."'[74] Other officers were similarly drawn to their former haunts, clearly relishing both the companionship derived from the connection but also the contrast between former lives and the present. Arthur Pick, writing to his father in July 1918, was like Mills in using a school publication as a means of maintaining the links. He also highlighted the significance attached to the place: 'I should like the magazine from Worcester sent on please. I am very glad that I went down to see them all at the school when I was at home. It is almost four years now since I left, but to me it seems much longer.'[75]

There was a long history of celebrating this important sense of community and these ties by dining together. Any locality in which large numbers of public-school men had congregated would witness such entertainments. George Cecil, writing for the *Public School Magazine* in 1901 about the Annual Eton Dinner held in Simla, noted that the sizeable population of public-school men in India also gave the alumni of a range of different public schools similar chances to congregate and celebrate their *alma mater*.[76] Things were no different on the Western Front when there were many dinners of varying sizes, providing another engine for officer sociability.[77] Many of these events were small and 'informal'. Kenneth Evans reported to Trant that 'We had a small Old Wykehamist dinner in the summer, just a divisional show, 18 in number: it turned out to be a most cheery affair.'[78] Henry Dundas enjoyed 'a delightful Etonian dinner-party' in June 1917: 'J. Holmesdale and Ralph came, and the Brigadier was superb. Never have I met a better raconteur. His stories of Old Eton, 1880-1885, are perfect.'[79] The larger formal dinners provided officers with excellent opportunities to meet numerous friends and to socialise more widely with people who might not otherwise have crossed their paths during the war. These new contacts further expanded the range of their social activities. Invitations spread across the length of the British front. Dinners became increasingly grand. Lt. Rod Swayne of the 1st Battalion Wiltshire Regiment was involved in a dinner for 'OMs' (Old Marlburians) in January 1917 which was attended by '4 Major-Generals & one Brigadier with the VC + DSO among others. There were 68 people present ... We had the Divisional Band & a sing-song + speeches by the GOC Division who was an OM & acted as president.'[80] At the time, Swayne was quite proud that the 'OMs' had almost matched an Etonian tally of 70, an acknowledgement that – as in so many respects – that school was regarded as setting the standard. Certainly formal Etonian social activities, particularly the annual 4 June celebrations, were amongst some of the most stylish of the war. Arthur Gibbs looked forward to the 1917 event with keen anticipation:

> There is going to be a big dinner for Old Etonians, on the Fourth of June, in St. Omer, which we are going to. It ought to be splendid fun. Douglas Gordon, Davies and I are going. Our other Etonians, Bonn, Benson, Lisveral, are away on leave. We ought to meet a tremendous lot of friends. I think Cavan, the Corps Commander, is getting it up.[81]

Lt. Costas Blacker attended this function, where the 300 guests were seated according to the dates they had been at school, rather than by seniority.[82] This inversion of hierarchy clearly indicates which of the two organisations represented – Eton and the

Army – was deemed to have primacy! Blacker and Major Heathcoat-Amory report that the company became rather rowdy, and that all chairs and tables were smashed.[83]

Whatever their size, the various social activities and habits enjoyed by junior infantry officers were tremendously important throughout the period of their active service. In the first instance, a degree of continuity in social practices was extremely useful in facilitating the journey from the civilian world to the military. Moreover, while the 'clubbability' of the upper classes manifested itself in social activity, it seems clear that the two were part of a cycle, the one nourishing the other, and there can be no doubt that 'clubbability' eased the entry which thousands of young officers had to make into a group of potentially tight-knit strangers. Examining the factors which made Graham Greenwell well-disposed towards a new mess-mate, it is clear that he approached him primarily as a companion, rather than as a professional partner, and defined the relationship on the basis of social activity. He described the new man as 'a very welcome addition to the Mess' principally, it seems, because he 'knows a lot of people; also he has many of the same tastes as myself, including literature, in which he is very well read; he also appreciates good food keenly, which pleases me.'[84]

Following the initial period of integration, this continuity of Edwardian-style social activity went on supporting officers and sustaining their morale. John Fuller's central argument is that the export of working-class entertainments and cultures to France was of vital importance in maintaining the morale of the rank and file.[85] The same applies to their commanders. It was perfectly natural that these young men should enjoy the company of their peers and that this enjoyment should have made a significant contribution to their overall wellbeing. Some officers went so far as to suggest that it was the only thing that kept them going after a number of years' service. Henry Dundas joined the Scots Guards in September 1915 and was posted to France in February 1916 as soon as he was of age. By August 1917 he was thoroughly disillusioned and was 'rather coming round to the theory that the main object of life out here is to have as good a time as possible … one can amuse oneself trotting about and seeing one's friends with a certainty that no one can imagine one is an embusqué'.[86] The debate about morale is certainly more complex than that, but social activity made its contribution both in this and practical, professional areas. It could facilitate an officer's work, oil the wheels of command and reinforce his soldierly identity, combating the Western Front's threat to traditional concepts of soldiering.

The practical benefits should not be underestimated. Junior officers, lacking the benefits of experience or, in many cases, the depth of training available to pre-war regulars, needed to use all the skills at their disposal to operate effectively within the complicated hierarchies of the armed forces and the challenging environment of the Western Front. As Chapter 6 described, they had to find their niche alongside the various personalities within their company or battalion. Social skills could be an important determinant of success or failure. They could also be used to overcome barriers between junior and more senior members of the military hierarchy. William Villiers was clearly initially uncomfortable when, to his 'amazement', he found himself breakfasting with the brigadier in his chateau headquarters one morning, 'but he was very genial & I soon felt at ease & had a rattling good breakfast.' He was fortunate also to have a familiar figure present: 'The Bde Major was a Winchester master so that helped a lot.'[87]

Good inter-personal skills helped ensure the smooth running of relationships between the ranks within the officer corps, with social forms and hospitality setting the tone. It is not surprising (especially given his parentage) that, when offered a job at GHQ, Raymond Asquith discussed the matter with Brigadier-General John Charteris over lunch.[88] Some young officers from more privileged backgrounds were particularly well prepared for situations in which they might need to converse with Brigadiers and Generals, having been granted access to rarefied gatherings while still at school. Sam Paget, who was the senior scholar at Winchester College in his final year, moved in impressively elevated social circles when the Assizes were on, lunching with the Judges and their Marshals one afternoon and then dining with them and the college Warden a couple of days later.[89] The ability to be at ease in such company would stand an officer in good stead if he had to engage with superiors outside the comparative familiarity of the regimental mess.

On the battlefield, where the campaign was largely defined by trench stalemate, it could be similarly important to have an edge. By 1918 it was possible to achieve tactical success through co-ordinated use of the different weapons systems which the armed forces possessed. While this was eventually directed from the top down and became a part of the established military doctrine, inter-arm co-operation was also a matter of inter-personal relationships.[90] Through the creation of social links, junior infantry officers such as Paget could forge alliances which were directly useful to them in their work in the trenches. A 'great friendship' with the Forward Observing officers of the batteries to his rear, founded on shared messing arrangements, gave him the opportunity to influence the fire plan of the guns to his advantage: 'We have only to ask to get anything we like smashed up at any hour of the day or night.'[91] This technique could also operate effectively across national divides, facilitating liaison and co-operation.[92]

Sociability had other benefits. Historians such as Eric Leed have argued that trench warfare turned soldiers from active agents into passive victims of impersonal forces.[93] This idea will be discussed in much greater detail in subsequent chapters, but there is a brief comment to be made at this point in connection with the social habits of officers. An adherence to traditions of messing and dining, especially if all the customs of the regimental mess were maintained, could act as a powerful reminder and reinforcer of a soldierly identity. This point is closely associated with the debate around morale, which is Leed's principle focus, but it is more subtle than the suggestion, as made above by Dundas, that social activity could be an officer's main emotional prop. Despite the fact that the work of the infantry officer on the ground bore comparatively little resemblance to the work of his predecessors in the 19th Century, he was able to use the institutions and customs of the mess to locate himself within that same parade of honourable soldiers. This was most apparent at the more elaborate and formal end of the spectrum of military social activity. Harold Mellersh joined the 3rd Reserve Battalion of the East Lancashire Regiment in Portsmouth and was very impressed by the ceremony of the weekly Guest Night, which incorporated regimental traditions like taking snuff:

> On the table, between shining and immaculate glass fingerbowls, rested a long row of the first and second battalion's silver centre-pieces, elaborate affairs, gifts of retiring colonels, showing anything from a hunting scene to a bayonet infested and cannon-scarred battlefield.[94]

Fighting has never accounted for the majority of a soldier's time and was not the only sphere in which characteristically soldierly behaviour could be exhibited. Mellersh recognised that the Regular soldiers 'were clinging consciously to their customs'. Some would undoubtedly have derived some emotional benefit from this, although the extent to which this a significant factor in maintaining morale is unclear.

Similarly, it is difficult to know how genuine any wartime friendships may have been. A letter sent by Captain Charles Sorley of the 7th Battalion the Suffolk Regiment in July 1915 suggested that many were quite ephemeral: 'The existence is incredibly peaceful: till suddenly some officer whom one had known and not disliked – dies: one wonders; and forgets about him in a week'.[95] Similarly Henry Ogle, who survived the war, believed that, for the most part, sociability was essentially an affectation, and that officers were frightened of any but superficial friendships, affecting a brightness which did not fool anybody.'[96]

There is, however, evidence to suggest that friendships might be of real significance. Edwin Vaughan lamented that 'One of the most pathetic features of the war is this continual forming of real friendships which last a week or two, or even months, and are suddenly shattered for ever by death or division.'[97] Referring to non-commissioned soldiers, Joanna Bourke has argued that 'men on active service were rendered dependent upon each other for emotional as well as physical sustenance.'[98] Psychologists and historians of numerous conflicts would probably incline to the view that the friendships formed between men under these most difficult of circumstances were not casual. Bereavement might be a traumatic experience even if the dead man was only a relatively brief acquaintance. Since men lived and died in very close proximity, friendships were often more intense than they might have been during peace time. Veterans reminiscing about the comradeship of those days often cite 'the friendships of the firing line' as being one of the things they miss the most. Such associations, in the words of an anonymous officer, were 'simple and honest as the comradeship of schooldays, brief and splendid as the trail of a mid-night meteor.'[99] However, as Bourke argues, 'the same wholesale physical turmoil that yearned to be soothed also necessitated emotional hardening. Men could not get too close – and if they did, they learnt to withdraw their affections just as wholeheartedly.'[100]

Within this complicated tangle of emotions, the officer corps' habits of 'easy sociability' can be seen as decidedly disadvantageous. The maintenance of wide-spread social networks inevitably ensured that large numbers of acquaintances were at risk at any given time. The danger of bereavement was consequently heightened. A battle or an attack could lead to the almost total destruction of a battalion's complement of officers at a stroke, with inevitable sensations of loss for those who survived or, for various reasons, had been left out of the fighting. Lt. Edward Tennant of the Grenadier Guards wrote in shocked terms to his mother following a particularly traumatic episode in September 1916: 'I suppose you have heard who are dead? Guy Baring, Raymond Asquith, Sloper Mackenzie, and many others. It is a terrible list. Poor Olive will be heart-broken – and so will Katherine. Death and decomposition strew the ground'.[101]

The reference to Raymond Asquith's wife Katherine is an important reminder that, in an elite and exclusive regiment such as the Grenadier Guards, pre-war social ties as well as university or school associations were likely to be carried over into military service. Raymond's father, Prime Minister Herbert Asquith, was married to Margot Tennant and the families were consequently rather more closely connected than more distant school friends or wartime acquaintances. The loss of any friend could be traumatic, however, and efficient modern communications, high casualty rates and the culture of publicising deaths ensured that officers received tragic news almost constantly. Casualty lists were published in *The Daily Telegraph* and *The Morning Post* until the end of 1916. *The Times* restricted its coverage to officers only after the end of 1917, but continued to cover these casualties until the end of the war.[102] Officers regularly scanned these lists for familiar names. Raymond Asquith himself was 'sorry to see in today's list the name of Foster Cunliffe, whom I was rather fond of at All Souls. I forget if you knew him – a most agreeable civilized man, very good, but laughing always louder than anybody at one's foulest jokes.'[103] Modern methods of communication also ensured that these lists kept officers serving in France up to date with the fates of their friends serving in other theatres. Douglas Gillespie was particularly distressed by news from the Near East: 'This has been a black day for me ever since I saw Bay Balfour's name in the lists from the Dardanelles … He was the most lovable of men – so lively and full of zest and joy in living that he made all his friends feel glad to be alive.'[104]

Information was also spread, as Chapter 1 noted, by school and university networks. The magazines which could play such an important part in developing a sense of community regularly contained lists of ex-pupils who had been killed, wounded, honoured or decorated, and often published short obituaries as well. News was also disseminated by contacts amongst one's circle of school friends, current pupils or school staff. 2nd Lt. William Mills' sources included 'a letter from the Head, one from Greenwood and another from Mrs. K. The casualties in College have been awfully heavy. Well over two hundred Wykehamists have been killed. You remember Gibson: I was his 'valet' four halves. He's dead, and so is Ware who came to College on my roll. Johnstone, Prefect of Hall my first year, is wounded and missing: Sladen, who went into the Rifles a year ago is wounded, and two more men killed who were in College with me. It was an awful budget to get in one evening.'[105] Ironically, the act of socialising itself – though a tried and tested way of rebuilding morale after such news – kept one's networks broad and therefore carried with it the danger that one might encounter a bearer of bad news, with potentially damaging effects. Captain Norman Taylor met an Old Wellingtonian who 'rather depressed me with tales of O.W.s killed among them a delightful master [apparently called Powell] who used to teach me French and keep me in after school many a time – killed as [a Second Lieutenant].'[106]

Officers were nevertheless arguably better positioned to endure the losses of war than their men for two reasons. First, their social networks, although more susceptible to damage, were potentially more resilient than those of their men. A private's primary social network – comprising the men he shared most of his time with – was typically situated in the trench with him. Moreover, particularly in the early stages of the war, he might have especially close ties to his colleagues which pre-dated their shared service thanks to the traditional policy of recruiting regiments from distinct geographical areas. This occurrence was notably pronounced in the case of the famous Pals' Battalions formed in 1914 by men linked by professional, recreational, or educational ties.[107] Officers, on the other hand, had much more diffuse social networks. School friends might come from totally different parts of the country and often served in very different regiments. It was comparatively rare for an officer to serve alongside long-standing acquaintances in any other than elite regiments, whereas attacks such as those on the Somme in 1916 could result in very significant damage to battalions which had practically grown up on the same streets or worked in the same factories. With more freedom of movement and the ability to pick and choose their associates from a wider pool than their men, officers could ensure that their social networks were not localised and were therefore less liable to be entirely shattered.

Secondly, the habit of 'easy sociability' and a constantly widening group of acquaintances ensured new groups were quickly and instinctively formed which could, if necessary, provide some replacement for battle casualties. Bereavement continued to be traumatic but many friendships, if brief, were real and powerful. Often further removed from the death of a friend, rather than in the next fire-bay, officers could be confident of the survival, and rapid repopulation, of their circle of acquaintances. This provided another source of emotional strength which, for many, represented an extension or augmentation of pre-war practices.

9

Luxuries and Logistics

The sociable behaviour which formed such a significant part of the lives of young officers on the Western Front was facilitated by their enjoyment of more comfortable living standards and greater access to goods and services than the men under their command. Their habits of consumption were, however, more important than simply providing a convivial context for communal interactions. The more comfortable an officer could make himself the better able he might be to endure the privations and stresses of active service. As with all parts of the transition from civilian to soldier, it was important to learn what was feasible and effective. The officer's attempts to use such mechanisms as the postal service to keep him supplied with necessary items were set against a background of increasingly sophisticated commercial activity which tried to define officer status through material possessions. At first, many new officers were unsure of their surroundings and consequently kept both their consumption and their social activities within fairly narrow limits. Once they had settled into routines and learnt the effective limitations on their actions their habits of consumption and socialising expanded according to their means and opportunities. Another important determinant was the military system which accorded officers certain privileges, and consequently assisted them in their efforts to maintain certain standards. Out of the line, officers were always given the best available billets, which were allocated according to seniority. On the march, they were usually able to get their valises and other items of kit transported on the mess cart, or taken by the battalion's transport wagons.[1] 'We (the bloomin' orficers)', explained Keith Henderson to his wife Helen, 'have a "mess-cart" for all our absurd wines and tinned peaches and things, but the men often have nothing but the contents of their haversacks.'[2] This was an important privilege since, in addition to lessening their physical burdens, it dramatically increased the amount of personal kit – basic luxuries like spare clothes, if nothing else – that officers might possess on active service.

Very few young officers appear to have questioned or criticised the privileges they enjoyed. Some young men from the upper classes decided to enlist and remain in the ranks, inspired by utopian, socialist or even romantic ideals, but the majority accepted the implications of a class-based hierarchy. This is not surprising since it represented a continuity of the social order to which many of them belonged and was reinforced by military traditions (particularly views about the officer's paternalistic duties and consequent entitlements) with which they were being indoctrinated. There were some dissenting voices within the ranks of the officer corps which, although neither particularly common nor loud, deserve recognition since they reflect some understanding within that body of men that the modern army was unlike any previous British force. Lieutenant Arthur Adam, serving with the territorial Cambridgeshire Regiment, is an example of an officer who disliked an official over-emphasis, as he saw it, on the comfort of platoon and company commanders: 'too much energy is spent in making officers comfortable and too little in making men'.[3] During the course of the war, many young men of different social and class backgrounds were thrown together for long periods of time. This social mingling was to have a profound impact on British society in the coming decades.

It should not, however, be forgotten that, in the utmost exigencies, the officer's advantages were swept away. If transport was lost or unavailable, or if troops were involved in strenuous operations then all men were likely to suffer equally. Letters and diaries describe numerous occasions on which officers, like their men, had to subsist on something like 'just a cold snag of meat and bread and cheese'. This was Graham Greenwell's experience simply when he returned (apparently rather suddenly) to the front-line trenches in May 1916.[4] In certain circumstances or times of crisis, especially during the retreat and subsequent advances of 1918, matters were even worse. On 26 March 1918, as the British Army reeled under the onslaught of the German Spring Offensive, James Neville was reduced to the following circumstances:

> Ellam and I scrounged about and found an old dug-out, which had partially collapsed at the bottom. It was damp and cold and musty at the bottom, and smelt of decay, rats, and putrescent vegetation and food. But, here I found a half-opened tin of bully beef, and picking out the biggest pieces of chalk with my penknife, ate the remainder of the contents. How the tin had got there, or how long it had been there, I never stopped to consider. We had been through strenuous days, marching far over shell-torn country on underfed stomachs, never knowing if or when we should see food again, and here, at least, was a form of food! But never shall I forget the taste in my mouth after it! For four days I had a dry stickiness in my mouth, incessant heartburn, and a feeling of overwhelming depression, which almost blotted out the instinct of life. Ellam would not touch it, and, therein he was wiser than I.[5]

By 27 March Neville was extremely unwell. He was eventually evacuated to a base depot to recover, his story contrasting sharply with tales of the extravagant lifestyles of officers.

The officer's status as an active consumer was established immediately by the requirement to clothe and equip himself for his new life in the army. This in itself was an important delineation of the differences between leaders and led. Privates were issued with uniform and personal equipment. Officers were expected to be more self-reliant, acquiring necessary kit for themselves (albeit aided by government funds) and ensuring that they conformed to all relevant dress codes and gentlemanly standards of presentation. Chapter 2 has described the nature of this challenge. The system obliged them to use their judgement but inexperienced officers typically had very little idea as to what they would actually need. Many embarked on a flurry of over-consumption which was, at best, unnecessary and, at worst, rendered them objects of ridicule, as Eliot Crawshay-Williams described in his *Leaves from an officer's notebook*:

Where the individual has plenty of money, the zeal finds one of its outlets in the purchase of every imaginable form of campaign equipment. One officer (I will not even disclose his rank) became quite notorious in this way. Day after day the Battery office was piled with his parcels. Canvas boots, prismatic compasses, cap-covers, waterproofs, special socks, waders, water-proof breaches, trenchoscopes, mackintosh sheets, woolly waistcoats, leather jackets, fluffy underclothes, tremendous gloves, under-gloves, revolvers, ammunition – the place swarmed with his equipment, most of it destined to defy the rigours of trench life at Christmas. Eventually two of the other officers sent a card intimating to their opulent comrade that, having entered the furniture-removing trade, they were in a position to supply him with a pantechnicon for the period of the war at a very reasonable cost, and soliciting his patronage.[6]

Some of those who did succumb to such acquisitive urges failed to jettison whatever useless paraphernalia they had picked up and tried to take substantial quantities of equipment with them. Others were able (or forced) to rationalise their possessions in preparation for their journey overseas. Doubtless they did not always correctly indentify those items which were essential, rather than merely desirable, but it would be wrong to suppose that this was an entirely individual process undertaken without reference to external authorities.

On entering the army, any individual officer might have had access to advisers who could assist him in the task of preparation, especially in the later phases of the war when military experience and knowledge became more widely distributed throughout the population. In John Hay Beith's *The First Hundred Thousand* a young officer called Bobby is taken in charge by the more knowledgeable Wagstaffe, who reduces his 'military museum' to a more compact and useful collection.[7] Gilbert Nobbs encountered an old acquaintance who, dandy-ish as ever, had packed very little 'he would really need; but a curious mixture of strange articles which would fill a fancy bazaar. There were hair-brushes with ebony backs and silver monograms, silk handkerchiefs with fancy borders, a pinky tooth-paste oozing out of a leaden tube crushed between a comb and a pair of silk socks' and much more besides.[8] Nobbs kindly assisted his re-packing.

Once on active service food and drink quickly became a central part of the officer lifestyle – bordering on an obsession for some. Dining, as opposed to merely eating, would have been extremely familiar to many who were commissioned having attended public schools or universities and had been part of an Edwardian society which was characterised by ceremony and epicurean tastes. Extravagant and somewhat ritualised consumption was a recognised social practice, with ancient historical antecedents. The fashion was set at the very top of society and the habits of the professional officer corps were a reflection of wider trends.[9] Dining combined luxury with theatricality and naturally lent itself to ever greater heights of culinary sophistication as hosts strove to impress with their generosity, ingenuity or refined tastes. The trophy-like recollections of courses found in Edwardian accounts are exactly mirrored in later accounts of elaborate dugout dinners. Fine dining was also the apogee of society, the context for companionship and entertainment.

Public schools also encouraged an interest in food, but for a different reason. Young boys learned at an early age how to supplement their ration fare in a manner which found its echo in the later habits of officers on active service. Stuart Cloete was born in 1897 and educated at Lancing College. He described taking a tuckbox back with him each term:

> I always took a big seven-pound jar of marmalade, several pots of assorted jams, a variety of potted meats, such as shrimp paste, chicken and ham, and bloater paste. One round flat white china of Gentleman's Relish, tins of sardines, corned beef, pilchards in tomato sauce, and a very big and rich fruit cake, the kind that will keep for months. These foods were used to supplement the meals we got – particularly in giving us something to spread on our bread. There was plenty of bread.'[10]

There are definite parallels between the schoolboy's yearning for tasty foods and the subaltern's close interest in his victuals on the Western Front. Cloete later described how, during his military career, he drew rations with his colleagues and supplemented them with 'imported luxuries from shops like Fortnum and Mason, Harrods and Selfridges. We bought our wine from local wine-merchants behind the lines.'[11] As when he was at school, it was seldom the quantity of food that was the problem. (In fact, many poorer men were significantly better nourished during their time in the Army than they were previously.) It was necessary, rather, to vary the monotony of a dull diet. In the relatively Spartan environment of an Edwardian public school edible treats could also provide some material comfort. The trench fighter would quickly come to recognise the morale-boosting value of something tasty amid so many other physical discomforts. As Donald Hankey pointed out, 'Every one knows that war means to the soldier a big measure of deprivation.'[12] Lt. Brian Lawrence, serving with the Grenadier Guards in December 1916, found it strange that 'in this country, particularly when one is in a camp in a part where there are no civilians or natural domestic life, one's only aim is the acquisition of creature comforts. By far the most important item for contentment is good food and plenty of it, so that the mess boxes and a supply of delicacies from the mess man, and plenty of drink, are one's first thought on arrival at any new camp, billet, or dug-out.'[13]

Schoolboys also appreciated that food could be used as an adjunct to specific social activity. Opportunities – perhaps in the form of some special event – for enjoyment were eagerly seized upon. At Winchester, John Baines was a member of a house sports team in November 1910. He reported to his sister that on completion of the competition he and his friends would 'regale themselves on veal and ham pie, fruit salad and lemonade until late at night.'[14] These habits continued to develop as the young man moved to a university, where access to necessary supplies remained crucial. Fortunately, this was seldom a problem for those with means. At Oxford, Owen Buckmaster remembered, 'anything from Turkish cigarettes gold-tipped with the buyer's initials specially printed on them, to a case or two of wine would be delivered in college without demur and without delay.'[15] Desmond Young recounts dining in Markham Square and drinking, 'horribile dictum, innumerable bottles of sparkling Burgundy. Then we returned to college. No one could quite resist the effects of topping up this concoction with tumblers of port and brandy mixed.'[16]

It is unsurprising, given these social antecedents and a strong interest in maintaining an appealing diet, that details of menus and arrangements for dinners (both formal and relatively unimportant) fill letters and diaries throughout the period of the war. (Such details could also be shared entirely safely with relatives, providing reassurance that a young man was well and, perhaps equally importantly to an Edwardian mother, well fed.) Graham Greenwell, who clearly considered himself something of a gastronome, provides some good examples, regularly regaling his relatives with detailed accounts of his extravagant dinner parties such as this one in Courcelles in January 1916:

> We have evolved the following menu:
> Oysters,
> Consommé Courcelles,
> Rôti de Veau de Sailly: Möet et Chandon 1906,
> Poulet Conybeare,
> Asperges des tranchées,
> Rum omelette à la Q.M. et Macédoine,
> Welsh Rarebit.
> Coffee. Liqueurs. Cigars.[17]

The food can seldom have been up to the standards officers might have expected in civilian life, given the comparatively basic cooking arrangements available, but it is rare to find them explicitly discussing the quality of a meal. The menu is allowed to stand on its own as an evocation of elegance and luxury, almost in defiance of any suggestion that

Luxurious meals played an important role in the lives of officers. The men pictured belong to the Royal Army Medical Corps, September 1916. (Imperial War Museum Q 1150)

it might not deliver all that would be required in a normal dinner in civilian life. The list of multiple courses also helped the officers to assert civilisation and domesticity despite the conditions of active service. Greenwell's attention to the detail of the delights on offer demonstrates the importance of maintaining appearances (although it is not clear whether this is for his or his correspondent's benefit).

As was the case when moved into the relative ease of rest or the greater comfort of more distant leave from the front line, anything which restored more cultured standards was most welcome, but food seems to have occupied a particularly important place in the hierarchy of civilised behaviours. This is not surprising. As Rachel Duffett has pointed out, food is seldom merely the satisfaction of a biological need, occupying a much more important place in our culture and personal rituals.[18] It is often one of the very first things mentioned in an account of a period of leave, a clear indication that it was regarded as a priority, and played a significant role in establishing a separation between trench-duty and a more civilised existence. When Captain James Neville surprised his relatives with a letter from the Hotel Continental in Paris in May 1917 he did not dwell long on the wonders of the city: 'Yesterday we went to the Tuileries and Louvre. This hotel overlooks the Tuileries Gardens,' he wrote, before rapidly moving on. 'We also did a lot of shopping and feeding, perhaps most of the latter! It's good to have a civilised meal.' That other great delight of the officer at rest – the luxurious bath – was soon brought up, along with some of the social pleasures on offer, but food could only be sidelined briefly: 'Grover and I are sharing a room together with a bath adjoining, which is heaven. It is the first time since I left home that I have had a bath in a big bath, and not had to hang my legs over the side. You can imagine what an effect all this luxury has on me after five months' absence from civilisation. Some of the Staff Officers have got their wives over here, and it is glorious to hear the language spoken by an English lady. Altogether I am amazed at my surroundings. Grover and I do the hell of a lot of eating and sleeping. That in itself is a great change!'[19]

The range of food presented (as opposed to the food itself) in Greenwell's mess would not have disgraced a formal dinner party in London and would certainly have been very acceptable in a regimental or battalion mess behind the lines, which is in fact where it was served. What is most startling about the dining habits of the officer corps on the Western Front is the tenacity with which they clung to them in all but the most difficult and dangerous circumstances. Standards were not lightly allowed to slip even when in the line. Bernard Long wrote to his sister in August 1916 describing 'quite a swanky dinner' he had enjoyed one evening 'in a dug-out in the front line – three course meal you'd wonder how it was done wouldn't you but you see an officer's servant sets off in the morning and gets out of the trenches and walks back to the nearest village and makes his purchases and then gets back into the trenches.'[20]

Long's letter highlights the importance of assistance in maintaining these living standards. The Army provided officers with a full-time servant – known as a batman – able to devote time and energy to acquiring and preparing food. Many officers from lower-class backgrounds would not have been accustomed to such an arrangement, and they did not always satisfy the expectations of regular officers in their manners towards their servants.[21] Nor should it be assumed that batmen were universally competent or familiar with the duties required of them. It was no doubt with this in mind that Desmond Young's friend Dink Horsfall interrogated the two Riflemen who reported to them as batmen. "'Have you ever had any previous experience of private service?" he asked. "Yes, sir," was the reply. "Before enlisting I was second footman to His Grace the Duke of Devonshire." I gulped as I turned to my smaller and less formidable one. "And you, Rifleman Groves, have you too been in service before?" "Yes, sir," said Groves, "until last week I was valet to the Prime Minister." "Good God," said Dink as they saluted smartly and left, "I've only got three khaki shirts."[22]

Since batmen were excused various duties the officer seldom had to worry that the preparation of his evening meal might be unduly time-consuming. In addition, the officer never had to worry about cleaning cooking utensils and cutlery either. A servant had more time available for acquiring stores and often had access to better provisions, whether from rations or private suppliers including nearby villages away from the unit, as Long's letter reveals. When rations were brought up from supply depots and distributed, he was able to have his pick before anybody else, exercising his commander's prerogative to demand special consideration. In R.C. Sherriff's play *Journey's End* Captain Stanhope's servant Mason laments the fact that, owing to an unlabelled tin and an incorrect (or possibly mendacious) storeman, the Captain must have peaches for dinner, which he does not care for, rather than pineapple. It is extremely unlikely that an ordinary Tommy could have expressed a preference of any sort when drawing his rations. Similarly, when buying provisions from a café, shop or estaminet the privileges of the officer corps effectively devolved on to their servants, making a wider selection of goods available. The consumer choices of the rank and file were seriously restricted but the officers, or their servants acting on their behalf, had access to a wide range of delicacies. The stock of an Expeditionary Force Canteen in Louvencourt, and the restrictions placed on access to it, were described in the semi-autobiographical novel *The Middle Parts of Fortune* by the Australian war veteran Frederick Manning:

> ... the shop-window was as rich in delicacies as any in London. Hams, cheeses, bottled fruits, olives, sardines, everything to make the place a paradisal vision for hungry men. Shem and Martlow continued down the street, and Bourne went inside and stood at the counter ... He wanted sweet things, macaroons, cake, and crystallized fruit, all of which he had seen displayed; and when a shopman dignified by uniform came up to him, he began by asking for these things. The man merely asked him for a chit; and when Bourne replied that he had not got a chit, that he would pay cash, the other man turned away superciliously, saying that they only served officers.[23]

Moreover, while military regulations banned rankers from possessing commodities such as spirits, there were no official proscriptions on the private stores that could be accumulated by their superiors.

There was therefore less logistical difficulty than might be supposed in maintaining refined habits, even in the front-line trenches. In fact, it is often hard to tell purely from a menu whether or not it was consumed within a few hundred yards of the enemy or much further back. Thomas Heald celebrated a round of promotions by treating three fellow officers to a dinner of seven courses. The menu, apparently served with champagne, consisted of: Hors d'oeuvres; Consommé Argentine; Lobster Mayonnaise; Pâté, Canard rotie au 'George'; Petit pois, Sauce des Pommes; Pomme de terres brouille; Fruits, Gateau;

'Un petit piece de moutard'; Liqueurs; Café; Music.[24] Although there was nothing in the design of the menu to indicate it, this dinner was eaten in the largest dug-out available in Heald's section of trench.

Officers could acquire various provisions in France, but many items were mailed to them. It is generally recognised that an efficient postal service is an important adjunct to a modern army. Chapter 5 notes the benefits to morale of receiving letters. Richard Holmes has highlighted a second benefit: the recipient's morale is further increased by the demonstration of organisational efficiency; this efficiency was demonstrated during the war by the speed with which letters could arrive despite the most rudimentary address.[25] Of greater significance to the officer's habits of consumption – if not to the morale of the individual, although surely there was a strong correlation – was the supply of parcels. Official statistics record that 320,409 tons of mail and parcels were shipped to the army in France between 1914 and 1920.[26] Although the system was robust parcels were sometimes delayed, when submarine threats prevented channel crossings, or lost in the extensive depots and lines of communication. Major events such as the German advance of 1918 caused considerable interruption.[27] Moreover, there could be no guarantee that some light-fingered individual, far removed from the officer's personal jurisdiction, would not help themselves.[28] Consequently, numerous officers made special arrangements to try to reduce the likelihood of theft, or at least to prevent them from missing out without realising. Sam Paget suggested that his mother 'might number your parcels – then I shall see whether they all arrive.'[29]

It is scarcely possible to estimate how much of the mail was intended for officers as opposed to other ranks, or for infantrymen as opposed to other branches of the armed forces, but it is apparent that the infantry officers who are the focus of this book were usually able to use the postal system more extravagantly than their men. It is also apparent that the extent to which they did so was related to their broader transition from civilian to experienced soldier. Their use of the mail system seems in many cases to have evolved over time as they became increasingly aware of the ways in which they could make themselves comfortable on active service and support those requirements by mail. Oliver Lyttelton's earliest requests from the front in February 1915 for socks, tinned potted meat, port, and a few bottles of beer were simple (even if rather in excess of the requests normally made by the rank and file) and in fact very typical of such letters – in no way extravagant for an officer, even though his regiment, the Grenadier Guards, was one of the more socially exclusive.[30] Within a couple of weeks the list had expanded considerably, the accompanying explanation indicating that he might himself have learned more about his unit's practices on active service, or at least recognised that he wanted (or needed) to change his own behaviours:

> All messing is done by Companies and all supplies are common property (practically all). There are three of us, so if sending anything bear this in mind. Half a dozen strong knives and forks, the knives with steel handles would be very useful, and some horn cups, very small for port, etc., say 4 of these, I think you can get them quite cheap. Chocolate etc. we nearly always have to excess, but sort of things like tongue (tinned), tinned lamb and peas, pate, or even a cold chicken are very popular. I shouldn't order a fixed show from F. and Mason but if you could send say

once a week a selection of the above kind of things together with a bottle of port (F. and M. No. 4) it would be splendid.[31]

This request is typically mindful of the size of the mess. Those who were in the habit of receiving parcels regularly seem to have taken care to cater for their comrades as well as themselves, sharing provisions in the same manner as other ranks.[32] William Villiers of the King's Royal Rifle Corps explained to his mother shortly after arriving at the front that 'we each supply a certain amount if possible from home of things we can't get here.'[33] This had obvious benefits for unit cohesion and comradely feeling.

While learning how far they could go in facilitating their own comfort, officers also found they needed items which few gentlemen could have considered vital in everyday life but which soon became indispensable in the world of the trenches. Douglas Gillespie was one of many officers who asked for insect powder or liquid: 'so far I have only met the skirmishers, but supports and reinforcements can't be very far behind, and I think a whole new army will begin to move when the weather gets warmer'.[34] What must genteel Edwardian mothers have felt when faced with such requests? The system also occasionally conveyed items which gave a very different impression of the conditions. Captain Norman Taylor arranged for a soda machine to be dispatched to him, although it apparently initially arrived 'minus bulbs with which to inject air'.[35] In December 1915 Edgar Matthews revealed details of a new delivery in a letter to his friend E.J. Dent. He began by enquiring if Dent was familiar with *Les Gobelins*, a restaurant which stood in Heddon Street, just off Regent Street, and which sported a particular type of coffee machine made of glass:

> A Polish friend of mine (now interned in the Isle of Man) told me that the Russians always use them. I sent for the largest sized one to make coffee for our mess – (i.e. for the five officers in the company). It arrived when I was in a front-line trench and as it was made entirely of glass I thought it wise to send it to a place of safety. While we were on the march back another mysteriously arrived. It was really rather fortunate because on the first time of use the globe of one broke. Certainly it makes excellent coffee. As it boils the water rises from the globe to the bowl and then comes down again. As the 'officers' active service' coffee machine it amuses me much.[36]

Both Matthews and Taylor can be seen testing the limitations imposed on them by front line service and apparently refusing to accept that the military world might not accommodate their civilian tastes and ideas. It is also apparent that they were learning the extent to which these luxuries were practical; Taylor had previously asked for a more modest apparatus for boiling water using solid methylated spirits.[37]

Officers commissioned from the ranks had, in most cases, already become experienced combatants. They still had to undergo a transition, but theirs was a different process of growing accustomed to their newly-elevated positions. Increased consumption seems to have been a part of this. Robert Harker enlisted in the 1st Battalion The Honourable Artillery Company, a 'class corps', at the start of the war. His earliest letters from the ranks to his sister Ethel included relatively small requests. In October 1914 he asked for 'every week 6 slabs or big squares of the superior plain chocolate from the Army &

Navy Stores'.[38] In November he requested 'some large pots or tins of potted meat twice a week and chocolate twice a week'.[39] In 1915 he was commissioned into the 1st Battalion the North Staffordshire Regiment and, although still asking for similar articles, clearly began looking to increase his level of consumption in accordance with his new status (even if his new colleagues were more frugal than some in their messing arrangements). This can be seen in his letter of 16 March 1915:

> The officers of the two companies are messing together here and they run things very cheaply about 4 francs a day. You might send out the old Army & Navy chocolate, say 8 slabs a week, as Waterall is sharing half of it with me and the 1 tin of Smiths Glasgow mixture every fortnight with the yellow paper round it. Oxford sausage, tongue and potted meat are the best things in the way of food and if any of my friends and relations should think of sending a cake, the plainer the better, sort of Sultana cake and shortbread also but not the very rich heavy Xmas cake full of currants etc.[40]

The Honourable Artillery Company was different to other units in that, like the Artists Rifles, it was composed of well-educated and potentially relatively well-off young men who opted for enlistment and therefore rapid service in preference to waiting and trying to get a commission. Once commissioned, the fact that Harker began to make greater use of the postal system suggests that the circumstances of private soldiers and the expectations of the officer community played a role alongside relative wealth levels in determining patterns of consumption.

Experience was important in fields other than the culinary. As they were initiated into the mysteries of active service and trench warfare, new officers quickly learned more efficient ways in which to make themselves more comfortable. They did not necessarily become more frugal. Even experienced officers still carried a tremendous amount of kit, ultimately the only limiting factor being the tolerance of the quartermaster. Charles Dudley-Ward considered it impossible to endure winter 'with the regulation weight of 35lbs. One must have warm things for the night.' Some of his colleagues clearly took things significantly further, placing a burden on the unit which could create friction:

> Still old campaigners like Aldridge are rather impossible when they arrive out here with two valises, two saddle bags and a camp kit bag – and then collect other things on the top of all that![41]

Sometimes a 'general jettison' was required, in which case the surplus kit might be stored in a convenient location with a guard.[42] Officers also constantly discarded or sent home items which turned out to serve little or no useful function or which were too heavy or bulky to be easily transported. Simultaneously they learned which articles were essential and therefore worth investing in. Conscientious subalterns might supplement army issue equipment with better-quality items. Stores like the Army & Navy would usually have a Weapon Department which could cater for all these needs.[43] Siegfried Sassoon bought a set of wire-cutters whilst on leave in London, borrowing his Aunt's store card to gain entry to the Army & Navy Stores.[44] In January 1916 Arthur Gibbs, having gained some experience of trench warfare, requested a pocket-sized sidearm which would be more practical than an additional service revolver.

> I think a small automatic pistol to go in one's pocket would be very useful out here. The Service revolver is rather big, and you can't carry more than one of them around. You want something handy after you have fired the 6 rounds from your revolver. It should be small enough to put in your pocket, as there are such a lot of things to put on your belt already. Could you get one? A small Colt automatic, which I think are as good as any, also 100 rounds of ammunition?[45]

Experience of mutable tactical realities also influenced his culinary requests when in the trenches in March of that year:

> It is very difficult to get water or fuel up here so I shall want some cold things sent, which don't need any cooking, such as tongues, ham, chicken etc. We can't show any fires as the Bosch shells them at once. He is much more wide awake here than he was in the other line. A small Primus stove would be jolly useful.[46]

Clearly the task of equipping oneself was never definitively completed. Constant fine-tuning was required to maximise comfort. Since infantry units were frequently moved between sectors in which very different conditions might prevail – as indicated by Gibbs's comment on the difficulty of getting water or fuel *up here* – these specific requests for food and kit might have to be acted on relatively quickly. The postal system was apparently efficient enough to enable these adjustments to the individual's supply chain and make them worthwhile.

Experience was also extremely useful in preventing officers' servants from taking too many liberties with whatever supplies had arrived by post or been purchased locally, as the memoir of Captain Alfred Pollard makes clear. Pollard, who enlisted in the Honourable Artillery Company at the start of the war, was commissioned in January 1916, but not before a lengthy stint as a mess servant during which time he and his colleagues mercilessly took advantage of their masters – crucially, because they were inexperienced:

> Of course the officers were very raw or they would never have stood the treatment we gave them. Later on when I held a commission myself, I was in a position to out-general my servant in all the tricks he tried on me.[47]

Pollard's pilfering was eventually stopped by the arrival of a Captain Boyle who ordered lots of provisions but announced from the first that servants were to have a share: 'Wise Captain Boyle. He placed us in a position which honour prevented us from abusing.'[48]

As the war progressed, newly-commissioned officers were more likely to be able to benefit from the experience of family members or friends who had already gained some experience of active service. Clifford Platt joined the Oxford University OTC in January 1915 and was commissioned into the 19th Battalion Lancashire Fusiliers in July. By

March 1916 he was writing to his brother Glyn, who had recently been commissioned, with useful advice concerning equipment:

> Yes, bring your Sam Browne out! As for mess staff, you will probably have company messes, if you don't have a battalion mess. In the former case you have a company mess cook and a waiter who pack and look after the stuff, and see it on the limber or mess cart. So there is no need to trouble about it, but I carry a Tommy's cooker to heat shaving water and that and have a billy can to boil it in and clean my teeth and shave out of etc. And of course I should bring out a canteen in case you want it on detachment duty.[49]

His letter, with its relative uncertainty about messing arrangements, further highlights the ways in which the lack of uniformity in army practices, although a source of great regimental strength and esprit de corps, hampered the attempts of new officers to get things right first time. While it seems highly likely that this sort of informal instruction became increasingly common as the war progressed and military knowledge accumulated within the population, ultimately there could be no substitute for experience.

Purchases and consumption habits were also influenced by monetary considerations. Many officers had private means, although the proportion decreased as the war progressed and the social base of the officer corps became broader. They were also better paid than their men. In 1916 a newly-commissioned subaltern received 7s. 6d a day with a field allowance of 2s. 6d, the same allowance for lodgings and a 9d allowance towards his mess bill.[50] A full lieutenant received 8s. 6d and a captain 12s. 6d.[51] By comparison, a private earned a basic daily rate of a shilling.[52] Spending power was, however, eroded quite significantly by inflation. By 1918 prices in Britain were almost two and a half times their level in 1914.[53] Inflation in France was even more severe; over the same period prices increased by 344 per cent.[54] Despite wartime conditions, officers like Lancelot Spicer could find that there was a 'tremendous quantity of food to be had' in places like Amiens – 'almost peace time luxuries' – but also that 'everything was very expensive.'[55] The military authorities did respond to these inflationary pressures to some extent by adjusting pay rates. By 1918 a 2nd lieutenant's pay had increased to 10s. 6d, a lieutenant's to 11s. 6d and a captain's to 13s. 6d.[56] Although this was in no way commensurate with the level of inflation, few complaints are found in primary sources. This may in part reflect the fact that the War Office supplied officers with their basic requirements and operated schemes designed to keep the price of clothing as low as possible, as described in Chapter 2.

It must also be remembered, as Michael Roper notes, that many an officer was sent food and other items by his parents – and that they met the costs. Some officers received parental allowances, which potentially amounted to the same thing. Roper argues that these arrangements reflected the way in which many officers, only recently out of school, retained the attitude of dependents and did not think of providing for themselves, even though they were now earning their own money.[57] Harold Mellersh clearly demonstrated this lack of adult self-reliance when attending a Young Officer's Course at Oxford: 'One evening I was so tired that I went to sleep in my room and totally missed my dinner. I was very sorry for myself, but it did not occur to me that I might do anything so rash and expensive and grown-up and sophisticated as go out and buy myself a meal.'[58] Though examples of material parental support are common, some officers were capable of breaking the habit of dependency. Very quickly after arriving in France, Lancelot Spicer, who went straight into the Army after Rugby and Cambridge, wrote home with a request that his father 'knock off that £5 a month which he gives me. I don't want it now, as I can quite easily live on my pay.' That this was only a partial loosening of his grip on the parental apron strings was made apparent by his next comment: 'I shall also feel less guilty about asking you for things for myself and for the men.'[59] Perhaps Spicer realised that there was little point his having money at the front, but that it would be unwise to undermine the flow of support from Britain.

He may equally have been thinking of the circumstances of those at home. When Robert Harker went to war he left his son in the care of his sister Ethel. His attitude towards money suggests that he was concerned about the well-being of his family and the importance of not leaving them in straightened circumstances. 'Some large pots or tins of potted meat twice a week and chocolate twice a week would be most useful,' he wrote in November 1914, 'but they are all to be paid for out of my account'.[60] Harker was presumably a widower, whose decision to enlist may have been seriously complicated by his family responsibilities. Having dependents of one's own certainly seems to have played an important part in defining the officer's attitude to money. Jack Oughtred's concerns about pay (noted in Chapter 6) seem to have been linked to his impending marriage. Montie Carlisle, who married in April 1914 shortly after his 25th birthday, insisted that his wife use funds drawn from his own account when he sent her a list of requirements.[61] It is also notable that Carlisle, with his pre-war experience of financial dealings at the Baltic Exchange, seems to have had a more practical approach to monetary issues than many of his colleagues. Neither Arthur Gibbs nor Arthur Pick shared Carlisle's background, but both took an interest in savings and investments while at the front. 'Can you tell me what dividends are due to me next quarter day? Are the War Loan dividends half yearly?' asked Gibbs in May 1916. 'How much War Loan have I got now? I can't remember if it is £200 or £300. I should like my next quarter's allowance invested too.'[62] Arthur Pick wrote repeatedly about War Bonds, asking his family on a number of occasions to invest his money for him. His motivation is unclear, although he does refer at one point to a war savings campaign in his Corps.[63] Since officers sometimes only began earning money when they took their commissions it is not surprising that some should similarly have started to think more seriously about what to do with it. The apparent popularity of War Loan or Bonds probably reflects the success of appeals such as the one to which Pick subscribed rather than any financial acumen.

Of course, not everything had to be paid for. Any useful article left lying around was liable to acquire a new owner before too long. Pilfering and petty larceny were widespread and probably not significantly less prevalent amongst officers than any other group.[64] Billy Congreve wrote in his diary in May 1915, apparently without any embarrassment, that he and the General for whom he was working had spent some time that day seeing what they could acquire in a local town. Their loot on this occasion was limited to a beer mug and a mirror.[65] Stuart Cloete describes a dug-out 'well furnished with the loot of abandoned houses.'[66] Even if it took some men a little while to get used to this habit of helping oneself, it could become an enduring custom.[67]

This willingness to appropriate others' belongings was a reflection of the destructive nature of their environment. Soldiers quickly appreciated that any possessions, whether gained easily or at great trouble and expense, might be lost almost instantaneously. Food supplies could run out or go missing. Belongings could be smashed, stolen, mislaid or simply dumped. Anything available could justifiably be used because a failure to do so could result in its being irrevocably lost. Even if it were not, a sad fact of the time was that there could be no guarantee that its new owners would enjoy it for long. Erich Maria Remarque satirised this transience in *All Quiet on the Western Front*. He describes the fate of a pair of highly-prized leather boots noting that, although they enjoy a lengthy career, their successive owners do not.[68] Under such circumstances it seemed reasonable to make use of almost anything that came to hand. Possession could have little real meaning amid such danger and uncertainty – and yet it is striking that officers should so often have felt the need to excuse their actions in some way. Cloete referred to the abandoned state of the houses. Billy Congreve contrasted his needs and those of his mess with the likely waste which would have resulted from leaving items behind to be smashed up.[69] These small acts of self-justification demonstrate the officer's enduring need to demonstrate – both to his civilian audience and to himself – that he retained civilised standards and sensibilities despite his circumstances.

The high levels of consumption displayed by numerous officers were also facilitated by commercial developments. The static nature of trench warfare on the Western Front and the fact that the postal service was so efficient ensured that there was a potentially vast captive market in the trenches and behind the lines. There were also large numbers of anxious relatives at home who would be more than willing to buy staples, favourites and the latest product tweaked and primed for active service for their loved ones. Advertisers and businesses quickly realised the extent of the opportunity presented by the war, and responded with alacrity.[70] Although advertising space was quickly rationed, campaigns with a specifically military flavour were rapidly instigated. Initially their purpose was to sell products to soldiers in their existing forms.[71] From the outset, there were clear links between officers and an idealised, high-consumption lifestyle. Officers might find themselves encumbered with a plethora of articles which they had been given by well-meaning relatives, 'who are themselves', according to John Hay Beith's account, 'the victims of those enterprising tradesmen who have adopted the most obvious method of getting rid of otherwise unsaleable goods by labelling everything *For Active Service* – a really happy thought when you are trying to sell a pipe of port or a manicure set. Have you seen our Active Service Trouser-Press?'[72]

The emergence of the new military-themed notices was all the more striking for being essentially unprecedented. Mainstream advertising for military products was uncommon in the Edwardian era, even in the period immediately prior to the outbreak of war. There are no advertisements fitting this description in July 1914 editions of *The Times,* May to July 1914 editions of *The Daily Chronicle* or pre-war 1914 editions of *The Illustrated London News*. Then, as now, it would not apparently have been normal to see military advertising in the national press. The armed forces simply did not occupy that sort of space within mainstream culture, another challenge to interpretations of the

Edwardian period which emphasise popular militarisation. Despite this, it is apparent that advertisers quickly latched on to the commercial possibilities presented by the conflict when it began. On the day that Britain declared war the tailoring firm Thresher & Glenny placed a small advertisement for active service kits in *The Times*.[73] It was very basic (suggesting either a hurried decision to launch a campaign of this kind or a severe lack of copy-writing imagination) but was rapidly followed by more sophisticated adverts similarly reflecting the emergence of a new wartime market. Suppliers of 'Overland' cars encouraged territorial officers – theoretically remaining in Britain as a home defence force – to equip themselves with motor transport as soon as possible. The advert did not attempt to explain why this was desirable, but did offer to deliver within 30 minutes of ordering.[74] Such helpful suggestions were not only directed at the military. The general public were exhorted to demonstrate their patriotism by purchasing almost any commodity that could claim a war-time function. Sutton & Sons, seed merchants, were more prescient than they may have realised, thoughtfully encouraged the planting of important vegetables against possible shortages.[75] Soon battles were raging in the pages of the papers and, throughout the war, advertisers used patriotism to boost their clients' products and denigrate the competition's.[76]

Thereafter commercials with an explicitly wartime content typically had one of two distinct purposes: to market custom military products to serving and prospective soldiers; or to link brands and wares which were not explicitly military in nature to the fighting men, very often on the Western Front. Different companies attempted to sell products designed to satisfy a perceived military need – for example, a wide range of lavish field accessories. A typical advertisement of the period, printed in *The Times* in August 1915, directed the reader to the Junior Army and Navy Stores where he could purchase a supposedly complete kit for the officer on active service, which included such articles as a combined bath and washstand and a collapsable lounge chair.[77] Products presented in this way as camp essentials were not always particularly successful. In his short story *The Lieutenant*, 'Sapper' pokes fun at his hero, Gerald Ainsworth, who is sadly over-equipped, and burdened with one item in particular: 'Prominent among it was that abomination of desolation the fitted mess-tin. Inside it reposed little receptacles for salt and pepper and plates and dinner napkins and spirit lamps that explode like bombs. Aunts are aunts, and there was none to tell him that the roads of Flanders are paved with fitted mess-tins.'[78]

No doubt the relatives and friends who so burdened the real life Gerald Ainsworths were reading these newspapers and were influenced by the idea they propagated: that military (or at least officer) status was defined by the possessions which enabled a young man to function to the required standard and present the correct appearance. Reflecting the upper-class bias of the officer corps, the more exclusive emporiums launched a range of expensive goods specifically aimed at wealthier officers.[79] As well as seeking to gold-plate – sometimes literally as well as metaphorically – the officer's personal effects, businesses and advertisers were also keen to generate long-term custom. The desired outcome was to establish a routine line of supply, either by selling a service to the officer or mess directly or by persuading a proxy, usually the officer's family, to subscribe on a soldier's behalf. Stores such as the Junior Army and Navy loudly proclaimed their ability to tailor their service to any tastes or requirements.[80] Details of these arrangements are not common in letters and diaries but the occasional mention does shed some light on common practices. Raymond Asquith briefly explained to his wife Katherine in October 1915 that 'we have an arrangement for hampers to be sent twice a week from Fortnum and Mason with delicatessen etc. At present we have an assortment of cakes and sweets which Rumpelmayer might envy.'[81] Asquith seemed to wish to keep business and family matters separate, possibly because this order was for the mess as a whole, rather than for him personally. In contrast, when Montie Carlisle wanted a regular order for himself placed with Fortnum and Mason he asked his wife Kitty to make the arrangements.[82]

The personalised service which Asquith, Carlisle and others utilised was a continuation of pre-war business methods and a hallmark of the gentlemanly lifestyle. Officers who were used to having their needs catered for in this way could maintain not only living standards similar to those they had left behind but also comparable commercial or logistical arrangements. Moreover, it seems likely that entrenched links between class, the officer corps and commercial interests played their part in ensuring that changes in the demographics of the officer corps were not accompanied by more significant changes in culture. As earlier chapters have argued, the military hierarchy still expected certain standards of officers, even if it recruited them from a wider pool. The army did seek to train new officers to emulate the "right sort" of behaviour. New lieutenants would also have been influenced both by the example and expectations of colleagues and by widespread, socialised models for officer behaviour and lifestyles. Advertisers and a host of shopkeepers were then on hand to provide assistance and to encourage officers to follow established consumerist patterns. The provision of a personalised (or at least regularised) service enabled new officers to surrender to tastes which were set for them, to a large extent, by a social elite.

Brands remained important. Like modern consumers, officers wanted specific products to make military life more comfortable and familiar. Lieutenant Bernard Pitt expressed a preference for *Bivouac* cocoa tablets and *Lazenby* or *Crosse & Blackwell* soup squares.[83] Robert Harker specified that he wanted the 'superior' plain chocolate from the Army & Navy Stores.[84] It seems likely that this consumer loyalty on the part of officers reflected established preferences rather than the success of advertising campaigns linking certain products to an active service context; when writing home to request particular articles from family or friends, they did not, as a rule, refer to advertising. Moreover, serving soldiers were not usually the target of these promotions. While the *end-user* was usually on active service, the new packaging and advertising campaigns typically targeted *civilians* (who were, after all, more likely to be reading the advertisements), creating a product designed to appeal to relatives anxious to do what they could to help the fighting men, or to the more generally patriotically inclined.

The product itself often seemed essentially unchanged except for packaging designed to give the impression that it would be particularly useful to the man on active service. While some of the new uses suggested for established products may have seemed somewhat spurious, branding did at least offer the consumer some protection. With such a wide range of products on offer and such a large market to satisfy, it was inevitable that some less reputable entrepreneurs would attempt to exploit the new military consumers or that attempts to render certain consumables portable and practical for military service would sometimes be less than successful – or safe. In 1915 *The Lancet* published a warning about products appearing on the market in Germany which apparently provided innovative solutions to the challenges of active service but were in fact potentially hazardous. It also alerted readers to the possibility of food adulteration, whereby commodities might be mixed or diluted with other substances.[85] These fraudulent activities could present a threat to consumers, but as the war continued there was increasingly no avoiding some deterioration in the quality of food. Substitution effectively became military policy, with the qualities of available supplies generally falling over time. Towards the end of the war the contents of official rations became increasingly uncertain, with (for example) rabbit substituted for more typical meats, and herrings instead of bacon.[86] This did not, of course, pass unnoticed at the front and was often a cause for complaint. The writers of *Blackadder Goes Forth* memorably used Baldrick's inventive recipes to satirise both the officers' pretensions of fine dining and the war's impact on the availability of certain products. Nevertheless, the hapless batman's attempts to produce something that could pass for coffee without actually containing any still serve as a reminder that the familiar – for example, a cup of something that resembles coffee, even if only superficially – could continue to provide comfort and reassurance.

10

Morale, Identity and Heroism

One of the most difficult aspects of the transition from civilian to officer was the creation and maintenance of the mentality required of a soldier. Civilians are encouraged to obey laws which prohibit violence. Military personnel are required to discard inhibitions relating to the use of force. The primary function of an infantryman in the Victorian army was to engage with the enemy at close quarters. Members of the professional army were habituated to this role over time through a combination of training and socialisation. Many volunteer or conscripted British soldiers in the First World War were consequently disadvantaged in comparison to their professional counterparts because they had to start carrying out the duties of a front-line combatant without the same depth of physical and mental preparation. Moreover, the type of warfare which developed after 1914 would have challenged the resilience of any army. In previous wars the individual soldier had been a powerful agency on the battlefield, his performance and ability largely determining his own survival and the outcome of encounters. Heroic endeavour in personalised combat was a fundamental element of masculinity. By the time soldiers arrived on the Western Front, however, they had substantially lost that active role on which martial traditions and masculine self-confidence had been built. Rather than closing with the enemy, they were required to spend much of their time in the combat zone minding their positions. Many of the tools which dominated the line required a purely technical ability to operate rather than the physical skills used at extremely close quarters over centuries of warfare.[1]

The deployment of immensely powerful defensive weapons like artillery and machine guns, whose efficiency in killing vastly outstripped that of riflemen, created a deadly environment in which soldiers were deprived of the traditional warrior role of active combatant. Their martial identities were also challenged and frustrated by the way in which modern weapons dispensed an impersonal violence. Death frequently came suddenly and unexpectedly from a high-velocity shell, fired by unseen hands some distance away. Enemy combatants might not be seen for months at a time. In the absence of a personalised foe, aggressive instincts were frequently thwarted. It was particularly difficult to witness comrades being killed and to suffer the strain of being under fire oneself without having any opportunity for revenge on the enemy or even escape from the killing zone. In August 1915 the men of Francis Hitchcock's company 'were very bitter to think they had been shelled all day by an invisible foe, and had lost some of their best pals, without a chance of retaliation.'[2] Soldiers, once the active participants of battles, were now apparently reduced to near-passive victims and the slaves of technology. Trench warfare, in Eric Leed's analysis, 'eroded officially sponsored conceptions of the soldierly self as an act of aggression. It produced a ... defensive personality, moulded by identifications with the victims of a war dominated by "impersonal" aggressors of chemicals and steel.'[3] Rather than focusing on killing the enemy, soldiers became primarily concerned with one thing – survival in the face of what was literally a killing machine. Morale – confidence in one's role and consequent willingness to perform tasks determined by commanders – was threatened, simply because the soldier could not assert his personal agency and therefore could not maintain a positive conception of his status as a combatant. If disillusionment became extreme, soldiers might decide that it was no longer worth fighting and either desert or mutiny.

It is a striking feature of the First World War that, alone among the major European combatants, the British army did not suffer any hugely significant incidents of mutiny or unrest. The explanation for this is a complicated one. Morale has always depended on various factors ranging from the difficult psychological problems identified by Leed to the provision of rations. Numerous historians, attempting to explain the maintenance of British morale on the Western Front, have identified particular components and their contributions. John Baynes concluded that the foundations for high morale were unit loyalty and pride, strong inter-rank relations, sound administration, a sense of duty, and strict military discipline.[4] This latter was certainly as applicable to officers as it was to their men. There were 5,952 courts-martial on officers at home and abroad from 4 August 1914 to 31 March 1920, with offences including fraud (113), desertion (46), cowardice (10), drunkenness (1,856), theft (16), indecency (23), self-inflicted wound (12) and scandalous conduct (206).[5] Three officers were executed during the war, one of whom had been found guilty of murder, the other two for desertion.[6] The army did not, however, rely entirely on compulsion. In fact, if it had attempted to it would almost certainly have undermined cohesion and effectiveness in large parts of the army, as Helen McCartney has argued with reference to the Liverpool Territorials. Units like these – which were socially more diverse, had their own internal hierarchies based on pre-war society and had volunteered – would have responded badly to a harsh disciplinary regime because they 'retained a stake in civilian society and carried their civilian expectations and attitudes with them when they joined their unit.' Their officers 'were aware that the punitive discipline system was a necessary component in maintaining an efficient battalion in the face of horrendous fighting conditions, but they also understood that it took far more than the threat of a court-martial to motivate their men to continue fighting the war.'[7] This sensitivity sits along the paternalistic role of junior officers which, Gary Sheffield argues, played such an important part in ameliorating conditions for their men.[8] The sole serious mutiny in the British army, at Étaples in September 1917, took place at a time when the men had been separated from their usual officers.[9]

Other factors also played their part. Niall Ferguson has emphasised the importance of everyday pleasures such as smoking. He and Joanna Bourke have both explored the idea that soldiers might have been sustained by their enjoyment of killing.[10] John Fuller suggests that the export of working-class cultural pursuits to France was significant.[11] Junior officers certainly seem to have drawn significant moral support from their social networks and the retention of their familiar cultural activities.

Alongside theories stressing such factors are others which address the problems associated with the maintenance of positive 'conceptions of the soldierly self'.[12] Despite the conditions on the Western Front, soldiers in the ranks could restore a sense of personal agency and reassert a degree of control over their lives. Leonard Smith's study of the French mutinies of 1917 provides an example of how this might be done in the most dramatic way. France's Commander-in-Chief Robert Nivelle, who had succeeded Joseph Joffre in December 1916, decided to launch an offensive on the River Aisne. The French

Army, which was already exhausted and demoralised by the experience of the Battle of Verdun in 1916, suffered heavy casualties. Once it was clear that Nivelle's offensive was failing, French soldiers waiting to attack decided that another assault would probably be futile and that further losses were consequently unnecessary. Despite this refusal to attack, Smith notes, they remained committed to their defensive lines, having established their own sense of when they should and should not engage in aggressive action and succeeded in making their commanders comply with their wishes.[13] In a British context, as has already been indicated with reference to McCartney's work, soldiers were not entirely passive; good inter-rank communications and an element of negotiation were crucial.[14] Moreover, as Tony Ashworth has argued, soldiers were often able to control the fighting in particular sectors through a system of tacit truces and ceasefires, dubbed 'live and let live'.[15] They thwarted the higher command's more aggressive impulses through inactivity, thereby improving not only their chances of survival but also their confidence in their own ability to preserve themselves.

Junior British officers could similarly benefit from the reassertion of some measure of control which was made possible by the 'live and let live' system. Ashworth cites an episode from the history of the 15th Division in which two infantry captains argued vehemently with a trench mortar officer, each claiming that the *other's* sector was the more appropriate mortar site. They did not wish to host any aggressive action as they recognised that it would probably provoke a retaliation against them and their men. They appealed to the CO, who decreed that the officer should take his contraption to an altogether different spot away from the battalion.[16] Lancelot Spicer would have approved of this judgement from his vantage point on the Somme in February 1916: 'for every trench mortar we throw over to the Hun (and a great deal of damage they do), the Huns returns us an "aerial torpedo" as they are called. The aerial torpedo is the nastiest thing I have come across yet. It is like a large cigar, has about 170 lbs of H.E. and makes a hole about 14 ft deep by 30 ft across. So you can understand why we don't want any more trench mortars!'[17] He qualified this remark by claiming that he did not seriously mean it, but the sentiment is quite common in the letters and diaries of young officers, especially in connection with trench mortar officers.

This should not come as any surprise, even though officers were the personification of officialdom in the front line and might have been expected to maintain more aggressive postures. After all, they faced the same psychological problems associated with impersonal industrialised warfare as their men. Unlike more senior colleagues, they lived alongside their troops in the forward trenches when in the line. They were subjected to the same dangers and could have the same instincts for self-preservation. They had to be sensitive to the feelings of the men under their command and sometimes respect their desire to limit aggressive activity. These considerations arguably made a coping strategy like 'live and let live' all the more valuable.

Some historians have suggested that junior officers were peculiarly vulnerable to losing a positive conception of their soldierly character in comparison with the other ranks by virtue of their class and educational background.[18] There certainly seems to be a marked discrepancy between the vision of war inculcated by Edwardian society and the public schools, and the reality of the Western Front. Many a young officer entered the war with an image of soldiering derived from the 19th Century, from the works of George Henty, Henry Newbolt and Rudyard Kipling and from the stories in such magazines

That Sword.

How he thought he was going to use it——

——and how he did use it.

'That Sword' by Bruce Bairnsfather. (Copyright Barbara Bruce Littlejohn)

as *The Boy's Own Paper*.[19] At the same time, some philosophers were drawing on Social Darwinian ideas, arguing that war was a necessary element of international relations that ensured the vigour and spiritual health of the nations.[20] Conflict, in Edwardian culture, despite the turmoil of the Boer War, was consequently portrayed as and considered to be chivalric, ennobling and heroic. Even if a young man had been in an Officer Training Corps at school or university or in some other form of militaristic organisation, he could still have had very little conception in 1914 of the sort of war which awaited him *in the trenches*. Bruce Bairnsfather and other satirists joked about the contrast between the chivalric imaginings of public-school men and the harsher reality of life on active service, but this romanticism can be found in letters and diaries. Bertram Medley began writing his war diary in April 1915 with the sadly un-prophetic phrase 'The Tale of the Adventures of Sir Bertrame the Knight from the day when he set forth on his perilous voyage until he returned safely back home again.'[21] He was killed that September. The contrast with the bitter, disillusioned tone of Wilfred Owen's *Dulce Et Decorum Est* is striking.[22] This poem neatly encapsulates the historiographical case against public-school officers. By taking as its theme and title the traditional expression of an ideal of self-sacrifice – a central pillar of the public-school ethos – and juxtaposing it with the agonised death of a gassed soldier, Owen's work powerfully highlights the enormous gulf that separated the heroic idealism associated with the Edwardian public school and the harsh nature of warfare. It was because the disparity between an imagined war and a real one could be so stark for a young officer that he was so vulnerable, according to the theories of Leed and others, to psychological damage. Realising that they had been deceived, they became disillusioned.

The war therefore supposedly witnessed the end of idealism.[23] So apparently self-evident was it that the acolytes of the public-school ethos should have become demoralised under such circumstances that the history of this type of officer is closely associated with the language and ideas of disillusionment. This is partly because of the enduring myth of the 'lost generation' of a pre-war elite, because of the fame and literary importance of disillusioned officers such as Siegfried Sassoon and Wilfred Owen, and also because of persistent arguments between historians about the value of public-school-educated officers (as opposed to those selected on more rigorously meritocratic lines). A widespread impression that the war was characterised by unmitigated waste, futility and horror has also hindered a more balanced reading of the motivations and ideologies of these officers.

Revisionist military historians have recently challenged this last conception, detailing tactical developments and successful innovations rather than seeing only failure and incompetence.[24] It is, moreover, generally accepted that, although many officers were rendered cynical and bitter by their experiences, many *did* keep faith with their traditional ethos and ideas and were able to regard their careers as soldiers in a generally positive light.[25] John Bourne, for example, has acknowledged that, despite the blunting of idealism, those fighting the war did not succumb to disillusionment in large numbers, nor did they abandon the ideas which had inspired them.[26] Peter Parker similarly states that 'Chivalric notions about the War were those which were most difficult to relinquish'.[27] In Samuel Hynes's analysis, 'men at the Front continued to believe in the ideals for which they had enlisted, because only if those ideals were valid could their sufferings be justified; it was the people at home who abandoned them.'[28] The final two chapters of this book explore how that faith survived and the ways in which officers avoided disillusionment.

This chapter examines the threat presented by modern warfare to an officer's identity as a soldier. It argues that newly-commissioned public-school-educated officers were less powerfully influenced by a 19th Century attitude to war than may have been supposed, that there was no sudden shock or moment of revelation which could produce a collapse of their value system and that officers, in comparison to their men, had certain advantages which helped to prevent them from being overwhelmed by trench warfare. Moreover, whilst a 19th Century heroic idiom *did* continue to inform these officers' attitudes towards soldiering, it was subtly altered and remoulded by their experiences of 20th Century warfare, creating a new version of heroism which was applicable to the Western Front and achieved a wider influence, informing the creation of images and narratives of combat both during and after the war. Chapter 11 will examine officers' changing ideas and attitudes concerning the war, the public-school ethos and their own mortality.

⁊⁊

The familiar narrative of disillusionment usually places great emphasis on the naivety of the generation which volunteered in 1914, often overstating the case. Admittedly, nothing could have entirely prepared the most imaginative or well-informed new officer for the Western Front. There could be no substitute for experience.[29] Most young officers would therefore have agreed to some extent with James Neville when he wrote that 'I never knew what war was like when I first came out.'[30] There seems, however, to be a tendency for historians – themselves inevitably increasingly removed from events – to imagine that there was something about the trenches that remains totally incomprehensible to those who did not experience them, reinforcing the idea that young subalterns must therefore have been psychologically extremely ill-prepared for active service.

Some contemporary writers have reinforced this conception. 'In my childhood,' wrote Charles Douie in his 1929 memoir *The Weary Road*, 'I had often perused magazines in which the departure of troops for the front was depicted. It had seemed to me an occasion likely to give much satisfaction. Bands played. Crowds cheered. Generals shook private soldiers by the hand. The same troops on arrival in the field appeared also to have certain consolations. Battles undoubtedly were exhilarating affairs in which batteries came into action at the gallop and cavalry made gallant, and so as could be judged, not too expensive charges. A degree of excitement clearly obtained which might mitigate any sense of inherent danger. I had already learned that there were no bands playing, nor colours flying, nor any panoply of war in modern battle; only the roar of the barrage, the deadly rat-tat-tat of machine guns, and a sea of reeking mud.'[31] A tendency to emphasise this sort of pre-war innocence with the awfulness of the Western Front (often imagined at its worst all the time) has tended to create a strong presumption of shock and subsequent collapse.

In reality, information and practical knowledge could be collected from numerous sources, making the soldier's new life more familiar than might be supposed. Interestingly, as Jeffrey Richards has noted, public-school fiction had long provided prospective public-schoolboys with a picture of what to expect on reaching their new schools in a comparable fashion. He cites the experiences of preparatory school pupils like Alec Waugh and H.E. Bates, who developed their impressions of what public-school life would be like from the writings of authors like Talbot Baines Reed.[32] The process of becoming a soldier consequently contained elements which were strikingly similar to other aspects of growing up.

With regards to an understanding of the nature of trench life, a wealth of material rapidly became available which at least gave young or prospective officers a broad conceptual framework.[33] As soon as the front lines had solidified, newspapers and magazines were reporting the fact and circulating stories and images. Photographs appeared in papers like *The Illustrated London News* which fixed certain images of war in readers' minds.[34] 'No one who has carefully read the daily press for the first years of the war,' argues Ted Bogacz, 'can fail to see that the nature of combat on the Western Front was known very early on.'[35] *The War Illustrated*, a weekly paper first issued on 26 August 1914, immediately carried evocative images of harsh conditions on the front line.[36] Costing only twopence, it was intended to appeal to lower-middle-class and working-class readers.[37] Its information and images may still have had some impact on the officer classes, especially in the later stages of the war when the class base of the officer corps became much broader. It is not unreasonable to suppose either that it may have been read by public-schoolboys destined shortly for the army, for whom price may have been more of a determining factor. Harold Mellersh certainly had access to it amongst a range of periodicals: 'There were the newspapers and magazines, supplied for us to read; and I think a new one appeared, with the rather curious title, *Land and Water*, in which Hilaire Belloc reviewed the strategy of the war in weekly articles. But I doubt whether many of us read them. We looked more at the illustrated weeklies, the *Graphic* and *Illustrated London News*. Those were the days of the imaginative artists rather than the photographer, and their efforts were often to our liking. There was one of the pilot of a British aeroplane, who, having landed behind the enemy lines, was starting up his engine and flying off in the nick of time, with a German Uhlan galloping madly after him.'[38]

Material of this kind was soon supplemented by authors like John Hay Beith, whose novel *The First Hundred Thousand*, published under the pseudonym 'Ian Hay', was based on his experiences in the BEF. Peter Buitenhuis has argued that writing of this kind was fundamentally unrealistic and that Beith's work was essentially fantastical and misleading.[39] All the same, such stories were regarded by at least some serving officers as a useful source of information. Billie Nevill wrote to his family in January 1916 encouraging them to investigate Hay's work in order to gain a greater insight into his own war experience: 'if you do want to know exactly what the 'Front' is like, read the First Hundred Thousand by Ian Hay, The Junior Sub. It's the best thing I've seen & describes exactly what we've been doing for the last six months.'[40] (This is admittedly the same Billie Nevill who so famously used footballs as an inspirational aid on the first day of the Somme battle.)

Published material was supplemented by information from friends, relatives or acquaintances who were already serving. This may, in fact, have carried the greatest weight of all by virtue of its more personal nature and lack of association with government channels or external influences.[41] The existence of a strong connection and information flow between the front line and the home front runs contrary to what Helen McCartney calls the 'traditional view': that civilians 'remained largely ignorant of the nature of the war, retaining a glamorized, idealistic impression of the fighting.'[42] Her study of the Liverpool Territorials supports a revisionist interpretation, as does much of the material cited in this book. While some correspondents never advanced beyond colourless platitudes and requests for more chocolate or cake, others consistently wrote in graphic detail. Advice and assistance was sought and given when young men with serving relatives found themselves on the point of joining up or preparing for their first deployment abroad. In April 1916 Clifford Platt wrote to his brother Glyn, who was undergoing divisional training, saying he hoped that he (Glyn) would be posted to France rather than Belgium, 'which by all accounts is a land of rotten billets and almost continual strafing'.[43] Officers also made a point of calling on friends and acquaintances when back in the UK – often returning to their old schools or universities. Given the candour many were prepared to employ in their letters, it is highly likely that they were equally forthcoming with at least some of these contacts. They also wrote articles and letters which found their way into school magazines and other publications. Contact with discharged and serving soldiers can only have become more frequent as the war continued and the armed forces expanded. Those new officers who had to wait some months before embarking for France could have learned a great deal. Increasingly sophisticated and realistic training techniques also helped to acclimatise them ahead of their eventual initiation into trench life.

Furthermore, many Edwardians knew something of what to expect thanks to certain experiences at school. It would almost certainly be stretching a point to claim that their team games or the Spartan regimes of many boarding houses really conditioned pupils to be as hardy as they would need to be in the army. Many, however, had spent time in the OTC, and there can be little doubt that this practical experience did have some value. It introduced cadets to the rigours of route marches carrying heavy equipment and to some of the discomfort, fatigue and hunger associated with life in the field.[44] One should not exaggerate the degree to which this was an adequate preparation for the rigours of the Western Front. In most cases, thanks to army training, it did not need to be – but it should at least be taken into account.

All those who did not find themselves on the front line within the first few months quickly had ample evidence of the potential lethality of their undertaking. Adrian Gregory has argued that the seriousness of the nation's plight was evident as early as September 1914; it was the realisation of the tough fighting needed to defend the nation which pushed recruiting to new highs.[45] The significant losses incurred by the public-school classes were also all too evident to prospective officers. As has already been noted in Chapter 1, the schools went to great lengths to mark and commemorate the passing of their alumni. Family and social networks also ensured that officers frequently prepared to go out to the continent having only just received news of the death of yet another acquaintance. In Sam Paget's case the casualty was actually his grandfather, who succumbed to illness in January 1915, about six months before Paget's battalion finally crossed over to France. 'My own feeling is that death today is a far less strange and unfamiliar thing than ever before', he wrote to his mother. 'I was thinking of it this evening; for with whatever attitude one looks forward to going out to Belgium or Germany one must realize that we shall take our lives in our hands and that so many of one's most intimate friends have done and are doing so at this moment: "omne ignotum pro magnifico" [everything that is unknown appears magnificent] and certainly death today is no unknown thing.'[46] On

9 May 1915 Ian Melhuish received 'v. sad news', probably concerning the death in battle of a close (but unidentified) relative. Interestingly, the main conduit for information, his mother, was supplemented by his broader awareness of developments. The news came 'as a great shock, though it was not altogether unanticipated, owing to the fact that I knew the Colonel of the 1st Essex had been killed in action, and that therefore the Battalion had probably suffered.'[47]

With these sorts of tragedies constantly unfolding before them, and with the many different sources of information available to them through the media, acquaintances and their own military training, it is not unreasonable to suppose that many were quite well prepared psychologically for what awaited them, even if aspects of the experience were still unexpected. Sometimes, in fact, young men seemed to imagine things would be far worse than they turned out to be. They were surely quite fortunate.

While romantic notions did persist amongst the ranks of the newly-commissioned, an erosion of high concepts about war arguably began long before young officers reached the front line as they came to understand more and more about the realities of active service and how these might challenge their expectations. In the first instance, soldiering was frequently both mundane and tedious. Far from finding army life either highly exciting or horrific, officers had to get used to the normality and routine. Both training and the overall experience of living in uniform in military establishments in the UK must have habituated them quite well to this before they left for the continent. It is apparent that expectations could reach a higher pitch once this frustrating period of waiting was over, and that transposition to France presented its own challenge to officers imagining that this was the 'proper' start of their military careers. Edwin Vaughan's account of his first experiences of active service in January 1917 reveals both the detail of the mental image he had been able to create and its divergence from the more mundane reality:

> I tried hard to convince myself that the moment I had lived for had arrived and that I was now a real Service man. But this was difficult: there was no band playing, no regiment bearing the old colours into the fray, only little *me*, sitting behind an unwashed, unshaven driver, finding my way alone because I had been told to.

On turning his attention to the setting for his first experience of real soldiering (as he imagined it), the discrepancy was even more jarring. As he travelled he questioned his driver about the circumstances of the battalion, picturing it 'in the midst of fire and smoke.' He was told instead that it was stationed in a rather pleasant area well away from the lines: 'I, with my eyes prepared to meet a scene of wire entanglements, shell bursts and trenches, was confused by his references to the estaminets the men frequented, the girls they met, and the cushy time they were having … It was a drastic disillusionment and I did not know whether to be annoyed or relieved.'[48] It appears as though the first experiences of many officers really were not as bad as they had been expecting. This protected them from the potentially shattering consequences of being pitched headlong into a significant action and enabled them to recalibrate their sense of the normal and the soldierly identity on which morale depended. Vaughan's experience in joining an experienced unit must have been an increasingly common one as the war progressed. Whatever the standard of formal unit induction, simply being around men for whom trench service had long since ceased to be a strange experience must have had quite a profound impact. As previous chapters have shown, the development of a soldierly identity could then proceed in accordance with the passage of certain defining events, for example going up the line for the first time, or witnessing death or wounding.

Once stationed in France, officers had various advantages over the rank and file with regards to the maintenance of morale. One of the chief psychological problems associated with trench warfare – comparative helplessness and lack of control over one's fate – was countered by officer status itself. While they may not ultimately have been in control of their destinies, they were in charge of the platoons or companies in which they lived and worked. This brought particular benefits. Men of all ranks seem to have found it easier to cope with danger and stress when occupied. John Nettleton realised that the 'mere fact of doing something or, at least having to think what to do, blunted the sharp edge of fear.'[49] Possibly a key distinction between men like Nettleton and those under his command was that Nettleton usually had more occupying his mind because of the nature of an officer's work. Moreover, as has already been noted in Chapter 5, officers were buoyed by the responsibility of being in charge of men and the knowledge that they must set an example.[50]

Thanks to their membership of the command hierarchy and their contacts, often at quite senior levels, junior officers were also potentially much better informed than the men in their units. Those at the bottom of the pile could be kept in almost total ignorance. James Hawke enlisted in the Royal Warwickshire Regiment in 1909, eventually taking a commission and rising to the rank of Major. As he pointed out while still in the ranks in the trenches, 'Ordinarily, we didn't know what was happening or exactly what part of the line we were in. Why should the private soldier know? There was no question of movement, and his job was to hold the trenches.'[51] The knowledge with which the officer was privileged did not necessarily have to concern high level tactics or strategy. The most apparently unimportant information could make a tremendous amount of difference to the man on the ground; knowing when one will have a chance to stop, rest, eat or get dry helps the soldier to persevere in a way that may not be possible if there is no end to his discomforts in sight. Charles Dudley-Ward, commenting on the disciplinary failings resulting from a long march, recognised this:

It was a hard march and I don't know what I should have done if we had been told to do another five miles, still some of the men did lay down rather soon and several only came in two days after. I believe the reason for so much falling out was partly due to the unexpectedness of the distance. The rumour was that it was only ten miles and it turned out to be twenty thanks to the staff.[52]

While officers were just as vulnerable as their men to staff errors, they were more likely to have this sort of basic information which could help them endure. Their access to much more information about the status, plans and movements of their company or battalion would have given them a much greater ability to place their own experiences into context, as would staff appointments and perhaps also contact with well-placed acquaintances in other units or higher command formations.

Furthermore, the life of the junior officer was inherently more varied than that of the soldier serving in the ranks. A private had relatively little to look forward to. His periods of leave were less frequent, he was unlikely to be moved to radically different duties unless he was commissioned, and he was at all times subservient to military authority in the person of his NCO or officer. Officers, on the other hand, possessed greater freedom of movement and job flexibility. They were treated much more generously by the army with regards to periods of rest and leave. (Lt. Maurice Peters related to his mother how one of his men complained that it took him 19 months to get any leave, in which time some of the officers had had four or five periods.[53]) Consequently, officers were less likely to endure the most unpleasant aspects of the Western Front for as long as their men. While they still had responsibilities and were subject to the authority of senior officers, these restrictions tended to be much less over-bearing.

The psychological threats associated with the particular characteristics of industrialised and entrenched conflict were still present. It has been argued that one of the most substantial challenges to a positive soldierly identity was the physical and arduous nature of the work. Trench warfare was extremely labour intensive, involving significant amounts of digging, carrying and building. Eric Leed has suggested that the debasement of combatants to the level of the industrial proletariat, becoming workers rather than soldiers, was particularly threatening to morale.[54] It is certainly the case that many officers resented the change in status which manual labour could engender. Charles Douie was particularly struck by the way in which certain tasks were at odds with the ordinary soldier's self-conception:

> In all the monotony of trench warfare there was no greater tedium than that of the carrying parties which were needed for the supply of material to the front-line trenches, and no greater patience and tact than that of the officers and non-commissioned officers of the Royal Engineers, on whose behalf the carrying parties for the most part worked. The infantry soldier regarded himself as a fighting man and could not be persuaded to take kindly to the role of pack animal. Soldiers who could be relied on to remain cheerful in the most exposed trenches in the front line became unwilling and resentful on fatigue.[55]

Clearly the laborious nature of trench warfare presented officers with a challenge in terms of man-management. It was also a challenge to their own soldierly identity, although it is difficult to know how officers reacted because of varying circumstances. Certainly they had no automatic exemption from this 'social descent' because of their rank, but different units had different philosophies. Some were content for their officers to accompany their men to a work site and then simply leave them there, returning to whatever comforts might await them. Others expected the officers to work alongside the men, therefore arguably undergoing the full process of 'proletarianisation', or to supervise and direct.[56] Raymond Asquith vividly expressed the irritation of officers from elite units when afflicted in this way: 'It is really rather bloody to have the responsibility of a captain, the pay of a subaltern, and the work of a coolie – if not indeed of an elephant piling teak in a muddy slushy creek. Really they might find some more suitable work for the 1st regiment of Foot Guards than dunging.'[57] This attitude may well have applied even more forcefully to newly-enlisted men who had joined up with a prejudice against any but combat duties.

Officers were not, however, implacably opposed to labour. Some of those who were expected to pitch in alongside their men actually seem to have found the experience rewarding, enhancing both their respect for the men and also their own self-conceit.[58] Furthermore, as they learnt about the job of soldiering and developed increasingly professional attitudes they began to incorporate a strong work ethic into their own activities, increasingly discarding (as Chapter 3 has noted) romantic expectations of chivalry and adventure. Importantly, the type of work described above – which was usually ordered by more senior commanders, often supervised by Royal Engineers and inflicted on units stationed behind the lines – was unpopular because it was carried out *on behalf of an external authority* and allowed officers little opportunity to use their own judgement or initiative, and arguably therefore contributed to a sense of proletarianisation. In contrast, suitably motivated officers could choose, when in control in their own trenches, to focus on non-aggressive but still traditional aspects of the soldier's craft, thereby reinforcing their soldierly bearing and a positive self-conception. The maintenance of appropriate military standards of work was as important as the heightened aggression which historians have correctly associated with elite units and was similarly beneficial to morale.[59] Oliver Lyttelton, who volunteered in August 1914 following an education at Eton and Trinity College, Cambridge, served with the Grenadier Guards:

> I had a burying party at work and also every other man over the parapet of the trench we had taken over making them bullet-proof. The line had been in these trenches for six weeks and at no place would the parapet stop a bullet and everywhere the parados was quite inadequate. These regiments showed the utmost gallantry in the attack, but their ways are not ours at other times. When it comes to bayonet work they are as courageous as we are, but they haven't got the method, the care or the discipline to make good their gains, or to show the same steadiness in success and reverse as the Brigade.[60]

The Guards had long been self-consciously elitist. Their corporate ethos revolved around maintaining high standards. Other regiments and units, although lacking their heritage, were able to bolster their own sense of soldierly worth through emulation. When Douglas Bell wished to indicate his pride in the immaculate condition into which his men had restored his trenches, he cited the famous Guards as defining the standard which he felt had been achieved.[61] In other words, soldiers could choose to maximise opportunities (however presented) to demonstrate their soldierly character, and officers were particularly well placed to take advantage of this.

Another expression of the adherence to military work ethics was an insistence on maintaining high standards of turnout, drill and discipline when out of the lines.[62] The rank and file generally referred to such activities as 'Bull' and they could be extremely unpopular.[63] Graham Greenwell, however, was 'a firm believer in polish and smartness as an aid to discipline, as it undoubtedly is.'[64] Oliver Lyttelton too remained certain of the importance of discipline and the retention of the correct attitude: 'I am afraid that the New Army is trained too much with the idea "Oh we don't need discipline. These are not recruits driven into the ranks by hunger, they are patriots, it's ridiculous to ask a well educated man of forty to salute an officer of twenty", and so on. The alpha and omega of soldiering and training is discipline and drill.'[65] This attitude, which naturally matched official military thinking, was deliberately inculcated in potential officers. In a 1916 pamphlet entitled *Moral – The Most Important Factor in War*, Lieutenant Colonel W. Shirley published a speech which he gave in his capacity as commandant of the 2nd Artists Rifles, OTC. In it he particularly advocated high standards of personal appearance, arguing that the discipline required to achieve and maintain these standards would probably also have a beneficial effect on a man's professional conduct.[66]

The element of comparison remained important at all levels, as it had been at public school where sports matches and pride in one's boarding house associations were important elements of the education and the development of a corporate identity. The competitive edge, noted in Chapter 3, which encouraged pupils to ascend any available hierarchical ladder was also a valuable stimulant. Robert Hamilton wanted to keep his platoon smart partly 'because I want other platoons to look up to it, as one wants one's team to win.' He admitted there were other considerations: 'also I get cussed by COs and Brigadiers if it's not smart, and also it's better for the chaps and better for the job.'[67] Nevertheless, a perception of differences between units could play an important part in determining how much an officer enjoyed being a member of it. Clifford Platt moved from a Kitchener to a regular battalion and commented that 'It is simply top-hole being in a battalion where things are done properly and all the officers are gentlemen. It is so very different to the 19th [Lancashire Fusiliers].'[68]

Many officers consequently succeeded in maintaining (or developing) a broad view of the military craft, rather than focusing on the way in which the Western Front frustrated the aggressive instincts more traditionally associated with soldiering. Psychological survival could be promoted by identifying activities and standards, on whatever level, which seemed suitably military or professional in character. This required the development of a more expert attitude towards soldiering and the acquisition of knowledge relating to conventional military practices. Both were achieved under the intense pressures of wartime service. Officers who had grown up imagining glorious cavalry charges or advancing with a sword in their hand did learn the value of other aspects of soldiering. Some tasks were vital in ensuring the smooth day-to-day running of their units. Others assisted them in shaping the soldierly characters of their men and their own task of providing leadership. In some cases, ambition and a growing sense of careerism reinforced these lessons.

The army also retained and even expanded traditional techniques for judging and rewarding performance. In the words of an anonymous 'Amateur Officer', 'there exists a military provision by which this craving for individual achievement is also appeased, and to some extent satisfied. The soldier who accomplishes a personal feat of military importance is promised recognition. Medals and decorations are the prizes which, by their significance, made it possible for the solider to look forward to a realization of his own personality, in the teeth of death.'[69] The Military Cross was created in December 1914, partly because so many officers had already been made companions of the

Distinguished Service Order (DSO) in the earliest months of the war. The new award was only for warrant officers and commissioned officers with the substantive rank of captain or below.[70] Receiving some sort of decoration or being mentioned in dispatches was an important form of validation, not least because it was such a public declaration of achievement – which would undoubtedly be celebrated by schools, colleges or employers as well as friends and family.[71] It is significant that Captain Lionel Crouch should have complained that the company commander had a really tough job 'but he never has a chance of a "mention," much less of a medal.'[72] Many officers earnestly desired some sort of award, usually for self-validation but in some cases hoping that it would provide justification for their subsequent move to quieter and safer occupations.

As Crouch's words suggest, the system for allocating awards and recognising service was placed (like so much within the armed forces) under severe strain by the conditions of modern warfare. To retain their credibility in the eyes of fighting men, medals had to be seen to go to the most deserving. Too wide – or, indeed, too narrow – a distribution could lead to a general devaluing of the system, as could an apparently arbitrary process. Unfortunately, some of the ways for determining the allocation of medals did exactly that. There was a set quota for DSOs and MCs until May 1918, which potentially prevented men from being recognised despite impressive service.[73] At the same time, units were sometimes allotted a particular number of awards after a battle and then asked to submit recommendations for recipients.[74] This made getting a medal potentially an emotionally ambiguous event. When Douglas Bell was given an MC in August 1916 he was both pleased and self-deprecating. His diary entry clearly shows the effects of different sentiments and his awareness of the different constructions that could be placed on his honour. He could not conceal his own sense of pride, or the realisation that the honour would be appreciated by his family, but he also recognised that he might have been the recipient of an honour which had not been bestowed for any particularly meritorious service.[75] Bell's modesty is understandable. Officers seem to have appreciated that numerous honours were indeed distributed in a somewhat haphazard fashion. Bell himself thought that his battalion had probably been allocated a medal, and then had to find somebody to receive it. Moreover, many decorations effectively rewarded the artistic flair of the officer submitting the recommendation rather than the heroic act itself. Officers knew this because they themselves had to do the paperwork.[76] 'Your first job', a colleague told Guy Chapman, 'is to sit down and compose stories for decorations. Have a drink and let your imagination rip.' Chapman excused this sort of behaviour by arguing that 'all the men in the line who were decorated had done deeds which in South Africa or on the Indian frontier would have seemed superhuman, but in France were a job of ordinary routine.'[77]

A perceived lack of rigour in the system also made it vulnerable to problems of personal antipathy. If unpopular or inefficient officers received awards it could cause their colleagues to be even more dismissive of them. Charles Dudley-Ward bitingly observed in June 1916 that 'Evans has an MC and we all laugh. The thing is no longer worth anything.'[78] (Exactly one month previously month he had described this officer as having 'an enviable position in the Battalion. He is sniping officer which apparently means he is never to sleep in the trench and may attempt to direct all matters except sniping. There is much grousing about Evans and I think he is beginning to notice it.'[79]) Since the system was capable of being discredited even when the awards were going to front-line fighters, it is no surprise that its inability to differentiate sufficiently well between various types of service should be another major source of contention. Trench warfare, the defining feature of the Western Front, physically separated soldiers into distinct spheres of operation and influence. These were not entirely closed communities; soldiers interacted and moved between them, but there was a clear line between front-line combatants and those who worked in the rear areas and supply lines. The mystique and power of the trenches as the war's focal point simultaneously reinforced these perceptions in the minds of servicemen and the wider population. It was this perception of 'otherness' which rendered initiation into trench warfare and one's status as a 'trench fighter' so important. The existing honours system did not, however, take these differences into account. Many officers serving in the trenches were frustrated and angry that the awards for which they might be eligible could also be obtained for (in their view) comparatively insignificant non-combat performances.

They were particularly irritated by the perception that the system would actually favour those who were in the least danger. The argument – advanced, for example, by an anonymous military contributor to the letters page of *The Times* in May 1916 – was that those who enjoyed the safest jobs were more likely to survive long enough to obtain an award than the men who had done the most to earn one.[80] There was a further suggestion that this bias (if not, in fact, the giving of *any* commendations to support elements rather than combat soldiers) was breaking an essential connection between decorations and valorous service. This was seen by some officers as potentially damaging, given the importance of incentivising men to undertake the inherently less pleasant duties of the combat arms and an apparent belief that mere financial reward was less effective a motivation than higher concepts of honour and glory.

Increasingly, the perception that military honours were failing to recognise genuinely notable service threatened to bring the whole system into disrepute. A.J. Sansom incredulously related to his wife how a chaplain in his Division had received the MC in January 1917: 'he hasn't been in or near the front line, but he ran a Divisional canteen, and by charging sufficiently exorbitant prices he produced a good profit. Just fancy a Military Cross suffering such degradation!'[81] As Charles Messenger has pointed out, however, such awards were perfectly proper. Both the DSO and the MC were instituted to acknowledge 'distinguished' or 'meritorious' services in time of war, which did not have to mean bravery.[82]

Infantry officers continued to cling to the idea that their particular form of service should eclipse most others in matters of honours and recognition. This problem – that the system was undermined if perceptions or attitudes did not match purpose or process – could have unexpected effects. In July 1916 the War Office started issuing a 'wound stripe' made of gold braid. They were worn on the left arm and soldiers were entitled to one for each time they appeared as wounded on a casualty list since the start of the war.[83] Unfortunately, there was a flaw in the system as far as the fighting men were concerned. It honoured something generally regarded in trench circles as a positive occurrence, when their chief interest was in seeing that their endurance of hardships was properly recognised. As Frederick Keeling, the Fabian who had rejected the chance to take a commission, explained: 'The gold braid for the wounded is not at all popular out here, where everyone regards any wound, except a serious one, as a stroke of luck. What would have been popular is a trench medal, distinguishing the men who have been under fire, for say a hundred days, from the Staff job men.'[84] This view that the system should be modified to recognise trench service specifically did find some advocates. For example, *The Times*' anonymous letter-writer of May 1916 proposed that men who performed the most dangerous and onerous duties should be easily identifiable both in terms of their uniforms and in the creation of a new award indicating a particular period of trench service or a wound.[85] Such a scheme was never instituted although, Charles Messenger argues, the system had been made fairer by the end of the war. The creation of the Order of the British Empire, for example, made it possible to acknowledge the service of non-combatant servicemen without recourse to those awards seen as the preserve of combat soldiers.[86]

Promotion, the other method by which the army could mark distinction, has been discussed both in Chapter 3, which described the development of careerism within the officer corps, and in Chapter 6, which examined the issues surrounding professional advancement. As with medals and other awards, the creation of a mass *citizen* army created particular pressures. Former civilians – and by extension their families and friends – were less familiar than experienced soldiers with the gradations of military honours. They required unambiguous distinctions to explain and validate their actions, and a lot of ill-feeling was created within the officer corps by an over-rigid application of a system of promotion which was not designed for a force as large and complex as the BEF. As part of the work of his 1917 committee on promotions, Winston Churchill had himself floated a scheme designed to grade officers accurately and fairly. Having commanded a battalion of Royal Scots Fusiliers (albeit relatively briefly) in 1916, he was probably well aware of the general feelings of his fellow officers in the field. In any case, both he and Lord Derby, the Secretary of State for War, received evidence and petitions from the relatives and acquaintances of officers who had experienced some unfair treatment.

Churchill's suggestion was for a system of point-scoring by which every officer could compute his own personal 'Figure of Merit', providing 'a flexible means of guiding and encouraging the efforts and aspirations of officers into whatever channels were most desirable.' Each year's pre-war service in the regular army was worth five points. Each year's war service 'elsewhere than at the front for all branches alike' earned 12 points, but each *month's* service at the Front earned two. 'At the front' was defined as a zone within 15 kilometres of the firing line. A month in command of a company was worth a point, a wound five points and so on.[87] Although it would certainly have placed considerable emphasis on regimental service in the combat arms, Churchill's scheme did not find favour with military men like Major-General F.C. Shaw, who struggled 'to understand how such a system could be worked with fairness to officers generally and for the general good of the public service.' Shaw had a better understanding of the totality of military endeavour than Churchill. A particular complaint was that such a scheme would penalise 'staff and others who are absolutely essential, and who are placed in these positions in the interests of the service through no fault of their own. They are encouraged to do all they can to escape from these essential posts so as to get up to the front to earn "points".'[88] Essentially, for all Churchill's calculations, it was hardly possible to standardise trench and military experience, something many junior officers readily appreciated after they had themselves gained broader experience of life on active service. Major-General Shaw was effectively providing the professional perspective on a scheme derived from an amateur or voluntarist perspective. The fault lay not in the system but in the public understanding of the relative merits of different aspects of military service. Many junior officers, developing their own sense of professionalism, reached the same conclusion.

The existing system was not, however, altogether without its merits. Promotion, when it came, was usually gratefully received. If decorations were sometimes the butt of jokes they were still, as Richard Holmes points out, prized by most recipients and sometimes pursued with maniacal enthusiasm.[89] Critics and those tasked with investigating any deficiencies did not advocate sweeping the system away, but instead tried to find ways of adjusting it to make it seem more equitable. The persistence of well-known forms was further ensured by their familiarity and acceptability to generations brought up on stories of heroism and consequently disposed to honour them. The fact that they existed at all as performance markers automatically made them appeal to the public-school mentality. A medal was recognisably another rung on the familiar ladder of achievement discussed in Chapter 3. Sassoon's desire to win an MC, thereby proving himself the equal of his contemporaries was the same, argues Jean Moorcroft Wilson, as his pre-war determination to achieve sporting prowess.[90]

In this way the enduring cultural legacy of an Edwardian education helped officers to maintain positive conceptions of their actions and criteria against which to judge their efforts. These traditional elements of soldiering harmonised particularly well with their expectations. They could also reinforce a soldierly identity by adopting those quintessentially soldierly traits less commonly found in their Homeric tales. A young officer cannot have been in the army for very long before he realised that the archetypal activity of the pre-war regular and, by extension, the rank and file of the New Armies was complaining and grumbling about their lot. Lionel Sotheby, who joined the Argyll and Sutherland Highlanders in August 1914, realised by January 1915 that the ordinary soldier 'grouses as all true soldiers do, if he did not grouse, then he could not be a true Tommy.'[91] Appreciating that this was usually indicative of a relative degree of satisfaction, officers like Andrew Buxton were tolerant: 'It is a very fortunate thing that when life is uncomfortable an English soldier is always cheerful and jovial; when comfortable he grouses.'[92] As they absorbed this kind of traditional military vocabulary, former civilians began applying it to themselves, thereby identifying themselves with centuries of British soldiers who were proverbial 'grousers'.[93] There is certainly plenty of grumbling to be found in officers' letters and diaries. Since this fitted into a recognised military pattern it could contribute towards the construction of a soldierly identity, as well as fostering a sense of corporate solidarity.

❧

Young officers also had an advantage over professionals in this unprecedented war in that they were not encumbered by any significant pre-war experience of soldiering. They may have laboured under the delusion that war was inherently glorious, chivalrous or romantic but these ideas began to evaporate almost immediately and they had no practical experience to provide unfavourable comparisons. Professionals, on the other hand, had to adjust to the idea that the type of warfare they knew and had trained for was temporarily redundant, if not totally extinct. Gerald Burgoyne, who had served in the

Boer War, thought trench warfare 'rotten ... tedious, uninteresting, and ever death waits behind the curtain, thrusting out a hand to clutch some poor careless lad.' Admittedly, this comment could easily have been made by any number of British officers. While it is not possible, however, to say for certain that Burgoyne's dislike of the trenches was substantially influenced by previous experiences of warfare, it is striking that he should highlight the omnipresence of death and his own lack of interest in the business. It is also significant that he should go on to present a trio of 'high ideals' as particular casualties of the Western Front: 'Little of honour or glory apparent to us here, yet of course it's all in the day's work, and we are really jolly well paid for it, to put our duty on it's very lowest level.'[94] The difficulty experienced by longer-serving professional soldiers in adjusting to the new type of warfare can further be guessed at from the positive reactions of a new generation of officers to the outbreak of open warfare in the later stages of the 1918. Desmond Young found it 'dramatic and exciting'.[95] Lancelot Spicer described it as 'interesting' and 'much more pleasant', even if it was more strenuous at times.[96]

Newly-commissioned officers were usually able to abandon their pre-conceptions and resign themselves to the fact that, no matter what they had been *expecting*, this was what conflict was really like. Ralph Bickersteth, writing home to his family, told them 'I am very fit indeed – in fact, if this is War – give me War!!'[97] Acquiescence is another common theme in their writings. Christopher Stone, describing the suffering of wounded men in battle, noted 'However it's war, & there's an end of it.'[98] A.J. Sansom noted stoicism of this sort operating more widely:

> The French have a wonderful way of curing depression, satisfying complaints and accepting the conditions; it consists simply of the words "C'est la Guerre," and it acts like a charm – over and over again I have seen angry people pacified, grumblers satisfied and wrongs rectified by the use of that little phrase, accompanied by a smile and a shrug of the shoulders.[99]

Leslie Peppiatt and Charles Dudley-Ward both employed this formula after detailing certain professional annoyances.[100]

While a degree of resignation was important, officers also needed to engage, where possible, in action which did conform more readily to their pre-conceived ideas of soldierly behaviour. In other words, they had to find ways to operate in an aggressive or adventurous fashion and, in so doing, exert a greater degree of control over their lives. The trenches and No Man's Land provided the stage on which these performances had to be presented. Although they were dominated by machine guns and artillery which prevented military operations from taking place according to previous patterns of open warfare, they still provided the most scope for traditionally soldierly behaviour because their occupants were in the closest proximity to the enemy. Consequently they were both in the greatest danger and had the best opportunity for taking the fight to the enemy in a more personal way, both of which were key ingredients in traditional military conceptions of heroism.

Officers were encouraged by the military hierarchy to regard the front line as a sphere of personal martial endeavour. An aggressive posture was considered to be a useful stimulant of morale, and the maintenance of an 'active front' was consequently a regular element of British policy.[101] Operations directed by a higher authority were potentially unpopular, since individual officers might have a very different perception of their desirability or advisability.[102] However, tactical commanders could place a very different construction on action that they themselves had initiated, even if it was fundamentally the same type of activity. Personally motivated aggressive or adventurous activity would invariably be considered desirable, whether it was confined to the trench itself, or carried out in No Man's Land in front. As tactics evolved, individualism was increasingly able to re-assert itself through officially-sponsored operations; the development of the platoon as the main tactical unit and the integration within it of different weapon systems gave the junior officer much greater scope to dominate the battlefield.

The ability of the individual to interact with and dominate the machine warfare environment has been described by Dennis Showalter as 'a new wave of heroic vitalism'. His argument about the significance of individual performances is illustrated with particular reference to elite German assault battalions and the Italian *arditi* equivalents which emerged during the course of the war, but he also stressed their importance from 'the earliest stages of trench warfare'.[103] Junior British officers were ideally placed to demonstrate this heroic quality, and did indeed do so from the beginning of the war despite the testing conditions. They may not have had complete and autonomous power over their own section of the line – being subject both to the authority of more senior officers and the less formal, but potentially equally effective, influence of their NCOs – but they did have quite a lot of control. This enabled them to instigate or personally conduct activity in ways which would typically be unavailable to non-commissioned soldiers.

Shooting at the enemy from the safety of one's trenches was the most basic assertion of an aggressive soldierly character which is why, as Chapter 3 describes, so many trench newcomers were eager to try it. Officers could easily participate in or order such actions. One morning James Neville described taking a shot at 'two Boche walking about in their support line … They ducked, and I had another shot at them and they ran like hell. I wish I had killed them … However, I am going to register some rifle grenades on that spot and see if I can't catch them tomorrow.' Such activities may not have displayed much heroic vitalism, certainly when compared to later stormtrooper tactics, but they were attempts to dominate the battlefield and deny elements of it to the enemy. They also re-personalised the conflict; Neville's aggression was directed against identifiable combatants, tempered by the hope that 'they won't return the compliment and try to snipe me!' It was this sense of deadly competition which provided both an incentive to further action and potentially a boost to morale. Neville won the contest the next morning, mercilessly following up a presumed kill with 'six rounds rapid with rifle grenades'.[104]

As the variation in his weapon of choice indicates, as an officer he also had access to all the different weapons systems which the trenches had to offer. Selecting the appropriate tool for the job was both a mark of professionalism and an opportunity to tailor aggressive activity to satisfy personal conceptions of soldierly behaviour. As a trench mortar officer, Bernard Pitt might well have done more damage to the enemy with indirect mortar fire than with direct rifle fire. He felt, however, that 'It was good to get a rifle in one's hand and plaster the Hun sniper's loophole plate with bullets so that he dared not open the shutter'.[105] This he could do thanks to his more autonomous status as an officer. In this instance he seems to have been less interested in the actual utility of his aggression than in engaging the enemy directly, thereby reasserting his aggressive soldierly agency and 're-personalising' the conflict.

As officers became slightly more senior their abilities to take aggressive action increased proportionately. Opportunities to command companies could fall to very young or comparatively inexperienced individuals. William Villiers of the King's Royal Rifle Corps temporarily commanded a company in 1916 at the age of nineteen, having only been at the front for six months. A company usually consisted of four platoons, each containing some 40 men, all armed with rifles, bombs and rifle-grenades. The company commander would also have had access to the specialist services of heavy and light machine gunners, trench mortars and snipers. His control over all these modern weapons systems, combined with his enhanced freedom of action, gave him numerous opportunities to exercise his initiative in a traditionally soldierly and aggressive fashion. One company commander with access to a military band reportedly marked the first anniversary of the beginning of the war by staging a concert in a front-line trench, drawing the enemy into their own forward areas. 'Then, as the last note sounded, every bomber in the battalion, having been previously posted on the fire-step, and the grenade-firing rifles, trench-mortars, and bomb-throwing machine, all having registered during the day, let fly simultaneously into the German trench; and, as this happened, the enemy, who had very readily swallowed the bait, were clapping their hands and loudly [shouting] "encore."'[106] In this instance, initiative overcame the tactical constraints imposed by trench warfare, thereby maximising the effectiveness of British firepower.

Going 'over the top' – or 'over the bags', as it was sometimes called – to take part in a large-scale attack was a relatively rare occurrence for most soldiers.[107] Aggressive activity in No Man's Land most commonly took the form of raiding and patrolling. Raids were the more aggressive of the two, being attempts to get into the enemy trenches, usually to take prisoners and gather intelligence but potentially also to destroy defensive positions or simply to inflict casualties. Patrols were sometimes similarly intended to gather intelligence, but could equally be used to provide cover for soldiers working in No Man's Land or, in their most aggressive form, to dominate the ground and challenge enemy operations. In 1915 these practices developed as *ad hoc* battalion tactics. From 1916 they were increasingly directed by the higher command.[108] Although highly-motivated officers retained the ability to carry out localised operations on their own account, the actual level of activity was therefore likely to be related to the phase of the war and the level of hostilities within a sector.

Although leaving the protection afforded by a trench was inherently risky, going out into No Man's Land was comparatively safe at night and not particularly unpopular. Some officers clearly regarded it as another defining activity, separating veterans from less experienced soldiers. Moreover, recognising that they might just as easily be killed doing nothing in a trench by a stray bullet or shell, officers appreciated the chance to behave in a way that at least seemed more traditionally soldierly than waiting underground. Lieutenant Stephen Hewett commented that 'the general feeling is a desire to do something active, and we all welcome the minor risks of patrol work, etc. as a relief from the monotony of trench routine, which combines passivity with quite enough dangers of its own.'[109] Raids were also frequently carried out in daylight. These were, of course, substantially more perilous but this does not seem to have deterred motivated officers like James Neville. 'There are great stunts going on now, on this small piece of front,' he wrote in August 1917. 'Officers seem to have the habit of going over the top on daylight patrols to try and snaffle a Boche. I am itching to try to make a prisoner, and am going to evolve a scheme to effect this.'[110] His enthusiasm for the active soldierly role seems to have been boosted by the apparent introduction of an element of competition. Validation was frequently a matter of their perceived standing relative to their colleagues, and operations in No Man's Land called for both the initiative and courage which were the hallmarks of the ideal officer. Accounts also convey a sense of enjoyment, the officer revelling in the excitement, the risk or simply the challenge.

Deeds did not always need to be aggressive to be personally satisfying, contribute to a sense of soldierly worth and build morale. Small and even apparently pointless acts, for example, of exploration or reconnaissance could be equally valuable. A number of good examples of this can be found in the letters of Sam Paget. On first arriving at the front in 1915 Paget appears to have taken every opportunity to explore his new surroundings. On taking over a new part of the line, he commented that he had spent most of the morning exploring, joking that he could now act 'as a competent Cooks Guide to our Sector.' This was constructive work in its own right, consciously developing his tactical awareness. During the course of the morning he identified a useful vantage point to which he returned when he had more time: 'needless to say you can't do much in the way of looking over the parapet in the front line. But I found a place – an old shell hole just off a communications trench – into which you can crawl and use a telescope through the long grass; and here I had a great time.' He had a clear view of a German-held village and their lines of communication up to the trenches.[111] The value of this sort of investigation was demonstrated in the letter written to his mother several days later. Paget reckoned that he now knew 'more about (a) Germans and (b) trenches after the last few days than I ever learnt during a year's training with incessant lectures from authorities "back from the front".' By this time he had got into even closer proximity to the enemy:

> This place here is rather a salient and at the very apex here where we are there is a small wood which you can get into by tunnels from our trench. From here you can hear the [Boche] not only working but talking – they are about 250 yards away I suppose. I spent a whole day there putting up wire and observing and it was certainly very interesting: at times especially about 6am you can almost hear the words the Germans are saying and when I wish to exaggerate I say that we can hear them eating soup.

Other than the wiring, his actions seem to have had relatively little wider utility, unless he was more assiduous in collecting hard intelligence than his letter suggests. Clearly, however, he saw it as instructive and therefore a useful part of his education and development as a soldier. His tone, although potentially distorted in consideration of his audience, also suggests he derived some emotional benefit from his efforts. Moreover, he was being active, pushing forward into No Man's Land and recognisably behaving in a traditionally soldierly manner – effectively scouting. Some of the soldiers under his command – 'two poaching boys who kept pestering me to let them go' – were similarly impelled to investigate their new environment but they could not act with as much autonomy and had to wait for Paget's approval.[112]

These sorts of private and individually motivated operations and excursions enabled officers to become more familiar with the ground and the experience of being out of the trenches. They were consequently useful in developing the confidence needed to maintain the aggressive spirit demanded by British doctrine. When Edwin Vaughan, in company with a colleague called Radcliffe, decided to go out into No Man's Land he 'felt awfully frightened and my heart beat very high as for the first time I passed through the wire into the silence and mystery of the unknown ground.' His nerves, already stretched by the appearance on the scene of a small party of Germans, can't have been helped by the discovery that Radcliffe was essentially unarmed, but getting through the ordeal gave him a taste for more aggressive action: 'I was so pleased at having broken the ice that I felt quite anxious to get out again with a fighting patrol behind me.'[113]

Vaughan's expedition was spontaneous and even rather casual – it had not been ordered and had no specific military objective beyond acclimatising himself to his new environment. He was using his initiative and his independence for some personally-identified purpose. Precedent for this behaviour can be found in the educational institutions of the pre-war era. Junior officers, in taking advantage of their comparative freedom and organising their spare time to their own advantage, were reflecting the everyday habits of the senior public-schoolboy. Owen Buckmaster, recalling his experiences at Winchester, commented in his autobiography that 'no normal man can ever again be in such a happy position as the prefect at a great public school, free to play any game that he may choose, able to take up any one of many pursuits'.[114] If a distinction is drawn between officially-sponsored work and activities which officers were obliged to undertake and the privately-conceived activities which have been described, it can be seen that active service mirrored life as a prefect in some respects – one had responsibilities and work but also privileges and quite a lot of time for self-indulgence. In other words, public-school men were already familiar (in terms of role recognition) with the essence of an officer's lifestyle and circumstances. They could therefore maximise any available opportunities for activities which reinforced their soldierly self-conception.

Despite the strategic stalemate and the transformation in soldiering it produced, the Western Front did not preclude activities which placed a satisfying emphasis on personal performances. The value of these performances, other than the moral fillip provided by the adrenalin rush of excitement or the satisfaction derived from seeing some personal goal achieved, lay in the construction of personal combat zone narratives and identities which harmonised with pre-existing or developing models of good or valid behaviour. These standards were defined by the prevailing culture which stressed personal agency, physical prowess and the high ideals of glory and heroism which acted as both motivation and reward. Any aggressive action was potentially beneficial, since it had been the defining characteristic of the soldier throughout the ages. Similarly, activities in the nature of stalking or reconnaissance harked back to stories of big game hunting or military scouting which always stressed manly virtues of courage and heroism. These activities were highly prized by Lord Baden-Powell, the founder of the Boy Scouts, who had a significant influence on the creation of the Edwardian ethos of manliness.[115] By remaining active, utilising their initiative and taking advantage of their freedom from immediate authority, officers could continue to fashion a positive sense of their worth as soldiers.

The experiences themselves were clearly different from what young officers might have expected. The Western Front did not conform to many of the characteristics of warfare on which the traditional image of soldiering and heroic idioms had been based. It was undoubtedly anti-heroic in the sense that it generally denied combatants personalised contests within defined periods of battle which marked out the episodes of a grand strategic narrative. It required mass armies, many of whose soldiers were substantially still undertrained civilians compared with the pre-war martial elite. The environment was dominated by mud and filth, which detracted from any supposed nobility while also threatening to conceal individual characteristics under a uniform layer of sludge. It was too dangerous much of the time to operate in the open during the day, so a lot of activity had to take place in the darkness and anonymity of night. Moreover, trench warfare as a doctrine was an inherently limiting enterprise. It emphasised patience and labour and restricted individual spheres of action and perception. Offensives or big battles, even if strategically successful, were characterised by noise, smoke and confusion which isolated soldiers. At these peaks of its intensity, the Western Front was a chaotic space which defied overall orderly explanation from the individual's perspective. Clearly, certain disastrous episodes like, for example, the opening of the Somme battle, could not credibly be interpreted according to a heroic idiom in any case for other reasons, the sheer awfulness of the occasions invalidating the traditional high-concept rhetoric.

As has been argued, officers partly overcame this problem by adopting officially-sponsored modern notions of good soldiering. They may have had no idea of such a thing when dreaming of a career in the army, but professionally-minded officers in the trenches would ensure that their men took appropriate care of their feet and that their section of the line was well maintained and tidy, precise standards being dictated by formal or cultural codes of practice. Thanks to these codes, they could also rely on their superiors to challenge their worth as soldiers and officers if they fell below certain standards. They did not, however, find that their pre-conceived notions of heroism were entirely invalid and replaced by such managerial conceptions. They typically could not make sense of warfare on a large scale – because it was too big, too horrific, too confusing or rendered the individual too insignificant – but the traditional grand concepts (and the sense of self-worth derived from them) could survive in the personal sphere, the microcosm of military activity in which they could continue to be the central characters. Significantly, the activities described above by Sam Paget, Edwin Vaughan, James Neville and others are all fundamentally small-scale and localised.

To some extent, scale did continue to exert an influence on the way officers perceived combat. While large assaults were understandably a major cause of anxiety and fear for many, letters or diaries expressing a desire to be involved in major actions are relatively common. This can be partly ascribed to the genuine wishes of many officers not to be parted from their men or their colleagues. In July 1917 Arthur Gibbs was disappointed to be designated part of the 'left out of battle' (LOOB) contingent, a residuum of officers and men left behind to enable a battalion to reconstitute itself in the event of heavy losses, because he had 'had the training of the company for so long.'[116] Charles Douie saw a subaltern become publicly distraught at the news that he was to be left out.[117] Some examples in correspondence may also be ascribed to prevailing cultural expectations and attempts at self-definition; the audience of any writings might have expected the young officer to be enthusiastic about a 'big push', and the officer himself may have preferred to give this impression. Nevertheless, it is also apparent that some genuinely wanted to be at the epicentre of activity. In addition to his feelings about his men, Gibbs had also attributed his disappointment to the fact that he 'was rather looking forward to a real good scrap.'[118] Back in late July 1916 he had expressed similar feelings about the major offensive of the moment: 'I certainly rather wish that we could have a go on the Somme. It is certainly one of the shows of the war, and we feel rather out of it at present.'[119] When Geoffrey Fildes commiserated with his company sergeant-major about being, like him, part of the LOOB the disappointment at having to abandon the men is clearly apparent, but the CSM's parting shot ('Twelve years with the Colours, sir! Sergeant at Mons, company sergeant-major since Loos, and now – this!') similarly suggests that a soldier's positive self-conception partly depended on participating in what were considered to be the defining events of the campaign.[120]

Although the prospect of large-scale operations might have been attractive to some, officers seem to have found it difficult to maintain an impression of large-scale heroism once they were underway. When Oliver Lyttelton went over the top with his battalion in 1916 the overall impression was one of confusion and chaos. His account, written while on leave, begins with a clear description of the final minutes before the start ticking away:

> 6.15 I announced to the Commanding Officer – 5 minutes to go. Not an anxious five minutes: the fight was for those five minutes beyond our control: nothing could be altered, no more orders given, 4 mins. I hope sincerely the barrage if it does not come down at the right time will be late & not early. 3 mins. Silence complete except for the faint stir of nature at dawn. 2 mins. A flash of one or two bayonets. 1 min . . . .
>
> "The front line is off" I said. The Commanding Officer smiled as if to say "I am well aware that it was likely to happen at 6.20" and so up we got yelling to the men to watch the dressing.

The narrative then begins to become somewhat sketchy as the initial phases of the assault gather momentum – descriptions of specific moments as the battalion encounters and overcomes a small number of Germans giving way to the rush of men, the impersonal machine gun fire, and finally 'a blurred image of slaughter' as the battalion pours into the German lines. Lyttelton's somewhat disordered state of mind is revealed when called to report to his colonel following the conclusion of one phase of the action: '"This is great fun I must say" was all the report I could give.' The fog of war clears to some extent as the battalion focuses on specific tactical challenges during the course of the day. Lyttelton has clear recall of particular tactical engagements like leading a bombing party to clear a specific objective.[121] His story is most coherent when dealing with comparatively minor events.

Heroic vitalism consequently found its place on the Western Front within personal stories which were inherently concerned with small scale occurrences. The initial interest and excitement with which many new officers approached the trenches, combined with their youthful exuberance, predisposed them to undertake the sorts of expeditions embarked on by Paget or Vaughan. Since almost any activity in the vicinity of the front line was inherently dangerous and since any aggressive behaviour or minor expedition out of the comparative safety of the trenches could be interpreted as being in accordance with familiar stories and images, young officers were able to imagine themselves in heroic roles. It is surely no coincidence that Lyttelton recalled encouraging his men by shouting 'like a man in a novel'.[122]

Officers who cast themselves at the centre of their own personal stories were automatically reducing the scale on which heroism and soldierly endeavour were seen to be operating, thereby minimising the importance of a grand strategic narrative. Subsequently, when the war did not reveal itself to be any more romantic or heroic on the larger strategic scale, they were able to continue to regard the personal sphere (which was always available, even in major operations, as Lyttelton indicates) as their most fertile source of inspiration for a positive soldierly self-conception. The prominence which episodes of this kind enjoy in letters certainly suggests that they were regarded as being particularly significant, both to writers and to their audiences, who would probably have similar preconceptions. They would not have featured if they were regarded as unsoldierly.

This emphasis upon unimportant actions, set against a hostile landscape and the absence of a personalised enemy, suggests that the existence of a grand narrative arc was less significant in defining Western Front heroism than an officer's ability to establish an appropriate pattern of behaviour. It was the continuing activity of being a soldier that mattered, not the effect or utility of any action taken. In other words, the function of soldiering was changed. Hitherto, military work had typically been defined by successful (or even valiantly unsuccessful) attempts to perform specific deeds. In this campaign, however, there was very little traditional purpose on an individual level. Ironically, even killing the enemy was invested with a form of pointlessness because, in the clash of such huge armies, isolated pin-pricks became insignificant – a problem magnified by the occasional killer's empathetic realisation that the individual combatant "had done him no harm". If a man could not be classed as a genuine agent of the enemy state, he ceased to be an appropriate target for violence. The 'storm of steel' itself was left as the identifiable enemy, yet it was vital for the overall success of the war effort that that storm be weathered. Endurance and activity within it consequently became endowed with heroic and soldierly qualities.[123]

These changes in the structures of accounts of warfare brought young officers and their writings into a close relationship with the contemporary print media, both informing it and being influenced by it. Large-scale battles and attacks excluded, the type of warfare usually described by officers has several main characteristics, some of which match traditional press practices, some of which appear to be importantly different. Officers' stories are characterised, in the first place, by their focus on episodes in which they were the central exponents. This was entirely typical of the usual Victorian press method of focusing on the heroic incident, where possible involving an individual.[124] Secondly, the enemy seldom appears as a distinct personality. Unless a soldier was in a position to identify and engage with a specific enemy directly with a rifle, or in hand-to-hand combat, he was merely adding to the latent lethality of his environment. Even those soldiers who admit to shooting at identified targets seldom report that the target was attempting to engage them; a soldier caught off guard by a sniper is scarcely a formidable opponent in that moment. Instead, the environment itself is a hostile presence, more dangerous than any obvious human agency. In many of the stories the main protagonists are not themselves opposed in any active sense, although there is an ever-present threat. Vaughan's expeditions encountered no enemy at all. Paget could hear Germans talking but there is no suggestion that they were in a position to attack him or that he felt threatened. Finally, each story has very little sense of any ultimate success or victory, at least on any large scale. Nor could it hope to. The Western Front may fundamentally have been an attritional contest but isolated kills could scarcely be seen as significant in the grand scheme of things. Similarly, expeditions into No Man's Land, even if they led to violent exchanges, could not hope to alter the course of the war.

There were some similar changes in the representations of the war in popular culture. Admittedly, few writers adopted a policy of strict realism. Wartime newspapers have been heavily criticised, both at the time and in subsequent years, for their failure to report the events on the Western Front more accurately.[125] Jay Winter has particularly criticised the civilian paper *The War Illustrated*:

> The drawing on the cover of the issue of 28 April 1918 is of 'British Cavalry Charging the Oncoming Germans in the Great Battle in the Somme Area'. In the time-honoured (and totally outdated) tradition of the Bengal Lancers, British horsemen are shown 'Getting In With the Point' of their lances, thus scattering a cluster of terrified Germans. The articles which followed were all hortatory and full of the rhetoric of war as adventure.[126]

Certainly, the traditional heroic tone displayed on the cover of this edition and found in the articles of many newspapers is at odds with the more sombre note struck by the average letter writer. Many soldiers would themselves consider this a propagandist or distorted perspective. Images of soldiers striking a heroic pose in various settings, with no apparent enemy or activity in view, would probably also fall into that category, censoring out danger, squalor or any other negative aspects of war in favour of an implied manliness and stolidity. Dan Todman has suggested that this retention of a traditional style reflects the extent to which the purported war aims of the Allies conformed to the heroic, chivalric style.[127] While often blatantly propagandist, many images in *The War Illustrated* also have various features in common with accounts from the trenches in terms of their focus and the scale on which participants see heroism operating. Most are still stirring portrayals of events and the overall tone across the series is certainly emphatically pro-war, but there are surprisingly few images that could be described as conforming to a straight-forward 19th Century idiom of heroic and glorious warfare, especially amongst those that deal specifically with the British war on the Western Front.

At the lower end of the heroism scale are a number of images apparently intended to offer the civilian reader a glimpse of the daily routine in the trenches. "A Quiet Day In The Trenches" (16th January 1915) features soldiers smoking, blowing on their hands, writing letters or gazing moodily over the parapet. "The Coming Of Winter On The Battlefield" (5th December 1914) shows troops huddling behind a low wall in the snow. Some scenes of disappointment and dismay are included – the edition dated 22 May 1915 carries a picture of bedraggled soldiers, some of whom have obviously been wounded, taking roll-call in the trenches after a 'desperate counter-attack' (although the text provides an implied heroism, amplified by the use of the word 'desperate'). There are also images showing typical military tasks such as wiring parties. There is still clearly a sanitising hand at work, rendering trenches neat and dry and Tommies apparently contented.

Most interesting are those that portray action. Many of the images of front-line activity which appear in *The War Illustrated* match certain characteristics of the accounts of officers like Paget and Vaughan. They tend to focus on individuals or small groups of people, avoid depicting a personalised enemy, and largely remove any sense of achievement or utility. 'After the Knock-out Blow: Taking Possession of an Overturned German Gun' (4 November 1916) is interesting in that all the Germans visible are dead. There is no suggestion either in the picture or in the caption that the British soldiers depicted had any part to play in their deaths or in the capture of the gun. They have simply arrived on the scene and look totally unconcerned, merely 'taking possession'. 'Fighting Foul Fumes and Fiends: The British Soldier still a match for coward Germans' (15 May 1915) shows a small group of soldiers advancing, with protective pads in place, through a cloud of poisoned gas. It is noticeable that the men depicted moving through the fumes cannot be seen to be heading for any readily apparent enemy or objective and that the reader is given no information about the success or otherwise of their mission. While the caption and the fixed bayonets suggest that the soldiers are attacking, the artist contains them in a de-personalised microcosm of action which is common in such drawings. A similar example is 'Hand Grenades to the Fore! British Bombing Party attacking a German Trench' (10 July 1915) in which no live Germans are visible.

Moreover, when depicting the foe artists often avoided creating images of an opponent whose defeat could be considered particularly glorious. This was not the normal practice during the 19th Century, when cartoons occupied a form of visual rhetoric in which the foe was rendered as menacing, brutal and frightening as possible.[128] The point was to emphasise the evident heroism of the cartoon's chief protagonist. During the war, however, as Lawrence James notes, artists working for papers like *The War Illustrated* took their cues from propaganda photographs. The German was consequently often portrayed as a cowardly, brutish and ineffectual figure.[129] National chauvinism may have demanded this denigration of the opposition, but it hardly enhanced the impression that the enemy combatant was the real threat.

Even those pictures in *The War Illustrated* which seem to offer a more heroic vision of the war manage to deflate the traditional glorious idiom (presumably unintentionally, given the propagandist overtones) by removing any sense of ultimate utility. An example is 'One against Many: How Corporal Pollock won the VC near the Hohenzollern Redoubt' (4 December 1915). A bomber is depicted in the act of assaulting an occupied German trench. Once again, the inhabitants of this position are, for the most part, stricken with fear as Pollock throws his bombs with a look of grim determination on his face. However, in accordance with the trends so far identified, any sense of real achievement is strikingly absent. There is no supplementary biographical information. The reader is not even informed whether or not the corporal survived. The presence of three Germans and the mention of the VC do set it apart from similar images but in other respects it is similar to the anti-traditional images found not only on the covers but more generally throughout the magazine. 'An Unnamed Hero-Officer's Great Bombing Exploit' (6 November 1915) is another example of a microcosm of battle. The officer in question is said to have ensconced himself behind a barricade and kept up a steady bombardment of the enemy line for a prolonged period during an attack on the Hohenzollern Redoubt. The narrative accompanying the picture does little to connect it to wider operational developments and does not recount whether or not anything was actually achieved by these actions. In all of these cases, the image is of a brief moment in time which has been separated from any sense of historical or military sequence, or any over-arching story.

Illustrations of this kind are clearly attempts to present the war in a particular light, constructing a version of events and conditions which could conform to certain preconceived ideas. On that basis it is perhaps appropriate that their work should so often have chimed, in certain respects, with the way young officers – so many of whom were the children of that ideology – created their own narratives of conflict. This does not make them any more appropriate or less deceitful as depictions of combat, but it does reinforce the impression that there was a natural evolution in the application of the traditional high concepts. The Western Front did not provide artists with many prospects which naturally lent themselves to heroic representations. There were some – massed troop assaults, for example – which might impress through their scale or comparisons to earlier modes of combat, if nothing else, but fundamentally it was necessary to scale back some of the traditional modes of expression to fit the new circumstances. Rather than twist various episodes to fit the old mould, it is striking that artists should instead have found ways of co-opting the non-traditional scenes which were created in abundance and finding within them the same kernel of heroism or personal satisfaction which officers themselves seemed to find. The creation of these images and others like them may have influenced the soldiers whose exploits provided the inspiration, supplying the fantasy which they could then seek to emulate.

Some comparable developments may be observed in the field of popular literature, which may have had a similarly symbiotic relationship with the combatants themselves. The fiction of the Edwardian era had been dominated by narratives of 'derring-do'. Volunteers and commentators alike imagined that the war would provide a theatre in which the fighting population could rediscover their martial vigour and emulate their literary heroes. Not all authors abandoned these ideas, clinging on to the high concepts as tenaciously as some of the doomed combatants themselves. Writers like P.F. Westerman and F.S. Brereton published stories which continued to depict the war in the Edwardian style.[130] It is notable, however, that others chose to avoid the Western Front – the locality expected to be the centre of world events – altogether in order to maintain the ability to write stories about *significant* individual heroic endeavour. John Buchan provides a good example. His most famous character, Richard Hannay, first appeared in 1915, winning his spurs not as the officer he would subsequently become but as a civilian. The difficulty of emulating the heroism and dynamism shown in *The Thirty-Nine Steps* in wartime is actually reflected in that book's final line: 'But I had done my best service, I think, before I put on khaki'. *Greenmantle*, Hannay's only other adventure published during the war, took him to the Near East. It was only in 1919 that Buchan finally published a story showing him in the role of a more conventional Western Front soldier, and even then much of the action in *Mr Standfast* takes place in the UK.

Although attempts were made during the inter-war years to remember and present the war in the traditional terms which trench warfare had rendered redundant, many chose to focus on the exponents of the new forms of warfare, exemplified by the actions of the Royal Flying Corps, which seemed better suited to the old idioms of valour and chivalry.[131] Alternatively, writers such as C.S. Forester of *Hornblower* fame could delve into the past for inspiration and a setting in which they might keep the conventions alive and relevant. The period is now particularly famous for the appearance of a large number of anti-war books, especially the famous autobiographical and semi-fictionalised works by writers like Sassoon and Graves. Mirroring the letters and diaries produced during the war, these texts tended to concentrate on the exploits of individuals. Some historians have argued that this focus on the experiences of isolated soldiers was a deliberate strategy designed to bolster the 'myth' that the war was characterised by futility, waste and horror since, in contrast to the much less ambiguous story of big battalions and grand strategies, the individual's account could not help but convey an impression of chaos and powerlessness.[132] Others criticise apparently deliberate attempts to reintroduce romanticism into a type of warfare that was notably lacking in elevated sentiments. Sassoon's *Memoirs of an Infantry Officer* contains several descriptions of personal heroic actions including a lone assault on a German trench and an attempt to rescue a wounded man following a raid for which he won the Military Cross. Samuel Hynes interprets this deployment of essentially trivial episodes which formed no part of any collective military action and had no military consequences as a literary conceit, a form of commemoration for a type of heroic warfare that no longer existed.[133] He suggests that Sassoon's choices as a story-teller reveal an intention to present the war in an unrealistic fashion:

> In making his war personal and heroic, Sassoon made it recognisable to readers who knew war only in its literary forms. Other personal narratives of modern war could defamiliarise it; Sassoon made it familiar. A reader could imagine himself acting as Sassoon acted, being romantic out there in no man's land, as he could imagine acting like other heroes in books.[134]

Hynes is correct to argue that the episodes at the centre of *Memoirs of an Infantry Officer* are essentially without point. However, the intention was arguably not to inject a long-lost romanticism back into the account but to reflect a form of heroism that still had meaning for the participants. These passages of the book reflect the tone and content of contemporary officer accounts and the type of images published in *The War Illustrated*. In fact, Sassoon's activities might easily have provided subject material for the artists employed by that paper. They certainly have similar characteristics. His attempt to rescue an injured man closely matches aspects of 'The Wounded Comrade and the proper method of carrying him out of action' (17 April 1915). In the picture, as in Sassoon's description, there is no apparent enemy.[135] There is no information in the paper relating whether or not the wounded man survived. Sassoon's unfortunate casualty died before they reached safety. In both cases, therefore, the exercise is invested with a degree of pointlessness. Even survival could only make a difference within a very narrowly-defined sphere and could not matter within the context of the war as a whole. Sassoon's work is therefore an ideal example of the 'new heroism' which developed when romantic traditions came into contact with total war.

Rather than trying to create a specific version of the war for a particular audience, Sassoon was trying, according to Michael Thorpe, to avoid universality.[136] While that may have been his intention, in effect he reproduced the accounts which were typical of young officers throughout their periods of service, focusing on the small episodes which stood out in his memory because they supplied him with a central and active role. They may therefore be interpreted as having played the most important part in reinforcing his conception of what it was to be a soldier. It is striking that a literary work published some twelve years after the end of the war should appear to conform to descriptive trends which grew so organically on the Western Front out of the frustration of traditional soldierly characteristics. This suggests that this subtly modern way of interpreting the war had become pervasive. There was no glory, chivalry or heroism in the trenches except that which the individual was able to wrap around his own private actions. Personal standards continued to be important – Sassoon's own highly developed sense of duty acts as an indicator – since, in a world stripped of ultimate purpose, only the manner in which one behaved carried any real significance and the only real form of failure was the loss of an ability to endure which was demanded by abstract notions of heroism and duty.

The emphasis on narrowly-focused personal episodes with little wider significance reflects the young officer's understanding of the nature of the trench deadlock and the improbability of any major breakthrough. This appreciation coloured all attitudes towards the war and the subaltern's role in it and will be discussed in the next chapter. It also reflects the comforting orthodoxy propagated by soldiers and commentators both contemporaneously and subsequently (even if it was undermined in practice by careerism and other factors described in Chapter 3) that one's primary duty was to avoid abandoning colleagues and therefore simply to persevere. If the soldier's obligations to deliver operational success could not be wholly discharged because of the operating environment then success became less important than the manner in which a man performed his duties. War became a sort of lifestyle, rather than a distinct episode characterised by significant happenings and with a relatively defined conclusion. The shift demanded of millions of civilians, who had become soldiers when they had never previously considered that eventuality likely, was not that they become professionalised, because even professional soldiers are not expected to endure a state of constant warfare. Instead they had to come to terms with a profoundly challenging idea – that this was not a distinct episode or phase in their lives; this *was* their life. Moreover, permanent release only seemed likely through disablement or death.

11

War, Death and the Public-School Ethos

The public schools saw it as their mission to instil a particular ethos into their charges, described by Peter Parker as 'a gentlemanly tradition of loyalty, honour, chivalry, Christianity, patriotism, sportsmanship and leadership'.[1] That ethos found widespread expression in the Victorian and Edwardian concept of the gentleman, ensuring that even those who had never been to a public school had a common reference point. This was important for officers from non-traditional backgrounds and their ability to adopt the expected mantle was reinforced by specific training, their own indoctrination into the mentality and methods of the upper classes.

The public schools' success in inculcating a sense of duty and responsibility was proved when the war started and young British men with public-school educations answered the nation's call in impressive numbers. All but eight of the 539 boys who left Winchester College between 1909 and 1915 volunteered.[2] Official policies to recruit new officers from such sources were driven by a deep-seated class-based perspective on the social order. The authorities also recognised that the public schools' Officer Training Corps had created a reservoir of military skills which should be utilised. The system seems to have been effective. Whatever their failings, the new officers seem generally to have adapted promptly to the demands of active service. The challenge inherent in developing a mass army without suffering either severe dislocation or a breakdown in order should not be underestimated and the men commanding platoons and companies in the trenches can take some of the credit.

Given the system's achievement in inspiring volunteers and creating a leadership paradigm within which the British army achieved notable eventual success, it is striking that it should have received so much subsequent criticism. The most relevant to this study is the accusation that it left junior officers singularly ill-equipped to survive the psychological pressures of the Western Front. One suggestion is that the emphasis on stoicism and the 'stiff upper lip' was a significant handicap, denying men any legitimate way of expressing fear and consequently placing them under severe strain. Alternatively, it has been suggested that the attempt to believe in the elevated concepts used by the Victorians to describe warfare amidst the sordid realities of the Western Front promoted the disillusionment which has so frequently been associated with junior officers.

The ethos may have contributed to certain psychological maladies but it was not simply a liability. The previous chapter has argued that it remained possible to experience heroic episodes in which personal performance played an important part, and that this could boost morale. Furthermore, as many historians have appreciated, many officers did not become disillusioned – in that they retained both their faith in the justice of their cause and a traditional belief in honour, glory and the virtues of self-sacrifice.[3]

The survival of this ethos cannot just be explained in terms of the doggedness of its adherents. As this chapter argues, in exploring the complicated interaction between traditional ways of understanding warfare and the modern reality, it had to have some resonance or provide some meaning. It is necessary to begin, however, by acknowledging that many officers did indeed become disillusioned, especially in the later phases of the war. Generally this does not seem to have been that type of disillusionment which caused them to reject the war. Those who did become opposed to government policy – Siegfried Sassoon is the most famous example – found that the strains of modern warfare had altered their political outlook. A much more common form of disillusionment was a depression or weariness, often caused by specific experiences of suffering or bereavement. This was not an irreversible process and most officers were able to continue supporting the war despite it. Confidence, both in the justice of their cause and in the final outcome, was a vital emotional support to many. This continued commitment to the war and the ability to persevere despite periods of low morale has to be seen in the context of growing knowledge and understanding of the nature of life on the Western Front which acted on the traditional ethos in several powerful ways. Certain elements, for example a belief in a distinction between an honourable and an ignoble death, retained their validity. Others, especially ideas relating to the virtue of sacrifice, were actually emphasised and given a special contemporary resonance by the prevailing conditions. Consequently, as with other parts of the transition from civilian to soldier, junior officers synthesised traditional and familiar factors with new experiences and ideas.

꙳

Young officers, Chapter 10 has argued, were relatively well-equipped or pre-disposed to maintain positive images of themselves as soldiers. Their war may not have resembled the battles or heroic exploits they had learned about while growing up but it could still provide them with satisfying episodes to demonstrate their prowess or experience excitement. Still, many did become disillusioned. No study of the lives and experiences of junior British infantry officers should overlook this, especially given the prominence this issue has attracted in modern public interpretations of the war. The narrative of disillusion has exercised a tremendous and ongoing influence over perceptions and understandings of the war, either directly or through the creation of works of popular culture such as *Oh! What A Lovely War* and *Blackadder Goes Forth*.

Primary sources do reflect a variety of types of dissatisfaction but the element of transition remains a common feature. Disillusionment was a process, a change which took place over time as the war eroded a soldier's belief in the cause for which he was fighting. Frequently it manifested itself as a temporary loss of spirit or a period of depression to which many officers succumbed. In Raymond Asquith's case this much may be inferred from the following comment: 'I have read some letters from Indian troops: one man says: "I never think about the chance of being killed, nor do I feel any particular satisfaction at the idea of going on living." This is a mood one recognises.'[4] Such despondency could be caused by a number of factors. The way in which the campaign itself was developing was inevitably an important determining factor, as Oliver Lyttelton indicated in 1915: 'There is some depression here among the officers at the failure of the great offensive.'[5] Bad news from home or other parts of the front inevitably also had a dispiriting effect.

Officers could not be immune to the emotional traumas caused by so many casualties among their circle of friends and acquaintances and were usually all too aware of recent deaths. Douglas Gillespie was very upset to hear in July 1915 of the death of his friend Bay Balfour. 'I can remember him so well as I first saw him, on that hot July day outside school at Winchester, before he and I went in to do our papers at the same table.' Several days later he wrote 'for the time everything is stale and flat to me, since I heard of Bay Balfour's death ... The world is a poorer place without Tom and Bay Balfour, and I do feel that, if it wasn't for all of you at home, I should be quite content to follow them. If "getting used to it" means that one slowly forgets how much there was to love in them, I would rather keep the pain for ever.'[6]

Morale and motivation were also inevitably eroded by the unpleasant conditions and experiences which officers had to endure in the line, although it is difficult to gauge to what extent from letters and diaries. 'I wonder when I shall get out of these trenches,' wrote Jack Oughtred in June 1916. 'I shall shortly have been longer in them than ever before. I must try and establish a record. Time hangs very heavy on your hands'. There is in the same letter, however, a counterpoint to this tone of weariness: 'I had a bath yesterday not in the usual civilised manner but in a big shell hole. It is very strange what circumstance one can get accustomed to.'[7] More damaging were particularly shocking episodes or periods of sustained stress. Arthur Adam, who so notably struggled to reconcile himself to the carnage around him, found his resolve to continue fighting dramatically undermined by his experiences of the front line. After coming out of a stint in the trenches during which his company suffered fourteen casualties he wrote: 'I feel a quite new hatred of war and all its ways, and also an even stronger desire than aforetime to get out of company commanding.'[8] Rowland Feilding similarly found his conviction wavering after experiencing a battlefield in late 1915: 'I confess that the first sight of the reckless slaughter brings a sense almost of shame. I find myself half wondering if the people at home can possibly realize what is going on here.'[9] The loss of a particular comrade could trigger a period of depression, as Christopher Stone discovered in June 1916: 'Black's death has rather taken the guts out of me for the moment; it's such wanton murder, almost without a redeeming feature.'[10]

Those who suffered most, unsurprisingly, were those who had failed to harden themselves to the more disagreeable aspects of war and had not developed any emotional insulation. Disillusionment, however, was not an irreversible process. Recovery was possible. The often episodic nature of periods of depression is revealed by Graham Greenwell, whose disillusionment was a temporary aberration, a brief episode brought on by extreme conditions. Despite seeming consistently quite comfortable with life on active service, he endured several episodes in horrific areas such as the Somme in August 1916 which sapped his enthusiasm. 'You wouldn't be able to conceive the filthy and miserable surroundings in which I am writing this note – not even if you were accustomed to the filthiest slums in Europe', he wrote as he sat in an old German dug-out. He described the corpses, the stench and the desolation. 'I shall never look on warfare either as fine or sporting again,' he concluded. 'It reduces men to shivering beasts: there isn't a man who can stand shell-fire of the modern kind without getting the blues. The Anzacs are fine fellows, but they say Gallipoli was a garden party to this show.' Escape from this nightmare seems to have worked wonders on his spirits. A week later he was reassuring his correspondent that he was not 'a bit depressed or downhearted.'[11] Perhaps he was simply trying to write in a style which he thought would be expected of him, but the tone still stands in marked contrast to that of the previous missive. Within a few months, moreover, he seemed to have recovered his former attitude: 'The war is developing along the strangest lines and God knows what the end of it will be. But I am once more persuaded that military life is full of excitement and romance. It is something to be able to spend one's youth gloriously in France, Flanders, Italy, Egypt and Palestine visiting the scenes of the victories and defeats of one's ancestors instead of living at home and being hustled round the Continent once a year *via* Cooks. Should I ever have seen Arras and Ypres, Albert and Peronne under such interesting conditions if there had been no war? I doubt it.'[12]

The fact that these changes in Greenwell's circumstances should have had such an impact is not surprising, given the contrasts that existed on the Western Front. Even coming out of relatively quiet trenches for a period of comparatively safety and comfort in billets might be cause for relief. That was, after all, part of the reason for a policy of troop rotations. What this also suggests is that the potentially varied nature of an officer's career could play a significant part in warding off depression. As Chapter 3 has noted, officers might move quite frequently between different posts, undertaking and finding refreshment in widely differing roles and thereby potentially reducing their exposure to those activities which were liable to be the most dispiriting. In addition, as they became more professional in their outlook they were able to re-imagine their service in these terms, recognising that they need not be stuck in one unchanging role. They could consequently make plans to alter their circumstances to suit their inclinations. Naturally this could not affect the greatest causes of depression – the apparently unending nature of the conflict, the separation from their families, the high casualty rates – but it could make a difference. Duty of a particular type may have been distasteful but it could also be regarded as finite and therefore more bearable.

The temporary disillusionment of men like Stone, Greenwell and Asquith was essentially a function of emotional fatigue or their revulsion at the horrors of the war. The type of disillusionment associated with officers like Siegfried Sassoon was much more political. Its existence illuminates both the power of Edwardian society to create officers who would be loyal to the war effort (to which it is a contrast) and the development of a more recognisably modern attitude towards the relationship between the state and the individual. Before the war, the state operated in a distinct sphere which did not overlap extensively with the rest of society.[13] After 1914 it became increasingly active in citizens' daily lives, not least because so many Britons joined the armed forces. Large numbers of civilians consequently became part of the corporate body waging the war. Many volunteers automatically and genuinely identified with the state's dispute and war aims, despite the impression held by some politicians like David Lloyd George that the time had passed when politicians could count on the unquestioning acceptance of the population.[14] Official propaganda and decades of cultural conditioning had created an extremely powerful imperative, especially for the middle and upper class men who had gone through the public-school system. Raymond Asquith – the son of the Prime Minister, and therefore perhaps more likely than most to identify with state action – was one of many who believed that they had a civic responsibility to engage with the war. To deny this obligation was to forfeit the rights commensurate with citizenship, hence Asquith's contempt for conscientious objectors: 'they are too far beyond the pale to be taken notice of. Besides they will, I hope, all be disfranchised and therefore [be] politically as well as morally and socially negligible. Whatever you may think about War (and no one thinks worse of it than I do) it is fatuous to refuse to fight and yet claim to vote.'[15] These ideas remained potent and were formally incorporated into the political culture in 1918, when the Representation of the People Act granted Asquith's wish. Conscientious objectors, in a dramatic condemnation of their failure to serve, were disenfranchised and were not entitled to vote again until 1926.[16]

The imperative to join in the national war effort could be summarised in a single word: duty. The public-school ethos clearly elevated corporate good above that of the individual and in wartime this translated into a strong message of commitment, endurance and sacrifice. Many officers wholeheartedly accepted this perspective. Some expressed it fervently, drawing on all the abstractions of honour and duty. Leslie Yorath Sanders was one of the enthusiastic volunteers who enlisted immediately rather than return to university or wait for a commission, only becoming an officer in July 1915. Despite his experiences, which included a wound and slight shell-shock while serving in the ranks, he continued to cling passionately to a creed of devotion and sacrifice: 'The individual matters little; the race is everything. The soldier in battle cannot stop to succour his wounded comrade; he must callously press on to the attack. So also I: let others palliate the bitterness of the fruit, but I must strike at the roots.'[17] More prosaically, Douglas Gillespie wrote in April 1915 that stories of German gas attacks 'make me lose all regret, except the personal one, for lives lost on our side in this war; they are necessary sacrifices for the lives of all the rest, and for finer principles.'[18]

In contrast to these notions of duty and obligation, those who disagreed with the war were in various ways attempting to question a relationship between citizen and state which had heavy presumptions in favour of the latter's interests and policies. Harold Parry railed against 'a doctrine of frightfulness' which caused ordinary men with no personal animosities to fight each other, noting that the 'real evil in this conflict is not of the individual so much as of the powers that be.'[19] His earnest hope, and that of many fellow officers and soldiers in the ranks, was that those responsible for the war be sent out to experience it, causing them to change their minds. Protests of this kind were often bolstered by accusations that the government had deviated from its original justifications for war. An officer called Robert Maltby of the Rifle Brigade made this charge in an anonymous letter to *The Cambridge Magazine*. A letter written in October 1915 seems to date his original bitterness to 'that fated day' in September 1915, since when 'all my letters, and there have been very few, have done nothing but deplore the criminal stupidity of those commanding the British army here. Wherever one goes, wherever there has been an attack, there is the same tale told (if there happens to have been an intelligent observer) – blunder after blunder, costing innumerable lives – and all glossed over in the manner approved by British officialdom.'[20] His principal preoccupation at that time consequently seems to have been the scale of the losses being incurred and the wellbeing of his men, a stunned reaction to the impact of battle, but his published protest introduced different themes of official and national deceit:

> We officers and men enlisted or took commissions in our genuine enthusiasm for a true fighting cause ... we shall not go back on it, nor betray our oath. I shall return to my battalion and shall be sufficiently a coward silently to assist in killing as I

promised … Is the reason for our continuing this war the same as the reason for which we agreed to fight? Of course not … You people at home are responsible for continuing this slaughter. Secretly you know it. Individually you mostly acknowledge it. But publicly there is but one cry: "War, War to the death, till we exterminate our foes; and after the war, more war. Economic, social war." Hateful, detestable cry. Not even expedient! And we enlisted to rescue Belgium! That will go on as long as you speak as individuals, and so long as you do that, shall we continue to make war without hope of peace. And my letter is only to entreat for some organisation of this vast body of scattered opinion, in order that it may make itself felt, become powerful, recover our rights of speech and opinion, defeat our political immorality, and stop this slaughter. All this it may do.[21]

Criticisms of this sort, although impugning the higher authority, did not automatically challenge its right to wage the war on behalf of the citizenry. Maltby did not advocate a revolution, and he still seems to have accepted the legitimacy of the state's actions – hence blaming the civilian population at home for not asserting itself and effecting a change in policy.

By an interesting coincidence, Maltby and Sassoon were both correspondents of the Cambridge musicologist Edward J. Dent. They clearly also shared homosexual tendencies, Maltby writing before going into action that he 'would like to be tended afterwards by the fair hands of Clive'.[22] If this was in any way a common factor contributing to the development of their opposition, Sassoon's disenchantment ultimately found expression in the more radical political message. His earliest war poems reflect a strong sense of patriotism and heroic idealism and are much more like the poems of Rupert Brooke than of Wilfred Owen. Yet Sassoon was eventually driven to issue a public protest against the war in June 1917.[23] The opening passage of his statement established his intention to reassert his individuality, separating himself from the military machinery to whose laws he was subject. There is a suggestion, in the way he juxtaposes ideas about the noble concepts initially used to justify the war with his revised views about its true purpose, that his disillusion is at least partly driven by a collapse in his self-esteem as a soldier. It is also clear, both in this extract and subsequent lines, that this is an intervention on behalf of his men. Paul Moeyes argues that this concern was evident early on in his career, revealed in poems as yet untouched by his eventual bitterness.[24] It was a similar political evolution to that which Alec Waugh believed had affected his contemporaries: 'The young officer began to feel differently about the men he led into action. What voice had they had in determining their present fate? They had been taken from their homes and jobs; a gun had been put into their hands, and they had been told to kill Germans with it. What were they getting out of it? Had any government the right to do this to them? Many young officers carried back with them to civilian life a number of unanswered questions.'[25]

Whereas Waugh considered this awakening of social conscience to have flowered during the inter-war period, Sassoon answered that same question about the rights of the state by seeking to remove his consent and dissociate himself from its actions.[26] By specifying that he was not complaining about the way in which the government was prosecuting the campaign, he placed some distance between himself and complainants like Parry who were essentially shocked by the nature of the conflict. By attacking its justification, accusing the government of having altered its aims, he and Maltby explored the idea of a contractual relationship between the state and the individual, rather than a straightforward obligation which devolved on the citizen. Maltby's protest was limited by the fact that he considered that he was still bound by an oath. Sassoon, in contrast, effectively argued that he (and, by extension, the population generally) had chosen to support war on a specific justification and that there was therefore no mandate for any military action which deviated from that which was originally proposed. The idea that the government has no right to make war other than that which it is given by its citizens is radically different to Raymond Asquith's concept of duty.

This message failed to resonate widely, partly because the authorities were able to use Sassoon's psychiatric treatment as a cover. In the words of a colleague from his battalion, the medical officer James Dunn, 'Sassoon's quixotic outburst has been quenched in a "shell-shock" retreat. He will be among degenerates, drinkers, malingers, and common mental cases, as well as the overstrained. It is an astute official means of denying our cold-blooded, cold-footed, superior persons the martyr they are too precious to find from their own unruly ranks.'[27] Furthermore, other friends and fellow officers, including Dunn, denied that Sassoon was giving an accurate representation of the views of men at the front.[28] He eventually abandoned his protest in order to return to his troops, impelled by his desire to be with his men.[29] There were some parallels in Maltby's own position. He seemed to regret his outburst quite quickly, writing to Dent in an apparent attempt to have it withdrawn: 'In a fit of fanatical depression at Folkstone I sent you what I now imagine was a sheet of perfect nonsense – I am sure you will have destroyed it by now – it will do no use, and I don't really believe in anonymous letters.' He continued to rail occasionally against the war, but less vehemently than previously. Like Sassoon, he also seemed to find both meaning and solace in the company of his men.[30]

⋇

As Sassoon's capitulation, Maltby's recantation and Asquith's comments vividly illustrate, Edwardian culture had powerfully programmed public-school men and their ilk to support the war effort. Consequently, it is not surprising that the type of cynicism and opposition associated with Sassoon, Maltby and others does not appear to have been particularly common amongst officers during the war itself, despite the growth of anti-war literature in the years between the two world wars. While temporary periods of depression and disillusionment were much more common, as was heartfelt disgust at the nature of warfare, they did not usually break down officers' loyalty to the state and its war aims.[31] The very fact that few sources contain explicit expressions of disillusionment may indicate widespread support for government policy. Many who believed firmly in the justice of their cause also stated their views explicitly. Douglas Gillespie, for example, argued that 'we must get the Germans driven out of France and Belgium before we begin to talk of peace, and we shall do it too, though, of course, the cost will be very heavy.'[32] Captain John Coull wrote his farewell letter to his son in April 1917: 'You will understand better as you get older that your daddy came out to France for your sakes and for our Empire's sake.' This letter was eventually forwarded home after he was killed in September 1918.[33] Either Coull genuinely retained his faith in such sentiments over the course of many months, or he was unwilling to break that faith by admitting anything to the contrary.

Presumably many young officers did not really bother to question their reasons for continuing to support the war. Those who did, and who recorded their thoughts in their letters or diaries, offer a variety of justifications – even if they are sometimes difficult to identify accurately. Gillespie's own bellicosity appears to have stemmed particularly from revulsion at what he perceived to be German barbarism. Where his most anti-German statements occur, his judgements are very often based on specific stories or observations of enemy actions such as the use of poison gas or unrestricted U-boat warfare:

> How pleased the Germans will be that they have sunk the *Lusitania*! … It's no use protesting against them now, except with the bayonet; their leaders must have lost their heads in their rage, and I think it's a sort of just judgement for their gospel of hate.[34]

He was not alone in reacting against unpalatable news by expressing antipathy for the German people as a whole. From the start of the war many in the officer class were strongly motivated by a sense that Germany had transgressed against the code of civilised nations. Successful government propaganda denigrated German national characteristics, causing a significant number of young officers to cast themselves unambiguously as defenders of civilised values and therefore to adopt a heroic view of the conflict. In the words of one anonymous officer:

> The nations of Europe have chosen, not to enter into a contest of arms with Germany, but have taken it upon them to sit in righteous judgment upon Germany, to call her to account for a great and barbarous crime against humanity, and to pronounce her doom. We are not engaged in a duel of swords. We are not engaged in a duel at all. We are but carrying out what has always been dormant at the heart of Christianity, but has never before been so fully translated into the life and action of nations and of men – "he that taketh the sword shall perish by the sword."
>
> Germany must perish because of all she stands for. There are certain things which cannot be. The final triumph of inhumanity in a world which has turned its face toward chivalry and gentleness and the succour of the fallen cannot be. There are certain events which must be. The failure of evil is a necessity of the universe. Evil has already failed in a world which has sentenced evil to destruction. Victory is ours not, indeed, because we thought ourselves worth to champion the right, but because men have proved their nations worthy with their own blood.[35]

In combination with the recollection of recent pre-war antagonisms, these ideas enabled officers to regard the Germans as an historic enemy whose ideology was irrevocably hostile to Britain. 'We went into this war because we believe our country to be the upholder of certain ideals and beliefs which we and our fathers before us have held for centuries,' wrote Lancelot Spicer in February 1918. 'Germany never did believe in these ideals of ours, and showed us so quite openly. Consequently when she overran Belgium we had either to accept her doctrines or uphold our own. Fortunately we chose the right path.'[36] By placing the conflict within a longer sequence of history, soldiers could more easily identify values which had been presented as 'traditionally' British by an extensive lineage of popular heroes. Consequently they were able to view themselves as perpetuating the same line. These various constructions and a firm belief that the cause was just powerfully enhanced morale.[37] It also made it easier for officers to reconcile any lack of personal animosity towards most German soldiers, as discussed in Chapter 4, with a necessary willingness to kill: 'We want to exterminate, not so much the Germans as individuals, for they are harmless enough,' wrote James Neville, 'but their methods and principles: and the worst of it is, that there is only one way to do this, and that is to kill the individuals.'[38]

Officers did not forget that these perceived German traits presented a direct threat to their homeland. Although it is less common to find an officer writing explicitly in terms of the balance of European power or the security of the British Isles or Empire, such considerations were clearly present within the officer corps. Many years after the war a veteran, Richard Hawkins, expressed it in the following terms. The subject of the discussion is the Battle of the Somme, but the understanding of the geopolitical reality is still relevant:

> Something had to be done. Belgium had gone. France had nearly gone. We'd lost most of our regular army at Mons. We had to move at the Somme, even though it meant terrible losses. We had to attack. If we hadn't the French would have soon surrendered and the Kaiser would have overrun us.[39]

An understanding that soldiers were fighting to defend British interests and security has similarly been identified by Helen McCartney as a major psychological prop for the men of the Liverpool Territorials: The 'scenes of destruction and death they encountered on the Western Front strengthened their determination to prevent such scenes being replicated in their homeland, and militated against the effects of war-weariness.'[40]

Widespread faith in the justice and necessity of the war was matched, for the most part, by confidence in the final outcome. Initially this was the product of upbringing. The men who came from the public schools and the universities were an elite who had been taught to believe in the strength of the British Empire. Defeat was to them almost unthinkable. 'All we must do is to wait until we have sufficient men and munitions for a terrific offensive simultaneously on every front, and the end will come,' believed William Fraser in May 1916. 'It will cost much blood, but it's a sure thing. Absolutely certain. We are fools and we make many mistakes, but we are a "chosen people" and we shall not lose. That is my view anyway.'[41]

Many found, however, that the war took a toll on such optimism, confidence and a sense of destiny. Alfred Pollard described his 'distinct shock' on first seeing troops taking part in an unsuccessful attack: 'I had always believed British Infantry to be invincible; to see them rendered impotent was a revelation which dismayed me.'[42] A series of military reverses even prompted some to think that the nation should seek peace terms. In December 1916, at a time when the Conservative leader in the House of Lords, Lord Lansdowne, was privately arguing for a compromise peace, Henry Dundas likewise suggested considering negotiation: 'My views about peace are simply these. If we don't consider the German terms, and, if they are reasonable, accept them, we shall probably be in a far worse position this time next year. Due in a great measure to the late

Government's two years. Granted, but unfortunately this departure doesn't undo the harm done. What have we to set against the German victories – except their Colonies, and the stifling of their trade – upon which they didn't depend, as we do utterly.[43] Even though two official surveys of censored mail in 1917 indicated that morale remained relatively sound, Richard Holmes notes that certain dark episodes like the Battle of Passchendaele did undermine confidence in the eventual outcome.[44]

Yet, despite such periods of gloom, officers managed to cling to optimism. Confidence undoubtedly varied episodically, but usually seems to have reasserted itself. By February 1918, Dundas had recovered his own conviction sufficiently to play down the importance of the expected German offensive.[45] Stephen Hewett, writing in July 1916, similarly wavered only briefly: 'There were times when the issue of this war seemed doubtful: do you realise what is implied by any doubt on that score? Now it is certain: and, if we have to suffer the heaviest losses, and even have a hard time for the rest of our lives, we should consider ourselves not unlucky.'[46] Leslie Sanders would have agreed, writing in February 1917 that 'The Boche knows as well as we that our ultimate victory is certain.'[47]

This confidence, which was to exert a tremendous influence over the young officers of the British Army, was part of the legacy of an Edwardian education rooted in the public-school ethos. Subalterns did not cling stubbornly to this code in the face of its blatant irrelevance. It survived instead because it was able to remain both valuable and viable on some levels, despite the appalling suffering. The change was comparable to that described in the last chapter, whereby traditional concepts of heroism more suited to an earlier era of warfare were not abandoned altogether but were re-adjusted in order to remain relevant. This chapter makes a similar argument for ideas of service, duty and sacrifice. As with notions of heroism, the process was shaped by the transition from civilian to soldier, the acquisition of genuine knowledge and understanding of the strategic and tactical realities of the Western Front, and a growing military professionalism.

The front line was a lethal environment, characterised by deadlock between well-entrenched enemies. Many officers were fortunate enough to spend long periods essentially just holding sections of line where casualties were sustained on a regular basis but only in the arbitrary, attritional way of trench warfare and normally at a low rate. Offensive operations, which had to be attempted if the Allies were to break the German line, were very different. Officers quickly understood that substantial progress was impossible unless the army was prepared to suffer much greater numbers of dead or wounded. Officers consequently had to come to terms with two challenging ideas: first, that suffering was an unavoidable and even necessary part of bringing the war to a close and, secondly, that they might be called upon to lay down their lives at some point in the near future. The public-school ethos deemed sacrifice virtuous. The Western Front made it functional.

Few who were experienced in the ways of the front line could doubt that it would be impossible to break the deadlock without suffering. Even in February 1915 Lionel Sotheby seemed to have appreciated the true extent of what would be required:

To drive the Germans out of Belgium and of west France I think that from now, we shall at the lowest figure lose a million men. Yes, I know the figure is large to people outside, but to anyone who knows the Germans, their obstinacy, pluck, endurance and marvellous patriotism, men who for their country are content to be slaughtered like a hundred sparrows in line if a gun is fired at them from the side, it is the lowest figure one could place.[48]

William Fraser knew all too well in July 1917 what lay in store for those men whom he had wished '*bon success*' a few hours earlier: 'some must be killed, that is the sad part of it all. One cannot make omelettes without breaking eggs, and they are fine fellows.'[49] Leslie Sanders appreciated that 'In war you must always pay for whatever advantage you gain. You must always expend munitions; you must almost always sacrifice life.'[50] Douglas Bell seemed similarly clear about the task that lay ahead and the soldier's prospects, consequently adopting a stoical posture and preferring to focus on his immediate circumstances rather than the future.[51] This tone filtered through into trench journalism, with a writer in *The Gasper* declaring in February 1916 that 'the business will be costly … We don't whine at the cost of seeing the business through.'[52]

For junior officers this was not a theoretical or dispassionate consideration. They understood that their role on the battlefield made them particularly vulnerable. Sotheby, commenting on how the 'idea prevalent in England is that the Subalterns or Second Lieutenants are foolish and get quickly cut up through foolishness', noted that 'a Platoon Commander has a great responsibility, acting on initiative etc. He has to encourage his men and expose himself more than anyone.'[53] As the war went on, prospective subalterns became more and more aware of the risks they would be running, their understanding fed by the numerous different sources of information about the war to which they had access. In his autobiography Guy Chapman reckoned that by September 1917 'none except perhaps the very young joined the infantry without knowing that his chance of life was at best about 4 to 1 on'.[54] Some were actually arguably overly pessimistic, employing a strikingly fatalistic language in their letters. Leslie Sanders departed for France in February 1915. On the eve of sailing he wrote to his mother: 'I estimate my chance of getting wounded at one in four, of getting killed or totally disabled at one in ten. These are pretty heavy averages, and I should be foolish not to go out prepared for the worst. In a sense, therefore, I count myself already dead.'[55] Sanders, who did not explain how he calculated these probabilities, was admittedly killed in 1917. He is, however, one of many officers who seemed to believe that their lives were forfeit almost as soon as they stepped onto French soil. An element of pessimism is discernible in Bernard Long's news after about two months abroad: 'We've had still another officer wounded in my battalion and a pal of mine in the 14th at Brocton went to another battalion of the West Yorks out here and was killed a week after landing, so you see I am doing quite nicely.'[56] Whether it came as a shock or, perhaps in a few cases, even as a reassurance, officers had to come to terms with the true nature of fighting on the Western Front and what this might mean for them personally.

⁂

An appreciation of the likely costs of success also informed wider understandings of the conduct of the war. In military terms, many officers began to think that all niceties should be disposed of and that ends justified means. The Battle of Loos prompted Lancelot Spicer to change his opinions: 'From what I saw that day, I am inclined to think that we shall never have a real advance in this war, unless we are a great deal more ruthless than we are at present. It may seem very cruel, but I certainly think that when an advance like that has started everything on the road must give way to three things – first ammunition for the guns, secondly fresh troops, and thirdly small arms ammunition. In other words, the wounded must be left till there is time to attend them, which may mean two or three days.'[57] Similar sentiments removed some of the moral impediments hampering the use of such weapons as poison gas. Ralph Bickersteth was cheered to learn that British developments in this area were 'absolutely deadly': 'It sounds awful, but dash it all, one's got to pay back the blighters in their own coin, with interest!'[58] Thomas Pratt, writing in May 1915, did not feel the need to maintain any moral superiority over the enemy, frankly advocating 'the utmost cruelty and inhumanity' on the grounds of utility: 'It is my opinion that the utmost cruelty and inhumanity must be practiced and thought out on our side – gases and all the devilish things we can imagine. We shall lose if this is not done.'[59] Dennis Neilson-Terry supported bombing 'all the open towns of Germany till they cried out for mercy, its all part of War & it must be carried through. We're beginning to doubt a bit out here whether the Government & the Staff are fighting a war to win.'[60] Officers justified this hardening of their sentiments with reference to the cost that they and their colleagues were paying. The anonymous *Gasper* contributor criticised the Lord Chancellor, Lord Buckmaster, for arguing against retaliatory bombing of German cities:

> … the principle applies equally to the use of unsanctioned means of warfare against combatants … One of these days the Germans will try a new and more powerful gas on us. Then the government will say, "Oh! We had the recipe for that, only we didn't like to use it, because it was naughty." There will be a local German success, hospitals full of agonised victims, a new gas-helmet; and the war will go on till we have muddled through. … For good reason (and equally if it were bad) we are in this war. Now there is just one aim and one necessity – to win it. The only important modification is that we must win with as little loss of life as possible to ourselves and our Allies. Quixotism is expensive – in lives. But not the lives of the Quixotes. … We merely object to fighting with one hand tied to some sanctimonious old frump's apron-strings.'[61]

In these ways, Daniel Pick argues, the officer corps, like wider British society, was increasingly reflecting the qualities that were abhorred in the enemy.[62] It was the fear of this eventuality which prompted Lord Lansdowne's peace initiative.[63]

An uncompromising stance also predisposed officers to criticise the efforts made by the rest of society. They knew that the war could not be won easily but the home front did not, in the eyes of many combatants, respond accordingly. A sentiment commonly expressed by troops was that England needed to emulate her allies and opponents and really focus on the war. As early as December 1914 Gerald Burgoyne pronounced himself satisfied with the German shelling of Scarborough: 'It will wake England up and do more for recruiting than all the posters in the world.'[64] One of the more constant complaints before the introduction of conscription in 1916 was that too few people were volunteering, apparently not realising the danger that the country was in. It was this resentment, combined with the strong pride and soldierly identity derived from volunteer status, which made more experienced troops suspicious of new arrivals. Sotheby was clearly more concerned, however, about the available numbers, rather than their reasons for serving:

> How mad people must be in England not to have conscription, nothing but that can possibly defeat Germany. It is no good getting troops by the voluntary system, as although they may be a better class, you will never get enough.[65]

Once this specific fear had subsided and compulsion had been introduced, the behaviour of the remaining civilian population – rather than the lack of volunteering spirit – became open to particular criticism, especially those industrial workers who engaged in strike action. Christopher Stone heard a lecture by his Corps commander, General Sir Charles Wilson, in April 1916 and sympathised with the views expressed:

> He implored us to try and make England as a whole come into the war and to take part in it as the French & the Russians & the Germans do – It's all very true and I don't see how we can finish the war this year unless we can put a stop to strikes & conscientious objectors and party politicians.[66]

Striking was typically seen by officers in the front line as despicable and a very real threat to the war effort. Not only were strikers failing in their duty but they were doing so when they had to face none of the real hardships and dangers of the fighting men. In some cases criticism also seems to have been driven by class-derived antipathies towards organised labour. A.J. Sansom complained in 1915 that 'the men are drawn from a class which nowadays is simply taught to "down tools" on the slightest provocation, and looks upon employers as natural enemies!'[67]

As the years of conflict dragged on there began to emerge a fear that civilian resolve might crumble, with disastrous effect.[68] Opposition to the war was found throughout the duration at all levels of British society and took a number of different forms. The activities of campaigners such as Bertrand Russell and organisations such as the Union of Democratic Control and the No Conscription Fellowship achieved the greatest prominence within the domestic political firmament but were ultimately unsuccessful.[69] Conscientious objectors attained a status within the popular imagination that was far in excess of their numbers.[70] Officers were typically more concerned about a more general malaise setting in. Oliver Lyttelton appreciated that the attitude of those back home in Britain could have a dramatic impact on the ability of the army to fight successfully, writing in January 1917 that 'despondency in England if allowed to get going will quite counteract say 10,000 prisoners and a couple of miles of ground.'[71]

The worst possible scenario, from many an officer's point of view, was that civilian dissatisfaction might force the government to concede a compromise peace, something to which many were fundamentally opposed. Concern about the resolve of the civilian population became a regular feature of officers' writings, such as this letter from Billie Nevill:

> The only danger to my mind is that some near sighted and fat headed people will say 'oh anything to stop the War' and when Germany proposes terms of peace,

jump at them & make peace, on the pretext that we've lost so much already & so many valuable lives. I do hope that won't happen.[72]

These fears were directly related to the certainty with which officers believed in the cause for which they were fighting. To a large number of men like Christopher Stone, for whom the defeat of Germany was the only sure method of preventing any further conflict, such a move would have been folly: 'You can't earnestly and sincerely pray for a peace which is only the menace of a future war – a mere truce: and a peace that involves victory must also involve the crushing of the prayers that rise to Heaven from the enemy! No, in a war like this where it is not for men to decide what is right and what is wrong, I think the only prayer is Fiat voluntas tua – Thy will be done: and forgive us our trespasses etc.'[73] In Lyttelton's not unprophetic view, an early peace would have been disastrous. The German nation not only had to be defeated but also had to have real and painful experience of that defeat: 'Until the actual population have seen khaki, the Hun will be entitled to say that the army is unbeaten and they will merely prepare for a more favourable opportunity, when say Russia or ourselves will not be involved in the next 40 years, to have another shot. Everybody in Germany dislikes militarism even when successful but when it is unsuccessful demonstrably and patently and obviously then and not till then they will chuck it.'[74] The idea of a 'war to end war' was not mere empty rhetoric, even if its meaning changed. The patriotic volunteers of 1914 imagined that they might genuinely take part in the modern world's last conflict; the hardened trench warriors of 1917 feared that war would resume all too quickly if they did not finish the job properly. Winning was a way of ensuring that it would not be repeated.

Some officers, scorning mere perseverance, advocated still more strenuous efforts which would have substantially increased the burden on the civilian population. Writing in February 1917, Leslie Sanders felt that the country had got off lightly and should prepare for worse eventualities: 'If English people want to win this war, they must be prepared for things scarcely dreamed of as yet – for starvation rations; for unremitting labour of man, woman and child; for death in every home in the land. These things may not come, but unless they are faced and accepted in spirit, we cannot truly win.'[75] Sanders's ominous predictions in this passage appear to carry an almost religious flavour, creating a link to the concept of a 'blood sacrifice' and an image of penitence and suffering. These are elements which have subsequently been attributed to the British experience of the First World War, usually through the processes of commemoration, and the connections with Christian notions of sacrifice had an important influence on junior British officers adjusting to the difficulties of life on the Western Front.

While developing this understanding of the cost of victory and these different perspectives on the war, many officers repeatedly used the vocabulary of the public-school ethos to rationalise and justify their experiences despite the potential difficulties of applying such concepts to the Western Front. For Douglas Gillespie, glory and justification came from the conviction that fighting was right and noble: 'After all, to be killed fighting for a cause like ours is the greatest honour a man can win, and that is how we should try to look at it, as something far greater than a VC or any other honour to the living.'[76] This belief that glory would be the reward of the fallen was one of the most persistent beliefs. Lancelot Spicer was so impressed by the splendour of the deeds attempted that he found in them solace for the awful casualties suffered:

> It was the most marvellous show I've ever seen or had anything to do with! If it wasn't for that our losses would be unbearable, for we have suffered, particularly in officers, Lynch, Griffen, Haswell, Head and Walker all killed, not to mention many others killed or wounded. But they all died a magnificent death, and if they know, as I am sure they must do, what they have achieved by sacrificing their own lives, they would be perfectly satisfied.[77]

Using this language as a guide to their true feelings is problematic, given the myriad conventions, audience expectations and authorial intentions affecting every piece of writing. It is possible, however, as Janet Watson has argued, to see their retention of these ideas as both natural and credible:

> Within a society where the idea of service was so highly valued for specific social classes, happiness in uniform was a real possibility, not simply a self-delusion. This idea affected not just how soldiers portrayed the war to non-combatants, but how they understood their own war experiences themselves. They worked within the terms available to them.[78]

It was entirely appropriate, in other words, for officers to talk about enjoying the war, usually focusing on the masculine characteristics of activity, fitness and health. Having been brought up to honour physical prowess they could not interpret the outdoor military lifestyle as anything other than invigorating. When talking about their motivation, they similarly reached for the high concepts that had inspired them to volunteer and which genuinely formed a significant part of their world-view. When addressing pain, suffering and sacrifice they employed a creed which both consoled and encouraged, provided purpose and validation.

The importance of some transcendent meaning was considerably accentuated by the scale of the casualties. The traditional Christian ideal of the 'good death' remained an important element of the Victorian and Edwardian gentlemanly philosophy.[79] There was always consolation in the right sort of end, but until the First World War this had been the final fall-back position of the public-school ethos, which had never been a suicide cult. Honour and glory were active and vigorous. Only a comparative few received the accolade of a hero's death, often after taking their heroism to extreme lengths. Those who gave their lives were exemplary in their devotion to duty. They provided a lesson in constancy, not a model for complete emulation. During the Edwardian era most upper and middle class men did not have to worry about a 'good death'. They knew how they might be expected to behave, but were seldom called on to put their beliefs into practice.

On the Western Front, by comparison, death was common and dutiful in an unprecedented way. This was not realised at first. The expansion of the army by voluntary recruitment created an example of sacrifice and selflessness which resonated throughout the country. In fact, the impact upon a society unused to such displays may have been disproportionate, as Gillespie believed:

It's one disadvantage of our voluntary system that the press and every one else try to persuade officers and men that they are little heroes to have come out here at all, and that they deserve the best of everything; whereas they are just doing what every Frenchman has got to do as a matter of course.[80]

In other words, soldiers might have been forgiven for believing that, through their very presence in the army and in the line, they were doing enough. However, as an understanding of the strategic deadlock eventually made clear, they had to accept or even *embrace* greater suffering if they were to achieve their desired ends. For the volunteers (and those who were strongly imbued with the same ethos but entered the army after the introduction of conscription), this created a particularly potent fusion of ideas. They had chosen to place themselves in this extreme danger for a greater good. It was therefore important to distinguish between an honourable and an ignoble end, since they had to accept that they probably could not avoid a death of some sort. As Sotheby commented:

To be stricken down on the battlefield is much nicer than to be stricken down in billets with some awful disease. To die a glorious death is the former & to die a glorious death when dying for one's country, but at the same time a horrid one to fall foul of is the latter.[81]

These feelings were expressed even in the face of the grimmest calamities of the trenches and not just in an abstract or academic sense. Gilbert Talbot's reaction to the death of a cherished member of his unit seems genuine:

A tragedy has happened: one of the very best and jolliest of my platoon was shot through the head ... I was sorry for it, as he was a very favourite little fellow, infinitely cheery and conscientious, perfectly simple ... I think I felt in him for the first time by personal experience how fine a soldier's death is.[82]

Leslie Hill's response in 1917 to the death of his brother Austen was couched in similar terms: 'It was a rotten blow to us all: of course, I do not miss him so much yet as I have seen him so very little during the past three years, but it will be a pretty empty space after the war. There is one great consolation – he could not have died a better death than in scrapping out there.'[83] More significantly still, the language did not change when writers considered their own deaths. They continued to use – and presumably, therefore, to think on some levels in terms of – the same concepts. On the eve of his first action, three days before he was mortally wounded on 1 July 1916, Eric Heaton wrote his last letter: 'I have no regrets save for my loved ones I leave behind. It is a great cause and I came out willingly to serve my King and Country.'[84]

Thoughts of the potential necessity or inevitability of self-sacrifice were powerfully affected by the knowledge that so many others had already laid down their lives. The men who accepted commissions were acutely aware of the service of large numbers of their peers. The officer corps was particularly characterised, as Chapter 8 detailed, by a large number of overlapping social networks, both those which had been formed before the war and those which were forged on active service through habits of easy sociability. The tendrils of war reached even further into British society once conscription was introduced. Thanks to high casualty rates, most young officers serving in the front line would consequently have suffered some form of bereavement from within a close circle on top of any operational losses suffered by their own unit within their own experience. They may have lost relatives or particularly close friends. There will also have been a category that is slightly harder to define, people they perhaps knew less well, but whose example could exert an equally potent influence: the prefects or captains of sport who had been exalted within the public-school or university system. In some cases, this category may even have included some of those national sporting heroes who were killed in the war.[85]

It became impossible for young officers to be unaware of colleagues who had made the ultimate sacrifice. They were profoundly attached to these fallen soldiers by family ties, friendship, admiration, and maybe hero worship. The public-school ethos and wider cultural influences declared their deaths to be noble, gallant and virtuous. Many officers still serving would have had little wish to disbelieve any of this (even if their experiences of death in the trenches were rather less edifying) as to do so would rob them of valuable consolation. As the deaths of friends, relatives and colleagues mounted, the extent of their apparent unselfishness and the magnitude of the debt and obligation owing to them accumulated. Self-sacrifice and its ramifications were consequently elevated into a form of creed. Ironically, while junior members of the officer corps became increasingly professional in their attitudes and regarding the war as *work*, they became in this respect progressively more and more dominated by emotional concepts of *service*.

This bolstered their support for national war objectives, placing serving officers potentially under two particular obligations. In the first place, some will have understood that, without the sacrifices already made, the war might have been lost or, at the very least, they themselves might be fighting from even less advantageous positions. Their lines, their daily strategic and tactical realities, were the often hard-won dividends of these losses. Secondly, they were required to ensure that the sacrifices of the hallowed dead were not rendered useless. The most obvious way in which this had to be done was by defeating Germany. It would obviously be extremely painful for Britain to lose. Breaking faith and giving up the fight because of the suffering, on the other hand, would devalue the deaths of many friends and relations as well as being a fundamental breach of the code and expectations drummed into them at school.[86] Not only did that objective have to be achieved, but it also had to be accorded the status of a sacred duty, largely because the sacrifice was constantly eulogised in high concept terms. As Chapter 1 noted, the creation of this sense of obligation in the minds of younger officers began at school with an institutional emphasis from August 1914 onwards on the sacrifice and service of alumni. The war also needed to retain some grander purpose to elevate and validate so much suffering.

There was a further dimension. As Hew Strachan has noted, certainly by 1917 it had become common to predict the war's continuation in terms of years rather than months.[87] The likely ramifications were obvious to all initiated trench fighters who had attained this understanding that their lives were potentially forfeit in any attempt to make progress. Even before 1917, when officers seem to have found it easier to believe that strategic success was just around the corner, it must have been clear to many that the 'big pushes' to which some of them looked forward were hardly likely to succeed without significant losses. Their experience of the trench stalemate and, in some cases, the efforts required and casualties endured in making quite limited tactical gains suggested that, at best, many of them were only preserving a position of comparative advantage from which their successors, rather than they themselves, would advance to ultimate triumph. By performing their duty they could believe, in the words of an anonymous officer reviewing an action, that they had 'already participated in the final victory through yesterday's contribution to it.'[88] (It is significant that he chose the title *After Victory* when publishing his account in 1917.) This logic had to be accepted because it seemed so plausible that the most anybody could realistically hope for was to pave the way for others who would follow and, it was hoped, eventually be in a position to finish the job. There was a darker side to this bargain, however. Breaking faith would also invalidate their own deaths, were they themselves to fall in the attempt.

The burden of preserving some higher purpose and meaning lay heavily on the officer corps. It was as if the list of war aims had been expanded to include validation of all the deaths that had taken place and that would take place before the conflict was over. The compounded effect of these different influences was further to enhance the officer corps' dedication to winning the war. Comments such as this one from Douglas Gillespie might initially sound like an expression of the impulse to retribution that prompted much hatred of the Germans, although it seems to be really a re-iteration of this central creed:

> I believe the dead are still lying thick out in front, just where they fell. However, I don't think such things are really depressing, for they just leave you with the determination to reward all these past efforts by success at the last, and I never doubt myself that success is coming, though it may be long in coming.[89]

Many officers typically believed that a compromise peace would constitute failure, or at the very least entail taking an enormous risk, and hence devalue the sacrifice. This was one argument that the psychologist W.H.R. Rivers used to bring Sassoon round to the idea of returning to France.[90] It is sadly ironic that their emotional turmoil only compelled them to undergo more fighting and death as surely as if they were acting under very different motives of anger and revenge.

This obligation was not limited to wartime objectives. It also prompted officers to reflect on the construction of the post-war world – the future for which so many were laying down their lives. This tendency was described by Thomas Wentworth Pym, chaplain of Trinity College, Cambridge, who went out to France with the BEF: 'We have recently been engaged in very heavy fighting, and have lost a large number of our friends; those who have survived do undoubtedly feel a relief which is akin to thankfulness, a sense of "being spared for a purpose," but at present it is very hard for them to return thanks for deliverance to God. Better men, they feel, have been killed.'[91] Geoffrey Fildes addressed this point towards the end of his memoir of his services with the Coldstream Guards: 'What did it all mean? Why had this appalling Thing come about? Why were men so monstrously afflicted? "The War that shall end War" – the trite headline of a newspaper came back to me. But would it? Every war in history had been a wasted catastrophe, in that the germ had still survived. To think of the sacrifice around as fruitless was almost unbearable. We, the living, must battle on to prevent that; surely this was the message of the dead. Death and glory this eviscerated land contained, but greater than these was its summons to the living!'[92] Christopher Stone actually refuted present military objectives in favour of these future considerations:

> I do not honestly consider that a peace based on the present situation and balance of successes would be an act of treachery to the men who have given their lives, though no doubt a good many of them dreamed of British troops marching into Berlin. The dead are in another and a better world; our job is to see if we can't save something out of the wreckage of this one.[93]

He remained extremely conscious of his debt and it prompted him to speak of dedicating his remaining life to the memory of his fallen comrades: 'If I come home to you safe etc I must see to it and so must you that I don't misuse opportunities. This sounds priggish but you know what I mean. All the sacrifices that have been made should be justified by those who survive, in their lives. I don't want ever to forget what I owe to them and I pray that I shall never be self-complacent again, as I am apt to be.'[94] After the war these sentiments were institutionalised in various different ways. Veterans became marginalised at commemorative occasions and the mothers and wives of fallen soldiers received greater prominence, thereby ensuring that the greatest cultural emphasis was placed on loss rather than victory.[95]

Various emotions of guilt, remorse and bereavement also contributed to a tendency to 'elevate the fallen'. Impelled by a form of collective modesty, the natural impulse of many officers faced with the loss of friends was to ascribe to them special qualities of personality, skill and courage. Stone himself reacted in this way in March 1918 to the death of his close friend Brigadier-General Randle Barnett Barker, for whom he was working:

> I miss the General terribly, and the more I survive the more I realize it is because I am not fit to be taken. Otherwise there's no sense in the thing. I don't think it has occurred to us that one of us would be taken and the other left: we were so much together that only a fluke separated us at the moment of his death.[96]

Raymond Asquith expressed himself more bitterly on the death of his friend Hugo Charteris:

> A blind God butts about the world with a pair of delicately malignant antennae to detect whatever is fit to live and an iron hoof to stamp it into the dust when found. It seems amazing that the bony fingers of fate and spite should push into what seemed the safest field of the War and nip the finest flower in it. One's instinct that the world (as we know it) is governed by chance is almost shaken by the accumulating evidence that it is the best which is always picked out for destruction.[97]

Asquith was writing a letter of condolence to a close friend, Lady Diana Manners, Hugo's sister-in-law. Although this particular example has little of the ring of convention about it, these sorts of sentiments were often found, naturally enough, in letters of condolence and were presumably intended to assuage grief. An officer in the 1st Battalion, King's Shropshire Light Infantry, writing to the widow of Company Sergeant Major

John Redford, assured her that 'It is always the best people who are taken', which could not be entirely true, however well meaning the sentiment.[98] Having said that, while it is difficult to lose sight of the fact that death in the trenches or on the field of a major battle was potentially so arbitrary as to render any suggestion of selection ridiculous, Douglas Gillespie's experience suggested to him that there might have been some truth in the idea; the military system did indeed seem peculiarly capable of culling talented individuals: 'That's the worst of this damnable war; it just lops off the bravest men as you might lop off the tallest heads of bracken with your stick, and once a man gets a reputation for keeping his head, and doing difficult jobs, he's bound to be picked for them.'[99]

Whether rhetorical or sincere, these expressions of personal inadequacy and indebtedness added further psychological weight to the officers' sense of duty and obligation. They also gave considerable momentum to the development of the concept of the 'lost generation'. Decades after the war had finished politicians like Harold Macmillan, Anthony Eden and Clement Attlee all promoted the idea that the country's rulers were only in power by the sufferance of those who had died and who were the better men.[100] Ironically, of course, by this time the exact same group of subalterns were being accused of possessing 'enthusiasm and little else' by A.J.P. Taylor.[101] Sassoon's poem 'The Hero' bitterly reconciles these two contradictory positions. In it, a failed officer is posthumously elevated to a heroic status by a bereaved mother's desire for a consoling image of virtue and a fellow officer's tacit collusion.[102] The reverence for the fallen which seemed to evolve naturally during the course of the war may have been self-deceiving, but it had a dramatic effect on those who remained alive.

The language of suffering, penitence and redemption was informed by two fundamentals of an Edwardian public-school education. The first was the encouragement of manliness, because of the virtues of endurance and commitment which it embodied. The second – organised religion – was the foundation of the education provided by the public schools, many of which were originally religious foundations. At an institution like Winchester College, founded in 1382 by William of Wykeham, Bishop of Winchester, chapel attendance remains compulsory to this day. George Moberly, headmaster of Winchester College between 1836 and 1867, believed that religion 'was for underpinning the moral conduct of the school, and its development … set the Public Schools apart from other teaching establishments where authority simply acted as an instrument of repression.'[103]

While organised religion was clearly an integral part of the public-school ethos, it is difficult to say how strongly it influenced young officers as a collective. It is possible that many pupils sincerely absorbed the religious instruction which they received at school. This may then have been significant in sustaining them in wartime, despite arguments that traditional religious teachings struggled to cope with the horrors of modern industrialised conflict.[104] Alternatively, previously more secular-minded young men may have experienced a rebirth of faith in the face of the suffering of the trenches. Letters and diaries generally provide little detailed information about the writers' religious views. Passing references or use of religious terminology – such as 'thank God', 'God bless you', 'God knows' and so on – are extremely common, but these may simply reflect prevailing habits of expression.[105] It is rarer to find texts of explicit religiosity, such as this example written by Gilbert Talbot: 'I'm in God's Hands, and I trust in His mercy.'[106] While the sincerity of this sort of writing seems undeniable, it would only be fair to ascribe to religious allusions the same problems of convention, audience expectation and authorial intention which affect the interpretation of other expressions of tropes derived from the public-school ethos. Talbot was, after all, the son of the Bishop of Winchester.

Whatever the overall level of faith within the officer corps, it was through religious imagery and ideas that the connection between suffering and glory was made most explicit. This association was an inherent part of the elevated status of trench-fighters. Their nobility and heroism came from their acceptance to debase themselves for the cause. The purgative effect of this was recognised within popular culture. John Buchan's character Wake, the pacifist in *Mr. Standfast*, is dignified and redeemed by a self-imposed immersion in the discomforts and dangers of the Western Front. Religious ideas of sacrifice and renewal were also employed by politicians. From the beginning of the conflict Liberals and some Socialists looked forward to a national renewal, the price of which would be sacrifice, and set the tone for the whole war using biblical and apocalyptic language.[107]

Consequently, service on the Western Front became associated with a moral and spiritual development in addition to that personal growth which was a feature of the transition from civilian to soldier. Christopher Stone felt in 1918 that, 'if I were killed now I should die a much better man than if I had died in 1914.'[108] The possibility of deriving good from evil had been noted at an early stage by the Church, Bishop Talbot writing that 'catastrophe has been historically one of the means in the hand of Providence for growth … out of destruction comes creation; out of the old the new. God's face is towards the future. And, unless the higher faith is altogether delusive, that way lies promise and hope.'[109] Rhetoric of this kind spontaneously fused with imagery of suffering to suggest to impressionable young soldiers that by performing their duty, especially if it culminated in their deaths, they could achieve a personal apotheosis. Talbot's audience within the establishment, the upper classes and consequently the ranks of public-school educated men were able to construct a complete moral code. By keeping faith with the war aims of their predecessors and honouring their sacrifices they could avoid rendering death pointless, meaningless and therefore insupportably tragic, whilst a further strong incentive was added by simultaneously interpreting the suffering of the war as a period of cleansing or purgatory, with redemption potentially achieved either through victory or an honourable death.

Further factors might also help, in the Christian idiom, to remove or at least blunt death's sting. Eric Leed has suggested that death might be welcomed 'as a resolution to an insupportable, continuous mourning', itself a kind of redemption.[110] That certainly seemed to be so in a case witnessed by Bertram Medley:

> … about midday I heard of the awful HLI casualties i.e. at Festubert, including Crossley. He is one of those to whom a lasting sorrow made life almost unbearable; and yet I am inclined to believe that that same sorrow sweetened his whole being. "If you had met me a year ago, you would have found me very disagreeable" he once said to me, and I half believe it. But I only knew him when grief had laid hold of his life – the man who from the first helped me, whom I learnt to love and look

up to, as few others that I have known. He went out hoping to die, but in his last letter to me he wrote "I went out, as you know, very eagerly; but now, I confess it, I as everyone else, would be pleased if it finished tomorrow." God has granted him his first wish and, though I know that a great thing has been taken out of my life, I cannot regret his great happiness.[111]

Charles Douie described a similar episode, the more romantic prose of his memoir contrasting with Medley's diary entry:

Sometimes on a walk, or in the solitude of a billet or dug-out, a man might unburden his soul to another. Once I went for a walk with a subaltern, one of my contemporaries at Rugby, whom I had always regarded as among the most cheerful and care-free of my friends. I was surprised when he told me that life meant nothing to him, that he had hardly known a happy hour, that he cared very little whether he lived or died. Being very young, I had not previously realised how much of unhappiness the laughter of a brave man may conceal. Death waited for this subaltern on the Somme. He kept his rendezvous without flinching and without dismay. He did not apprehend the majesty, or recognise the dominion of Death. To him, as to the Guards Ensign in *The Way of Revelation*, Death gave not a summons, but a welcome, 'arms wide to embrace, sleep strong to enfold, a friend there faithful and true.'[112]

Both of these cases involve intensely personal exchanges between people who clearly knew one another very well. They suggest a type of depression or war-weariness which could well have been difficult to detect. This could consequently have been a relatively common mentality. A further point which should not be overlooked is that acclimatisation had the power to normalise ideas and experiences that would seem strange or frightening to the civilian or uninitiated mind. The psychologist Charles Moran argued that a combatant became habituated to the idea or the threat of death, mastering their fear by a natural progression.[113] Andrew Buxton's comment – 'Death is looked on as such a small thing out here' – was partly a reflection of the almost inevitable callousness which soldiers developed.[114] Alfred Bonadeo has noted that Moran is rather inclined to see this as a serene process of surrender. His own analysis of Graves and Sassoon suggests that these two phenomena – welcoming and surrendering to death – were potentially quite similar psychologically.[115]

Keith Henderson, a cavalry officer, gave a similar insight into the officer's psyche, emphasising more the sense of foreshortening of perspective: 'Death is such a little thing. A change of air – no more. Death is the last day of Term, the last day of the Year. Regret? That's because we don't understand, quite.'[116] Lt. Edward Living, recollecting the moments before attacking on the first day of the Somme, felt 'to its intensest depth the truth of the proverb, "Carpe diem." What was time? I had another twenty minutes in which to live in comparative safety. What was the difference between twenty minutes and twenty years? Really and truly what was the difference? I was living at present, and that was enough. I am afraid that this working of mind will appear unintelligible. I cannot explain it further. I think that others who have waited to "go over" will realise its meaning.'[117] The future Prime Minister Anthony Eden remembered praying that, if hit, his fate would be either death or only a slight wound. He admitted that he could not fully account for this feeling. While he quoted the words of the 17th Century French tragedian Pierre Corneille – *Mourir pour le pays n'est pas un triste sort; C'est s'immortaliser par une belle mort* – in an effort to explain what he did not think, his choice of text suggests that he may have subscribed to a somewhat similar perspective about a 'good death'. More importantly, he certainly seemed to feel that the deaths of many of his friends had normalised the idea that he himself might die in battle. Furthermore, he found the threat of being killed much less frightening than the possibility of disablement or disfigurement, and living with the consequences.[118] Faced with such an awful prospect, death on the battlefield might have its consolations. Within the prevailing conventions it would be dignified by society and rendered purposeful. As these various comments indicate, the loss of one's future could seem a less terrible prospect when that future was so dominated by the awfulness of the war and its effects, particularly the grief it was generating. Moreover, having witnessed the injuries which modern weapons could inflict, it is hardly surprising that men like Eden, whose lives had been built around concepts of masculinity and physical prowess, should dread disfigurement or disablement more than death.

Personal attitudes shifted and evolved. While the loss of a friend could be devastating, in certain cases there seems to have been a curious effect on the attitudes of the men involved. Bertram Medley experienced Crossley's death as a form of epiphany:

> He is to me a type of the great Sweetness of Sorrow; and here, where there is so much bitter sorrow, I thank my God that he showed me that Death has two faces.[119]

In other words, death could become a highly complex and not necessarily wholly negative eventuality. Many officers, reflecting the wartime and post-war growth of spiritualism, seem to have believed or felt that they were sustained and supported by the spirits of former comrades. These ideas, which are clearly connected to the continuing influence of dead comrades as expressed through the powerful and common sense of obligation, were often brought into clearest focus when officers contemplated their parts in forthcoming actions. When awaiting an attack, these feelings could give comfort, as they apparently did to Douglas Gillespie, writing what was to prove his last letter:

> I have no forebodings, for I feel that so many of my friends will charge by my side, and if a man's spirit may wander back at all, especially to the places where he is needed most, then Tom himself will be here to help me, and give me courage and resource and that cool head which will be needed most of all to make the attack a success.[120]

Gillespie's brother Tom had been killed in October 1914 near La Bassée. Jack Oughtred expressed a similar belief after the death of his older brother Harold: 'I often feel in times of danger that he is with me. Strange, isn't it? I have never mentioned it to a soul – except to you now – but he went over the top on Oct 4th with me – and kept me safe – and gave me strength and determination to carry on as I should. He was with me again this time up. Don't think I am uncaring – I don't mean it that way – but we have always been such a lot to one another that even death cannot put a stop to it.'[121]

Sentiments of this kind partly explain the extraordinary letters which were often their last communications. Bernard Long told his parents 'We're fighting hard now and it's a serious game. We're all ready to lay down everything if need be, and if God wills I'm ready.'[122] Edward Tennant, in a remarkable valedictory letter to his mother, expressed his renewed sense of duty using biblical imagery: 'I feel rather like saying "If it be possible let this cup pass from me," but the triumphant finish "nevertheless not what I will but what Thou willest," steels my heart and sends me into this battle with a heart of triple bronze.'[123] Gilbert Talbot told his mother: 'It's easier for me than for you. Death is not so formidable or awful in a way here. Soldiers put it in its right place somehow. I know it's not the end – only an incident – and that the love that unites us lives through and will triumph over all.'[124] Lionel Sotheby wrote his final missive after attending an Old Etonian dinner marking the traditional 'Fourth of June' celebration at the Coldstream Guards' headquarters in Béthune. This occasion doubtless stimulated many emotions planted deep by his upbringing. He addressed parents, school and relatives, re-asserting one last time his membership of that kinship which was so important to junior officers, emphasising the values which still inspired him, and mixing the language of honour and rejoicing with a more romantic and peaceful notion: 'The cables are cut and I slip away, fading into pinky mists as at early dawn, remembering you all.'[125] After Douglas Gillespie's death on 25 September 1915, the copy of Bunyan's *Pilgrim's Progress* which was returned with his kit had a particular page marked. This was its closing sentence:

> Then I entered into the Valley of the Shadow of Death, and had no light, for almost half the way through it. I thought I should have been killed there, over and over; but at last day broke, and the sun rose, and I went through that which was behind with far more ease and quiet.[126]

These letters, diaries and other indicators cannot reveal the emotions that were passing through their minds at or shortly before the fateful moment. What seems certain is that many continued to understand and conceptualise their experiences in a way that was consistent with their formative ethos, even if that ethos had to adapt when it came into contact with the Western Front.

Conclusion

Once the war had finally ended demobilisation marked the start of a new period of transition for thousands of officers still serving on the Western Front, this time back from soldier to civilian. This was no less a momentous journey for many than the progress from civilian to soldier described in this book. Some found that their wartime service had transformed their outlooks and prospects for the better. Others were left shattered by wounds, illness or psychological traumas. Both types of veteran officer can be found in the literature of the inter-war years. Hugh 'Bulldog' Drummond and his friends, the creations of veteran Herman Cyril McNeile, are vigorous warriors, ready and willing to spring into action when danger threatens. George Fentiman, the shell-shocked friend of Lord Peter Wimsey in Dorothy L. Sayers' *The Unpleasantness at the Bellona Club* (1928), is a casualty of the war, angry and resentful, bedevilled with financial difficulties. In fiction as in real life, there was a wide and recognised diversity of experience.

For many, the readjustment to a life outside the army was also the start of a process of reappraising the war, an attempt to understand it and become reconciled to personal suffering and bereavement. It took time for narratives and interpretations to emerge, for participants to make sense of the sheer scale of events. Some of the most famous and influential accounts of the war emerged in the late 1920s and early 1930s, by which time the energy and focus dedicated to commemorative efforts had dissipated to some extent. Having marked the sacrifice of the war, Britain was finally ready to start internalising and understanding it.

How this was done is a much bigger story, one that is not within the scope of this book except when it touches upon enduring perceptions of British officers. It is worth noting that the gap between the Armistice and these periods of intense debate about the war, its purpose and its costs was filled by a process of memorialisation which was rooted in the same ideology that had held sway in the Edwardian era. Many memorials were actually the culmination of discussions begun at an early stage during the war, when it was already apparent that special commemorative efforts would be needed to mark tragedy on such a dramatic scale. The design eventually chosen for the Winchester College War Cloisters was actually proposed by Wykehamist Douglas Gillespie, writing from the trenches in 1915.[1] In the 1920s many memorials, both locally and nationally, used the high concepts of the pre-war era to give them their meaning, a further reminder that the ethos which inspired many British officers retained its power.[2] If it had not done so these designs would not have been chosen and would not have been effective.

Continuity of older ideas and practices has proved to be a persistent theme throughout the careers of junior officers. The survival of recognisable elements of the public-school ethos amidst the carnage of the Western Front is perhaps the most striking example of this, but there were many others. The young men who went off to war did not abandon everything they had known in civilian life in so doing. The fact that many documented their experiences so thoroughly in letters to family and friends is testament to enduring habits of communication established (in many cases) at school or university and the importance of emotional ties to the civilian world. The significance of home was further reinforced in hundreds of small ways in the officer's daily life and the domesticated existence he fashioned for himself in or behind the lines. His social life, which also provided important psychological nourishment, was built around pre-war patterns and substantially populated by exactly the same types of acquaintances who inhabited his pre-war social networks. His enduring connection with the life of the nation was reinforced by occasional periods of leave, access to newspapers and correspondence, and a steady flow of consumer goods which enabled him to maintain many of his old tastes and interests.

These elements of continuity were offset by the acquisition of unfamiliar military knowledge and understanding, the development of which defined the transition alongside processes of personal maturation. At the start of the story many prospective officers had virtually no conception of what life in the army would really be like. This much is evident when, inspired by the dramatic events unfolding in the early days of the war, they hopefully applied for commissions or attended interviews with potential COs without any real understanding as to the significance of their choices. Distinctions between different regiments, corps or types of service were relatively unimportant to many. What mattered was getting into the army somehow. Their subsequent reactions to new lifestyles and roles suggest that enthusiasm and novelty carried them through many of their early experiences in the military and even active service, before the grim reality of the war revealed itself to them, sometimes in the most shocking ways imaginable. This disillusionment (the word used without the stark connotations often associated with the First World War) was probably less common as the war progressed and it became ever more apparent to new officers that they faced an unpleasant future. Nevertheless, all those who made it to the Western Front still had to acclimatise themselves if they were to cope with the demands of their new working environment and learn how to soldier for real. The tactical realities of trench life demanded it.

The acquisition of military knowledge and experience inevitably had a substantial impact. Some officers struggled with their new responsibilities or with the requirement to kill. Others found that they were relatively comfortable with their work, a revelation which must have had a profound effect on them (and on their families too, if these changes were apparent in letters or when they finally met once again). For many the biggest change was the development of a new, more professional attitude towards soldiering and the war than that with which they volunteered or accepted their call-up papers. Janet Watson's differentiation between the values and outlooks of professionals and volunteers is a valuable starting point from which to consider this transition.[3] Volunteers as a group did tend to have a distinctive perspective on the war, usually defined at the start of the conflict by a sense of duty and an expectation that soldiering was ultimately a necessary but temporary diversion from their set path in life. Even when it became apparent that the struggle was likely to be a more protracted and serious business, the concept of service, and therefore selflessness in the face of a great national cause, remained important.

This attitude was not wholly incompatible with experiences of front-line soldiering, but accumulated knowledge and military proficiency steadily stripped away significant elements of this volunteering identity. In particular, it altered young officers' perceptions of the importance of front-line service as a contribution to the war effort. Culturally-sanctioned definitions of masculinity placed great emphasis on combat, especially in the earlier phases of the war. The Edwardian and Victorian heroes, both real and literary, whose exploits were a key formative influence on many a prospective officer, were willing to test themselves on the front line. The volunteer warriors of 1914 and 1915 were similarly keen to get involved, encouraged further by the extent to which the trenches soon came to dominate the popular imagination. At any stage of the war, soldiers were defined by whether or not they had been 'there', and many men technically subject to conscription from 1916 onwards retained the volunteer mentality to some extent, especially if they belonged to the officer class. Professionals, men who had been in the regular army before the war, were not immune to such sentiments, but they were far less likely to have as narrow a view of the activities which could be considered to constitute 'valid' soldiering. They also recognised that a successful career depended on broader experiences; chateaux generals are rather a cliché of the First World War, but they do illustrate the obvious point that seniority tends to distance the soldier from the combat zone. Young officers learned about the broad range of tasks that were required of the competent officer and developed a greater understanding of the internal workings and eco-system of the armed forces, in which the fighting man is dependent on a large number of other supporting and command elements. In many cases this knowledge weakened their attachment to trench service, leading to greater willingness to seek out alternative employment, at which point the process of professionalization was accelerated by the development of still broader military competences.

While it is striking that some young volunteer officers should have aspired to careers in the regular army despite their experiences of the Western Front (or, rather, despite modern perceptions of what the Western Front must have been like), their professionalization, seen as part of the transition from civilian to soldier, is arguably less important for the effect it had on their careers than the impact it had on almost every other aspect of their lives. While continuity of experience or practice characterised the lives of many a subaltern or captain, the retention of these familiar aspects of life were always conditional on their successful incorporation into a military context or environment. For instance, on the domestic level, officers could continue to have access to items which reminded them of home or enabled them to recreate a more homely setting, but only if they could be accommodated logistically. On the emotional level, ties to friends and family could still be powerful, provided they were not distorted or destroyed by the changes wrought in one party or the other by the war. The prominence of continuity as a theme in narratives of war experience despite these difficulties or pressures is testament to its significance or resonance.

It would be wrong, however, to see military professionalization as only hampering or weakening links to the traditional, the latter only enduring where the former permitted it. In many respects officers' reliance on these elements was stimulated by their immersion in unfamiliar and emotionally challenging new roles and situations. They actively sought out comforting remnants of their previous lives in the face of new hardships and stresses. Moreover, a better understanding of the nature of life on active service made it easier to incorporate the familiar into their daily routines. The inexperienced young officer was less likely than a more thoroughly initiated colleague to appreciate that the Western Front could accommodate unmilitary practices or articles. This can be seen perhaps most clearly in officers' growing abilities to make themselves comfortable, but this development was as much about perspective as the provision of luxuries. Officers typically learned over time that soldiering and civilian sensibilities were not incompatible – indeed, that it was necessary to create a balance. The idea of a form of symbiotic relationship between the old and new is reinforced by the extent to which certain experiences from pre-war life can be seen as having a value in rendering new roles and responsibilities more familiar from the outset, thereby promoting the transition.

This inter-dependency can also be seen in the extent to which the set of high ideals summarised under the heading 'the public-school ethos' endured and were even reinvigorated by experiences on the Western Front. The juxtaposition of Victorian notions of honour and glory with the desolation and carnage of many a Flanders field is strikingly incongruous, but many officers seem to have been able to adapt their expectations of soldiering and their sense of military virtue so that this dislocation was not insupportably stark. They did not do so consciously. They may have instinctively felt that they should have continued to believe in the old creed, but it seems likely that disillusionment would have been the result of any recasting of these ideas which was not more organic and automatic. What seems more likely is that their initial experiences of soldiering in the area of the front line were sufficiently satisfying (and insufficiently incompatible with their imaginings of warfare) for them to understand them in accordance with traditional values. As they gained greater experience, which might have threatened this fundamentally naïve perspective, their growing professionalism filled the gap. A better understanding of their roles as soldiers enabled them to maintain a more positive conception of their actions. They were further assisted by a contraction in their sense of military scale. If large operations defied real comprehension, there continued to be smaller spheres for personal heroism and martial endeavour which could continue to satisfy their need for validation. The shift is perceptible in this capacity to find military purpose in their actions, while their continued adherence to the 'big words' of their traditional moral framework is demonstrated in their persistent choice of language and imagery.

This book is not fundamentally about the officer's ability to survive the psychological pressures of the war, but some areas which it explores do seem to have a role to play in answering that difficult problem. The retention of emotionally-nourishing elements of continuity from a former civilian life seems to have been significant, as does the possibility that a well-engrained set of values might endure in a slightly adapted form. Simple human resilience also seems to have been important. As many officers would themselves have said, they coped because there was no alternative. A host of other explanations cannot be overlooked, including small-group dynamics and loyalties. These were clearly immensely important to the junior officers of the Western Front, both in terms of their affection for and devotion to their men and their sense of belonging to a fellowship of likeminded people.

As has been argued in Chapter 11, this sense of group solidarity was instrumental in the moulding of the public-school ethos into a powerful and binding code which provided meaning and inspiration. Young officers did not merely cling blindly to an outdated creed. As they became increasingly experienced they achieved an understanding of the nature of the Western Front, retaining their conviction in the justice of their cause and subtly (and unconsciously) remoulding their ethos to enhance its relevance. Sacrifice was traditionally considered praiseworthy and ennobling. In the trenches, in possession of the legacy of their fallen comrades but with no immediate prospect of success, many young officers elevated sacrifice still higher, making it a validation for all their own sufferings and all that had preceded them. Sacrifice ceased to be merely a virtue in itself, becoming an essential link in a chain which, if broken, would render their whole world meaningless. In this way the public-school ethos – the epitome of tradition – was at the heart of the young officers' experience of the First World War.

Another way of interpreting this would be to say that they were trapped, their indoctrination proving so effective that even experience of some of the worst sufferings imaginable was not enough to make them re-think their position and rebel against it, as perhaps they ought to have done. Siegfried Sassoon certainly seemed ensnared, his willingness to challenge the prevailing ethos ultimately stifled as much by his own sense of propriety and obligation as any action on the part of the state. It is important to remember that junior officers were not entirely homogenous in their outlook and that there were Sassoons. It is also perfectly appropriate that such an interpretation should be considered, especially if one is debating the merits (or otherwise) of a particular social or educational model. That is, however, a debate for another time. This book is about the lives and experiences of a particular group of men. If they were able to endure it does not mean that they did so for the right reasons, or that there was no personal cost in so doing. If they were sincerely inspired or sustained by a particular philosophy that does not mean that it is one which should be perpetuated. The pages of history are filled with stories of men and women who believed that they were doing the right thing. There will always be differing opinions as to whether or not they were correct, but it should always be right to understand them as fully as possible on their own terms.

In the context of the young British officers of the Western Front, a group that has been often been marginalised in histories of the war or lionised behind obfuscatory labels such as the 'lost generation', it feels particularly important to try to see them in this way. Time and the distinctive nature of the trenches have drawn a veil between them and modern society which obscures what they, and all those who fought, really were: ordinary people who responded as best they could to extraordinary circumstances.

Notes

Introduction

1   A.P. Linder, *Princes of the Trenches – Narrating the German Experience of the First World War*, p. 46.

2   G.D. Sheffield, *Forgotten Victory – The First World War: Myths and Realities*; G. Corrigan, *Mud, Blood and Poppycock – Britain and the First World War*.

3   P. Simkins, 'Everyman at War: Recent Interpretations of the Front Line Experience', in B. Bond (ed.), *The First World War and British Military History*, pp. 290-294.

4   J. Bourke, *An Intimate History of Killing – Face-to-face Killing in Twentieth-Century Warfare*; J. Bourke, *Dismembering the Male – Men's Bodies, Britain and the Great War*.

5   J.G. Fuller, *Troop Morale and Popular Culture in the British and Dominion Armies 1914-1918*.

6   M. Roper, *The Secret Battle – Emotional Survival in the Great War*; I.M. Brown, *British Logistics on the Western Front 1914-1919*; G.D. Sheffield & D. Todman (eds.), *Command and Control on the Western Front – The British Army's Experience 1914-18*.

7   J. Lewis-Stempel, *Six Weeks – The Short and Gallant Life of the British Officer in the First World War*.

8   For example see D. Winter, *Death's Men – Soldiers of the Great War*, pp. 67-8.

9   G. DeGroot, *Blighty. British Society in the Era of the Great War*, p. 164.

10 Simkins, 'Everyman at War', p. 312.

11 J.S.K. Watson, *Fighting Different Wars – Experience, Memory, and the First World War in Britain*, pp. 48-51.

12 R. Holmes, *Tommy – The British Soldier on the Western Front 1914-1918*, p. xxiii.

13 H.E.L. Mellersh, *Schoolboy into War*, pp. 14, 36.

14 A. Simpson, *Hot Blood And Cold Steel: Life And Death In The Trenches of the First World War*, p. 119; G.D. Sheffield, *Forgotten Victory – The First World War: Myths and Realities*, p. 122.

15 G.D. Sheffield, *Leadership in the trenches – Officer-Man Relations, Morale and Discipline in the British Army in the Era of the First World War*, p. 44.

16 P. Parker, *The Old Lie – The Great War and the Public School Ethos*, pp. 283-4.

Chapter 1

1   *The Wykehamist*, No. 574, 3 June 1918, p. 241.

2   War Office, *Statistics of the military effort of the British Empire during the Great War 1914-20*, p. 234.

3   J.M. Bourne, *Britain and the Great War 1914-1918*, p. 160. See also K. Simpson, 'The Officers', in I.F.W. Beckett & K. Simpson (eds.), *A Nation in Arms – A Social study of the British army in the First World War*, p. 71.

4   W.J. Reader, *At Duty's Call – A Study In Obsolete Patriotism*, p. 100.

5   G.D. Sheffield, *Leadership in the Trenches – Officer-Man Relations, Morale and Discipline in the British Army in the Era of the First World War*, pp. 35, 38-9.

6   G.D. Sheffield, *Forgotten Victory– The First World War: Myths and Realities*, p. 122.

7   H. Strachan, *The Politics of the British Army*, pp. 24-5.

8   A. Shepperd, *Sandhurst – The Royal Military Academy Sandhurst and its Predecessors*, p. 77; E.M. Spiers, *The Army and Society 1815-1914*, p. 24; J.S.K. Watson, *Fighting Different Wars – Experience, Memory, and the First World War in Britain*, p. 22.

9   Strachan, *Politics of the British Army*, p. 25; Sheffield, *Leadership in the Trenches*, p. 2.

10   Spiers, *The Army and Society*, p. 24; E.M. Spiers, 'The Regular Army in 1914', in Beckett & Simpson, *A Nation in Arms*, p. 41.

11   G. Harries-Jenkins, *The Army in Victorian Society*, pp. 140-1.

12   Sheffield, *Leadership in the Trenches*, p. 2.

13   P. Parker, *The Old Lie – The Great War and the Public School Ethos*, p. 85.

14   Harries-Jenkins, *Army in Victorian Society*, p. 44.

15   Sheffield, *Leadership in the Trenches*, p. 2.

16   Spiers, *Army and Society*, p. 2.

17   Simpson, 'The Officers', p. 65.

18   Sheffield, *Leadership in the Trenches*, p. 6.

19   Spiers, *Army and Society*, p. 2.

20   S.C. Tucker (ed.), *The European Powers in the First World War – An Encyclopaedia*, p. 599.

21   Spiers, *Army and Society*, p. 3.

22   Spiers, *Army and Society*, p. 3.

23   The National Archives, *Scheme for promotion of non-commissioned officers from the ranks: Question of further education and comparison with French system'*, pp. 7-8.

24   *Scheme for promotion of non-commissioned officers from the ranks*, p. 4.

25   *Scheme for promotion of non-commissioned officers from the ranks*, p. 7.

26   *Scheme for promotion of non-commissioned officers from the ranks*, pp. 10-11.

27   L.E. Jones, *An Edwardian Youth*, pp. 8-9.

28   *Scheme for promotion of non-commissioned officers from the ranks*, p. 20.

29   *Scheme for promotion of non-commissioned officers from the ranks*, Minute 25. See also Sheffield, *Leadership in the Trenches*, p. 24.

30   *Scheme for promotion of non-commissioned officers from the ranks*, Minute 25.

31   Sheffield, *Leadership in the Trenches*, p. 56.

32   R. Ross (ed.), *The First Collected Edition of the works of Oscar Wilde – The Importance of Being Earnest*, p. 42.

33   C.Ó. Gráda, 'Agricultural decline 1860-1914', in R.C. Floud & D. McCloskey (eds.), *The Economic History of Britain since 1700 – Volume 2: 1860 to the 1970s*, p. 178.

34   R.C. Floud, 'Britain 1860-1914: a survey', in Floud & McCloskey, *Economic History of Britain since 1700 – Volume 2*, p. 2; D. Read, *The Age of Urban Democracy – England 1868-1914*, p. 215.

35   D. Cannadine, *The Decline And Fall Of The British Aristocracy*, p. 27.

36   Read, *Age of Urban Democracy*, p. 387.

37   Cannadine, *Decline and Fall*, p. 27.

38   M. Wiener, *English Culture and the Decline of the Industrial Spirit 1850-1980*, pp. 7-9.

39   J. Stevenson, *British Society 1914-45*, p. 30.

40   P. Thane, 'Social History 1860-1914', in Floud & McCloskey, *The Economic History of Britain since 1700 – Volume 2*, p. 216.

41   Read, *Age of Urban Democracy*, p. 230; Thane, 'Social History 1860-1914', p. 215.

42   Wiener, *English Culture and the Decline of the Industrial Spirit*, p. 127.

43   Wiener, *English Culture and the Decline of the Industrial Spirit*, p. 12.

44   W. Ewart, *Way of Revelation*, pp. 13-18.

45   J.A. Mangan, *Athleticism in the Victorian and Edwardian Public School: The Emergence and Consolidation of an Educational Ideology*, pp. 1-2.

46   Mangan, *Athleticism in the Victorian and Edwardian Public School*, pp. 1-2.

47   V. Ogilvie, *The English Public School*, p. 164.

48   E.C. Mack, *Public Schools and British Opinion since 1860 – The Relationship Between Contemporary Ideas and the Evolution of an English Institution*, p. 119.

49   P. Mason, *The English Gentleman – The Rise and Fall of an Ideal*, p. 9.

50   B. Darwin, *The English Public School*, p. 19.

51   J.R.de S. Honey, 'Tom Brown's Universe: The Nature and Limits of the Victorian Public Schools Community', in B. Simon & I. Bradley (eds.), *The Victorian Public School – Studies in the Development of an Educational Institution*, p. 21.

52   For an example see C. Barnett, *The Collapse of British Power*, pp. 36-7.

53   Reader, *At Duty's Call*, p. 94.

54   *Report of the Royal Commission to inquire into Revenues and Management of certain Colleges and Schools, Studies and Instruction*, pp. 12, 31-32.

55   Mangan, *Athleticism in the Victorian and Edwardian Public School*, pp. 211-12.

56   P. Jones & H. Jones, *War Letters of a Public-Schoolboy*, p. 17.

57   P. Earle, 'God, the Rod, and Lines from Virgil', in G. Macdonald Fraser, *The World of the Public School*, p. 54.

58   P. McIntosh, *Physical Education in England since 1800*, p. 132.

59   Mangan, *Athleticism in the Victorian and Edwardian Public School*, p. 128.

60   Reader, *At Duty's Call*, p. 96; McIntosh, *Physical Education*, p. 167. See also J. Lowerson, *Sport and the English Middle Classes – 1870-1914*, p. 21.

61   Parker, *The Old Lie*, p. 56; Spiers, 'The Regular Army in 1914', p. 41.

62   Mack, *Public Schools and British Opinion since 1860*, p. 219.

63   W.E. Cairnes, *The Army from Within*, p. 157.

64   B. Congreve, *Armageddon Road – A VC's Diary, 1914-1916*.

65   J.A. Mangan, *The Games Ethic and Imperialism: Aspects of the Diffusion of an Ideal*, p. 18; M. Moss, *Manliness and Militarism*, p. 16.

66   *Report of the Royal Commission to inquire into Revenues and Management of certain Colleges and Schools*, pp. 28, 38.

67   Mangan, *Games Ethic and Imperialism*, p. 18; Barnett, *The Collapse of British Power*, pp. 34-5.

68   J. Richards, *Visions of Yesterday*, p. 44; Mason, *The English Gentleman*, p. 169.

69   M. Falkus, 'Fagging and Boy Government', in Macdonald Fraser, *The World of the Public School*, pp. 58-9; J.R.de S. Honey, *Tom Brown's Universe: The Development of the Victorian Public School*, pp. 216-8.

70   Ogilvie, *The English Public School*, p. 182.

71   Darwin, *The English Public School*, pp. 78-9.

72   Mack, *Public Schools and British Opinion since 1860*, p. 108.

73   T.J.H. Bishop & R. Wilkinson, *Winchester And The Public School Elite – A Statistical Analysis*, p. 70.

74   Mack, *Public Schools and British Opinion since 1860*, p. 180.

75   R. Pound, *The Lost Generation*, p. 83.

76   Parker, *The Old Lie*, p. 63.

77   A.R. Haig-Brown, *The O.T.C. and the Great War*, p. 12.

78   *The Wykehamist*: No. 522, 14 November, 1913, pp. 204-5; No. 529, May, 1914, p. 287; No. 524, 22 December, 1913, pp. 229-30; No. 523, December, 1913, pp. 217-18; No. 521, November, 1913, pp. 195-6.

79   E. Blunden, 'Infantryman Passes By', in G.A. Panichas (ed.), *Promise of Greatness – The War of 1914-1918*, pp. 25-6; D. Stevenson, *1914-1918 – The History of the First World War*, p. 7. Blunden is well

known as the author of *Undertones of War*, first published in 1928. He served with the Royal Sussex Regiment.

80   Hynes, *The Edwardian Turn Of Mind*, p. 354.

81   Wiener, *English Culture and the Decline of the Industrial Spirit*, p. 22.

82   R. Holt, *Sport and the British – A Modern History*, p. 75; P. Martland & M. Pattenden, *Corpus Lives*, p. 72.

83   B. Supple, 'The Two World Wars', in D. Reynolds (ed.), *Christ's – A Cambridge College Over Five Centuries*, p. 153.

84   War Office, *Regulations under which Commissions in the Regular Army may be obtained by University Candidates*, p. 3.

85   H. Strachan, *History of The Cambridge University Officers Training Corps*, pp. 123-5.

86   Haig-Brown, *The O.T.C. and the Great War*, pp. 21-2.

87   Sheffield, *Forgotten Victory*, p. 22; P. Clarke, *Hope and Glory – Britain 1900-1990*, p. 57.

88   E.M. Spiers, *The Late Victorian Army 1868-1902*, p. 312.

89   Read, *Age of Urban Democracy*, p. 401; M. Paris, *Warrior Nation – Images of War in British Popular Culture, 1850-2000*, p. 85.

90   N.F. Gullace, *"The Blood of Our Sons" – Men, Women, and the Renegotiation of British Citizenship During the Great War*, p. 40.

91   S. Hynes, *The Edwardian Turn Of Mind*, p. 348.

92   C. Dakers, *The Countryside at War 1914-1918*, p. 49; Lowerson, *Sport and the English Middle Classes*, p. 8; N. Hiley, 'Ploughboys and Soldiers: the folk song and the gramophone in the British Expeditionary Force 1914-1918', *Media History*, 4, No. 1, p. 62.

93   A. Marwick, *The Deluge: British Society and the First World War*, p. 26.

94   Clarke, *Hope and Glory*, pp. 56-7.

95   P. Kennedy, 'The development of German Naval Operations Plans against England, 1896-1914', in P. Kennedy (ed.), *The War Plans of the Great Powers*, pp. 174-6.

96   D. Pick, *War Machine – the rationalisation of slaughter in the modern age*, pp. 172-3.

97   S. Hynes, *A War Imagined – The First World and English Culture*, p. 7; M. Smith, 'The War and British Culture', in S. Constantine, M.W. Kirby & M.B. Rose (eds.), *The First World War in British History*, p. 172.

98   Gullace, *"The Blood of Our Sons"*, pp. 40-1.

99   A. Gregory, *The Last Great War – British Society and the First World War*, p. 161.

100 P. Howarth, *Play Up And Play The Game: The Heroes Of Popular Fiction*, p. 34.

101 Moss, *Manliness and Militarism*, p. 83; Howarth, *Play Up And Play The Game*, pp. 48-50; Richards, *Visions of Yesterday*, p. 41.

102 G.J. DeGroot, *Blighty. British Society in the Era of the Great War*, pp. 38-9; Moss, *Manliness and Militarism*, pp. 83-8; Paris, *Warrior Nation*, p. 87; M. Ferro, *The Great War 1914-1918*, p. 26.

103 E.S. Turner, *Boys Will Be Boys – the story of Sweeney Todd, Deadwood Dick, Sexton Blake, Billy Bunter, Dick Barton, et al*, p. 86.

104 Howarth, *Play Up And Play The Game*, p. 44.

105 M. Girouard, *The Return To Camelot – Chivalry and the English Gentleman*, p. 264.

106 Paris, *Warrior Nation*, pp. 101-2.

107 R. Kipling, *The Complete Stalky & Co*, p. 17.

108 Richards, *Visions of Yesterday*, p. 20. See also Richards, *Happiest Days*, p. 149.

109 Kipling, *Complete Stalky & Co*, p. 170.

110 Moss, *Manliness and Militarism*, p. 88.

111   G. Dawson, *Soldier Heroes – British adventure, empire and the imagining of masculinities*, p. 235.

112   S. Calloway, *The Golden Age of Shopping 1910-1940 – A miscellany of items from Harrods, Gamages and Army & Navy Stores*), p. 76.

113   Paris, *Warrior Nation*, p. 136.

114   Girouard, *The Return To Camelot*, pp. 13-14.

115   Sheffield, *Leadership in the Trenches*, p. 48; A. Lambert, *Unquiet Souls – The Indian Summer of the British Aristocracy 1880-1918*, pp. 155-6.

116   Strachan, *History of The Cambridge University Officers Training Corps*, p. 122.

117   Gullace, *"The Blood of Our Sons"*, p. 47.

118   Gregory, *The Last Great War*, p. 39.

119   *The Harrovian*, Vol. XXVII, No. 6, 17 October, 1914, p. 106.

120   M.C. Morgan, *Cheltenham College – The First Hundred Years*, p. 156.

121   McIntosh, *Physical Education*, p. 191.

122   J.D'E. Firth, *Rendall of Winchester – The Life and Witness of a Teacher*, pp.155-6.

123   *The Harrovian*, Vol. XXIX, No. 7, 18 November 1916, p. 102.

124   *The Harrovian*, Vol. XXXII, No. 5, 26 July 1919, p. 69.

125   Papers of Sir G. Lenanton, Imperial War Museum, Department of Documents, letter dated 29 October 1914.

126   Girouard, *Return To Camelot*, p. 282.

127   *The Wykehamist*, No. 521, November, 1913, p. 197.

128   *The Harrovian*, Vol. XXVII, No. 7, 21 November 1914, pp. 123-4.

129   *The Harrovian*, Vol. XXVII, No. 7, 21 November 1914, p. 117.

130   *The Harrovian*, Vol. XXIX, No. 5, 29 July 1916, p. 60.

131   R. Holmes, *Tommy – The British Soldier on the Western Front 1914-1918*, p. 93; Parker, *The Old Lie*, p. 260.

132   *The Harrovian*, Vol. XXXI, No. 1, 2 March 1918, p. 1.

133   M.J. Rendall, letter to Bishop Paget dated 10 March 1915, in the Papers of Captain S.J. Paget.

134   Papers of Major M.S.S. Moore, Imperial War Museum, Department of Documents, 'Third Supplement To *The London Gazette*', 6 November 1917.

135   Moore papers, R.W. Rice to Moore, 4 December 1917.

136   *The Harrovian*, Vol. XXIX, No. 3, 3 June 1916, p. 32.

137   *The Harrovian*, Vol. XXIX, No. 3, 3 June 1916, p. 23.

138   Paget papers, letter dated 23 May 1915.

139   Lenanton papers, letter dated 4 October 1914.

140   Parker, *The Old Lie*, p. 198.

141   G. Orwell, *My Country Right Or Left and other selected essays and journalism*, p. 199.

142   A. Waugh, *Public School Life – Boys, Parents, Masters*, p. 177.

143   *The Harrovian*, Vol. XXVIII, No. 6, 23 October 1915, p. 80.

144   Parker, *The Old Lie*, pp. 22-4.

145   Bourne, *Britain and the Great War*, p. 207.

146   A. de Jonge, letter to C.J. Moore-Bick dated 15 June 2003.

Chapter 2

1   A. Gregory, *The Last Great War: British Society and the First World War*, pp. 32, 74-81.

2   S. Hynes, *A Soldier's Tale – Bearing Witness To Modern War*, p. 49.

3   Papers of Major T.D. Pratt, Imperial War Museum, Department of Documents, memoir.

4   A.O. Pollard, *Fire-Eater – The Memoirs of a V.C.*, p. 22.

5   D. Hankey, *A Student In Arms*, p. 91.

6   J.S.K. Watson, *Fighting Different Wars – Experience, Memory, and the First World War in Britain*, pp. 42-3.

7   R. Harris, 'The "Child of the barbarian": Rape, Race and Nationalism in France During The First World War', *Past and Present*, No. 141 (1993).

8   Papers of Major-General D.N. Wimberley, Imperial War Museum, Department of Documents, *The Memoirs of Major-General Douglas Neil Wimberley*, Volume 1, p. 14.

9   Papers of Captain S.J. Paget, letter dated 23 December 1914.

10   The National Archives, *Report of Winston Churchill's Committee on Promotion; reports of meetings, Letters of enquiry concerning claims*, p. 3.

11   W.J. Reader, *At Duty's Call – A Study In Obsolete Patriotism*, p. 123.

12   J. Winter, *The Great War and the British People*, pp. 30 1.

13   K. Simpson, 'The Officers', in I.F.W. Beckett & K. Simpson (eds.), *A Nation in Arms – A Social study of the British army in the First World War*, p. 83. See also P.H. Liddle, *The Soldier's War*, p. 85.

14   R. Holmes, *Tommy – The British Soldier on the Western Front 1914-1918*, p. 145.

15   E. Townshend (ed.), *Keeling Letters and Recollections*, p. 257.

16   Townshend, *Keeling Letters and Recollections*, p. 185.

17   D. Wheatley, *The Time Has Come … The Memoirs of Dennis Wheatley: Vol 2: Officer and Temporary Gentleman 1914-1919*, p. 39.

18   G.D. Sheffield & G.I.S. Inglis (eds.), *From Vimy Ridge to the Rhine – The Great War Letters of Christopher Stone DSO MC*, pp. 24-7.

19   G.D. Sheffield, *Leadership in the Trenches – Officer-Man Relations, Morale and Discipline in the British Army in the Era of the First World War*, p. 37.

20   J. Brown, *Letters, Essays and Verses*, p. 88.

21   Brown, *Letters, Essays and Verses*, p. 93.

22   Brown, *Letters, Essays and Verses*, p. 96.

23   Brown, *Letters, Essays and Verses*, pp. 98-9.

24   Brown, *Letters, Essays and Verses*, pp. 98-9.

25   'O.E.' (G. Fildes), *Iron Times with the Guards*, p. 9.

26   Pollard, *Fire Eater*, p. 42.

27   C. Messenger, *Call To Arms: The British Army 1914-18*, pp. 296-7.

28   Messenger, *Call To Arms: The British Army 1914-18*, pp. 296-7.

29   Pollard, *Fire-Eater*, p. 42.

30   G. Gould Walker (ed.), *The Honourable Artillery Company in the Great War 1914-1919*, pp. 28-9, cited in Messenger, *Call To Arms*, pp. 300-1.

31   Papers of Captain A.B. Pick, Imperial War Museum, Department of Documents, letter dated 3 June 1915.

32   Wheatley, *The Time Has Come … Vol 2*, p. 41.

33   K.W. Mitchinson, *Gentlemen and Officers – The Impact and Experience of War on a Territorial Regiment 1914-1918*, p. 85.

34   D. Winter, *Death's Men – Soldiers of the Great War*, pp. 67-8.

35   Brown, *Letters, Essays and Verses*, p. 112.

36   Holmes, *Tommy*, p. 580.

37   Anon. (D. Bell), *A Soldier's Diary of the Great War*, p. 113.

38   Anon. (D. Bell), *A Soldier's Diary of the Great War*, pp. 114-15.

39   Holmes, *Tommy*, p. 140.

40   Sheffield, *Leadership in the Trenches*, p. 37.

41   H. Dundas, *Henry Dundas – Scots Guards – A Memoir*, pp. 12-13.

42   H. Macmillan, *Winds of Change 1914-1939*, p. 63.

43   Wheatley, *The Time Has Come … Vol 2*, p. 50.

44   Papers of Major W. House, Imperial War Museum, Department of Documents, *1914-1918 War Memoirs*, p. 1.

45   M. Middlebrook, *The First Day on the Somme: 1 July 1916*, pp. 8-9.

46   The National Archives, War Office Officers Files, Captain S.J. Paget, 'Application form M.T. 393'.

47   Sheffield, *Leadership in the Trenches*, p. 54.

48   F.W. Paish, *War As A Temporary Occupation – First World War Memoirs of a Second Lieutenant*, p. 9.

49   Papers of Captain A. Gibbs, Imperial War Museum, Department of Documents, letter dated 20 April 1916.

50   Papers of John Trant Bramston, undated letter from Maurice, E3/7/28/1.

51   K. Simpson, 'The Officers', p. 89.

52   Papers of 2nd Lt. R.P. Hamilton, Imperial War Museum, Department of Documents, letter dated 3 June 1915.

53   Pick papers, letter dated 25 March 1917.

54   E. Leed, 'Fateful Memories: Industrialized War and Traumatic Neuroses', *Journal of Contemporary History*, 35, No. 1 (2000), p. 88.

55   I. Bet-El, *Conscripts – Lost Legions of the Great War*.

56   Papers of Major C.H. Dudley-Ward, Imperial War Museum, Department of Documents, journal entry dated 28 November 1916.

57   P. Simkins, *Kitchener's Army – The Raising of the New Armies, 1914-16*, p. 267.

58   Papers of Sir G. Lenanton, Imperial War Museum, Department of Documents, letter to Mother dated 16 April 1915.

59   'O.E.' (G. Fildes), *Iron Times with the Guards*, p. 6.

60   R. Kipling, *The New Army In Training*, p. 5.

61   P. Jones & H. Jones, *War Letters of a Public-Schoolboy*, p. 104.

62   Wheatley, *The Time Has Come … Vol 2*, p. 57; Papers of Captain J.E. Crombie, Volume 2: War 1914-1917, p. 2.

63   H. Williamson, *A Fox Under My Cloak*, p. 130.

64   Anon. (T.D. Pilcher), *A General's Letters To His Son On Obtaining His Commission*, p. 2.

65   J. Lewis-Stempel, *Six Weeks – The Short and Gallant Life of the British Officer in the First World War*, p. 189.

66   Dudley-Ward papers, journal entry dated 2 March 1916.

67   P. Thompson, *The Edwardians – The Remaking of British Society*, p. 19.

68   Wheatley, *The Time Has Come … Vol 2*, p. 56.

69   *The Times*, 5 August 1914, p. 8; 14 August 1914, p. 9a.

70   War Office, *Statistics of the military effort of the British Empire during the Great War 1914-20*, p. 529.

71   *The Times*, 16 July 1918, p. 4ef.

72   'Regular', *Customs of the Army – A Guide for Cadets and Young Officers*, p. 6.

73   H.E.L. Mellersh, *Schoolboy into War*, p. 36.

74   Williamson, *A Fox Under My Cloak*, p. 131.

75   Simpson, 'The Officers', pp. 76-7.

76   'Regular', *Customs of the Army*, pp. 38-9.

77   *The Times*, 17 August 1915, p. 13f.

78   J. Nettleton, *The Anger of the Guns: An Infantry Officer on the Western Front*, p. 50.

79   Nettleton, *Anger of the Guns*, p. 15.

80   E.S. Turner, *Gallant Gentlemen – a portrait of the British Officer 1600-1956*, p. 275; Simkins, *Kitchener's Army*, p. 300.

81   Sheffield, *Leadership in the Trenches*, p. 53.

82   Paget papers, letter dated 23 December 1914.

83   Papers of Lt. W.B.P. Spencer, Imperial War Museum, Department of Documents, letter postmarked 1 December 1914.

84   Simkins, *Kitchener's Army*, pp. 313-14; B. Williams, *Raising and Training the New Armies*, p. 97.

85   R. Graves, *Goodbye to All That*, p. 203. Sheffield, *Leadership in the Trenches*, p. 53-4; Simpson, 'The Officers', p. 80.

86   Sheffield, *Leadership in the Trenches*, pp. 55-6.

87   "B" Company No. 2 Officer Cadet Battalion, *Summary of lectures, private study, and practical work for the 4 months' course, exclusive of drill, bayonet fighting and physical training.*

88   Jones & Jones, *War Letters*, p. 105.

89   'O.E.' (G. Fildes), *Iron Times with the Guards*, p. 15.

90   C. Douie, *The Weary Road – Recollections of a Subaltern of Infantry*, p. 34.

91   C. Carrington, *Rudyard Kipling: His Life And Work*, p. 432.

92   Hamilton papers, letter dated 14 March 1915.

93   E. Leed, *No Man's Land – Combat and Identity in World War I*, p. 61.

94   Papers of 2nd Lt. D. Neilson-Terry, Imperial War Museum, Department of Documents, *Letters from the Great War 1914-1918*, p. 2.

95   E.C. Vaughan, *Some Desperate Glory – The diary of a young officer, 1917*, p. 1.

96   Papers of Captain C.C. May, Imperial War Museum, Department of Documents, diary entry dated 23 November 1915.

Chapter 3

1   D.C. Richter (ed.), *Lionel Sotheby's Great War – Diaries and Letters from the Western Front*, p. 2.

2   J. Lewis-Stempel, *Six Weeks – The Short and Gallant Life of the British Officer in the First World War*, p. 72.

3   P.J. Campbell, *In the Cannon's Mouth*, p. 1.

4   O.S. Buckmaster, *Roundabout – The Autobiography of Viscount Buckmaster*, p. 127.

5   Papers of Captain J.E. Crombie, Volume 2: War 1914-1917, pp. 108-9.

6   Papers of Captain A.D. Chater, Imperial War Museum, Department of Documents, *A Memoir About Harrow and War Service.*

7   G.A. Burgoyne, *The Burgoyne Diaries*, p. 6.

8   C. Messenger, *Call To Arms: The British Army 1914-18*, pp. 265-6.

9   J. Brown, *Letters, Essays and Verse*, p. 111; D. Young, *Try Anything Twice*, p. 109.

10   R. Holmes, *Tommy – The British Soldier on the Western Front 1914-1918*, pp. 344-5.

11   E.C. Vaughan, *Some Desperate Glory – The diary of a young officer, 1917*, pp. 4-5.

12   S. Hewett, *A Scholar's Letters from the Front*, p. 25.

13   D. Todman, *The Great War: Myth and Memory*, p. 26.

14   J.M. Bourne, 'A personal reflection on the two World Wars', in J.M. Bourne, P. Liddle & I. Whitehead (eds.), *The Great World War 1914-1945. Vol. 1 – Lightning Strike Twice*, p. 20.

15   D. Stevenson, *1914-1918 – The History of the First World War*, p. 179.

16   G. Corrigan, *Mud, Blood and Poppycock – Britain and the First World War*, p. 78.

17   P. Jones & H. Jones, *War Letters of a Public-Schoolboy*, p. 105.

18   Papers of Captain G.N. Adams, Imperial War Museum, Department of Documents, undated letter to Elsie.

19   Holmes, *Tommy*, pp. 248-9.

20   Vaughan, *Some Desperate Glory*, pp. 5-6.

21   Anon. (D. Bell), *A Soldier's Diary of the Great War*, pp. 59-60.

22   Papers of Captain E.R. Hepper, Imperial War Museum, Department of Documents, diary entry dated 20 February 1916.

23   E.S. Woods (ed.), *Andrew R. Buxton, The Rifle Brigade, A Memoir*, p. 68.

24   Papers of Lt. W.B.P. Spencer, Imperial War Museum, Department of Documents, letter postmarked 26 December 1914.

25   L. Talbot (ed.), *Gilbert Walter Lyttelton Talbot*, p. 52. 'Terrier' is contemporary slang for Territorial.

26   G.H. Greenwell, *Infant In Arms*, p. 18.

27   Papers of Captain S.J. Paget, letter dated 17 August 1915.

28   Papers of 2nd Lt. R.P. Hamilton, Imperial War Museum, Department of Documents, diary entry dated 22 May 1915.

29   R.E. Harris, *Billie – The Nevill Letters 1914-1916*, p. 58.

30   R. Bickersteth, *Bickersteth War Diaries 1914-1919, Volume 2: 3/2/1915 – 2/2/1916*, The Bickersteth War Diaries and the Papers of John Burgon Bickersteth, BICK 1/2, p. 524.

31   R. Wohl, *The Generation of 1914*, p. 94.

32   H. Strachan, *The First World War – A New Illustrated History*, pp. 159-60; Bourne, 'A personal reflection', p. 18.

33   Strachan, *The First World War – A New Illustrated History*, pp. 160-1.

34   A.D. Gillespie, *Letters From Flanders*, p. 96.

35   Holmes, *Tommy*, pp. 235-6.

36   Harris, *Billie*, p. 54.

37   G.D. Sheffield & G.I.S. Inglis (eds.), *From Vimy Ridge to the Rhine – The Great War Letters of Christopher Stone DSO MC*, p. 35.

38   Holmes, *Tommy*, p. 66.

39   Papers of Lt. C.L. Platt, Imperial War Museum, Department of Documents, *The Great War At Close Quarters*, p. 14.

40   Papers of C.K. Ogden, Imperial War Museum, Department of Documents, bound copy of Lt. B.L. Lawrence war letters, p. 16.

41   J.C. Dunn, *The War the Infantry Knew, 1914-1918*, p. 22-3.

42   Holmes, *Tommy*, p. 300; J. Bourke, *An Intimate History of Killing – Face-to-face Killing in Twentieth-Century Warfare*, p. 37.

43   Spencer papers, letter dated 2 February 1915.

44   Harris, *Billie*, p. 65.

45   C. Barnett, *The Collapse of British Power*, p. 432. See also C. Barnett, *The Great War*, p. 131; D.E. Showalter, 'Mass Warfare and the Impact of Technology', in R. Chickering & S. Förster (eds), *Great War, Total War – Combat and Mobilization on the Western Front, 1914-1918*, p. 88.

46   Hewett, *A Scholar's Letters from the Front*, pp. 38-9.

47   Gillespie, *Letters From Flanders*, p. 42.

48   B. Long, *First World War Letters*, p. 25.

49   Papers of E.J. Dent, letter from A.H. Parry dated 2 June 1916, Add MS 7973/P/12.

50   Crombie papers, Volume 3: War 1914-1917, p. 43.

51   B.A. Medley, *April 1915 to September 1915*, pp. 74-5.

52   Anon (D. Bell), *A Soldier's Diary of the Great War*, p. 125.

53   Hewett, *A Scholar's Letters from the Front*, p. 76.

54   Papers of Major M.S.S. Moore, Imperial War Museum, Department of Documents, letter dated 19 April 1917.

55   Hewett, *A Scholar's Letters from the Front*, p. 40.

56   Ogden papers, B.L. Lawrence war letters, pp. 38-9

57   Vaughan, *Some Desperate Glory*, p. 30.

58   V.W. Germains, *The Kitchener Armies – The Stories of a National Achievement*, pp. 178-9.

59   Holmes, *Tommy*, p. 276.

60   M. Glover (ed.), *The Fateful Battle Line: The Great War Journals and Sketches of Captain Henry Ogle, MC*, pp. 30-1.

61   'O.E.' (G. Fildes), *Iron Times with the Guards*, p. 40.

62   G. Chapman, *A Passionate Prodigality – Fragments of Autobiography*, pp. 25-6.

63   P. Griffith, *Battle Tactics of the Western Front: The British Army's Art of Attack, 1916-18*; G.D. Sheffield, *Forgotten Victory – The First World War: Myths and Realities*, pp. 149-51.

64   Papers of Lt. R.L. Mackay, Imperial War Museum, Department of Documents, *The Personal Diary of Lieutenant Robert Lindsay Mackay, while serving in France with 11th Battalion, later the 1st/8th Battalion Argyll and Sutherland Highlanders, September 1916 to January 1919*, p. 74.

65   R. Graves, *Goodbye to All That*, p. 202.

66   J. Jolliffe, *Raymond Asquith – Life and Letters*, p. 293.

67   E. Blunden, *Undertones of War*, p. 161.

68   A.O. Pollard, *Fire-Eater – The Memoirs of a V.C.*, p. 179.

69   Woods, *Andrew R. Buxton*, p. 243.

70   J.E.H. Neville, *War Letters of a Light Infantryman*, p. 73.

71   Neville, *War Letters of a Light Infantryman*, p. 83.

72   M. Roper, *The Secret Battle – Emotional Survival in the Great War*, p. 122.

73   G. Nobbs, *Englishman, Kamerad! Right of the British Line*, pp. 29-30.

74   Holmes, *Tommy*, pp. 184-8.

75   L. Peppiatt, *The War Diary – January to September 1918 – of Major Leslie Peppiatt MC*, p. 35.

76   C. Carlisle (ed.), *My Own Darling: Letters from Montie to Kitty Carlisle*, p. 154.

77   B. Bairnsfather, *"The Bystander's" Fragments From France*, p. 33.

78   G.D. Sheffield, 'Officer-Man Relations, Discipline and Morale in the British Army of the Great War', in H. Cecil & P.H. Liddle (eds.), *Facing Armageddon – The First World War Experienced*, p. 415.

79   Peppiatt, *The War Diary*, p. 35.

80   J.G. Fuller, *Troop Morale and Popular Culture in the British and Dominion Armies 1914-1918*, pp. 54-5.

81   'I. Hay' (J.H. Beith), *The First Hundred Thousand – Being the Unofficial Chronicle of a Unit of "K(I)"*, p. 47.

82   Neville, *The War Letters of a Light Infantryman*, p. 44; Papers of Captain W.E. Villiers, Imperial War Museum, Department of Documents, letter dated 8 October 1916.

83   J. Nettleton, *The Anger of the Guns: An Infantry Officer on the Western Front*, p. 163.

84   Papers of Captain A. Gibbs, Imperial War Museum, Department of Documents, letter dated 25 July 1918.

85   K. Simpson, 'The Officers', in I.F.W. Beckett & K. Simpson (eds.), *A Nation in Arms – A Social study of the British army in the First World War*, p. 89.

86   Lewis-Stempel, *Six Weeks*, p. 262.

87   Peppiatt, *The War Diary*, p. 117.

88   Chapman, *A Passionate Prodigality*, p. 325.

89   F. Warren, *Honour Satisfied – A Dorset Rifleman at War 1916-18*, p. 65.

90   Papers of Captain C.C. May, Imperial War Museum, Department of Documents, diary entry dated 15 January 1916.

91   Papers of Major R.S. Cockburn, Imperial War Museum, Department of Documents, *Memoir*, pp. 98-100.

92   J. Hayward, *Myths & Legends of the First World War*, p. 151.

93   Corrigan, *Mud, Blood and Poppycock*, p. 59.

94   Dent papers, letter from E.C. Matthews dated 31 October 1915, Add MS 7973/M/30.

95   Greenwell, *Infant In Arms*, p. 81.

96   Nettleton, *The Anger of the Guns*, pp. 147, 191.

97   Peppiatt, *The War Diary*, p. 31.

98   Papers of 2nd Lt. F. Wollocombe, Imperial War Museum, Department of Documents, *In The Trenches With The 9th Devons*, p. 68.

99   Papers of Major C.H. Dudley-Ward, Imperial War Museum, Department of Documents, journal entry dated 1 December 1916.

100 G. Sheffield, *Leadership in the Trenches*, p. 54.

101 Paget papers, letter dated 13 September 1915.

102 F.C. Hitchcock, *"Stand To" – A Diary of the Trenches 1915-1918*, p. 43.

103 Gillespie, *Letters From Flanders*, p. 113.

104 A. Wilkinson (ed.), *Destiny: The War Letters of Captain Jack Oughtred M.C. 1915-1918*, p. 24.

105 Paget papers, letter dated 25 September 1915.

106 Sheffield & Inglis, *From Vimy Ridge to the Rhine*, p. 69.

107 Peppiatt, *The War Diary*, pp. 27-8.

108 Neville, *The War Letters of a Light Infantryman*, p. 41.

109 O. Lyttelton, The Papers of Alfred Lyttelton and Dame Edith Lyttelton, and their son Oliver Lyttelton (1st Viscount Chandos), letter dated 6 August 1916, CHAN 8/4.

110 Greenwell, *Infant in Arms*, p. 144.

111 Papers of J.R. Monsell, letter dated 30 July 1915.

112 May papers, diary entry dated 12 April 1916.

113 Jones & Jones, *War Letters of a Public-Schoolboy*, p. 153.

114 Dent papers, letter from E.C. Matthews dated 4 January 1916, Add MS 7973/M/37.

115 Nettleton, *The Anger of the Guns*, p. 37.

116 I. Sansom (ed.), *Letters from France – Written between June 1915 – July 1917*, p. 274.

117 Paget papers, letter dated 23 October 1915.

118 Platt papers, letter dated 29 March 1916.

119 Dent papers, letter from M.G. Davidson dated 7 Sept 1915, Add MS 7973/D/12.

120 Jolliffe, *Raymond Asquith*, p. 263.

121 May papers, diary entry dated 19 May 1916.

122 Greenwell, *Infant In Arms*, p. 150.

123 Neville, *War Letters of a Light Infantryman*, pp. 59-60.

124 Hewett, *A Scholar's Letters from the Front*, pp. 100-1.

125 Greenwell, *Infant In Arms*, p. 199.

126 Holmes, *Tommy*, p. 91.

127   Holmes, *Tommy*, pp. 374-6.

128   Anon. (D. Bell), *A Soldier's Diary of the Great War*, p. 174.

129   L. Macdonald, *1915 – The Death Of Innocence*, p. 474.

130   D. Richter, *Chemical Soldiers: British Gas Warfare in World War I*, p. 13.

131   Richter, *Chemical Soldiers*, p. 32.

132   Simpson, 'The Officers', p. 89.

133   These figures were compiled by the author from E.R Wilson & H.A. Jackson (eds.), *Winchester College: A Register 1901-1946*, pp. 46-203.

134   Greenwell, *Infant In Arms*, p. 89.

135   Platt papers, letter dated 15 April 1916.

136   Mackay papers, *The Personal Diary of Lieutenant Robert Lindsay Mackay*, p. 22.

137   Graves, *Goodbye To All That*, p. 202.

138   A.R. Godwin-Austen, *The Staff and the Staff College*, p. 264; B. Bond, *The Victorian Army and the Staff College 1854-1914*, pp. 303-4.

139   Young, *Try Anything Twice*, p. 98. 'British warm' is a reference to an overcoat.

140   D. Fraser (ed.), *In Good Company – The First World War Letters and Diaries of The Hon. William Fraser, Gordon Highlanders*, p. 67.

141   P. Glenconner, *Edward Wyndham Tennant, 4th Grenadier Guards – A Memoir*, p. 185.

142   Simpson, 'The Officers', pp. 85-6.

143   M. Stephen, *The Price of Pity: Poetry, History and Myth in the Great War*, p. 111.

144   Nettleton, *The Anger of the Guns*, p. 105.

145   M. Arthur, *Forgotten Voices of the Great War*, p. 200.

146   J.S.K. Watson, *Fighting Different Wars – Experience, Memory, and the First World War in Britain*, pp. 20-26.

147   Young, *Try Anything Twice*, pp. 97-8.

148   Young, *Try Anything Twice*, p. 80.

149   S. Foot, *Three Lives – An Autobiography*, p. 138.

150   Papers of Captain N.A. Taylor, Imperial War Museum, Department of Documents, letter dated 5 March 1916.

151   Taylor papers, letter dated 12 March 1916.

152   Gibbs papers, letter dated 21 December 1916.

153   Wilkinson, *Destiny*, p. 185.

154   A. Waugh, *Public School Life – Boys, Parents, Masters*, p. 212.

155   Nettleton, *The Anger of the Guns*, p. 113.

156   Nettleton, *The Anger of the Guns*, p. 113.

157   Lyttelton papers, letter dated 26 January 1917, CHAN 8/5.

158   Carlisle, *My Own Darling*, p. 189.

159   Watson, *Fighting Different Wars*, p. 23.

160   Paget papers, letter dated 9 September 1915.

161   Carlisle, *My Own Darling*, p. 168.

162   Taylor papers, letter dated 18 March 1916.

163   Taylor papers, letter dated 12 March 1916.

164   Gibbs papers, letter dated 21 December 1916.

165   R. Holmes, *Firing Line*, p. 323; M. Middlebrook, *The Kaiser's Battle – 21 March 1918: The First Day of the German Spring Offensive*, pp. 335-6.

Chapter 4

1   E.C. Vaughan, *Some Desperate Glory – The diary of a young officer, 1917*, p. 23.

2   Vaughan, *Some Desperate Glory*, pp. 30-1.

3   Vaughan, *Some Desperate Glory*, p. 32.

4   B.A. Medley, *April 1915 to September 1915*, p. 28.

5   L.D. Spicer, *Letters From France 1915-1918*, pp. 10-11.

6   S. Hewett, *A Scholar's Letters from the Front*, p. 39.

7   W. Moore, *The Thin Yellow Line*, p. 104.

8   A. Simpson, *Hot Blood And Cold Steel: Life And Death In The Trenches of the First World War*, p. 78.

9   B. Shephard, *A War of Nerves – Soldiers and Psychiatrists 1914-1994*, p. 33.

10   C. Moran, *The Anatomy of Courage*, p. 69.

11   L. Talbot (ed.), *Gilbert Walter Lyttelton Talbot*, p. 63.

12   M. Roper, *The Secret Battle – Emotional Survival in the Great War*, pp. 262-3.

13   Anon. (A.J. Dawson), *A Temporary Gentleman in France – Home Letters from an Officer in the New Army*, p. 86.

14   A. Wolff, *Subalterns of the Foot – Three World War I Diaries of Officers of the Cheshire Regiment*, pp. 10-11.

15   Shephard, *A War of Nerves*, pp. 33-4.

16   G.H. Greenwell, *Infant In Arms*, p. 116.

17   J. Nettleton, *The Anger of the Guns: An Infantry Officer on the Western Front*, p. 163.

18   D. Young, *Try Anything Twice*, P. 95

19   A. Gregory, *The Last Great War – British Society and the First World War*, p. 3.

20   Papers of Miss H. Gosling, Imperial War Museum, Department of Documents, letter from Lt. L. Hill to Gosling dated 8 February 1916.

21   R. Bickersteth, *Bickersteth War Diaries 1914-1919 Volume 2: 3/2/1915 – 2/2/1916*, The Bickersteth War Diaries and the Papers of John Burgon Bickersteth, BICK 1/2, p. 526.

22   Medley, *April 1915 to September 1915*, p. 38.

23   Medley, *April 1915 to September 1915*, p. 80.

24   B. Congreve, *Armageddon Road – A VC's Diary, 1914-1916*, p. 161.

25   A.D. Gillespie, *Letters From Flanders*, p. 197.

26   Papers of 2nd Lt. A.C. Clapham, Imperial War Museum, Department of Documents, diary entry dated 24 August 1915.

27   D.C. Richter (ed.), *Lionel Sotheby's Great War – Diaries and Letters from the Western Front*, p. 77.

28   J. Ellis, *Eye-Deep In Hell – The Western Front 1914-18*, p. 65; D. Richter, *Chemical Soldiers: British Gas Warfare in World War I*.

29   Shephard, *A War of Nerves*, p. 63; A. Wilkinson (ed.), *Destiny – The War Letters of Captain Jack Oughtred MC 1915-1918*, p. 58.

30   R. Holmes, *Firing Line*, p. 212.

31   G. Corrigan, *Mud, Blood and Poppycock – Britain and the First World War*, p. 173; J.M. Winter, *The Experience of World War I*, p. 122.

32   Papers of Captain C.C. May, Imperial War Museum, Department of Documents, diary entry dated 23 November 1915.

33   G.D. Sheffield & G. Inglis (eds.), *From Vimy Ridge to the Rhine: The Great War letters of Christopher Stone DSO MC*, p. 94.

34   J. Jolliffe, *Raymond Asquith – Life and Letters*, p. 269.

35   Shephard, *A War of Nerves*, pp. 63-4.

36   J. Bourke, *Dismembering the Male – Men's Bodies, Britain and the Great War*, p. 152; Holmes, *Firing Line*, p. 182.

37   Papers of Major-General D.N. Wimberley, Imperial War Museum, Department of Documents, *The Memoirs of Major-General Douglas Neil Wimberley*, Volume 1, p. 13.

38   M. Ponsonby, *Visions and Vignettes of War*, pp. 31-2.

39   R. Devonald-Lewis (ed.), *From the Somme To The Armistice – The Memoirs of Captain Stormont Gibbs, MC*, p. 62.

40   Holmes, *Firing Line*, pp. 181-2.

41   Hewett, *A Scholar's Letters from the Front*, p. 58.

42   M. Brown, *Tommy Goes To War*, pp. 86-9; Bourke, *Dismembering the Male*, pp. 83-4.

43   Anon., *A Glossary of Trench Terms*, in the Papers of Captain W.M.L. Escombe, Imperial War Museum, Department of Documents.

44   Medley, *April 1915 to September 1915*, pp. 18-19.

45   Gillespie, *Letters From Flanders*, p. 61.

46   Wilkinson, *Destiny*, p. 71.

47   Greenwell, *Infant In Arms*, p. 194.

48   M. Eksteins, *Rites of Spring – The Great War and the Birth of the Modern Age*, p. 174.

49   'Amateur Officer', *After Victory*, p. 68.

50   'Amateur Officer', *After Victory*, p. 30.

51   Hewett, *A Scholar's Letters from the Front*, p. 84.

52   A. Powell (ed.) *A Deep Cry: A Literary Pilgrimage to the Battlefields and Cemeteries of First World War British Soldier-Poets Killed in Northern France and Flanders*, p. 336.

53   D. Winter, *Death's Men: Soldier's of the Great War*, p. 131.

54   D. Cannadine, 'War and Death, Grief and Mourning in Modern Britain', in J. Whaley (ed.), *Mirrors of Mortality: Studies in the Social History of Death*, p. 193.

55   Young, *Try Anything Twice*, p. 59.

56   Medley, *April 1915 to September 1915*, pp. 110-11.

57   J.E.H. Neville, *The War Letters of a Light Infantryman*, p. 8.

58   T. Quinn, *Tales of the Old Soldiers. Ten Veterans of the First World War Remember Life and Death in the Trenches*, p. 24.

59   Vaughan, *Some Desperate Glory*, p. 32.

60   B.L. Lawrence, undated draft of 'Sense or Sentiment – A Review of the Moment', in the Papers of C.K. Ogden, Imperial War Museum, Department of Documents. Richard Holmes cites a similar incident in which a young officer used a pile of dead Frenchmen as a source of comfort. Holmes, *Firing Line*, p. 180.

61   Wilkinson, *Destiny*, p. 29.

62   Hewett, *A Scholar's Letters from the Front*, p. 47.

63   Neville, *War Letters of a Light Infantryman*, pp. 103-4.

64   Wimberley papers, *The Memoirs of Major-General Douglas Neil Wimberley*, Vol. 1, p. 72.

65   A.M. Adam, *Arthur Innes Adam 1894-1916, A Record Founded on his Letters*, pp. 153, 159, 214, 164.

66   Richter, *Lionel Sotheby's Great War*, p. 93.

67   R.E. Harris, *Billie – The Nevill Letters 1914-1916*, p. 108.

68   Powell, *A Deep Cry*, p. 17.

69   J. Bourke, *An Intimate History of Killing – Face-to-face Killing in Twentieth-Century Warfare*, pp. 147-8.

70   P. Glenconner, *Edward Wyndham Tennant, 4th Grenadier Guards – A Memoir*, p. 132.

71 Glenconner, *Edward Wyndham Tennant*, pp. 133-4, 167.

72 J.S.K. Watson, *Fighting Different Wars – Experience, Memory, and the First World War in Britain*, pp. 25-6.

73 E. Townshend (ed.), *Keeling Letters and Recollections*, p. 202.

74 P.H. Liddle, *The Soldier's War*, p. 208.

75 Gregory, *The Last Great War*, p. 68.

76 Gillespie, *Letters from Flanders*, p. 138.

77 Sheffield & Inglis, *From Vimy Ridge to the Rhine*, p. 92; J. Haywood, *Myths and Legends of the First World War*, pp. 112-126.

78 'O.E.' (G. Fildes), *Iron Times with the Guards*, p. 66.

79 Richter, *Lionel Sotheby's Great War*, p.38.

80 Richter, *Lionel Sotheby's Great War*, pp. 102-3.

81 Wilkinson, *Destiny*, p. 132.

82 Gillespie, *Letters From Flanders*, pp. 36-8.

83 Gillespie, *Letters From Flanders*, p. 224.

84 Gillespie, *Letters From Flanders*, p. 254.

85 Holmes, *Firing Line*, p. 380.

86 E.S. Woods (ed.), *Andrew R. Buxton, The Rifle Brigade, A Memoir*, pp. 137-8.

87 E. Sanger, *Letters From Two World Wars – A Social History of English Attitudes To War 1914-45*, pp. 65-6.

88 A.A. Hanbury-Sparrow, *The Land-Locked Lake*, pp. 91-2.

89 E. Leed, *No Man's Land – Combat & Identity in World War I*, p. 107; J.M. Winter & B. Baggett, *1914-18: the Great War and the Shaping of the 20th Century*, p. 216.

90 May papers, diary entry dated 1 December 1915.

91 May papers, diary entry dated 25 February 1916.

92 A. Bonadeo, *Mark of the Beast – Death and Degradation in the Literature of the Great War*, p. 2.

93 Wilkinson, *Destiny*, p. 132.

94 Bourke, *An Intimate History of Killing*, p. 226.

95 Papers of E.J. Dent, letter from M.G. Davidson dated 19 August 1915, Add MS 7973/D/11.

96 Bourke, *An Intimate History of Killing*, p. 226.

97 T. Ashworth, *Trench Warfare 1914-1918: The Live and Let Live System*.

98 J. Keegan, *The Face of Battle*, p. 274.

99 J. Bourke, 'The experience of killing', in J.M. Bourne, P. Liddle & I. Whitehead (eds.), *The Great World War 1914-1945. Vol. 1 – Lightning Strikes Twice*, pp. 298-9; G.D. Sheffield, *Leadership in the trenches – Officer-Man Relations, Morale and Discipline in the British Army in the Era of the First World War*, p. 47. Such language was not a creation of the First World War. Michael Adams highlights examples from the American Civil War and Boer War. M.C.C. Adams, *The Great Adventure – Male Desire and the Coming of World War I*, pp. 43-4.

100 Neville, *War Letters of a Light Infantryman*, pp. 55-6.

101 Anon. (D. Bell), *A Soldier's Diary of the Great War*, p. 151.

102 Papers of Captain S.J. Paget, War Scrapbook, p. 4.

103 C. Dakers, *The Countryside at War 1914-1918*, pp. 161-2.

104 Papers of J.R. Monsell, letter dated Summer 1915.

105 Dakers, *The Countryside at War*, pp. 161-3.

106 Adams, The Great Adventure, pp. 43-4; P. Howarth, *Play Up And Play The Game: The Heroes Of Popular Fiction*, pp. 44-5.

107   Sheffield, *Leadership in the Trenches*, p. 47; W.J. Reader, *At Duty's Call – A Study In Obsolete Patriotism*, pp. 33-4.

108   Papers of Captain A. Gibbs, Imperial War Museum, Department of Documents, letter dated 11 March 1916.

109   T.W. Pym & G. Gordon, *Papers from Picardy*, pp. 24-5.

110   Bourke, *An Intimate History of Killing*, pp. 235-8.

Chapter 5

1   G. Chapman, *A Passionate Prodigality – Fragments of Autobiography*, pp. 240-1.

2   A.M. Adam, *Arthur Innes Adam 1894-1916 A Record Founded on his Letters*, p. 164.

3   J.E.H. Neville, *War Letters of a Light Infantryman*, p. 77.

4   B.A. Medley, *April 1915 to September 1915*.

5   Neville, *War Letters of a Light Infantryman*, p. 44.

6   D. Winter, *Death's Men – Soldier's of the Great War*, p. 138.

7   A. Wilkinson (ed.), *Destiny: The War Letters of Captain Jack Oughtred MC 1915-1918*, p. 32.

8   M. Arthur, *Forgotten Voices of the Great War*, p. 184.

9   Chapman, *A Passionate Prodigality*, pp. 240-1.

10   J. Nettleton, *The Anger of the Guns: An Infantry Officer on the Western Front*, p. 194.

11   Papers of Captain N.A. Taylor, Imperial War Museum, Department of Documents, letter dated 12 March 1916.

12   Medley, *April 1915 to September 1915*, p. 46.

13   S. Hewett, *A Scholar's Letters from the Front*, p. 92.

14   Hewett, *A Scholar's Letters from the Front*, p. 93.

15   G. Corrigan, *Mud, Blood and Poppycock: Britain and the First World War*, p. 108.

16   P. Glenconner, *Edward Wyndham Tennant, 4th Grenadier Guards – A Memoir*, pp. 138-9.

17   H.E.L. Mellersh, *Schoolboy into War*, p. 23.

18   L.W. Crouch, *Duty And Service – Letters From The Front*, p. 44.

19   A. Wolff, *Subalterns of the Foot – Three World War I Diaries of Officers of the Cheshire Regiment*, p. 79.

20   Papers of E.J. Dent, letter from A.H. Parry dated 2 June 1916, Add MS 7973/P/12.

21   G.H. Greenwell, *Infant In Arms*, p. 131.

22   Greenwell, *Infant In Arms*, p. 219.

23   J. Merton, *Love Letters under Fire*, p. 265.

24   Arthur, *Forgotten Voices of the Great War*, p. 148.

25   A.O. Pollard, *Fire-Eater – The Memoirs of a V.C.*, p. 127.

26   Papers of Captain S.J. Paget, letter dated 8 March 1914.

27   Paget to Mother, 11 January 1916, Captain S.J. Paget papers.

28   L. Macdonald, *1915 – The Death Of Innocence*, p. 30; G.D. Sheffield, *Leadership in the trenches – Officer-Man Relations, Morale and Discipline in the British Army in the Era of the First World War*, p. 137; C. Moran, *The Anatomy of Courage*, p. 152; E. Sanger, *Letters From Two World Wars – A Social History of English Attitudes To War 1914-45*, p. 30.

29   A. Simpson, *Hot Blood And Cold Steel: Life And Death In The Trenches of the First World War*, p. 35.

30   Papers of Captain W.E. Villiers, Imperial War Museum, Department of Documents, letter dated 3 January 1917.

31   J. Ivelaw-Chapman, *The Riddles of Wipers – An Appreciation of* The Wipers Times, *A Journal of the Trenches*, p. 65.

32   Greenwell, *Infant In Arms*, p. 69.

33 Papers of 2nd Lt. R.P. Hamilton, Imperial War Museum, Department of Documents, diary entry dated 27 August 1915.

34 Neville, *War Letters of a Light Infantryman*, p. 27.

35 Vaughan, *Some Desperate Glory*, pp. 147-8.

36 Vaughan, *Some Desperate Glory*, p. 161.

37 Papers of Captain C.C. May, Imperial War Museum, Department of Documents, diary entry dated 24 March 1916.

38 R. Holmes, *Tommy – The British Soldier on the Western Front 1914-1918*, p. 300; J. Bourke, *An Intimate History of Killing – Face-to-face Killing in Twentieth-Century Warfare*, p. 37.

39 C. Clark, *The Tin Trunk: Letters and Drawings 1914-1918*, pp. 51-2.

40 E. Crawshay-Williams, *Leaves From An Officer's Notebook*, p. 22.

41 Papers of Captain A.B. Pick, Imperial War Museum, Department of Documents, letter dated 12 October 1916.

42 P. Brendon, *Eminent Edwardians*, p. 211.

43 H. Williamson, *A Fox Under My Cloak*, pp. 168-9.

44 A. Williamson, *A Patriot's Progress – Henry Williamson and the First World War*, p. 54.

45 H.B. McCartney, *Citizen Soldiers – The Liverpool Territorials in the First World War*, pp. 89-90; D. Englander, 'Soldiering and Identity: Reflections on the Great War', *War In History*, Volume 1, No. 3 (November 1994), pp. 317-8.

46 J. Meyer, *Men of War: Masculinity and the First World War in Britain*, p. 45.

47 May papers, diary entry dated 7 December 1915.

48 M. Roper, *The Secret Battle – Emotional Survival in the Great War*, p. 93.

49 Papers of Lt J.A. Talbot, Imperial War Museum, Department of Documents, letter dated 9 April 1917.

50 Wilkinson, *Destiny*, p. 202.

51 Paget papers, letter dated 14 August 1915.

52 Papers of Captain J.E. Crombie, Volume 2: War 1914-1917, p. 26.

53 Papers of 2nd Lt D. Neilson-Terry, Imperial War Museum, Department of Documents, *Letters from the Great War 1914-1918*, p. 15.

54 Nettleton, *The Anger of the Guns*, p. 101.

55 Paget may be referring either to scrambled eggs or pancakes.

56 Paget papers, letter dated 10 November 1915.

57 Dent papers, letter from E.C. Matthews dated 2 December 1915, Add MS 7973/M/33.

58 P.H. Liddle, *The Soldier's War*, pp. 83-4; Winter, *Death's Men*, pp. 167-9.

59 Papers of Lt. G.N. Holt, Imperial War Museum, Department of Documents, letter dated 24 December 1916.

60 Papers of 2nd Lt K.C. Macardle, Imperial War Museum, Department of Documents, diary entry dated 6 June 1916.

61 G.D. Sheffield & G.I.S. Inglis (eds.), *From Vimy Ridge to the Rhine The Great War Letters of Christopher Stone DSO MC*, p. 97.

62 Roper, *The Secret Battle*, p. 91.

63 K. Simpson, 'The Officers', in I.F.W. Beckett & K. Simpson (eds.), *A Nation in Arms – A Social study of the British army in the First World War*, p. 77

64 Nettleton, *The Anger of the Guns*, p. 15.

65 S. Cloete, *A Victorian Son – An Autobiography*, p. 192.

66 P. Simkins, *Kitchener's Army – The Raising of the New Armies, 1914-16*, p. 198.

67   J. Bourke, *Dismembering the Male – Men's Bodies, Britain and the Great War*, p. 151.

68   B. Willey, 'A Schoolboy in the War', in G.A. Panichas (ed.), *Promise of Greatness – The War of 1914-1918*, pp. 324-5.

69   Willey, 'A Schoolboy in the War', pp. 325-6.

70   Papers of Major-General D.N. Wimberley, Imperial War Museum, Department of Documents, *The Memoirs of Major-General Douglas Neil Wimberley*, Volume 1, p. 13.

71   W.R. Hicks, *The School in English and German Fiction*, p. 61.

72   H. Sackville Lawson, *Letter of a Headmaster Soldier*, p. 80.

73   N. Ferguson, *The Pity Of War*, p. 446; R. Holmes, *Firing Line*, pp. 248-9; E.M. Spiers, *The Army and Society 1815-1914*, p. 22.

74   M. Stephen, *The Price of Pity: Poetry, History and Myth in the Great War*, p. 101.

75   Wimberley papers, *The Memoirs of Major-General Douglas Neil Wimberley*, Vol. 1, p. 16.

76   D. Young, *Try Anything Twice*, pp. 5-6, 26.

77   Holmes, *Firing Line*, pp. 248-50.

78   B.W. Long, *First World War Letters*, p. 14.

79   F.C. Hitchcock, *"Stand To" – A Diary of the Trenches 1915-1918*, p. 116.

80   Sheffield & Inglis, *From Vimy Ridge to the Rhine*, pp. 105-6.

81   A.A. Hanbury-Sparrow, *The Land-Locked Lake*, p. 284.

82   A.D. Gillespie, *Letters From Flanders*, p. 38.

83   War Office, *Statistics of the military effort of the British Empire during the Great War 1914-20*, pp. 643, 669-70.

84   R. Graves, *Goodbye to All That*, p. 144.

85   J.R. de S. Honey, *Tom Brown's Universe: The Development of the Victorian Public School*, p. 177.

86   R. Holt, *Sport and the British – A Modern History*, p. 89.

87   M. Browne, *A Dream Of Youth – An Etonian's Reply to "The Loom of Youth"*, p. 64.

88   Wimberley papers, *The Memoirs of Major-General Douglas Neil Wimberley*, Vol. 1, p. 13.

89   Cloete, *A Victorian Son*, p. 163.

90   Young, *Try Anything Twice*, p. 26.

91   P. Parker, *The Old Lie – The Great War and the Public School Ethos*, p. 185.

92   Bourke, *Dismembering the Male*, p. 159.

93   Wimberley papers, *The Memoirs of Major-General Douglas Neil Wimberley*, Vol. 1, p. 16.

94   Mellersh, *Schoolboy into War*, p. 82.

95   Holmes, *Tommy*, p. 597.

96   P.J. Campbell, *In The Cannon's Mouth*, pp. 29-30.

97   Bourke, *Dismembering the Male*, pp. 158-9. See also Holmes, *Tommy*, p. 596.

98   Mellersh, *Schoolboy into War*, p. 123.

99   Arthur, *Forgotten Voices of the Great War*, p. 259.

100   Cloete, *A Victorian Son*, p. 245.

101   Bourke, *Dismembering the Male*, p. 157.

102   Graves, *Goodbye to All That*, p. 104.

103   C.S. Peel, *How We Lived Then 1914-1918 – A Sketch of Social And Domestic Life In England During The War*, pp. 66-7.

104   Corrigan, *Mud, Blood and Poppycock*, p. 95.

105   L.D. Spicer, *Letters from France 1915-1918*, p. 54.

106   Stephen, *The Price of Pity*, p. 18.

107   P. Fussell, *The Great War and Modern Memory*, p. 272.

108 The identity of this officer has been withheld in accordance with the wishes of the copyright holder.

109 J. Jolliffe, *Raymond Asquith – Life and Letters*, pp. 289-91.

110 Ferguson, *The Pity of War*, p. 349. Richard Holmes cites a figure of 8 officers and 153 soldiers court-martialled for 'indecency' on active service during the war. Holmes, *Tommy*, p. 598.

Chapter 6

1 T. Ashworth, *Trench Warfare 1914-1918: The Live and Let Live System*, p. 156.

2 J. Nettleton, *The Anger of the Guns: An Infantry Officer on the Western Front*, p. 84.

3 Nettleton, *The Anger of the Guns*, p. 84.

4 C. McCarthy, 'Queen of the Battlefield: The Development of Command Organisation and Tactics in the British Infantry Battalion during the Great War', in G.D. Sheffield & D. Todman (eds.), *Command and Control on the Western Front – The British Army's Experience 1914-1918*, p. 191.

5 I.F.W. Beckett, 'The British Army, 1914-18: The Illusion of Change', in J. Turner (ed.), *Britain and the First World War*, p. 109.

6 Papers of Major T.D. Pratt, Imperial War Museum, Department of Documents, typescript memoir, p. 2.

7 Papers of Major C.H. Dudley-Ward, Imperial War Museum, Department of Documents, journal entry dated 28 November 1916.

8 B.W. Long, *First World War Letters*, pp. 49-51.

9 R. Graves, *Goodbye to All That*, p. 116.

10 R. Holmes, *Tommy – The British Soldier on the Western Front 1914-1918*, p. 577.

11 Papers of Captain C.C. May, Imperial War Museum, Department of Documents, diary entry dated 18 December 1915.

12 C. Clark, *The Tin Trunk: Letters and Drawings 1914-1918*, p. 77.

13 Clark, *The Tin Trunk*, pp. 48-9.

14 L.D. Spicer, *Letters From France 1915-1918*, pp. 36, 45-6, 47-8.

15 A.A. Hanbury-Sparrow, *The Land-Locked Lake*, pp. 103-4.

16 Papers of J.T. Bramston, letter from S.J. Paget dated 31 October [1914], E3/5/82/2.

17 E.C. Vaughan, *Some Desperate Glory – The diary of a young officer, 1917*, p. 10.

18 Vaughan, *Some Desperate Glory* , p. 18.

19 Vaughan, *Some Desperate Glory*, p. 10.

20 Papers of 2nd Lt F Wollocombe, Imperial War Museum, Department of Documents, *In The Trenches With The 9th Devons*, p. 59.

21 Wollocombe papers, *In The Trenches With The 9th Devons*, p. 74.

22 Papers of Lt. W.B.P. Spencer, Imperial War Museum, Department of Documents, letter dated 15 February 1915.

23 Vaughan, *Some Deperate Glory*, p. 101.

24 D. Young, *Try Anything Twice*, p. 80.

25 G. Chapman, *A Passionate Prodigality – Fragments of Autobiography*, p. 256.

26 B. Shephard, *A War of Nerves – Soldiers and Psychiatrists 1914-1994*, p. 37.

27 Graves, *Goodbye to All That*, pp. 214-6.

28 B. Liddell Hart, 'Forced to Think', in G.A. Panichas (ed.), *Promise of Greatness – The War of 1914-1918*, p. 100.

29 J.R. de S. Honey, *Tom Brown's Universe: The Development of the Victorian Public School*, pp. 217-8.

30 Graves, *Goodbye to All That*, p. 109.

31 A.D. Gillespie, *Letters From Flanders*, p. 296.

32   Papers of Captain A.B. Pick, Imperial War Museum, Department of Documents, letter dated 25 July 1917.

33   Papers of Captain A. Gibbs, Imperial War Museum, Department of Documents, letter dated 20 April 1917.

34   Gibbs papers, letter dated 3 July 1917.

35   Holmes, *Tommy*, p. 201.

36   A. Wilkinson (ed.), *Destiny: The War Letters of Captain Jack Oughtred MC 1915-1918*, p. 112.

37   Graves, *Goodbye to All That*, p. 172.

38   Anon. (D. Bell), *A Soldier's Diary of the Great War*, p. 148.

39   May papers, diary entry dated 11 May 1916.

40   G. Dugdale, *"Langemarck" And "Cambrai" – A War Narrative 1914-1918*, p. 26.

41   Papers of J.R. Monsell, letter dated 6 April 1917.

42   Pick papers, letter dated 8 July 1918.

43   Gibbs papers, letter dated 15 August 1918.

44   Gibbs papers, letter dated 16 August 1918.

45   W.H. Matthews, *Diary Letters of Lieutenant Colonel W.H. Matthews D.S.O., April 6th 1917 – 28th June 1917, commanding 1/20th London*, in the Papers of Captain W.M.L. Escombe, Imperial War Museum, Department of Documents.

46   Holmes, *Tommy*, pp. 202-3.

47   Wilkinson, *Destiny*, pp. 116, 120.

48   Wilkinson, *Destiny*, p. 126.

49   Wilkinson, *Destiny*, p. 138.

50   Wilkinson, *Destiny*, p. 142.

51   Wilkinson, *Destiny*, p. 146.

52   'I. Hay' (J.H. Beith), *The First Hundred Thousand – Being the Unofficial Chronicle of a Unit of "K(I)"*, p. 297; P. Buitenhuis, *The Great War of Words: Literature as Propaganda 1914-18 and After*, p. 113.

53   Wilkinson, *Destiny*, p. 213.

54   The National Archives, *Report of Winston Churchill's Committee on Promotion; reports of meetings, Letters of enquiry concerning claims*, pp. 4-6.

55   GHQ British Army in France, *Instructions Regarding Promotion of Officers*, pp. 5-8.

56   E.S. Woods (ed.), *Andrew R. Buxton, The Rifle Brigade, A Memoir*, p. 2.

57   G.D. Sheffield & G.I.S. Inglis (eds.), *From Vimy Ridge to the Rhine: The Great War Letters of Christopher Stone DSO MC*, p. 49.

58   Papers of Major-General D.N. Wimberley, Imperial War Museum, Department of Documents, *The Memoirs of Major-General Douglas Neil Wimberley*, Volume 1, pp. 16-7.

59   Wimberley papers, *The Memoirs of Major-General Douglas Neil Wimberley*, Vol. 1, pp. 16-17.

60   Papers of Captain W.E. Villiers, Imperial War Museum, Department of Documents, letter dated 11 October 1916.

61   G.H. Greenwell, *Infant In Arms*, p. 175.

62   Dudley-Ward papers, journal entry dated 3 November 1915.

63   Dudley-Ward papers, journal entry dated 2 March 1916.

64   S. Foot, *Three Lives – An Autobiography*, pp. 136-8, 172-4, 148-9.

65   Survey of the Papers of Senior UK Defence Personnel, 1900-1975, Liddell Hart Centre for Military Archives, King's College London, webpages http://www.kcl.ac.uk/lhcma/locreg/FURSE1.shtml and http://www.kcl.ac.uk/lhcma/locreg/ALDERSON.shtml accessed 19 April 2011.

66   Young, *Try Anything Twice*, p. 52.

67   Young, *Try Anything Twice*, pp. 61-2.

68   May papers, diary entry dated 13 December 1915.

69   I.M. Brown, *British Logistics on the Western Front 1914-1919*, pp. 139-40; D. Todman, 'The General Lamasery revisited: General Headquarters on the Western Front, 1914-1918', in Sheffield & Todman, *Command and Control on the Western Front*, p. 54.

70   Dudley-Ward papers, journal entry dated 7 February 1917.

71   K. Simpson, 'The Officers', in I.F.W. Beckett & K. Simpson (eds.), *A Nation in Arms – A Social study of the British army in the First World War*, p. 75; J.S.K. Watson, *Fighting Different Wars – Experience, Memory, and the First World War in Britain*, p. 24.

72   Holmes, *Tommy*, p. 87. See also Simpson, 'The Officers', pp. 80-1; J.M. Bourne, *Britain and the Great War 1914-1918*, p. 216; K. Simpson, 'The British Soldier on the Western Front', in P.H. Liddle (ed.), *Home Fires and Foreign Fields: British Social and Military Experience in the First World War*, p. 144.

73   G.D. Sheffield, *Leadership in the trenches – Officer-Man Relations, Morale and Discipline in the British Army in the Era of the First World War*, p. 162.

74   Wimberley papers, *The Memoirs of Major-General Douglas Neil Wimberley*, Vol. 1, p. 17.

75   P. Glenconner, *Edward Wyndham Tennant, 4th Grenadier Guards – A Memoir*, p. 234.

76   O.S. Buckmaster, *Roundabout – The Autobiography of Viscount Buckmaster*, p. 43.

77   'O.E.' (G. Fildes), *Iron Times with the Guards*, p. 272.

78   Simpson, 'The Officers', p. 75.

79   Nettleton, *The Anger of the Guns*, p. 54.

80   J. Jolliffe, *Raymond Asquith – Life and Letters*, p. 227.

81   Jolliffe, *Raymond Asquith*, p. 231.

82   Jolliffe, *Raymond Asquith*, p. 282.

83   Papers of Captain N.A. Taylor, Imperial War Museum, Department of Documents, letter dated 11 October 1915.

84   R. Bickersteth, *Bickersteth War Diaries 1914-1919 Volume 2: 3/2/1915 – 2/2/1916*, The Bickersteth War Diaries and the Papers of John Burgon Bickersteth, BICK 1/2, p. 515.

85   L. Talbot (ed.), *Gilbert Walter Lyttelton Talbot*, p. 51.

Chapter 7

1   G.D. Sheffield, *Forgotten Victory – The First World War: Myths and Realities*, p. 118.

2   M. Middlebrook, *The First Day on the Somme: 1 July 1916*, pp. 143-4.

3   Middlebrook, *The First Day on the Somme*, p. 36.

4   G. Dugdale, *"Langemarck" And "Cambrai" – A War Narrative 1914-1918*, p. 26.

5   A.O. Pollard, *Fire-Eater – The Memoirs of a VC*, pp. 164-5.

6   D. Young, *Try Anything Twice*, p. 50.

7   Young, *Try Anything Twice*, pp. 110-1.

8   B. Congreve, *Armageddon Road – A VC's Diary, 1914-16*, p. 141.

9   Papers of 2nd Lt. R.P. Hamilton, Imperial War Museum, Department of Documents, diary entry dated 18 August 1915.

10   A.D. Gillespie, *Letters From Flanders*, p. 90.

11   P. Buitenhuis, *The Great War of Words: Literature as Propaganda 1914-18 and After*, p. 113.

12   'I. Hay' (J.H. Beith), *The First Hundred Thousand – Being the Unofficial Chronicle of a Unit of "K(I)"*, p. 191.

13   L. Peppiatt, *The War Diary – January to September 1918 – of Major Leslie Peppiatt MC*, p. 51.

14   E.S. Woods (ed.), *Andrew R. Buxton, The Rifle Brigade, A Memoir*, pp. 233-4.

15   'Hay', *The First Hundred Thousand*, p. 192.

16   Peppiatt, *The War Diary*, pp. 134-5.

17   'Hay', *The First Hundred Thousand*, pp. 192-3.

18   A. Behrend, *As From Kemmel Hill – An Adjutant in France and Flanders 1917 & 1918*, p. 12.

19   Behrend, *As From Kemmel Hill, p. 12.*

20   Gillespie, *Letters From Flanders*, p. 183.

21   G.H. Greenwell, *Infant In Arms*, p. 220.

22   A.A. Hanbury-Sparrow, *The Land-Locked Lake*, pp. 285-6.

23   Young, *Try Anything Twice*, p. 115.

24   G. Chapman, *A Passionate Prodigality – Fragments of Autobiography*, p. 168.

25   Anon. (D. Bell), *A Soldier's Diary of the Great War*, pp. 136-7.

26   Chapman, *A Passionate Prodigality*, p. 168.

27   R. Holmes, *Tommy – The British Soldier on the Western Front 1914-1918*, p. 240.

28   G. Corrigan, *Mud, Blood and Poppycock – Britain and the First World War*, p. 210.

29   Papers of Captain C.C. May, Imperial War Museum, Department of Documents, diary entry dated 13 June 1916.

30   Chapman, *A Passionate Prodigality*, p. 153.

31   P. Simkins, "Building Blocks': Aspects of Command and Control at Brigade level in the BEF's Offensive Operations, 1916-1918', in G.D. Sheffield & D. Todman (eds.), *Command and Control on the Western Front – The British Army's Experience 1914-18*, p. 147.

32   B. Bond & S. Robbins (eds.), *Staff Officer – The Diaries of Walter Guinness (First Lord Moyne) 1914-1918*, p. 13.

33   Bond & Robbins, *Staff Officer*, p. 13.

34   Simkins, 'Building Blocks', pp. 146, 155.

35   May papers, diary entry dated 24 February 1916.

36   Papers of Captain A. Gibbs, Imperial War Museum, Department of Documents, letter dated 22 May 1916.

37   Papers of Major C.H. Dudley-Ward, Imperial War Museum, Department of Documents, journal entry dated 22 July 1916.

38   May papers, diary entry dated 26 March 1916.

39   Holmes, *Tommy*, p. 242.

40   J.E.H. Neville, *The War Letters of a Light Infantryman*, p. 83.

41   C. Douie, *The Weary Road – Recollections of a Subaltern of Infantry*, pp. 110-11.

42   Gibbs papers, letter dated 1 August 1916.

43   Papers of 2nd Lt. A. Milligan, Imperial War Museum, Department of Documents, undated letter, envelope bearing date stamp 8 March 1917.

44   Papers of Lt. R. Swayne, Imperial War Museum, Department of Documents, letter dated 7 February 1917.

45   Hamilton papers, diary entry dated 11 May 1915.

46   Gibbs papers, letter dated 30 April 1918.

47   G. Nobbs, *Englishman, Kamerad! Right of the British Line*, pp. 26-7.

48   Milligan papers, undated letter, envelope bearing date stamp 8 March 1917.

49   H.W. Blackburne, *This Also Happened On The Western Front*, pp.103-4.

50   G.D. Sheffield, *Leadership in the Trenches – Officer-Man Relations, Morale and Discipline in the British Army in the Era of the First World War*, p. 96.

51   Papers of Lt. C.L. Platt, Imperial War Museum, Department of Documents, letter dated 9 January 1916.

52   M. Ponsonby, *Visions and Vignettes of War*, pp. 1-2.

53   Hanbury-Sparrow, *The Land-Locked Lake*, p. 204.

54   Gillespie, *Letters From Flanders*, p. 151.

55   Dudley-Ward papers, journal entry dated 6 August 1916.

56   J. Nettleton, *The Anger of the Guns: An Infantry Officer on the Western Front*, p. 161.

57   G.D. Sheffield, & G.I.S. Inglis (eds.), *From Vimy Ridge to the Rhine – The Great War Letters of Christopher Stone DSO MC*, p. 91.

58   G. Dallas & D. Gill, *The Unknown Army*, p. 33; K. Simpson, 'The Officers', in I.F.W. Beckett & K. Simpson (eds.), *A Nation in Arms – A Social study of the British army in the First World War*, pp. 70-1, 76-7.

59   Sheffield, *Forgotten Victory*, p. 122.

60   A. Simpson, *Hot Blood And Cold Steel: Life And Death In The Trenches of the First World War*, p. 119; Sheffield, *Forgotten Victory*, p. 122.

61   P.W. Turner & R.H. Haigh, *Not For Glory*, p. 80.

62   V.W. Germains, *The Kitchener Armies – The Stories of a National Achievement*, p. 202.

63   Papers of Captain A.B. Pick, Imperial War Museum, Department of Documents, letter dated 27 July 1917.

64   Papers of Lt. G.N. Holt, Imperial War Museum, Department of Documents, letter dated 11 January 1918.

65   Neville, *The War Letters of a Light Infantryman*, p. 6.

66   R. Devonald-Lewis (ed.), *From the Somme To The Armistice – The Memoirs of Captain Stormont Gibbs, MC*, p. 68.

67   J. Bourne, 'The British Working Man in Arms', in H. Cecil & P. Liddle (eds.), *Facing Armageddon: The First World War Experienced*, p. 336.

68   Gillespie, *Letters From Flanders*, pp. 170-1.

69   R. Bickersteth, *Bickersteth War Diaries 1914-1919, Volume 2: 3/2/1915 – 2/2/1916*, The Bickersteth War Diaries and the Papers of John Burgon Bickersteth, BICK 1/2, p. 520.

70   Greenwell, *Infant In Arms*, pp. 11-2.

71   G.J. DeGroot, *Blighty. British Society in the Era of the Great War*, pp. 164-8.

72   P. Parker, *The Old Lie – The Great War and the Public School Ethos*, p. 167.

73   M. Roper, *The Secret Battle – Emotional Survival in the Great War*, p. 166.

74   G.D. Sheffield, 'Officer-Man Relations, Discipline and Morale in the British Army of the Great War', in Cecil & Liddle, *Facing Armageddon*, pp. 415-7.

75   Peppiatt, *The War Diary*, p. 27.

76   D.C. Richter (ed.), *Lionel Sotheby's Great War – Diaries and Letters from the Western Front*, p. 103.

77   Sheffield, *Leadership in the Trenches*, p. 100.

78   Gibbs papers, letter dated 18 December 1916.

79   Papers of C.K. Ogden, Imperial War Museum, Department of Documents, bound copy of B.L. Lawrence war letters, p. 45.

80   Papers of Captain S.J. Paget, letter dated 27 December 1915.

81   Paget papers, letter dated 16 December 1915.

82   R.T. Rees, *A Schoolmaster At War*, p. 79.

83   Sheffield, *Leadership in the Trenches*, p. 46.

84   H.C. Adams, *Wykehamica: A History of Winchester College and Commoners, from the foundation to the present day*, pp. 382-3.

85   J.R. de S. Honey, *Tom Brown's Universe: The Development of the Victorian Public School*, p. 11; R. Wilkinson, *The Prefects: British Leadership and the Public School Tradition – A Comparative Study in the Making of Rulers*, pp. 30-1; H.C. Adams, *Wykehamica: A History of Winchester College and Commoners, from the foundation to the present day*, pp. 382-3.

86   A. Waugh, *Public School Life – Boys, Parents, Masters*, pp. 171-2.

87   Pollard, *Fire-Eater*, pp. 164-5.

88   Buitenhuis, *The Great War of Words*, p. 113;

89   M.V.W. Smith, *Drummer Hodge – The Poetry of the Anglo-Boer War*, p. 56.

90   Cited in J. Richards, *Happiest Days – The public school in English fiction*, p. 144

91   Spicer, *Letters From France*, p. 16.

92   Peppiatt, *The War Diary*, p. 8.

93   DeGroot, *Blighty*, p. 165.

94   Congreve, *Armageddon Road,* p. 171. Congreve became an officer in the Rifle Brigade in 1911.

95   Anon. (D. Bell), *A Soldier's Diary of the Great War*, p. 44.

96   Vaughan, *Some Desperate Glory*, p. 16.

97   Paget papers, letter dated 15 February 1914.

98   Anon. (T.D. Pilcher), *A General's Letters To His Son On Obtaining His Commission*, p. 57.

99   Papers of Major-General D.N. Wimberley, Imperial War Museum, Department of Documents, *The Memoirs of Major-General Douglas Neil Wimberley*, Volume 1, p. 31.

100   Cited in Simpson, *Hot Blood and Cold Steel*, p. x..

101   Neville, *The War Letters of a Light Infantryman*, p. 115.

102   Sheffield, *Leadership in the Trenches*, p. 83.

103   Richter, *Lionel Sotheby's Great War*, pp. 31-2.

104   J. Golder Burns, *Through A Padre's Spectacles*, p. 81.

105   May papers, diary entry dated 25 November 1915.

106   Dudley-Ward papers, journal entry dated 3 November 1915.

107   E.S. Turner, *Gallant Gentlemen – a portrait of the British Officer 1600-1956*, p. 278.

108   Douie, *The Weary Road*, pp. 51-2.

109   Hamilton papers, letters dated 1 & 8 July 1915.

110   C.E. Jacomb, *Torment – A Study in Patriotism*, p. 233.

111   Sheffield, 'Officer-Man Relations, Discipline and Morale in the British Army of the Great War', p. 419.

112   Hamilton papers, letter dated 5 July 1915.

113   Jacomb, *Torment*, pp. 229-30.

114   I. Bet-El, *Conscripts – Lost Legions of the Great War*, p. 161.

115   Holmes, *Tommy*, p. 580.

116   Sheffield, 'Officer-Man Relations, Discipline and Morale in the British Army of the Great War' in Cecil & Liddle, *Facing Armageddon*, p. 419.

Chapter 8

1   The National Archives, *Scheme for promotion of non-commissioned officers from the ranks: Question of further education and comparison with French system*', pp. 10-11.

2   H.E.L. Mellersh, *Schoolboy into War*, pp. 65-6.

3   R. Holmes, *Tommy – The British Soldier on the Western Front 1914-1918*, p. 354.

4 Papers of Major C.H. Dudley-Ward, Imperial War Museum, Department of Documents, journal entry dated 23 November 1915.

5 B.A. Medley, *April 1915 to September 1915*, p. 99.

6 Papers of Major T.D. Pratt, Imperial War Museum, Department of Documents, typescript memoir, pp. 2-3.

7 A. Wilkinson (ed.), *Destiny: The War Letters of Captain Jack Oughtred MC 1915-1918*, p. 16.

8 'Regular', *Customs of the Army – A Guide for Cadets and Young Officers*, p. 31.

9 D. Cannadine, *The Decline And Fall Of The British Aristocracy*, p. 13.

10 Dudley-Ward papers, journal entry dated 13 December 1916.

11 'Regular', *Customs of the Army*, pp. 28-9.

12 G.H. Greenwell, *Infant In Arms*, p. 130.

13 Papers of E.J. Dent, letter from E.C. Matthews dated 31 October 1915, Add MS 7973/M/30.

14 W.E. Cairnes, *Social Life in the British Army*, p. 164.

15 R. Graves, *Goodbye to All That*, pp. 75-6.

16 A.K. Yapp, *The Romance of the Red Triangle – The Story of the Coming of the Red Triangle and the Service Rendered by the YMCA to the Sailors and Soldiers of the British Empire*, pp. 180-1.

17 Holmes, *Tommy*, p. 592.

18 O. Lyttelton, The Papers of Alfred Lyttelton and Dame Edith Lyttelton, and their son Oliver Lyttelton (1st Viscount Chandos), letter dated 15 April 1917, CHAN 8/5; J.E.H. Neville, *War Letters of a Light Infantryman*, p. 42.

19 L.D. Spicer, *Letters from France 1915-1918*, p. 89.

20 C.S. Peel, *How We Lived Then 1914-1918 – A Sketch of Social And Domestic Life In England During The War*, p. 66; J. Walvin, *Leisure and Society 1830-1950*, p. 130.

21 Holmes, *Tommy*, pp. 604-5.

22 H. Macmillan, *Winds of Change 1914-1939*, p. 88; D. Winter, *Death's Men – Soldiers of the Great War*, p. 138.

23 T.W. Koch, *Books In Camp, Trench and Hospital*, p. 7.

24 A. Tapert (ed.), *Despatches from the heart – An anthology of letters from the Front during the First and Second World Wars*, p. 21.

25 Papers of Captain W.E. Villiers, Imperial War Museum, Department of Documents, letter dated 4 June 1916.

26 Papers of Captain L. Holt, Imperial War Museum, Department of Documents, letter dated 15 February 1917.

27 27. Papers of Captain S.J. Paget, letter dated 14 October 1915.

28 Winter, *Death's Men*, p. 149.

29 B.W.E. Alford, *W.D. & H.O. Wills and the development of the U.K. tobacco industry 1786-1965*, p. 321.

30 Winter, *Death's Men*, p. 149.

31 The National Archives, War Office Officers Files, Lt. R. Asquith, Standing Committee of Adjustment, G.H.Q. 3rd Echelon, BEF to Cox & Co., inventory.

32 'Is The Soldier Smoking Too Much?', *The Lancet*, 1915, Volume 2, 4 September, p. 584.

33 Papers of J.T. Bramston, letter from Dick dated 23 March 1916, E3/7/1/2.

34 Paget papers, letter dated 2 January 1916.

35 Dent papers, undated letter from X. Marcel Boulestin, Add MS 7973/B/84.

36 Dent papers, undated letter from F.K. Bliss, Add MS 7973/B/48.

37 Koch, *Books In Camp, Trench and Hospital*, p. 13.

38 E.S. Woods (ed.), *Andrew R. Buxton, The Rifle Brigade, A Memoir*, p. 223.

39   N. Hiley, 'Ploughboys and Soldiers: the folk song and the gramophone in the British Expeditionary Force 1914-1918', *Media History*, 4, No. 1 (June 1998), p. 62.

40   G.D. Sheffield & G.I.S. Inglis (eds.), *From Vimy Ridge to the Rhine The Great War Letters of Christopher Stone DSO MC*, pp. 79-80.

41   C.R. Stone, 'A Decca Romance', *The Gramophone*, August, 1923, p. 56.

42   Papers of Captain N.A. Taylor, Imperial War Museum, Department of Documents, letter dated 11 October 1915.

43   P. Martland, *Since Records Began. EMI: The first 100 years*, p.112.

44   Hiley, 'Ploughboys and Soldiers', p. 74.

45   Graves, *Goodbye to All That*, p. 108.

46   Dent papers, letter from M.G. Davisdon dated 28 June 1915, Add MS 7973/D/10.

47   Dent papers, letter from M.G. Davidson dated 19 August 1915, Add MS 7973/D11.

48   J.G. Fuller, *Troop Morale and Popular Culture in the British and Dominion Armies 1914-1918*, p. 88.

49   Anon. (T.D. Pilcher), *A General's Letters to His Son*, p. 44.

50   Papers of Lt. W.B.P. Spencer, Imperial War Museum, Department of Documents, letter dated 27 February 1914 [sic, presumably 1915].

51   Neville, *War Letters of a Light Infantryman*, p. 48.

52   Paget papers, letter dated 7 June 1914.

53   L. Talbot (ed.), *Gilbert Walter Lyttelton Talbot*, p. 56.

54   Greenwell, *Infant In Arms*, p. 173.

55   Cairnes, *Social Life in the British Army*, p. 168.

56   S. Cloete, *A Victorian Son – An Autobiography*, p. 159.

57   Paget papers, letter dated 29 June 1914.

58   Dent papers, letter from E.C. Matthews dated 2 December 1915, Add MS 7973/M/33.

59   Dent papers, letter from F.K. Bliss dated 21 April 1916, Add MS 7973/B/47.

60   G. Dugdale, *"Langemarck" And "Cambrai" – A War Narrative 1914-1918*, p. 32.

61   Papers of Captain A.B. Pick, Imperial War Museum, Department of Documents, letter dated 12 October 1916.

62   J.S.K. Watson, *Fighting Different Wars – Experience, Memory, and the First World War in Britain*, p. 26.

63   Medley, *April 1915 to September 1915*, pp. 54-5.

64   P. Parker, *The Old Lie – The Great War and the Public School Ethos*, p. 208.

65   D.C. Richter (ed.), *Lionel Sotheby's Great War – Diaries and Letters from the Western Front*, p. 23.

66   Papers of Captain A. Gibbs, Imperial War Museum, Department of Documents, letter dated 8 January 1916.

67   Villiers papers, letter dated 23 September 1917.

68   L. Talbot (ed.), *Gilbert Walter Lyttelton Talbot*, pp. 59-60.

69   Villiers papers, letter dated 4 June 1916.

70   Bramston papers, undated letter from A. Ferguson, E3/5/34/4.

71   Bramston papers, letter from L. Booth dated 16 August, year unknown, E3/5/11/2.

72   Bramston papers, letter from F. Luttman-Johnson dated 29 August 1918, E3/5/65.

73   Gibbs papers, letter dated 8 January 1916.

74   W.R.G. Mills, *Poems and Letters of William R.G. Mills*, pp. 93-4.

75   Pick papers, letter dated 29 July 1918.

76   G. Cecil, 'India, The Annual Eton Dinner', *Public School Magazine*, vol. VIII, July to December 1901, October 1901, p. 358.

77   Parker, *The Old Lie*, p. 209.
78   Bramston papers, letter from K. Evans dated 31st December, year unknown, E3/5/30/5.
79   H. Dundas, *Henry Dundas – Scots Guards – A Memoir*, p. 129.
80   Papers of Lt. R. Swayne, Imperial War Museum, Department of Documents, letter dated 17 January 1917.
81   Gibbs papers, letter dated 3 June 1917.
82   Holmes, *Tommy*, p. 601.
83   R. Whinyates (ed.), *Artillery & Trench Mortar Memories – 32nd Division*, pp. 620-1.
84   Greenwell, *Infant In Arms*, p. 113.
85   Fuller, *Troop Morale and Popular Culture in the British and Dominion Armies.*
86   Dundas, *Henry Dundas*, p. 181.
87   Villiers papers, letter dated 2 September 1916.
88   J. Jolliffe, *Raymond Asquith – Life and Letters*, p. 238.
89   Paget papers, letter dated 15 February 1914.
90   G.D. Sheffield, *The Somme*, p. 72; J. Terraine, *White Heat – The New Warfare 1914-18*, pp. 307-8; D.E. Showalter, 'Mass Warfare and the Impact of Technology', in R. Chickering & S. Förster (eds.), *Great War, Total War – Combat and Mobilization on the Western Front, 1914-1918*, pp. 85-6.
91   Paget papers, letter dated 13 September 1915.
92   A. Simpson, *Hot Blood And Cold Steel: Life And Death In The Trenches of the First World War*, pp.146-7.
93   E. Leed, *No Man's Land – Combat & Identity in World War I*, p. 106.
94   Mellersh, *Schoolboy into War*, pp. 44-5.
95   A. Powell (ed.), *A Deep Cry: A Literary Pilgrimage to the Battlefields and Cemeteries of First World War British Soldier-Poets Killed in Northern France and Flanders*, p. 34.
96   M. Glover (ed.), *The Fateful Battle Line: The Great War Journals and Sketches of Captain Henry Ogle, MC*, pp. 153-4.
97   E.C. Vaughan, *Some Desperate Glory – The diary of a young officer, 1917*, p. 137.
98   J. Bourke, *Dismembering the Male – Men's Bodies, Britain and the Great War*, p. 151.
99   'Amateur Officer', *After Victory*, pp. 50-1.
100 Bourke, *Dismembering the Male*, p. 151.
101 P. Glenconner, *Edward Wyndham Tennant, 4th Grenadier Guards – A memoir*, p. 233.
102 J.M. Bourne, *Britain and the Great War 1914-1918*, p. 206.
103 Jolliffe, *Raymond Asquith*, p. 277.
104 A.D. Gillespie, *Letters From Flanders*, pp. 234-5.
105 Mills, *Poems and Letters of William R.G. Mills*, p. 58.
106 Taylor papers, letter dated 5 September 1915.
107 H. Strachan, *The First World War: Volume 1 – To Arms*, p. 161.

Chapter 9

1   R. Holmes, *Tommy – The British Soldier on the Western Front 1914-1918*, p. 579.
2   K. Henderson, *Letters to Helen; Impressions of an Artist on the Western Front*, pp. 12-13.
3   A.M. Adam, *Arthur Innes Adam 1894-1916 A Record Founded on his Letters*, pp. 162-3.
4   G.H. Greenwell, *Infant In Arms*, p. 126.
5   J.E.H. Neville, *War Letters of a Light Infantryman*, p. 111.
6   E. Crawshay-Williams, *Leaves From An Officer's Notebook*, p. 15.
7   'I. Hay' (J.H. Beith), *The First Hundred Thousand – Being the Unofficial Chronicle of a Unit of "K(I)"*, pp. 218-20.

8   G. Nobbs, *Englishman, Kamerad! Right of the British Line*, p. 56.

9   D. Read, *Edwardian England 1901-15 – Society and Politics*, p. 47.

10   S. Cloete, *A Victorian Son – An Autobiography*, p. 166.

11   Cloete, *A Victorian Son*, p. 219.

12   D. Hankey, *A Student In Arms*, p. 241.

13   Papers of C.K. Ogden, Imperial War Museum, Department of Documents, bound copy of Lt. B.L. Lawrence war letters, p. 30.

14   Papers of Captain J.S. Baines, letter to Miss Honor Baines dated 10 November 1910.

15   O.S. Buckmaster, *Roundabout: The Autobiography of Viscount Buckmaster*, p. 68.

16   D. Young, *Try Anything Twice*, p. 6.

17   Greenwell, *Infant In Arms*, p. 102.

18   R. Duffett, 'A War Unimagined: Food and the rank and file soldier of the First World War', in J. Meyer (ed.), *British Popular Culture and the First World War*, pp. 48-9.

19   Neville, *War Letters of a Light Infantryman*, p. 42

20   B.W. Long, *First World War Letters*, p. 15.

21   K. Simpson, 'The Officers', in I.F.W. Beckett & K. Simpson (eds.), *A Nation in Arms – A Social study of the British army in the First World War*, p. 78.

22   Young, *Try Anything Twice*, p. 49.

23   F. Manning, *The Middle Parts of Fortune*, p. 189.

24   A. Wolff, *Subalterns of the Foot – Three World War I Diaries of Officers of the Cheshire Regiment*, pp. 116-7.

25   R. Holmes, *Firing Line*, p. 88.

26   War Office, *Statistics of the military effort of the British Empire during the Great War 1914-20*, p. 521.

27   E.B. Proud, *History of British Army Postal Service – Volume 2 1903-1927*, p. 31.

28   Winter, *Death's Men*, p. 67.

29   Papers of Captain S.J. Paget, letter dated 4 August 1915.

30   O. Lyttelton, The Papers of Alfred Lyttelton and Dame Edith Lyttelton, and their son Oliver Lyttelton (1st Viscount Chandos), letter dated 21 February 1915, CHAN 8/3.

31   Lyttelton papers, letter posted 4 March 1915, CHAN 8/3.

32   Holmes, *Tommy*, p. 325.

33   Papers of Captain W.E. Villiers, Imperial War Museum, Department of Documents, letter dated 26 May 1916.

34   A.D. Gillespie, *Letters From Flanders*, p. 54.

35   Papers of Captain N.A. Taylor, Imperial War Museum, Department of Documents, undated letter to Joyce.

36   Papers of E.J. Dent, letter from E.C. Matthews dated 2 December 1915, Add MS 7973/M/33.

37   Taylor papers, undated letter to Gertrude.

38   Papers of 2nd Lt. R. Harker, Imperial War Museum, Department of Documents, letter dated 14 October 1914.

39   Harker papers, letter dated 17 November 1914.

40   Harker papers, letter dated 16 March 1915.

41   Papers of Major C.H. Dudley-Ward, Imperial War Museum, Department of Documents, journal entry dated 11 February 1916.

42   Papers of Captain A. Gibbs, Imperial War Museum, Department of Documents, letter dated 8 September 1916.

43   A. Saunders, *Dominating The Enemy: War In The Trenches 1914-1918*, p. 86.

44   S. Sassoon, *Memoirs of an Infantry Officer*, p. 42. In 1907, wire cutters from the Army & Navy Stores cost between 2s. 6d and 3s. 6d. Adburgham, *Yesterday's Shopping*, p. 704.

45   Gibbs papers, letter 18 January 1916.

46   Gibbs papers, letter dated 21 March 1916.

47   A.O. Pollard, *Fire-Eater – The Memoirs of a V.C.*, p. 51.

48   Pollard, *Fire-Eater*, p. 52.

49   Papers of Lt. C.L. Platt, Imperial War Museum, Department of Documents, letter dated 7 March 1916.

50   P.H. Liddle, *The Soldier's War*, p. 83.

51   *Royal Warrant for the Pay, Appointment, Promotion, and Non-Effective Pay of The Army*, p. 52.

52   M. Middlebrook, *The First Day On The Somme, 1 July 1916*, p. 37.

53   B.R. Mitchell, *British Historical Statistics*, pp. 728-9.

54   T. Kemp, *The French Economy 1913-39 – The history of a decline*, p. 49.

55   L.D. Spicer, *Letters from France 1915-1918*, p. 106.

56   *Amendments, &c., to the Royal Warrant for the Pay, Appointment, Promotion, and Non-Effective Pay of the Army, published in Army Orders between 1st December, 1914, and 1st August, 1918, and including, besides Permanent Additions and Amendments, those of Temporary Application only*, p. 94.

57   M. Roper, *The Secret Battle – Emotional Survival in the Great War*, p. 101.

58   H.E.L. Mellersh, *Schoolboy into War*, p. 41.

59   Spicer, *Letters from France*, p. 2.

60   Harker papers, letter dated 17 November 1914.

61   C. Carlisle (ed.), *My Own Darling: Letters from Montie to Kitty Carlisle*, p. 153.

62   Gibbs papers, letter dated 23 May 1916.

63   Papers of Captain A.B. Pick, Imperial War Museum, Department of Documents, letter dated 10 January 1918.

64   Holmes, *Firing Line*, p. 354.

65   B. Congreve, *Armageddon Road – A VC's Diary, 1914-1916*, p. 140.

66   Cloete, *A Victorian Son*, p. 219.

67   R. Graves, *Goodbye to All That*, p. 235.

68   E.M. Remarque, *All Quiet on the Western Front*, pp. 12, 15, 24, 197.

69   Congreve, *Armageddon Road*, p. 140

70   W. Smith, *Spilt Ink*, p. 134.

71   C.S. Peel, *How We Lived Then 1914-1918 – A Sketch of Social And Domestic Life In England During The War*, p. 60.

72   'Hay', *The First Hundred Thousand*, p. 216.

73   *The Times*, 4 August 1914, p. 8f.

74   *The Times*, 5 August 1914, p. 8.

75   *The Times*, 6 August 1914, p. 9.

76   J. Hayward, *Myths & Legends of the First World War*, p. 7.

77   *The Times*, 17th August 1915, p. 13f.

78   'Sapper' (H. McNeile), *The Lieutenant and others*, p. 6.

79   *The Illustrated London News*, 21 November 1914, p. 718.

80   *The Times*, September 23rd 1915, p. 6.

81   J. Jolliffe, *Raymond Asquith – Life and Letters*, p. 205.

82   Carlisle, *My Own Darling*, p. 147.

83   B. Pitt, *Essays, Poems, Letters*, pp. 19, 34.

84   Harker papers, letter dated 14 October 1914.

85   'Food Fakes In War', *The Lancet*, 1915, Volume 2, 31 July, pp. 259-60.

86   A.O. Temple Clarke, *Transport and Sport in the Great War Period*, p. 154.

Chapter 10

1   G. Corrigan, *Mud, Blood and Poppycock: Britain and the First World War*, pp. 129-131.

2   F.C. Hitchcock, *"Stand To" – A Diary of the Trenches 1915-18*, p. 70.

3   E. Leed, *No Man's Land – Combat & Identity in World War I*, p. 106.

4   J. Baynes, *Morale – A Study of Men and Courage*, pp. 253-4.

5   War Office, *Statistics of the military effort of the British Empire during the Great War 1914-20*, pp. 643, 669-70.

6   W. Moore, *The Thin Yellow Line*, pp. 92-3; War Office, *Statistics of the military effort*, p. 648.

7   H.N. McCartney, *Citizen Soldiers – The Liverpool Territorials in the First World War*, pp. 122, 188.

8   G.D. Sheffield, *Forgotten Victory – The First World War: Myths and Realities*, p. 128.

9   G. Dallas & D. Gill, *The Unknown Army*, pp. 72-3.

10   N. Ferguson, *The Pity of War*, pp. 446-447; J. Bourke, *An Intimate History of Killing – Face-to-face killing in twentieth-century warfare*, pp. 14-16.

11   J.G. Fuller, *Troop Morale and Popular Culture in the British and Dominion Armies 1914-1918*.

12   Leed, *No Man's Land*, p. 106.

13   L. Smith, *Between Mutiny and Obedience: The Case of the French Fifth Infantry Division During World War I*, p. 91.

14   McCartney, *Citizen Soldiers*, pp. 122, 188.

15   T. Ashworth, *Trench Warfare 1914-1918: The Live and Let Live System*. Peter Simkins also notes Malcolm Brown and Shirley Seaton's examination of the 1914 Christmas Truce. P. Simkins, 'Everyman at War: Recent Interpretations of the Front Line Experience', in B. Bond (ed.), *The First World War and British Military History*, p. 296.

16   Ashworth, *Trench Warfare 1914-1918*, p. 166.

17   L.D. Spicer, *Letters From France 1915-1918*, p. 34.

18   See, for example, S. Hynes, *A Soldier's Tale – Bearing Witness To Modern War*, p. 64.

19   G.J. DeGroot, *Blighty. British Society in the Era of the Great War*, p. 45.

20   S. Hynes, *A War Imagined*, p. 7. Interestingly, Tim Travers notes the prevalence of these ideas in the late Victorian and Edwardian army corps, arguing that this encouraged an anti-intellectual tendency. T. Travers, *The Killing Ground – The British Army, the Western Front and the Emergence of Modern Warfare 1900-1918*, p. 39.

21   B.A. Medley, *April 1915 to September 1915*, p. 1.

22   W. Owen, *War Poems and Others*, p. 79.

23   J.M. Bourne, *Britain and the Great War 1914-1918*, p. 231

24   See works such as Sheffield, *Forgotten Victory*; Corrigan, *Mud, Blood and Poppycock*; J. Terraine, *White Heat – The New Warfare 1914-18*; P. Griffith, *Battle Tactics of the Western Front: The British Army's Art of Attack, 1916-18*. To see examples of the learning processes undergone by particular units and specialists, see: I.V. Hogg, *Allied Artillery Of World War One* or D. Richter, *Chemical Soldiers: British Gas Warfare in World War I*.

25   M. Stephen, *The Price Of Pity: Poetry, History and Myth in the Great War*, pp. 24-5; P. Parker, *The Old Lie – The Great War and the Public School Ethos*, pp. 283-4.

26   Bourne, *Britain and the Great War*, p. 231

27   Parker, *The Old Lie*, p. 226.

28   Hynes, *A War Imagined*, p. 119.

29   P.H. Liddle, *Voices of War – Front Line and Home Front*, p. 63.

30   J.E.H. Neville, *The War Letters of a Light Infantryman*, p. 45.

31   C. Douie, *The Weary Road – Recollections of a Subaltern of Infantry*, p. 37.

32   J. Richards, *Happiest Days – The public school in English fiction*, p. 17.

33   G.D. Sheffield, *The Somme*, p. 154.

34   Hynes, *A War Imagined*, p. 121.

35   T. Bogacz, '"A Tyranny of Words": Language, Poetry, and Antimodernism in England in the First World War', *Journal of Modern History*, 58 (September 1986), p. 652.

36   *The War Illustrated,* 3 October 1914, p. 157.

37   L. James, *Warrior Race – The British Experience of War from Roman Times to the Present*, p. 411.

38   H.E.L. Mellersh, *Schoolboy into War*, p. 25.

39   P. Buitenhuis, *The Great War of Words: Literature as Propaganda 1914-18 and After*, p. 116.

40   R.E. Harris, *Billie – The Nevill Letters 1914-1916*, p. 144.

41   D. Englander, 'Soldiering and Identity: Reflections on the Great War', *War In History*, 1, No. 3 (November 1994), p. 316.

42   McCartney, *Citizen Soldiers*, pp. 89-90.

43   Papers of Lt. C.L. Platt, Imperial War Museum, Department of Documents, letter dated 16 April 1916.

44   *The Wykehamist*, No. 473, March 1910, p. 205.

45   A. Gregory, *The Last Great War- British Society and the First World War*, pp. 32-3.

46   Papers of Captain S.J. Paget, letter dated 20 January 1915.

47   Papers of 2nd Lt. I.V.B. Melhuish, Imperial War Museum, Department of Documents, letter dated 9 May 1915.

48   E.C. Vaughan, *Some Desperate Glory – The diary of a young officer, 1917*, pp. 6-8.

49   J. Nettleton, *The Anger of the Guns: An Infantry Officer on the Western Front*, p. 192.

50   A. Wilkinson (ed.), *Destiny: The War Letters of Captain Jack Oughtred MC 1915-1918*, p. 32; M. Arthur, *Forgotten Voices of the Great War*, p. 184.

51   J. Hawke, *From Private to Major*, p. 97.

52   Papers of Major C.H. Dudley-Ward, Imperial War Museum, Department of Documents, journal entry dated 3 November 1915.

53   Papers of Lt. M.W. Peters, Imperial War Museum, Department of Documents, letter dated 11 July 1918.

54   Leed, *No Man's Land*, p. 91.

55   Douie, *The Weary Road*, p. 110.

56   R. Holmes, *Tommy – The British Soldier on the Western Front 1914-1918*, p. 308.

57   J. Jolliffe, *Raymond Asquith – Life and Letters*, p. 229.

58   Holmes, *Tommy*, p. 308.

59   D. Stevenson, *1914-1918 – The History of the First World War*, p. 214.

60   O. Lyttelton, The Papers of Alfred Lyttelton and Dame Edith Lyttelton, and their son Oliver Lyttelton (1st Viscount Chandos), leter dated 25 March 1915, CHAN 8/3.

61   Anon. (D. Bell), *A Soldier's Diary of the Great War*, p. 159.

62   Holmes, *Tommy*, p. 86.

63   Fuller, *Troop Morale and Popular Culture in the British and Dominion Armies*, p. 61.

64   G.H. Greenwell, *Infant In Arms*, p. 238.

65   Lyttelton papers, letter dated 9 October 1915, CHAN 8/3.

66   W. Shirley, *Moral – The Most Important Factor In War*, p. 15.

67   Papers of 2nd Lt. R.P. Hamilton, Imperial War Museum, Department of Documents, letter dated 20 July 1915.

68   Platt papers, letter dated 9 January 1916.

69   'Amateur Officer', *After Victory*, pp. 95-6.

70   Holmes, *Tommy*, p. 583.

71   Papers of Major M.S.S. Moore, Imperial War Museum, Department of Documents, letter from R.W. Rice dated 4 December 1917.

72   LW Crouch, *Duty And Service – Letters From The Front*, pp. 88-9.

73   Holmes, *Tommy*, p. 584.

74   C. Messenger, *Call To Arms – The British Army 1914-18*, pp. 491-2.

75   Anon. (D. Bell), *A Soldier's Diary of the Great War*, p. 171.

76   Holmes, *Tommy*, p. 585.

77   G. Chapman, *A Passionate Prodigality – Fragments of Autobiography*, pp. 326-7.

78   Dudley-Ward papers, journal entry dated 4 June 1916.

79   Dudley-Ward papers, journal entry dated 4 May 1916.

80   Anon., 'A Trench Ribbon – The Popularizing of the Infantry', *The Times*, 18 May 1916, p. 9e.

81   A.J. Sansom, *Letters from France – Written between June 1915 – July 1917*, p. 287.

82   Messenger, *Call To Arms*, p. 495.

83   Messenger, *Call To Arms*, p. 492.

84   E. Townshend (ed.), *Keeling Letters and Recollections*, p. 307.

85   Anon., 'A Trench Ribbon'.

86   Messenger, *Call To Arms*, p. 495.

87   The National Archives, 'Proposal from Mr. Winston Churchill, 28 February 1917', in the Report of Winston Churchill's Committee on Promotion; reports of meetings, Letters of enquiry concerning claims. 1917', pp. 1-2.

88   The National Archives, 'Major-General F.C. Shaw to Churchill re. 'Figure of Merit', 14 March 1917', in the Report of Winston Churchill's Committee on Promotion.

89   Holmes, *Tommy*, pp. 585-6.

90   J. Moorcroft Wilson, *Siegfried Sassoon – The Making Of A War Poet (A Biography 1886-1918)*, p. 258.

91   D.C. Richter (ed.), *Lionel Sotheby's Great War – Diaries and Letters from the Western Front*, p. 15.

92   E.S. Woods (ed.), *Andrew R. Buxton, The Rifle Brigade, A Memoir*, p. 107.

93   F.A. McKenzie, 'The War By Land', *The War Illustrated*, Vol. 2, No. 28, 27 February 1915, p. 42.

94   G.A. Burgoyne, *The Burgoyne Diaries*, p. 48.

95   D. Young, *Try Anything Twice*, p. 97.

96   Spicer, *Letters From France*, pp. 120, 122.

97   R. Bickersteth, *Bickersteth War Diaries 1914-1919, Volume 2: 3/2/1915 – 2/2/1916*, The Bickersteth War Diaries and the Papers of John Burgon Bickersteth, BICK 1/2, p. 515.

98   G.D. Sheffield & G.I.S. Inglis (eds.), *From Vimy Ridge to the Rhine The Great War Letters of Christopher Stone DSO MC*, p. 63.

99   Sansom, *Letters from France*, p. 274.

100   L. Peppiatt, *The War Diary – January to September 1918 – of Major Leslie Peppiatt MC*, p. 95; Dudley-Ward papers, journal entry dated 10 August 1916.

101   Sheffield, *Forgotten Victory*, p. 127; M. Brown, *Tommy Goes To War*, p. 62.

102   Sheffield notes that raiding was often unpopular because of the casualties sustained and a subsequent toll on the morale of the men. Sheffield, *Forgotten Victory*, p. 127.

103 D.E. Showalter, 'Mass Warfare and the Impact of Technology', in R. Chickering & S. Förster (eds.), *Great War, Total War – Combat and Mobilization on the Western Front, 1914-1918*, pp. 88-9.

104 Neville, *War Letters of a Light Infantryman*, pp. 55-6.

105 B. Pitt, *Essays, Poems, Letters*, p. 46; Bourke, *An Intimate History of Killing*, p. 61.

106 R. Feilding, *War Letters to a Wife, France and Flanders 1915-19*, p. 29.

107 Wilkinson, *Destiny*, p. 66; Holmes, *Tommy*, p. 275.

108 Ashworth, *Trench Warfare 1914-1918*, p. 96.

109 S. Hewett, *A Scholar's Letters from the Front*, pp. 84-5.

110 Neville, *War Letters of a Light Infantryman*, p. 58.

111 Paget papers, letter dated 5 September 1915.

112 Paget papers, letter dated 9 September 1915.

113 Vaughan, *Some Desperate Glory*, p. 117.

114 O.S. Buckmaster, *Roundabout – The Autobiography of Viscount Buckmaster*, p. 43.

115 P. Howarth, *Play Up And Play The Game: The Heroes Of Popular Fiction*, p. 171.

116 Papers of Captain A. Gibbs, Imperial War Museum, Department of Documents, letter dated 6 July 1917; J. Lewis-Stempel, *Six Weeks – The Short and Gallant Life of the British Officer in the First World War*, pp. 186-7.

117 Douie, *The Weary Road*, p. 164.

118 Gibbs papers, letter dated 6 July 1917.

119 Gibbs papers, letter dated 25 July 1916.

120 'O.E' (G. Fildes), *Iron Times with the Guards*, pp. 250-1.

121 Lyttelton papers, undated description of battle written at 16 Great College Street, Cambridge, CHAN 8/4.

122 Lyttelton papers, battle description, CHAN 8/4.

123 B. Shephard, *A War of Nerves – Soldiers and Psychiatrists 1914-1994*, p. 35.

124 I.F. Clarke, *Voices Prophesying War – Future Wars 1763-3749*, p. 60.

125 Buitenhuis, *The Great War of Words*, pp. 149-150.

126 J.M. Winter, *The Great War and the British People*, p. 285.

127 Dan Todman, *The Great War: Myth and Memory*, p. 14.

128 Clarke, *Voices Prophesying War*, p. 60.

129 James, *Warrior Race*, p. 418.

130 M. Paris, *Warrior Nation – Images of War in British Popular Culture, 1850-2000*, pp. 112-17.

131 Paris, *Warrior Nation*, p. 153-4; D. Todman, 'Representations of the First World War in British popular culture, 1918-1998', pp. 53-6; M. Girouard, *The Return To Camelot – Chivalry and the English Gentleman*, p. 291.

132 Cyril Falls and Douglas Jerrold, as cited in Hynes, *A War Imagined*, pp. 453-5; R. Wohl, *The Generation of 1914*, pp. 108-9; J. Wiśniewski, *Mars and the Muse: Attitudes to War and Peace in 20th Century English Literature*, p. 81.

133 S. Hynes 'Personal Narratives and Commemoration', in J.M. Winter & E. Sivan (eds.), *War and Remembrance in the Twentieth Century*, pp. 214-16.

134 Hynes, 'Personal Narratives and Commemoration', p. 216.

135 S. Sassoon, *Memoirs of an Infantry Officer*, pp. 29-30.

136 M. Thorpe, *Siegfried Sassoon – A Critical Study*, p. 96.

Chapter 11

1 P. Parker, *The Old Lie; the Great War and the Public School Ethos*, p. 17.

2   N. Ferguson, *The Pity of War*, p. 201.

3   Parker, *The Old Lie*, pp. 283-4; J.M. Bourne, *Britain and the Great War 1914-1918*, p. 231.

4   J. Jolliffe, *Raymond Asquith – Life and Letters*, p. 248.

5   O. Lyttelton, The Papers of Alfred Lyttelton and Dame Edith Lyttelton, and their son Oliver Lyttelton (1st Viscount Chandos), letter received on 14 May 1915, CHAN 8/3.

6   A.D. Gillespie, *Letters From Flanders*, pp. 234-8.

7   A. Wilkinson (ed.), *Destiny – The War Letters of Captain Jack Oughtred MC 1915-1918*, p. 56.

8   A.M. Adam, *Arthur Innes Adam 1894-1916, A Record Founded on his Letters*, p. 215.

9   R. Feilding, *War Letters to a Wife, France and Flanders 1915-19*, p. 53.

10   G.D. Sheffield & G.I.S. Inglis (eds.), *From Vimy Ridge to the Rhine – The Great War Letters of Christopher Stone DSO MC*, p. 58.

11   G.H. Greenwell, *Infant In Arms*, pp. 156-9.

12   Greenwell, *Infant In Arms*, p. 243.

13   J. Harris, *Private Lives, Public Spirit – A Social History of Britain 1870-1914*, p. 181.

14   N.F. Gullace, *"The Blood of Our Sons" – Men, Women, and the Renegotiation of British Citizenship During the Great War*, p. 47.

15   Jolliffe, *Raymond Asquith*, p. 278.

16   Gullace, *"The Blood of Our Sons"*, pp. 170-183.

17   L.Y. Sanders, *A Soldier Of England – Memorials of Leslie Yorath Sanders*, p. 71.

18   Gillespie, *Letters From Flanders*, p. 116.

19   A. Powell (ed.), *A Deep Cry: A Literary Pilgrimage to the Battlefields and Cemeteries of First World War British Soldier-Poets Killed in Northern France and Flanders*, p. 245.

20   Papers of E.J. Dent, letter from C.R.C. Maltby dated 17 October 1915, Add MS 7973/M/88.

21   Dent papers, draft anti-war letter by C.R.C Maltby, Add MS 7973/M91; Anon. (C.R.C Maltby), 'Thoughts From the Front – The Betrayal of the Young' in the Papers of C.K. Ogden, Imperial War Museum, Department of Documents, *Cambridge Magazine* correspondence file.

22   Dent papers, letter from C.R.C. Maltby dated 8 August 1915, Add MS 7973/M/79.

23   Quoted in P. Moeyes, *Siegfried Sassoon: Scorched Glory – A Critical Study*, pp. 44-5.

24   Moeyes, *Siegfried Sassoon: Scorched Glory*, pp.32, 44.

25   A. Waugh, 'A Light Rain Falling', in G.A. Panichas (ed.), *Promise of Greatness – The War of 1914-1918*, pp. 342-3. Gerard DeGroot has argued that this effect should not be overstated. G. DeGroot, *Blighty. British Society in the Era of the Great War*, p. 164.

26   *The Times*, July 31 1917.

27   J.C. Dunn, *The War the Infantry Knew, 1914-1918*, p. 372.

28   Moeyes, *Siegfried Sassoon: Scorched Glory*, pp. 46-7.

29   J. Moorcroft Wilson, *Siegfried Sassoon – The Making Of A War Poet (A Biography 1886-1918)*, p. 418.

30   Dent papers, undated letter from C.R.C. Maltby, reference Add MS 7973/M/92.

31   G.D. Sheffield, *Forgotten Victory – The First World War: Myths and Realities*, p. 130; Parker, *The Old Lie*, pp. 283-4; M. Stephen, *The Price of Pity: Poetry, History and Myth in the Great War*, pp. 24-5.

32   Gillespie, *Letters From Flanders*, p. 70.

33   A. Tapert (ed.), *Despatches from the heart – An anthology of letters from the Front during the First and Second World Wars*, p. 55.

34   Gillespie, *Letters From Flanders*, p. 138.

35   'Amateur Officer', *After Victory*, pp. 101-2.

36   L.D. Spicer, *Letters From France 1915-1918*, pp. 107-8.

37   Bourne, *Britain and the Great War*, p. 207.

38   J.E.H. Neville, *The War Letters of a Light Infantryman*, p. 51.

39   T. Quinn, *Tales of the Old Soldiers. Ten Veterans of the First World War Remember Life and Death in the Trenches*, p. 24.

40   H. McCartney, *Citizen Soldiers – The Liverpool Territorials in the First World War*, p. 241.

41   D. Fraser (ed.), *In Good Company – The First World War Letters and Diaries of the Hon. William Fraser, Gordon Highlanders*, p. 85.

42   A.O. Pollard, *Fire-Eater – The Memoirs of a V.C.*, p.59.

43   A.J.P. Taylor, *The First World War*, pp. 157-8; H. Strachan, *The First World War – A New Illustrated History*, p. 227; H. Dundas, *Henry Dundas – Scots Guards – A Memoir*, p. 103.

44   R. Holmes, *Tommy – The British Soldier on the Western Front 1914-1918*, pp. 60-1.

45   Dundas, *Henry Dundas*, p. 206.

46   S. Hewett, *A Scholar's Letters from the Front*, p. 112.

47   Sanders, *A Soldier Of England*, p. 106.

48   D. Richter (ed.), *Lionel Sotheby's Great War – Diaries and Letters from the Western Front*, p. 42.

49   Fraser, *In Good Company*, p. 136.

50   Sanders, *A Soldier Of England*, p.102.

51   Anon. (D. Bell), *A Soldier's Diary of the Great War*, p. 161.

52   Anon., 'Retaliation', *The Gasper*, No 14, February 28 1916.

53   Richter, *Lionel Sotheby's Great War*, p. 83.

54   G. Chapman, *A Passionate Prodigality – Fragments of Autobiography*, p. 214.

55   Sanders, *A Soldier Of England*, p. 6.

56   B.W. Long, *First World War Letters*, p. 24. Long was killed in August 1917. The fact that both he and Sanders were ultimately proved right in their pessimism is less a comment on their prescience than on the nature of the material. One of the most fertile sources of letters and diaries in print are compilations published as memorials.

57   Spicer, *Letters From France*, p. 15.

58   R. Bickersteth, *Bickersteth War Diaries 1914-1919, Volume 2: 3/2/1915 – 2/2/1916*, The Bickersteth War Diaries and the Papers of John Burgon Bickersteth, BICK 1/2, p. 683.

59   Papers of Major T.D. Pratt, Imperial War Museum, Department of Documents, letter dated 14 May 1915.

60   Papers of 2nd Lt. D. Neilson-Terry, Imperial War Museum, Department of Documents, *Letters from the Great War 1914-1918*, p. 16.

61   Anon., 'Retaliation'.

62   D. Pick, *War Machine – the rationalisation of slaughter in the modern age*, p. 151.

63   Strachan, *The First World War – A New Illustrated History*, pp. 227-8.

64   G.A. Burgoyne, *The Burgoyne Diaries*, p. 22.

65   Richter, *Lionel Sotheby's Great War*, p. 20.

66   Sheffield & Inglis, *From Vimy Ridge to the Rhine*, p. 48.

67   I. Sansom (ed.), *Letters from France – Written between June 1915 – July 1917*, p. 76.

68   M. Eksteins, *Rites of Spring – The Great War and the Birth of the Modern Age*, pp. 180-1.

69   B. Millman, *Managing Domestic Dissent in First World War Britain*; J. Vellacott, *Bertrand Russell and the Pacifists in the First World War*.

70   J. Rae, *Conscience And Politics – The British Government and the Conscientious Objector To Military Service 1916-1919*, p. 1.

71   Lyttelton papers, letter dated 9 January 1917, CHAN 8/5.

72   R.E. Harris, *Billie – The Nevill Letters 1914-1916*, p. 107.

73   Sheffield & Inglis, *From Vimy Ridge to the Rhine*, p. 40.

74   Lyttelton papers, letter dated 9 January 1917, CHAN 8/5.

75   Sanders, *A Soldier Of England*, p. 106.

76   Gillespie, *Letters From Flanders*, p. 210.

77   Spicer, *Letters From France*, p. 55.

78   J.S.K. Watson, *Fighting Different Wars – Experience, Memory, and the First World War in Britain*, pp. 49-50.

79   P. Jalland, *Death In The Victorian Family*, pp. 51-4; M.C.C. Adams, *The Great Adventure – Male Desire and the Coming of World War I*, p. 88.

80   Gillespie, *Letters From Flanders*, p. 254.

81   Richter, *Lionel Sotheby's Great War*, p. 53.

82   L. Talbot (ed.), *Gilbert Walter Lyttelton Talbot*, pp. 55-6.

83   Papers of Miss H. Gosling, Imperial War Museum, Department of Documents, letter from Lt. L. Hill dated 14 June 1917.

84   Tapert, *Despatches from the heart*, p. 38.

85   See C. Harris & J. Whippy, *The Greater Game: Sporting Icons Who Fell in the Great War*.

86   W.J. Reader, *At Duty's Call – A Study In Obsolete Patriotism*, p. 100.

87   H. Strachan, *The First World War: Volume 1 – To Arms*, p. 1014.

88   'Amateur Officer', *After Victory*, p. 96.

89   Gillespie, *Letters From Flanders*, p. 268.

90   M. Thorpe, *Siegfried Sassoon – A Critical Study*, pp. 101-2.

91   T.W. Pym & G. Gordon, *Papers from Picardy*, pp. 44-5.

92   'O.E.' (G. Fildes), *Iron Times with the Guards*, p. 355.

93   Sheffield & Inglis, *From Vimy Ridge to the Rhine*, p. 111.

94   Sheffield & Inglis, *From Vimy Ridge to the Rhine*, p. 65.

95   A. Gregory, *The Silence of Memory: Armistice Day 1919-1946*, p. 226.

96   Sheffield & Inglis, *From Vimy Ridge to the Rhine*, p. 119.

97   Jolliffe, *Raymond Asquith*, p. 273.

98   Tapert, *Despatches from the heart*, p. 14.

99   Gillespie, *Letters From Flanders*, p. 255.

100 H. Macmillan, *Winds of Change 1914-1939*, p. 78, P. Clarke, *Hope and Glory – Britain 1900-1990*, p. 81.

101 Taylor, *The First World War*, p. 133.

102 S. Hynes, *A War Imagined – The First World War and English Culture*, pp. 154-5.

103 J.P. Sabben-Clare, *Winchester College: After 600 Years, 1382-1982*, p. 82.

104 Bourne, *Britain and the Great War*, p. 234.

105 See, for example, the Papers of Captain W.E. Villiers, Imperial War Museum, Department of Documents, letter dated 4 July 1916; Greenwell, *Infant In Arms*, p. 29.

106 Talbot, *Gilbert Walter Lyttelton Talbot*, p. 65

107 Bourne, *Britain and the Great War*, p. 230.

108 Sheffield & Inglis, *From Vimy Ridge to the Rhine*, p. 121.

109 E. Talbot, *The War and Conscience*, pp. 6-7.

110 E. Leed, *No Man's Land – Combat & Identity in World War I*, p. 211.

111 B.A. Medley, *April 1915 to September 1915*, pp. 52-3.

112 Douie, *The Weary Road*, p. 84.

113 C. Moran, *The Anatomy of Courage*, p. 157. Cited in A. Bonadeo, *Mark of the Beast – Death and Degradation in the Literature of the Great War*, p. 104.

114 E.S. Wood (ed.), *Andrew R. Buxton, The Rifle Brigade, A Memoir*, p. 65.

115 Bonadeo, *Mark of the Beast*, p. 104.

116 K. Henderson, *Letters to Helen; Impressions of an Artist on the Western Front*, pp. 71-2.

117 E.G.D. Living, *Attack – An Infantry Subaltern's Impressions of July 1st, 1916*, p. 47.

118 A. Eden, *Another World 1897-1917*, pp. 137-8.

119 Medley, *April 1915 to September 1915*, pp. 52-3.

120 Gillespie, *Letters From Flanders*, p. 311.

121 Wilkinson, *Destiny*, p. 141.

122 Long, *First World War Letters*, p. 58.

123 P. Glenconner, *Edward Wyndham Tennant, 4th Grenadier Guards – A Memoir by his Mother*, p. 235.

124 Talbot, *Gilbert Walter Lyttelton Talbot*, p. 65.

125 Richter, *Lionel Sotheby's Great War*, p. 142.

126 Gillespie, *Letters From Flanders*, pp. 312-3.

Conclusion

1 R. Pound, *The Lost Generation*, p. 151.

2 A. Gregory, *The Silence of Memory: Armistice Day 1919-1946*, p. 24.

3 J.S.K. Watson, *Fighting Different Wars – Experience, Memory and the First World War in Britain*, pp. 20-26.

Bibliography

Manuscript Sources

(1) Private collections
Captain J.S. Baines
W.G. Baker
Captain J.E. Crombie
Sir George Dyson
Brigadier-General G.N.B. Forster
Captain S.J. Paget
Major L. Peppiatt
Captain R.C. Smith
Major R. Stowell
Captain J.L. Strain
Major-General F.V.B. Witts
Worthington family archive

(2) The National Archives, Kew
War Office Officer Files
Lt. A.I. Adam, WO 374/178
Lt. R. Asquith, WO 339/71879
Lt. A.D. Gillespie, WO 339/24045
Captain S.J. Paget, WO 339/13228
Lt. R.L. Sale, WO 339/42198
CONDITIONS OF SERVICE (Other Ranks): General (Code 72 (A)): *Scheme for promotion of non-commissioned officers from the ranks: Question of further education and comparison with French system*, WO 32/8386.
CONDITIONS OF SERVICE (OFFICERS): PROMOTION (Code 59 (B)): *Report of Winston Churchill's Committee on Promotion; reports of meetings, Letters of enquiry concerning claims. 1917*, WO 32/5953.

(3) University Library, Cambridge
(a) Department of Manuscripts
The World War I Correspondence of E.J. Dent, Add MS 7973.
The correspondence and papers of J.R. Monsell, Add MS 9437.
(b) Official Publications Department
"B" Company No. 2 Officer Cadet Battalion, *Summary of lectures, private study, and practical work for the 4 months' course, exclusive of drill, bayonet fighting and physical training* (1916), OP.2100.8.5.

(4) The Imperial War Museum, Department of Documents, London
The Papers of:
Captain G.N. Adams
Lt. F.A. Brettell,
Lt. P. Brown,
Captain A.D.Chater,
2nd Lt. A.C.Clapham,
Major R.S. Cockburn
Major C.H. Dudley-Ward
Captain W.M.L. Escombe
2nd Lt. J.W. Gamble
Miss H. Gosling
Captain A. Gibbs
2nd Lt. R.P. Hamilton
2nd Lt. R. Harker
Captain E.R. Hepper
Lt. G.N. Holt
Major W. House
Lt. R.G. Ingle
Lt. A. Knight
Lt. B.L. Lawrence
Sir G. Lenanton
Captain J.B. Lorimer
2nd Lt. K.C. Macardle
Lt. R.L. Mackay
Captain J.H. Mahon
2nd Lt. C.M. Marsh
Captain C.C. May
2nd Lt. I.V.B. Melhuish
2nd Lt. A. Milligan
Major M.S.S. Moore
Lt. H.A. Munro
2nd Lt. D. Neilson-Terry
C.K. Ogden
Lt. M.W. Peters
Captain A.B. Pick
Lt. C.L. Platt
Major T.D. Pratt
Lt. W.J.C. Sangster
Captain N.M. Saunders
Lt. H.J. Savours
Captain H. Siepmann
Captain F.H. Simms
Lt., W.B.P. Spencer
Captain G. Stewart
Lt. R. Swayne

Lt. J.A. Talbot
Captain N.A. Taylor
Captain W.E. Villiers
Lt. H. Wilson
Major-General D.N. Wimberley
2nd Lt. F. Wollocombe
2nd Lt. R.N. Wood

(5) Churchill Archives Centre, Churchill College, Cambridge
The Bickersteth War Diaries and the Papers of John Burgon Bickersteth, BICK
The Papers of Alfred Lyttelton and Dame Edith Lyttelton, and their son Oliver
    Lyttelton (1st Viscount Chandos)

(6) Winchester College, Winchester, Hants
Winchester College Archives
Medley, B.A., *April 1915 to September 1915* (privately produced, n.d.)
Beloe, E4
Bramston, John Trant, E3

Printed Sources

Adam, A.M., *Arthur Innes Adam 1894-1916 A Record Founded on his Letters*,
    Cambridge, Bowes, 1920.
Adams, H.C., *Wykehamica – A History of Winchester College and Commoners, from the
    foundation to the present day*, London, J. Parker & Co, 1878.
Adburgham, A., *Yesterday's Shopping – The Army & Navy Stores Catalogue 1907*,
    Newton Abbott, David & Charles, 1969.
'Amateur Officer', *After Victory*, London, Andrew Melrose, 1917.
Anon. (Pilcher, T.D.), *A General's Letters To His Son On Obtaining His Commission*,
    London, Cassell & Co., 1917.
Anon. (Bell, D.), *A Soldier's Diary of the Great War*, London, Faber & Gwyer, 1929.
Anon. (Dawson, A.J.), *A Temporary Gentleman in France – Home Letters from an Officer
    in the New Army*, London, Cassell & Co., 1916.
Anon., *Memoir – Lieutenant-Colonel John Collier Stormonth Darling DSO*, The
    Standard Press, Kilmarnock, 1923.
Bairnsfather, B., *"The Bystander's" Fragments From France*, 4th edn., London, n.d.
Behrend, A., *Make Me a Soldier – A Platoon Commander in Gallipoli*, London, Eyre &
    Spottiswoode, 1961.
Behrend, A., *As From Kemmel Hill – An Adjutant in France and Flanders 1917 & 1918*,
    London, Eyre & Spottiswoode, 1963.
Blake, R. (ed.), *The Private Papers of Douglas Haig 1914-1919*, London, Eyre &
    Spottiswoode, 1952.
Blunden, E., *Undertones of War*, London, Collins, 1965.
Bond, B. & Robbins, S. (eds.), *Staff Officer – The Diaries of Walter Guinness (First Lord
    Moyne) 1914-1918*, London, Leo Cooper, 1987.
Brown, J., *Letters, Essays and Verses*, Edinburgh, Andrew Elliot, 1921.

Browne, M., *A Dream Of Youth – An Etonian's Reply to "The Loom of Youth"*, London, Longmans, 1918.

Buchan, J., *Greenmantle*, Oxford, Oxford University Press, 1993.

Buchan, J., *Mr. Standfast*, London, Hodder & Stoughton, 1919.

Buchan, J., *The Thirty-Nine Steps*, London, 1915.

Buckmaster, O.S., *Roundabout – The Autobiography of Viscount Buckmaster*, London, Witherby, 1969.

Burgoyne, G.A., *The Burgoyne Diaries*, London, Harmsworth, 1985.

Cairnes, W.E., *The Army from Within*, London, Sands & Co., 1901.

Cairnes, W.E., *Social Life in the British Army*, London, J. Long, 1900.

Calloway, S., *The Golden Age of Shopping 1910-1940 – A miscellany of items from Harrods, Gamages and Army & Navy Stores*, London, Studio Editions, 1996.

Campbell, P.J., *In The Cannon's Mouth*, London, Hamilton, 1979.

Carlisle, C. (ed.), *My Own Darling: Letters from Montie to Kitty Carlisle*, London, Carlisle, 1989.

Clark, C., *The Tin Trunk: Letters and Drawings 1914-1918*, Hounslow, F.S. & J. Rhys, 2000.

Cloete, S., *A Victorian Son – An Autobiography*, London, Collins, 1972.

Congreve, B., *Armageddon Road – A VC's Diary, 1914-16*, London, Kimber, 1982.

Crawshay-Williams, E., *Leaves From An Officer's Notebook*, London, Edward Arnold, 1918.

Crouch, L.W., *Duty And Service – Letters From The Front*, London & Aylesbury, 1917.

Devonald-Lewis, R., (ed.), *From the Somme To The Armistice – The Memoirs of Captain Stormont Gibbs, MC*, London, Kimber, 1986.

Douie, C., *The Weary Road – Recollections of a Subaltern of Infantry*, Stevenage, Strong Oak Press with Tom Donovan Publishing, 1988.

Dugdale, G., *"Langemarck" And "Cambrai" – A War Narrative 1914-1918*, Shrewsbury, Wilding, 1932.

Dundas, H., *Henry Dundas – Scots Guards – A Memoir*, London, W. Blackwood & Sons, 1921.

Dunn, J.C., *The War the Infantry Knew, 1914-1918*, London, Janes, 1987.

Durell, J.C.V., *Whizzbangs and Woodbines – Tales of Work and Play on the Western Front*, London, Hodder & Stoughton, 1918.

Eden, A., *Another World 1897-1917*, London, Allen Lane, 1976.

Ewart, W., *Way of Revelation*, Gloucester, Sutton, 1986.

Feilding, R., *War Letters to a Wife, France and Flanders, 1915-1919*, London, The Medici Society Ltd, 1929.

Field, E., *Advertising – The Forgotten Years*, London, Ernest Benn, 1959.

Foot, S., *Three Lives – An Autobiography*, London, William Heinemann, 1934.

Fraser, D. (ed.), *In Good Company – The First World War Letters and Diaries of The Hon. William Fraser, Gordon Highlanders*, Salisbury, Michael Russell, 1990.

Gibbs, P., *Realities Of War*, London, Hutchinson & Co., 1929.

Gillespie, A.D., *Letters From Flanders*, London, Smith Elder & Co, 1916.

Glenconner, P., *Edward Wyndham Tennant, 4th Grenadier Guards – A Memoir*, London, John Lane, 1919.

Glover, M. (ed.), *The Fateful Battle Line: The Great War Journals and Sketches of Captain Henry Ogle, MC*, London, Cooper, 1993.

Golder Burns, J., *Through A Padre's Spectacles*, London, J. Clarke & Co., 1917.

Graham, S., *A Private in the Guards*, London, Macmillan, 1919.

Graves, R., *Goodbye to All That*, revised edn., London, Penguin, 1960.

Greenwell, G.H., *Infant In Arms*, London, Dickson & Thompson, 1935.

Grisewood, F., *The World Goes By*, London, Secker & Warburg, 1952.

Hanbury-Sparrow, A.A., *The Land-Locked Lake*, London, Arthur Barker, 1932.

Hankey, D., *A Student In Arms*, 4th edn., London, A. Melrose, 1916.

Harris, R.E., *Billie – The Nevill Letters 1914-1916*, London, MacRae, 1991.

Hawke, J., *From Private to Major*, London, Hutchinson & Co., 1938.

Hay, I. (Beith, J.H.), *The First Hundred Thousand – Being the Unofficial Chronicle of a Unit of "K(I)"*, London, Blackwood, 1915.

Henderson, K., *Letters to Helen; Impressions of an Artist on the Western Front*, London, Chatto & Windus, 1917.

Hewett, S., *A Scholar's Letters from the Front*, London, Longmans, Green & Co., 1918.

Hitchcock, F.C., *"Stand To" – A Diary of the Trenches 1915-1918*, London, Hurst & Blackett, 1937.

Housman, L. (ed.), *War Letters of Fallen Englishmen*, London, Victor Gollancz, 1930.

Huxtable, C., *From the Somme to Singapore – A Medical Officer in Two World Wars*, Tunbridge Wells, Costello, 1987.

Jacomb, C.E., *Torment – A Study in Patriotism*, London, Andrew Melrose, 1920.

Jolliffe, J., *Raymond Asquith – Life and Letters*, Norwich, Michael Russell Publishing, 1997.

Jones, L.E., *An Edwardian Youth*, London, Macmillan & Co., 1956.

Jones, P. & Jones, H., *War Letters of a Public-Schoolboy*, London, Cassell & Co, 1918.

Kernot, C.F., *British Public Schools' War Memorials*, London, Roberts & Newton, 1927.

Kipling, R., *The Complete Stalky & Co*, London, The Folio Society, 1996.

Kipling, R., *The New Army in Training*, London, Macmillan & Co., 1915.

Koch, T.W., *Books In Camp, Trench and Hospital*, London, J.M. Dent & Sons, 1917.

Langbridge, R.H., *Edwardian Shopping – A Selection from the Army & Navy Stores Catalogues 1898-1913*, Newton Abbott, David & Charles, 1975.

Liveing, E.G.D., *Attack – An Infantry Subaltern's Impressions of July 1st, 1916*, London, William Heinemann, 1918.

Livermore, B., *Long 'Un – A Damn Bad Soldier*, Batley, Harry Hayes, 1974.

Long, B.W., *First World War Letters*, London, David Hawgood, 1995.

Lyttelton, E., *Britain's Duty To-day*, London, Patriotic Publishing Co., 1915.

Lyttelton, O., *From Peace to War – a study in contrast 1857-1918*, London, Bodley Head, 1968.

Macmillan, H., *Winds of Change 1914-1939*, London, Macmillan, 1966.

Manning, F., *The Middle Parts of Fortune*, London, Penguin, 2000.

Mellersh, H.E.L., *Schoolboy into War*, London, Kimber, 1978.

Merton, J., *Love Letters under Fire*, London, Duckworth & Co., 1916.

Mills, W.R.G., *Poems and Letters of William R.G. Mills*, Oxford, B.H. Blackwell, 1918.

Mitchell, B.R., *British Historical Statistics*, Cambridge, Cambridge University Press, 1988.

Montague, C.E., *Disenchantment*, London, MacGibbon & Kec, 1968.

Needham, E.J., *The First Three Months – The Impressions of an Amateur Infantry Subaltern*, Aldershot, Gale & Polden, 1936.

Nettleton, J., *The Anger of the Guns: An Infantry Officer on the Western Front*, London, Kimber, 1979.

Neville, J.E.H., *The War Letters of a Light Infantryman*, London, Sifton Praed & Co., 1930.

Nobbs, G., *Englishman, Kamerad! Right of the British Line*, London, William Heinemann, 1918.

'O.E.' (Fildes, G.), *Iron Times with the Guards*, London, John Murray, 1918.

Owen, W., *War Poems and Others*, London, Chatto & Windus, 1973.

Paish, F.W., *War As A Temporary Occupation – First World War Memoirs of a Second Lieutenant*, Edinburgh, Alan Peacock, 1998.

Pitt, B., *Essays, Poems, Letters*, London, Francis Edwards, 1917.

Pollard, A.O., *Fire-Eater – The Memoirs of a V.C.*, London, Hutchinson & Co., 1932.

Ponsonby, M., *Visions and Vignettes of War*, London, Longmans & Co., 1917.

Powell, A. (ed.), *A Deep Cry: A Literary Pilgrimage to the Battlefields and Cemeteries of First World War British Soldier-Poets Killed in Northern France and Flanders*, Aberporth, Palladour, 1993.

Pym, T.W. & Gordon, G., *Papers from Picardy*, London, Constable, 1917.

Quinn, T., *Tales of the Old Soldiers. Ten Veterans of the First World War Remember Life and Death in the Trenches*, Stroud, Sutton, 1993.

'Regular', *Customs of the Army – A Guide for Cadets and Young Officers*, London, Harrison & Sons, 1917.

Rees, R.T., *A Schoolmaster At War*, London, Haycock Press, 1936.

Richter, D.C. (ed.), *Lionel Sotheby's Great War – Diaries and Letters from the Western Front*, Athens, Ohio University Press, 1997.

Ross, R. (ed.), *The First Collected Edition of the works of Oscar Wilde – The Importance of Being Earnest*, London, Dawsons, 1969.

Sackville Lawson, H., *Letter of a Headmaster Soldier*, London, H.R. Allenson, 1919.

Sanders, L.Y., *A Soldier Of England – Memorials of Leslie Yorath Sanders*, Dumfries, J. Maxwell & Son, 1920.

Sanger, E., *Letters From Two World Wars – A Social History of English Attitudes To War 1914-45*, Stroud, Sutton, 1993.

Sansom, A.J., *Letters from France*, London, Andrew Melrose, 1921.

'Sapper' (H.C. McNeile), *The Lieutenant and others*, London, Hodder & Stoughton, 1915.

Sassoon, S., *Memoirs of a Fox-Hunting Man*, The Folio Society, London, 1993.

Sassoon, S., *Memoirs of an Infantry Officer*, The Folio Society, London, 1993.

Sheffield, G.D. & Inglis, G.I.S. (eds.), *From Vimy Ridge to the Rhine – The Great War Letters of Christopher Stone DSO MC*, Marlborough, Crowood, 1989.

Sheridan Jones, C., *London In War-Time*, London, Grafton & Co., 1917.

Shirley, W., *Moral – The Most Important Factor In War*, London, Sifton, Praed & Co., 1916.

Smith, W., *Spilt Ink*, London, Ernest Benn, 1932.

Spicer, L.D., *Letters From France 1915-1918*, London, Robert York, 1979.

Stone, C., *Letters to an Eton Boy*, London, T. Fisher Unwin, 1913.

Talbot, E., *The War and Conscience*, London, 1914.

Talbot, L (ed.), *Gilbert Walter Lyttelton Talbot*, London, 1916.

Tapert, A. (ed.), *Despatches from the heart – An anthology of letters from the Front during the First and Second World Wars*, London, Hamish Hamilton, 1984.

Thomson, A.A., *Cheero! – The Army of To-day*, London, Cassell & Co., 1917.

Townshend, E. (ed.), *Keeling Letters and Recollections*, London, G. Allen & Unwin, 1918.

Turner, P.W. & Haigh, R.H. (eds.), *Not For Glory*, London, Maxwell, 1969.

Vaughan, E.C., *Some Desperate Glory – The diary of a young officer, 1917*, London, Warne, 1981.

Warren, F., *Honour Satisfied – A Dorset Rifleman at War 1916-18*, Marlborough, Crowood, 1990.

Wheatley, D., *The Time Has Come … The Memoirs of Dennis Wheatley: Vol 2: Officer and Temporary Gentleman 1914-1919*, London, Hutchinson, 1978.

Whinyates, R., (ed.), *Artillery & Trench Mortar Memories – 32nd Division*, London, Unwin Bros, 1932.

Wilkinson, A. (ed.), *Destiny: The War Letters of Captain Jack Oughtred MC 1915-1918*, Cherry Burton, Hutton Press, 1996.

Williamson, H., *A Fox Under My Cloak*, Bath, Chivers, 1983.

Wolff, A., *Subalterns of the Foot – Three World War I Diaries of Officers of the Cheshire Regiment*, Worcester, Square One, 1992.

Woods, E.S. (ed.), *Andrew R. Buxton, The Rifle Brigade, A Memoir*, London, Robert Scott, 1918.

Yapp, A.K., *The Romance of the Red Triangle – The Story of the Coming of the Red Triangle and the Service Rendered by the YMCA to the Sailors and Soldiers of the British Empire*, London, Hodder & Stoughton, 1919.

Young, D., *Try Anything Twice*, London, Hamilton, 1963.

Official documents

Amendments, &c., to the Royal Warrant for the Pay, Appointment, Promotion, and Non-Effective Pay of the Army, published in Army Orders between 1st December, 1914, and 1st August, 1918, and including, besides Permanent Additions and Amendments, those of Temporary Application only, London, HMSO, 1918.

Instructions Regarding Promotion of Officers, G.H.Q. British Army in France, October 1918.

Regulations under which Commissions in the Regular Army may be obtained by University Candidates, War Office, London, 1912.

Report of the Royal Commission to inquire into Revenues and Management of certain Colleges and Schools, Studies and Instruction, Parl. Papers, 1864, XX.

Royal Warrant for the Pay, Appointment, Promotion, and Non-Effective Pay of The Army, London, HMSO, 1914.

Statistics of the military effort of the British Empire during the Great War 1914-20, London, HMSO, 1922.

Printed Secondary Works

(1) Books

Adams, M.C.C., *The Great Adventure – Male Desire and the Coming of World War I*, Bloomington, Indiana University Press, 1990.

Addison, G.H., *The Work of the Royal Engineers in the European War, 1914-1918 – Miscellaneous*, Chatham, Institution of Royal Engineers, 1926.

Alderson, D., *Mansex Fine – Religion, Manliness and Imperialism in Nineteenth-Century British Culture*, Manchester, Manchester University Press, 1998.

Alford, B.W.E., *W.D. & H.O. Wills and the development of the U.K. tobacco industry 1786-1965*, London, Methuen, 1973.

Arthur, M., *Forgotten Voices of the Great War*, London, Ebury, 2002.

Ashworth, T., *Trench Warfare 1914-1918: The Live and Let Live System*, London, Macmillan, 1980.

Babington, A., *For the Sake of Example*, London, Leo Cooper, 1983.

Badger, A.B., *The Public Schools and the Nation*, London, R. Hale Ltd., 1944.

Bamford, T.W., *Rise of the Public Schools – A Study of Boys' Public Boarding Schools in England and Wales from 1837 to the Present Day*, London, Nelson, 1967.

Barnett, C., *Britain and Her Army 1509-1970*, London, Allen Lane, 1970.

Barnett, C., *The Great War*, London, Park Lane Press, 1979.

Barnett, C., *The Collapse of British Power*, Gloucester, Sutton, 1984.

Baynes, J., *Morale – A Study of Men and Courage*, London, Cassell, 1967.

Beckett, I.F.W. & Simpson, K. (eds.), *A Nation in Arms – A Social study of the British army in the First World War*, Manchester, Manchester University Press, 1985.

Beckett, I.F.W., *The Amateur Military Tradition 1558-1945*, Manchester, Manchester University Press, 1991.

Beckett, I.F.W., *The First World War: The Essential Guide To Sources in the UK National Archives*, Richmond, Public Record Office, 2002.

Beevor, A., *Inside the British Army*, London, Chatto & Windus, 1990.

Bet-El, I.R., *Conscripts – Lost Legions of the Great War*, Stroud, Sutton Publishing, 1999.

Bishop, T.J.H. & Wilkinson, R., *Winchester And The Public School Elite – A Statistical Analysis*, London, Faber, 1967.

Bonadeo, A., *Mark of the Beast – Death and Degradation in the Literature of the Great War*, Lexington, University Press of Kentucky, 1989.

Bond, B., *The Victorian Army and the Staff College 1854-1914*, London, Eyre Methuen, 1972.

Bond, B. (ed.), *The First World War and British Military History*, Oxford, Clarendon Press, 1991.

Bond, B., *The Unquiet Western Front: Britain's Role In Literature and History*, Cambridge, Cambridge University Press, 2002.

Boorman, D., *At the Going Down of the Sun: British First World War Memorials*, York, W. Sessions, 1988.

Bourke, J., *Dismembering the Male – Men's Bodies, Britain and the Great War*, London, Reaktion, 1996.

Bourke, J., *An Intimate History of Killing – Face-to-face Killing in Twentieth-Century Warfare*, London, Granta, 1999.

Bourne, J.M., *Britain and the Great War 1914-1918*, London, Edward Arnold, 1989.

Bourne, J.M., Liddle, P. & Whitehead, I. (eds.), *The Great World War 1914-1945. Vol. 1 – Lightning Strikes Twice*, London, HarperCollins, 2000.

Boyd, D., *Royal Engineers*, London, Cooper, 1975.

Brendon, P., *Eminent Edwardians*, London, Secker & Warburg, 1979.

Brooke, C.N.L. (ed.), *A History of the University of Cambridge*, Cambridge, Cambridge University Press, 1993.

Brown, I.M., *British Logistics on the Western Front 1914-1919*, Westport, Praeger, 1998.

Brown., M., *Tommy Goes To War*, Stroud, Tempus, 2001.

Buitenhuis, P., *The Great War of Words: Literature as Propaganda 1914-18 and After*, London, Batsford, 1989.

Cameron, J., *1916 – Year of Decision*, London, Oldbourne, 1962.

Cannadine, D., *The Decline And Fall Of The British Aristocracy*, London, Yale University Press, 1990.

Carrington, C., *Rudyard Kipling: His Life And Work*, London, Macmillan, 1955.

Ceadel, M., *Pacifism in Britain 1914-1945: The Defining of a Faith*, Oxford, Clarendon Press, 1980.

Cecil, H., *The Flower of Battle – British Fiction Writers of the First World War*, London, Secker & Warburg, 1995.

Cecil, H. & Liddle, P.H. (eds.), *Facing Armageddon – The First World War Experienced*, London, Leo Cooper, 1996.

Chapman, G., *A Passionate Prodigality – Fragments of Autobiography*, London, Nicholson & Watson, 1933.

Chickering, R. & Förster, S. (eds.), *Great War, Total War – Combat and Mobilization on the Western Front, 1914-1918*, Cambridge, Cambridge University Press, 2000.

Clarke, I.F., *Voices Prophesying War – Future Wars 1763-3749*, Oxford, Oxford University Press, 1992.

Clarke, I.F. (ed.), *The Great War with Germany 1890-1914 – Fictions and Fantasies of the War-to-come*, Liverpool, Liverpool University Press, 1997.

Clarke, P., *Hope and Glory – Britain 1900-1990*, London, Allen Lane, 1997.

Clayton, A., *The British Officer – Leading The Army From 1660 To The Present*, Harlow, Pearson Education Limited, 2006.

Coetzee, F. & Shevin-Coetzee, M. (eds.), *Authority, Identity and the Social History of the Great War*, Oxford, Berghahn Books, 1995.

Connelly, M., *The Great War, Memory and Ritual – Commemoration in the City and East London, 1916-1939*, Woodbridge, Boydell Press, 2002.

Constantine, S., Kirby, M.W. & Rose, M.B. (eds.), *The First World War in British History*, London, Edward Arnold, 1995.

Cooper Willis, I., *England's Holy War – A Study of English Liberal Idealism During The Great War*, New York, Knopf, 1928.

Corrigan, G., *Mud, Blood and Poppycock – Britain and the First World War*, London, Cassell, 2003.

Crawford, T.S., *Wiltshire and the Great War: Training the Empire's Soldiers*, Reading, DPF, 1999.

Cunningham, H., *The Volunteer Force – A Social and Political History 1859-1908*, London, Croom Helm, 1975.

Dakers, C., *The Countryside at War 1914-1918*, London, Constable, 1987.

Dallas, G. & Gill, D., *The Unknown Army*, London, Verso, 1985.

Dangerfield, G., *The Strange Death of Liberal England*, London, Macgibbon & Kee, 1966.

Darwin, B., *The English Public School*, London, Longmans, Green & Co., 1929.

Dawson, G., *Soldier Heroes – British adventure, empire and the imagining of masculinities*, London, Routledge, 1994.

DeGroot, G.J., *Blighty. British Society in the Era of the Great War*, London, Longman, 1996.

Dennis, P., *The Territorial Army 1906-1940*, Woodbridge, Boydell, 1987.

Donovan, T. (ed.), *The Hazy Red Hell – Fighting Experiences on the Western Front 1914-18*, Staplehurst, Spellmount, 1999.

Drotner, K., *English Children And Their Magazines, 1751-1945*, New Haven, Yale University Press, 1988.

Eksteins, M., *Rites of Spring – The Great War and the Birth of the Modern Age*, London, Bantam, 1989.

Elliott, B.B., *A History of English Advertising*, London, Business Publications Ltd, 1962.

Ellis, J., *Eye-Deep In Hell – The Western Front 1914-18*, London, Penguin, 2002.

Ferguson, N., *The Pity Of War*, London, Allen Lane, 1998.

Ferro, M., *The Great War 1914-1918*, London, Routledge & K. Paul, 1973.

Firth, J.D'E., *Rendall of Winchester – The Life and Witness of a Teacher*, Oxford, Oxford University Press, 1954.

Floud, R. & McCloskey, D. (eds.), *The Economic History of Britain since 1700 – Volume 2: 1860 to the 1970s*, Cambridge, Cambridge University Press, 1981.

Fraser, G.M., *The World of the Public School*, London, Weidenfeld & Nicolson, 1977.

Fuller, J.G., *Troop Morale and Popular Culture in the British and Dominion Armies 1914-1918*, Oxford, Clarendon, 1990.

Fussell, P., *The Great War And Modern Memory*, London, Oxford University Press, 1975.

Gander, T.J., *The Royal Engineers*, London, Ian Allen, 1985.

Gardner, B., *The Public Schools – An Historical Survey*, London, Hamilton, 1973.

Gathorne-Hardy, J., *The Public School Phenomenon 597-1977*, Harmondsworth, Penguin, 1979.

Germains, V.W., *The Kitchener Armies – The Stories of a National Achievement*, London, Peter Davies, 1930.

Girouard, M., *The Return To Camelot – Chivalry and the English Gentleman*, London, Yale University Press, 1981.

Godwin-Austen, A.R., *The Staff and the Staff College*, London, Constable, 1927.

Gordon, H., *The War Office*, London, Putnam, 1935.

Graham, D., *Against Odds: Reflections on the Experiences of the British Army, 1914-45*, Basingstoke, Macmillan, 1998.

Grainger, J.H., *Patriotisms – Britain 1900-1939*, London, Routledge & Kegan Paul, 1986.

Green, S.J.D. & Whiting, R.C. (eds.), *The Boundaries of the State in Modern Britain*, Cambridge, Cambridge University Press, 1996.

Gregory, A., *The Silence of Memory: Armistice Day 1919-1946*, Oxford, Berg, 1994.

Gregory, A., *The Last Great War- British Society and the First World War*, Cambridge, Cambridge University Press, 2008.

Griffith, P., *Battle Tactics of the Western Front: The British Army's Art of Attack, 1916-18*, New Haven, Yale University Press, 1994.

Griffith, P. (ed.), *British Fighting Methods in the Great War*, London, F. Cass, 1996.

Gullace, N.F., *"The Blood of Our Sons" – Men, Women, and the Renegotiation of British Citizenship During the Great War*, Basingstoke, Palgrave, 2002.

Haig-Brown, A.R., *The O.T.C. and The Great War*, London, G. Newnes, 1915.

Harries-Jenkins, G., *The Army in Victorian Society*, London, Routledge & Kegan Paul, 1977.

Harris, J., *Private Lives, Public Spirit – A Social History of Britain 1870-1914*, Oxford, Oxford University Press, 1993.

Hartcup, G., *The War of Invention*, London, Brassey's Defence, 1988.

Hayward, J., *Myths & Legends of the First World War*, Thrupp, Sutton, 2002.

Hicks, W.R., *The School in English and German Fiction*, London, Soncino, 1933.

Hirsch, F. & Gordon, D., *Newspaper Money – Fleet Street and the Search for the Affluent Reader*, London, Hutchinson, 1975.

Hogg, I.V., *Allied Artillery of World War One*, Marlborough, Crowood, 1998.

Höglund, J.A., *Mobilising the Novel – The Literature of Imperialism and The First World War*, Uppsala, Ubsaliensis s. academiae, 1997.

Holmes, R., *Firing Line*, London, Pimlico, 1985.

Holmes, R., *Tommy – The British Soldier on the Western Front 1914-1918*, London, HarperCollins, 2004.

Holt, R., *Sport and the British – A Modern History*, Oxford, Clarendon Press, 1992.

Honey, J.R.de S., *Tom Brown's Universe: The Development of the Victorian Public School*, London, Millington, 1977.

Horn, P., *Rural Life in England in The First World War*, Dublin, Gill and Macmillan, 1984.

Horne, D., *God Is An Englishman*, London, Angus & Roberston, 1970.

Howarth, P., *Play Up And Play The Game: The Heroes Of Popular Fiction*, London, Eyre Methuen, 1973.

Hynes, S., *The Edwardian Turn Of Mind*, Princeton, Princeton University Press, 1968.

Hynes, S., *A War Imagined – The First World War and English Culture*, London, Bodley Head, 1990.

Hynes, S., *The Soldier's Tale – Bearing Witness To Modern War*, London, Pimlico, 1998.

Hurst, H., *The Public Schools Battalion in the Great War*, Barnsley, Pen & Sword, 2007.

Ivelaw-Chapman, J., *The Riddles of Wipers – An Appreciation of The Wipers Times, A Journal of the Trenches*, London, Cooper, 1997.

Jalland, P., *Death In The Victorian Family*, Oxford, Oxford University Press, 1996.

James, L. *Warrior Race – The British Experience of War from Roman Times to the Present*, London, Little, Brown & Co., 2001.

Keegan, J., *The Face of Battle*, London, Jonathan Cape, 1976.

Kennedy, P. (ed.), *The War Plans of the Great Powers, 1880-1914*, London, Allen & Unwin, 1979.

Kemp, T., *The French Economy 1913-39 – The history of a decline*, London, Longman, 1972.

King, A., *Memorials of the Great War in Britain – The Symbolism and Politics of Remembrance*, Oxford, Berg, 1998.

Klein, H. (ed.), *The First World War in Fiction – A Collection of Critical Essays*, London, Macmillan, 1976.

Knox, C., *Heroes All*, London, Hodder & Stoughton, 1941.

Laffin, J., *British Butchers and Bunglers of World War One*, Gloucester, Alan Sutton, 1988.

Lambert, A., *Unquiet Souls: The Indian Summer of the British Aristocracy 1880-1918*, London, Macmillan, 1984.

Leed, E., *No Man's Land – Combat & Identity in World War I*, Cambridge, Cambridge University Press, 1979.

Lejeune, A., *The Gentlemen's Clubs of London*, London, Macdonal and Jane's, 1979.

Lewis-Stempel, J., *The Autobiography of the British Soldier – From Agincourt to Basra, in his own words*, London, Headline, 2007.

Lewis-Stempel, J, *Six Weeks – The Short and Gallant Life of the British Officer in the First World War*, London, Weidenfeld & Nicolson, 2010.

Liddle, P.H. (ed.), *Home Fires and Foreign Fields: British Social and Military Experience in the First World War*, London, Brassey's Defence, 1985.

Liddle, P.H., *The Soldier's War*, London, Blandford, 1988.

Liddle, P.H., *Voices of War – Front Line and Home Front*, London, Leo Cooper, 1988.

Linder, A.P., *Princes of the Trenches – Narrating the German Experience of the First World War*, Columbia, Camden House, 1996.

Lowerson, J., *Sport and the English Middle Classes – 1870-1914*, Manchester, Manchester University Press, 1995.

Luvaas, J., *The Education of an Army – British Military Thought, 1815-1940*, London, Cassell, 1965.

McCartney, H.B., *Citizen Soldiers: the Liverpool Territorials in the First World War*, Cambridge, Cambridge University Press, 2005.

McIntosh, P., *Physical Education in England since 1800*, London, Bell, 1952.

Macdonald, L., *1915 – The Death Of Innocence*, London, Headline, 1993.

Mack, E.C., *Public Schools and British Opinion since 1860 – The Relationship Between Contemporary Ideas and the Evolution of an English Institution*, New York, Columbia University Press, 1941.

Mangan, J.A., *Athleticism in the Victorian and Edwardian Public School: The Emergence and Consolidation of an Educational Ideology*, Cambridge, Cambridge University Press, 1981.

Mangan, J.A., *The Games Ethic and Imperialism: Aspects of the Diffusion of an Ideal*, Harmondsworth, Viking, 1986.

Mangan, J.A. & Walvin, J. (eds.), *Manliness and morality: middle class masculinity in Britain and America 1800-1940*, Manchester, Manchester University Press, 1987.

Martland, P., *Since Records Began – EMI: The First 100 Years*, London, Batsford, 1997.

Martland, P. & Pattenden, M., *Corpus Lives, 1352-2002*, Cambridge, Corpus Christi College, 2003.

Marwick, A., *The Deluge: British Society and the First World War*, London, Bodley Head, 1965.

Mason, P., *The English Gentleman – The Rise and Fall of an Ideal*, London, Deutsch, 1982.

Messenger, C., *Call To Arms: The British Army 1914-18*, London, Weidenfeld & Nicolson, 2005.

Meyer, J. (ed), *British Popular Culture and the First World War*, Leiden, Brill, 2008.

Meyer, J., *Men of War: Masculinity and the First World War in Britain*, Basingstoke, Palgrave Macmillan, 2009.

Middlebrook, M., *The First Day on the Somme: 1 July 1916*, London, Allen Lane, 1971.

Middlebrook, M., *The Kaiser's Battle – 21 March 1918: The First Day of the German Spring Offensive*, London, Allen Lane, 1978.

Millman, B., *Managing Domestic Dissent in First World War Britain*, London, Frank Cass, 2000.

Mitchinson, K.W., *Gentlemen and Officers – The Impact and Experience of War on a Territorial Regiment 1914-1918*, London, Imperial War Museum, 1995.

Mitchinson, K.W., *Pioneer Battalions In The Great War – Organised and Intelligent Labour*, London, Leo Cooper, 1997.

Mitchinson, K.W., *England's Last Hope – The Territorial Force, 1908-1914,*Basingstoke, Palgrave Macmillan, 2008.

Moeyes, P., *Siegfried Sassoon: Scorched Glory – A Critical Study*, Basingstoke, Macmillan, 1997.

Money, T., *Manly & Muscular Diversions – Public Schools and the Nineteenth-Century Sporting Revival*, London, Duckworth, 1997.

Money Barnes, R., *The British Army of 1914 – Its History, Uniforms & Contemporary Continental Armies*, London, Seeley, 1968.

Moorcroft Wilson, J., *Siegfried Sassoon – The Making Of A War Poet (A Biography 1886-1918)*, London, Duckworth, 1998.

Moore, W., *The Thin Yellow Line*, Ware, Wordsworth Editions, 1999.

Moran, C., *The Anatomy of Courage*, London, Constable, 1945.

Morgan, M.C., *Cheltenham College – The First Hundred Years*, Chalfont St. Giles, Sadler, 1968.

Moss, M., *Manliness and Militarism*, Oxford, Oxford University Press, 2001.

Mosse, G., *The Image of Man*, Oxford, Oxford University Press, 1996.

Myatt, F., *The British Infantry 1660-1945: The evolution of a fighting force*, Poole, Blandford, 1983.

Neillands, R., *Attrition – The Great War on the Western Front, 1916*, London, Robson, 2001.

Nevett, T.R., *Advertising in Britain – A History*, London, Heinemann, 1982.

Newsome, D., *Godliness and Good Learning: Four Studies on a Victorian Ideal*, London, Murray, 1961.

Ollard, R., *An English Education – A Perspective of Eton*, London, Collins, 1982.

Ogilvie, V., *The English Public School*, London, B.T. Batsford, 1957.

Panichas, G.A. (ed.), *Promise of Greatness – The War of 1914-1918*, London, Cassell, 1968.

Paris, M., *Warrior Nation – Images of War in British Popular Culture, 1850-2000*, London, Reaktion, 2000.

Parker, P., *The Old Lie – The Great War and the Public School Ethos*, London, Constable, 1987.

Peck, J., *War, the Army and Victorian Literature*, Basingstoke, Macmillan Press, 1998.

Peel, C.S., *How We Lived Then 1914-1918 – A Sketch of Social And Domestic Life In England During The War*, London, John Lane, 1929.

Pick, D., *War Machine – the rationalisation of slaughter in the modern age*, London, Yale University Press, 1993.

Pound, R., *The Lost Generation*, London, Constable, 1964.

Proud, E.B., *History of British Army Postal Service – Volume 2 1903-1927*, Brighton, Proud-Bailey Co., 1980.

Rae, J., *Conscience And Politics – The British Government and the Conscientious Objector To Military Service 1916-1919*, London, Oxford University Press, 1970.

Read, D., *Edwardian England 1901-15 – Society and Politics*, London, Harrap, 1972.

Read, D., *The Age of Urban Democracy – England 1868-1914*, London, Longman, 1994.

Reader, W.J., *At Duty's Call – A Study In Obsolete Patriotism*, Manchester, Manchester University Press, 1988.

Richards, J., *Visions of Yesterday*, London, Routledge & Kegan Paul, 1973.

Richards, J., *Happiest Days – The public school in English fiction*, Manchester, Manchester University Press, 1988.

Richards, T., *The Commodity Culture of Victorian England – Advertising and Spectacle, 1851-1914*, London, Verso, 1991.

Richter, D., *Chemical Soldiers: British Gas Warfare in World War I*, Lawrence, University Press of Kansas, 1992.

Robbins, K., *The First World War*, Oxford, Oxford University Press, 1984.

Roper, M., *The Secret Battle – Emotional Survival in the Great War*, Manchester, Manchester University Press, 2009.

Sabben-Clare, J., *Winchester College: After 600 Years, 1382-1982*, Southampton, Paul Cave, 1981.

Samuels, M., *Command or Control? Command, Training and Tactics in the British and German Armies, 1888-1918*, London, Frank Cass, 1995.

Sanger, E., *Letters From Two World Wars – A Social History of English Attitudes To War 1914-45*, Stroud, Sutton, 1993.

Saunders, A., *Dominating The Enemy: War In The Trenches 1914-1918*, Stroud, Sutton, 2000.

Searle, G.R., *The Quest for National Efficiency – A Study in British Politics and Political Thought, 1899-1914*, Oxford, Blackwell, 1971.

Sheffield, G.D., *Leadership in the trenches – Officer-Man Relations, Morale and Discipline in the British Army in the Era of the First World War*, Basingstoke, Macmillan, 2000.

Sheffield, G.D., *Forgotten Victory – The First World War: Myths and Realities*, London, Headline, 2001.

Sheffield, G.D., *The Somme*, London, Cassell, 2004.

Sheffield, G.D. & Todman, D. (eds.), *Command and Control on the Western Front – The British Army's Experience 1914-18*, Staplehurst, Spellmount, 2004.

Shephard, B., *A War of Nerves – Soldiers and Psychiatrists 1914-1994*, London, Jonathan Cape, 2000.

Shepperd, G.A., *Sandhurst – The Royal Military Academy Sandhurst and its Predecessors*, London, Country Life Books, 1980.

Showalter, E., *The Female Malady: women, madness and English culture, 1830-1980*, London, Virago, 1987.

Simkins, P., *Kitchener's Army – The Raising of the New Armies, 1914-16*, Manchester, Manchester University Press, 1988.

Simon, B. & Bradley, I. (eds.), *The Victorian Public School – Studies in the Development of an Educational Institution*, Dublin, Gill and Macmillan, 1975.

Simpson, A., *Hot Blood And Cold Steel: Life And Death In The Trenches of the First World War*, London, Tom Donovan, 1993.

Smith, L., *Between Mutiny and Obedience*, Princeton, Princeton University Press, 1994.

Smith, M.V.W., *Drummer Hodge – The Poetry of the Anglo-Boer War (1899-1902)*, Oxford, Clarendon Press, 1978.

Spagnoly, T., *The Anatomy of a Raid*, London, Multidream Publishing, 1991.

Spiers, E.M., *The Army and Society 1815-1914*, London, Longman, 1980.

Spiers, E.M., *The Late Victorian Army 1868-1902*, Manchester, Manchester University Press, 1992.

Stephen, M., *The Price of Pity: Poetry, History and Myth in the Great War*, London, Leo Cooper, 1996.

Stevenson, D., *1914-1918 – The History of the First World War*, London, Allen Lane, 2004.

Stevenson, J., *British Society 1914-45*, Harmondsworth, Penguin, 1984.

Strachan, H., *History of The Cambridge University Officers Training Corps*, Tunbridge Wells, Midas Books, 1976.

Strachan, H., *European Armies and the Conduct of War*, London, Allen & Unwin, 1983.

Strachan, H., *The Politics of the British Army*, Oxford, Oxford University Press, 1997.

Strachan, H., *The First World War: Volume 1 – To Arms*, Oxford, Oxford University Press, 2002.

Strachan, H., *The First World War – A New Illustrated History*, London, Simon & Schuster, 2003.

Taylor, A.J.P., *The First World War*, Harmondsworth, Penguin, 1966.

Temple Clarke, A.O., *Transport and Sport in the Great War Period*, London, Quality Press, 1938.

Terraine, J., *The Western Front 1914-1918*, London, Hutchinson, 1964.

Terraine, J., *White Heat – The New Warfare 1914-18*, London, Sidgwick & Jackson, 1982.

Thomas, H., *The Story of Sandhurst*, London, Hutchinson, 1961.

Thompson, P., *The Edwardians – The Remaking of British Society*, London, Weidenfeld & Nicolson, 1975.

Thorpe, M., *Siegfried Sassoon – A Critical Study*, London, Oxford University Press, 1966.

Todman, D., *The Great War: Myth and Memory*, London, Hambledon Continuum, 2005.

Travers, T.H.E., *The Killing Ground – The British Army, the Western Front and the Emergence of Modern Warfare 1900-1918*, London, Allen & Unwin, 1987.

Trebilcock, C., *The Vickers Brothers: Armaments and Enterprise, 1854-1914*, London, Europa, 1977.

Tucker, S.C. (ed.), *The European Powers in the First World War – An Encyclopedia*, London, Garland, 1996.

Turner, E.S., *Boys Will Be Boys – the story of Sweeney Todd, Deadwood, Dick, Sexton Blake, Billy Bunter, Dick Barton, et al*, London, Joseph, 1975.

Turner, E.S., *Gallant Gentlemen – a portrait of the British Officer 1600-1956*, London, Michael Joseph, 1956.

Turner, J. (ed.), *Britain and the First World War*, London, Unwin Hyman, 1988.

Vellacott, J., *Bertrand Russell and the Pacifists in the First World War*, Brighton, Harvester, 1980.

Waites, B., *A Class Society At War: England 1914-1918*, Leamington Spa, Berg, 1987.

Walford, G., *Life in Public Schools*, London, Methuen, 1986.

Walvin, J., *Leisure and Society 1830-1950*, London, Longman, 1978.

Warner, R., *English Public Schools*, London, Collins, 1945.

Watson, A., *Enduring the Great War: Combat, Morale and Collapse in the German and British Armies, 1914-1918*, Cambridge, Cambridge University Press, 2008.

Watson, J.S.K., *Fighting Different Wars – Experience, Memory, and the First World War in Britain*, Cambridge, Cambridge University Press, 2004.

Waugh, A., *Public School Life – Boys, Parents, Masters*, London, W. Collins, 1922.

Whaley, J. (ed.), *Mirrors of Mortality: Studies in the Social History of Death*, London, Europa, 1981.

Whitehead, I.R., *Doctors In The Great War*, London, Leo Cooper, 1999.

Wiener, M., *English Culture and the Decline of the Industrial Spirit 1850-1980*, Cambridge, Cambridge University Press, 1981.

Wilkinson, R., *The Prefects: British Leadership and the Public School Tradition – A Comparative Study in the Making of Rulers*, London, Oxford University Press, 1964.

Williams, B., *Raising and Training the New Armies*, London, Constable, 1918.

Williams, J., *The Home Fronts – Britain, France and Germany 1914-1918*, London, Constable, 1972.

Williamson, A., *A Patriot's Progress – Henry Williamson and the First World War*, Stroud, Sutton, 1998.

Winter, D., *Death's Men – Soldiers of the Great War*, London, Allen Lane, 1978.

Winter, J.M., *The Great War and the British People*, London, Macmillan, 1985.

Winter, J.M., *The Experience of World War I*, London, Macmillan, 1988.

Winter, J.M., *Sites of Memory, Sites of Mourning: The Great War in European Cultural History*, Cambridge, Cambridge University Press, 1995.

Winter, J.M. & Baggett, B. (eds.), *1914-18 – The Great War and the Shaping of the 20th Century*, London, BBC, 1996.

Winter, J.M. & Sivan, E. (eds.), *War and Remembrance in the Twentieth Century*, Cambridge, Cambridge University Press, 1999.

Wiśniewski, J., *Mars and the Muse: Attitudes to War and Peace in 20th Century English Literature*, Warsaw, Warsaw University Publishers, 1990.

Wohl, R., *The Generation of 1914*, Cambridge, Harvard University Press, 1979.

Young, M., *Army Service Corps*, Barnsley, Leo Cooper, 2000.

(2) Articles

Bogacz, T., "'A Tyranny of Words": Language, Poetry, and Antimodernism in England in the First World War', *Journal of Modern History*, 58, September 1986.

Englander, D., 'Soldiering and Identity: Reflections on the Great War', *War In History*, 1, No. 3, November 1994.

Graves, K., 'C.E. Montague and the Making of *Disenchantment*, 1914-1921', *War In History*, 4, No. 1, January 1997.

Hargreaves, R. 'Promotion from the Ranks', *The Army Quarterly and Defence Journal*, LXXXVI, April 1963-July 1963.

Harris, R., 'The "Child of the barbarian": Rape, Race and Nationalism in France During The First World War', *Past and Present*, No. 141, 1993.

Hiley, N., 'Ploughboys and Soldiers: the folk song and the gramophone in the British Expeditionary Force 1914-1918', *Media History*, 4, No. 1, June 1998.

Inglis, K.S., 'The Homecoming: The War Memorial Movement in Cambridge, England', *Journal of Contemporary History*, 27, No. 4, October 1992.

Leed, E., 'Fateful Memories: Industrialized War and Traumatic Neuroses', *Journal of Contemporary History*, 35, No. 1, 2000.

Travers, T.H.E., 'The Offensive and the Problem of Innovation in British Military Thought 1870-1915', *Journal of Contemporary History*, 13, 1978.

Travers, T.H.E., 'Learning and decision-making on the western front, 1915-16: the British example', *Canadian Journal of History*, April 1983.

Winter, J.M., 'Catastrophe and Culture: Recent Trends in the Historiography of the First World War', *Journal of Modern History*, 64, September 1992.

Unpublished dissertations

Goebel, S., 'Medievalism in the Commemoration of the Great War in Britain and Germany, 1914-1939', unpublished PhD. thesis, University of Cambridge, 2001.

Jamet-Bellier de la Duboisiere, C., 'Commemorating the Lost Generation – First World War Memorials in Cambridge, Oxford and some English Public Schools', unpublished MLitt. dissertation, University of Cambridge, 1994.

Mythen, J., 'The Revolution in British Battle Tactics July 1916 – June 1917: The Spring and Summer Offensives during 1917', unpublished MPhil. thesis, University of Cambridge, 2001.

Perry, F.W., 'Manpower and Organisational Problems in the Expansion of the British and other Commonwealth Armies During the Two World Wars', unpublished PhD. thesis, University of London, 1985.

Philpott, M., 'Disillusion During the Great War', unpublished MPhil. thesis, University of Cambridge, 2003.

Stryker, L.S., 'Languages of Sacrifice and Suffering in England in the First World War', unpublished PhD. thesis, University of Cambridge, July 1992.

Todman, D., 'Representations of the First World War in British popular culture, 1918-1998', unpublished PhD. thesis, University of Cambridge, 2003.

Index

Related titles published by Helion & Company

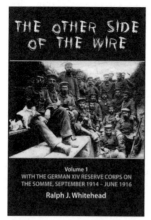

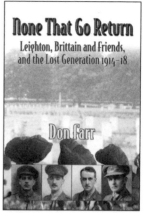

The Other Side of the Wire Volume 1.
With the German XIV Reserve Corps on
the Somme, September 1914-June 1916
Ralph J. Whitehead
616pp Hardback
ISBN 978-1-906033-29-3

None That Go Return. Leighton, Brittain
and Friends, and the Lost Generation 1914-18
Don Farr
232pp Hardback
ISBN 978-1-906033-83-5

Forthcoming titles

The Other Side of the Wire Volume 2. The Battle of the Somme.
With the German XIV Reserve Corps, 1 July 1916
Ralph J. Whitehead   ISBN 978-1-907677-12-0

The Science of War. A Collection of Essays and Lectures 1892-
1903 by the late Colonel G.F.R. Henderson, C.B.
Capt. Neill Malcolm, D.S.O. (ed.)   ISBN 978-1-906033-60-6

The Kitchener Armies. The Story of a National Achievement 1914-18
Victor Wallace Germains   ISBN 978-1-907677-17-5

HELION & COMPANY
26 Willow Road, Solihull, West Midlands B91 1UE, England
Telephone 0121 705 3393   Fax 0121 711 4075
Website: http://www.helion.co.uk

DATE DUE

Demco, Inc. 38-293